THE RE-EMERGENCE OF EMERGENCE

The Re-Emergence of Emergence

The Emergentist Hypothesis from Science to Religion

Edited by
PHILIP CLAYTON AND PAUL DAVIES

OXFORD
UNIVERSITY PRESS

OXFORD
UNIVERSITY PRESS

Great Clarendon Street, Oxford ox2 6DP

Oxford University Press is a department of the University of Oxford.
It furthers the University's objective of excellence in research, scholarship,
and education by publishing worldwide in

Oxford New York

Auckland Cape Town Dar es Salaam Hong Kong Karachi
Kuala Lumpur Madrid Melbourne Mexico City Nairobi
New Delhi Shanghai Taipei Toronto

With offices in

Argentina Austria Brazil Chile Czech Republic France Greece
Guatemala Hungary Italy Japan Poland Portugal Singapore
South Korea Switzerland Thailand Turkey Ukraine Vietnam

Oxford is a registered trade mark of Oxford University Press
in the UK and in certain other countries

Published in the United States
by Oxford University Press Inc., New York

British Library Cataloguing in Publication Data

Data available

Library of Congress Cataloging in Publication Data

The reemergence of emergence : the emergentist hypothesis from
science to religion/edited by Philip Clayton and Paul Davies.
p. cm.
Includes bibliographical references and index.
ISBN-13: 978-0-19-928714-7 (alk. paper)
ISBN-10: 0-19-928714-7 (alk. paper)
1. Emergence (Philosophy) 2. Science–Philosophy. 3.
Consciousness. 4. Religion and science. I. Clayton, Philip, 1956-
II. Davies, Paul, 1962-
Q175. 32. E44R44 2006
501–dc22
2006009453

Typeset by SPI Publisher Services, Pondicherry, India
Printed in Great Britain
on acid-free paper by
Biddles Ltd, King's Lynn, Norfolk

ISBN 0–19–928714–7   978–0–19–928714–7

3 5 7 9 10 8 6 4 2

Contents

IV. RELIGION AND EMERGENCE

Acknowledgments

The present volume was conceived in August, 2002, during a three-day consultation on emergence in Granada, Spain, at which most of the authors were present. The consultation was generously sponsored by the John Templeton Foundation. We gratefully acknowledge this financial support, without which this volume would not have come to press. Thanks are due in particular to Dr. Mary Ann Meyers, Director of the 'Humble Approach Initiative' programme at the Foundation, for her unfailingly professional work in organizing the conference, and her ongoing support of the efforts that resulted in the present book.

Although not explicitly represented in these pages, several other scholars were present at the original consultation and made substantive contributions to the background research that eventually led to these chapters. We wish to name in particular Dr. Rodney Brooks (Fujitsu Professor of Computer Science and Director of the Artificial Intelligence Laboratory at the Massachusetts Institute of Technology); Dr. Peter Fromherz (Director of the Department of Membrane and Neurophysics at the Max-Planck Institute for Biochemistry in Martinsried/Munich and an honorary professor of physics at the Technical University of Munich); Dr. Charles Harper (Executive Director and Senior Vice President at The John Templeton Foundation); Dr. Harold Morowitz (the Clarence Robinson Professor of Biology and Natural Philosophy at George Mason University and a member of its Krasnow Institute for Advanced Study); and Dr. Wojciech Zurek (a laboratory fellow at the Los Alamos National Laboratory).

In Oxford, Ms. Lucy Qureshi had the vision for a volume that would be both rigorous in its presentation of the relevant scientific results and bold to engage in philosophical and theological reflection on the basis of these results. To her, and to the superbly professional staff at Oxford University Press, we express our thanks.

Finally, we acknowledge the hard work and high standards of Zach Simpson, a biologist and graduate student in philosophy and religion at Claremont Graduate University, who invested countless hours as the Editorial Assistant for the volume.

Preface

Much of scientific history involves a succession of subjects that have made the transition from philosophy to science. Well-known examples are space and time, the nature of matter and life, varieties of causation, and cosmology, all of which were already the subjects of rich philosophical discourse at the time of ancient Greece. Of all the topics deliberated upon by the ancient Greek philosophers, the one which has had the greatest impact on the scientific view of the world is the atomic hypothesis. Richard Feynman once remarked that if all scientific knowledge were to be lost save for one key idea, then the atomic theory of matter would be the most valuable.

Today we may regard the early speculations of Leucippus and Democritus as the beginning of a two-and-a-half millenium quest to identify the ultimate building blocks of the universe. These philosophers proposed that all matter is composed of a handful of different sorts of particles—atoms—so that the universe consists merely of atoms moving in the void. According to this idea, physical objects may be distinguished by the different arrangements of their atoms, and all change is nothing but the rearrangement of atoms. Essential to the atomic theory was that the 'atoms' had to be non-decomposable particles, with no constituent parts, making them truly elementary and indestructible, otherwise there would be a deeper level of structure to explain. What we today call atoms are clearly not the atoms of ancient Greece, for they are composite bodies that may be broken apart. But most physicists believe that on a much smaller scale of size there does exist a set of entities which play the same role conceptually as the atoms of ancient Greece, that is, they constitute a collection of fundamental, primitive objects from which all else is put together. Today it is fashionable to suppose that this base level of physical reality is inhabited by strings rather than particles, and string theory, or its further elaboration as the so-called M theory, is held by some to promise a complete and consistent description of the world—all forces, all particles, space and time.

In spite of the persistent hype that physicists are poised to produce such a 'theory of everything', thereby allegedly relegating philosophy to a scientific appendage, there remain at least two areas of philosophy that still seem far from being incorporated into mainstream science. The first is the nature of consciousness and the second is emergence. Most philosophers regard the former as inextricably bound up with the latter.

The term 'emergence' was first used to define a philosophical concept by George Henry Lewes in his 1875 *Problems of Life and Mind*. Roughly speaking, it recognizes that in physical systems the whole is often more than the sum of its parts. That is to say, at each level of complexity, new and often surprising qualities emerge that cannot, at least in any straightforward manner, be attributed to known properties of the constituents. In some cases, the emergent quality simply makes no sense when applied to the parts. Thus water may be described as wet, but it would be meaningless to ask whether a molecule of H_2O is wet.

Emergence was embraced by the British school of philosophy in the late nineteenth and early twentieth century, particularly in the realm of chemistry and biology. At that time, many biologists were vitalists, adhering to the notion that living organisms possessed some form of additional essence that animated them. Vitalism came into conflict with orthodox physics, which suggested that organisms were merely highly complex machines, their novel behaviour being ultimately explicable in terms of basic physical laws operating at the molecular level. Emergentists sought a middle position, discarding vital essences but denying that all properties of living organisms could be completely reduced to, or 'explained away' in terms of, the mechanics of their components. According to this view, the property 'being alive' is a meaningful one, even if no individual atom of an organism is alive. Thus John Stuart Mill wrote:

All organized bodies are composed of parts, similar to those composing inorganic nature, and which have even themselves existed in an inorganic state; but the phenomena of life, which result from the juxtaposition of those parts in a certain manner, bear no analogy to any of the effects which would be produced by the action of the component substances considered as mere physical agents. To whatever degree we might imagine our knowledge of the properties of the several ingredients of a living body to be extended and perfected, it is certain that no mere summing up of the separate actions of those elements will ever amount to the action of the living body itself. (*A System of Logic*, bk. III, ch. 6, §1)

By extension, the same sort of arguments can be used in connection with the mind–body problem. Panpsychists and dualists assert that consciousness arises from additional mental essences ('mind stuff'), whereas mechanists seek to define consciousness (or define it away) in terms of the complex behaviour of brains. Emergentists take the position that brains—collections of interconnected neurons—really can be conscious, while maintaining that no individual neuron is conscious.

Over the years, emergence has waxed and waned in its impact on science. The middle years of the twentieth century saw spectacular advances in physics and biology, especially in the elucidation of the fundamental structure of matter (e.g. atomic, nuclear, and subatomic particle physics and quantum mechanics*) and the molecular basis of biology. This progress greatly bolstered the reductionist approach by explaining many properties of matter in terms of atomic physics and many properties of life in terms of molecular mechanisms. To a lot of scientists, emergence was regarded as at best an irrelevant anachronism, at worst, a vestige of vitalism. But during the last couple of decades, the mood has shifted again. In large part this is due to the rise of the sciences of complexity. This includes subjects such as chaos theory, network theory, nonlinear systems, and self-organizing systems. The use of computer simulations as an experimental tool to model complex systems has encouraged the view that many features of the world cannot be foreseen from contemplating a set of underlying dynamical equations. Rather, they are discovered only from a systematic study of the *solutions* in the form of numerical simulations.

In exploring the tension between reductionism and emergence, it is helpful to distinguish between weak and strong versions of each. Few would deny the power and efficacy of reductionism as a methodology. The icon of reductionism is the subatomic particle accelerator or 'atom smasher' by which the basic constituents of matter have been exposed. Without our ability to break apart atomic particles into smaller and smaller fragments, there would be little understanding of the properties of matter or the fundamental forces that shape it. As physicists have probed ever deeper into the microscopic realm of matter, to use Steven Weinberg's evocative phrase (Weinberg, 1992), 'the arrows of explanation point downward.' That is, we frequently account for a phenomenon by appealing to the properties of the next level down. In this way the behaviour of gases is explained by molecules, the properties of molecules are explained by atoms, which in turn are explained by nuclei and electrons. This downward path extends, it is supposed, as far as the bottom-level entities, be they strings or some other exotica.

While the foregoing is not contentious, differences arise concerning whether the reductionist account of nature is merely a fruitful *methodology*—a weak form of reductionism known as *methodological reductionism*—or whether *it is the whole story*. Many physicists are self-confessed out-and-out *strong* reductionists. They believe that once the final building blocks of matter and the rules that govern them have been identified, then all of nature

---

* Chapter 3 provides a detailed overview of the developments in quantum mechanics and their significance for the emergence debate. Although readers without a background in physics may find the presentation challenging, the relationship between quantum physics and classical physics remains a crucial piece of the emergence puzzle.

will, in effect, have been explained. This strong form of reductionism is sometimes known as *ontological reductionism*: the assertion that the whole *really is*, in the final analysis, nothing but the sum of the parts, and that the formulation of concepts, theories, and experimental procedures in terms of higher-level concepts is merely a convenience.

A minority of scientists—emergentists—challenge this account of nature. Again, it is helpful to distinguish between weak and strong versions. Weak reductionism recognizes that in practice the only way that the behaviour of many complex systems may be determined is by direct inspection or by simulation. In other words, one may not deduce merely from the principles that govern a class of systems how a specific individual system will in fact behave. Human behaviour, and even the behaviour of a simple organism such as a bacterium, probably falls into this category.

Strong emergence is a far more contentious position, in which it is asserted that the micro-level principles are quite simply inadequate to account for the system's behaviour as a whole. Strong emergence cannot succeed in systems that are causally closed at the microscopic level, because there is no room for additional principles to operate that are not already implicit in the lower-level rules. Thus a closed system of Newtonian particles cannot exhibit strongly emergent properties, as everything that can be said about the system is already contained in the micro-level dynamics (including the initial conditions).

One may identify three loopholes that permit strong emergence. The first is if the universe is an open system. This would enable 'external' or global principles to 'soak up' the causal slack left by the openness. The system as a whole would then be determined in part from the micro-level dynamics and in part from the constraints imposed by the global principles. The second possibility arises when the system is non-deterministic—quantum mechanics being the obvious example—and the system under consideration is unique rather than belonging to a homogeneous ensemble (in which case a statistical form of determinism would still apply). The final possibility is if the laws of physics operating at the base level possess intrinsic imprecision due to the finite computational resources of the universe. All three possibilities would be considered unorthodox departures from standard physical theory.

Emergence thus possesses a curious status. It has a long history within philosophy, but its position within science is both recent and tentative. For emergence to be accepted as more than a methodological convenience—that is, for emergence to make a difference in our understanding of how the world works—something has to give within existing theory. There is a growing band of scientists who are pushing at the straightjacket of orthodox causation to 'make room' for strong emergence, and although physics remains deeply reductionistic, there is a sense that the subject is poised for a dramatic paradigm shift in this regard. And where physics leads, chemistry and biology are likely to follow.

Why would this shift be important? If emergence (in the strong sense) were established as a bona fide part of physics, it would transform the status of the subjects within the hierarchy that physics supports. One might expect there to exist 'laws of complexity' that would augment, but not conflict with, the underlying laws of physics. Emergence in biology would open the way to biological laws that supplement the laws of physics, perhaps enabling scientists to pin down exactly what it is that distinguishes living matter from nonliving matter. The greatest impact would surely be in the field of consciousness studies, where the mind–body problem could be solved by appealing to mental causation as a legitimate category augmenting, but not reducible to, physical causation. This would enable scientists to take consciousness seriously as a fundamental property of the universe, and not as an irrelevant and incidental epiphenomenon.

Strong emergence would have a profound effect in ethics, philosophy, and theology too. Take, for example, ethics. In a reductionist world view, all that really matters are the base level entities and their laws, for example, subatomic particles and superstrings. Life, mind, society, and ethics are all regarded by reductionists as highly derivative special states of matter with no claim to represent basic aspects of reality. Those who argue that there is a moral dimension to the universe, that is, that there exist genuine ethical laws that may stand alongside the laws of physics in a complete description of reality, are dismissed by reductionists with the 'no-room-at-the-bottom' argument: how can there exist distinct ethical laws when the laws of physics already account for everything? But if mental, social, and ethical laws *emerge* at each relevant level of complexity, in a manner that augments but does not conflict with the laws of physics, there is room for the existence of ethical laws. Categories such as 'right' and 'wrong' could possess an absolute (law-like) rather than a socially relative status.

If emergence is eventually embraced by science, it raises an interesting theological issue. The founders of physics, such as Galileo, Kepler, and Newton, were all religious, and they believed that in doing science they were uncovering God's handiwork, arcanely encoded in mathematical laws. In this world view, God sits at the base of physical reality, underpinning the mathematical and rational laws of physics, constituting what Tillich calls 'the ground of being'. Religious emergentists might be tempted to locate God at the *top* of the hierarchy, as the supreme emergent quality. There is thus apparently a tension between reductionism and emergence in theology as well as in science. It is fascinating that no less a scientist than Richard Feynman felt moved to address this very issue as long ago as 1965, in a lecture

about levels of complexity leading from the fundamental laws of physics, up
and up in a hierarchy, to qualities such as 'evil', 'beauty', and 'hope.' I can do
no better than to close by using his words (*The Character of Physical Law*, 2nd
edn., Penguin, London, 1992, p. 125):

Which end is nearer to God, if I may use a religious metaphor: beauty and hope, or the
fundamental laws? I think that the right way, of course, is to say that what we have to
look at is the whole structural interconnection of the thing; and that all the sciences,
and not just the sciences but all the efforts of intellectual kinds, are an endeavour to
see the connections of the hierarchies, to connect beauty to history, to connect history
to man's psychology, man's psychology to the workings of the brain, the brain to the
neural impulse, the neural impulse to the chemistry, and so forth, up and down, both
ways. And today we cannot, and it is no use making believe that we can, draw carefully
a line all the way from one end of this thing to the other, because we have only just
begun to see that there is this relative hierarchy.

And I do not think either end is nearer to God.

Paul Davies

Sydney, 2006

1

Conceptual Foundations of Emergence Theory

Philip Clayton

The discussion of emergence has grown out of the successes and the failures of the scientific quest for reduction. Emergence theories presuppose that the once-popular project of complete explanatory reduction—that is, explaining all phenomena in the natural world in terms of the objects and laws of physics—is finally impossible.[1]

In one sense, limitations to the programme of reduction*ism*, understood as a philosophical position about science, do not affect everyday scientific practice. To do science still means to try to explain phenomena in terms of their constituent parts and underlying laws. Thus, endorsing an emergentist philosophy of science is in most cases consistent with business as usual in much of science. In another sense, however, the reduction-*versus*-emergence debate does have deep relevance for one's understanding of scientific method and results, as the following chapters will demonstrate. The 'unity of science' movement that dominated the middle of the twentieth century, perhaps the classic expression of reductionist philosophy of science, presupposed a significantly different understanding of natural science—its goals, epistemic status, relation to other areas of study, and final fate—than is entailed by emergence theories of science. Whether the scientist subscribes to one position or the other will inevitably have some effects on how she pursues her science and how she views her results.

---

[1] See, among many others, Austen Clark (1980), Hans Primas (1983), Evandro Agazzi (1991), and Terrance Brown and Leslie Smith (2003). Also helpful is Carl Gillett and Barry Loewer (2001), e.g. Jaegwon Kim's article, 'Mental Causation and Consciousness: The Two Mind–body Problems for the Physicalist'.

1. DEFINING EMERGENCE

The following definition of emergence by el-Hani and Pereira includes four features generally associated with this concept:

1. *Ontological physicalism*: All that exists in the space-time world are the basic particles recognized by physics and their aggregates.
2. *Property emergence*: When aggregates of material particles attain an appropriate level of organizational complexity, genuinely novel properties emerge in these complex systems.
3. *The irreducibility of the emergence*: Emergent properties are irreducible to, and unpredictable from, the lower-level phenomena from which they emerge.
4. *Downward causation*: Higher-level entities causally affect their lower-level constituents. (el-Hani and Pereira, 2000, p. 133)

Each of these four theses requires elaboration, and some may require modification as well. We consider them *seriatim.*

(1) *Concerning ontological physicalism.* The first condition does correctly express the anti-dualistic thrust of emergence theories. But if the emergence thesis is correct, it undercuts the claim that physics is the fundamental discipline in terms of which all others must be expressed. Moreover, rather than treating all objects that are not 'recognized by physics' as mere aggregates, it suggests viewing them as emergent entities (in a sense to be defined). Thus it might be more accurate to begin with the more neutral doctrine of ontological monism:

(1') *Ontological monism*: Reality is ultimately composed of one basic kind of 'stuff'. Yet the concepts of physics are not sufficient to explain all the forms that this stuff takes—all the ways it comes to be structured, individuated, and causally efficacious. The one 'stuff' apparently takes forms for which the explanations of physics, and thus the ontology of physics (or 'physicalism' for short), are not adequate. We should not assume that the entities postulated by physics complete the inventory of what exists. Hence emergentists should be monists but do not need to be physicalists in the sense that physics dictates their ontology.

(2) *Concerning property emergence.* The discovery of genuinely novel properties in nature is indeed a major motivation for emergence. Timothy O'Connor has provided a sophisticated account of property emergence. For any emergent property *P* of some object *O,* four conditions hold:

(i) *P* supervenes on properties of the parts of *O*;

(ii) *P* is not had by any of the object's parts;

(iii) *P* is distinct from any structural property of *O*;

(iv) *P* has direct ('downward') determinative influence on the pattern of behaviour involving *O*'s parts. (O'Connor, 1994, pp. 97–8)

Particular attention should be paid to O'Connor's condition (ii), which he calls the feature of *non-structurality*. It entails three features: 'The property's being potentially had only by objects of some complexity, not had by any of the object's parts, [and] distinct from any structural property of the object' (p. 97).

(3) *Concerning the irreducibility of emergence.* To say that emergent properties are irreducible to lower-level phenomena presupposes that reality is divided into a number of distinct levels or orders. Wimsatt classically expresses the notion: 'By level of organization, I will mean here compositional levels—hierarchical divisions of stuff (paradigmatically but not necessarily material stuff) organized by part-whole relations, in which wholes at one level function as parts at the next (and at all higher) levels...' (Wimsatt, 1994, p. 222). Wimsatt, who begins by contrasting an emergentist ontology with Quine's desert landscapes, insists that 'it is possible to be a reductionist and a holist too' (p. 225). The reason is that emergentist holism, in contrast to what we might call 'New Age holism', is a controlled holism. It consists of two theses: that there are forms of causality that are not reducible to physical causes (on which more in a moment), and that causality should be our primary guide to ontology. As Wimsatt writes, 'Ontologically, one could take the primary working matter of the world to be causal relationships, which are connected to one another in a variety of ways—and together make up patterns of causal networks' (p. 220).

It follows that one of the major issues for emergence theory will involve the question when exactly one should speak of the emergence of a new level within the natural order. Traditionally, 'life' and 'mind' have been taken to be genuine emergent levels within the world—from which it follows that 'mind' cannot be understood dualistically, *à la* Descartes. But perhaps there are quite a few more levels, perhaps innumerably more. In a recent book, the Yale biophysicist Harold Morowitz (2002), for example, identifies no fewer than twenty-eight distinct levels of emergence in natural history from the big bang to the present.

The comparison with mathematics helps to clarify what is meant by emergent levels and why decisions about them are often messy. Although mathematical *knowledge* increases, mathematics is clearly an area in which one doesn't encounter the emergence of something new. Work in mathematics involves discovering logical entailments: regularities and principles that are built into axiomatic systems from the outset. Thus it is always true that if you want to know the number of numerals in a set of concurrent integers, you subtract the value of the first from the value of the last and add one. It's not as if that rule only begins to pertain when the numbers get really big. By contrast, in the natural world the quantity of particles or degree of complexity in a system does often make a difference. In complex systems, the outcome is more than the sum of the parts. The difficult part, both empirically and conceptually, is ascertaining when and why the complexity is sufficient to produce the new effects.

(4) *Concerning downward causation.* Many argue that downward causation or 'whole–part influence' is the most distinctive feature of strong emergence—and its greatest challenge. As O'Connor notes, 'an emergent's causal influence is irreducible to that of the micro-properties on which it supervenes: it bears its influence in a direct, "downward" fashion in contrast to the operation of a simple structural macro-property, whose causal influence occurs *via* the activity of the micro-properties that constitute it' (O'Connor, 1994, pp. 97–8).

Such a causal influence of an emergent structure or object on its constituent parts contrasts with the claim that all causation is ultimately to be analysed in terms of micro-physical causes. The notion of emergent causal influences receives detailed exposition and defence—and its fair share of criticism—in many of the following chapters. Defenders of the notion often appeal to Aristotle's four distinct types of causal influence, which include not only efficient causality, the dominant conception of cause in the history of modern science, but also material, formal, and final causality. The trouble is that material causality—the way in which the matter of a thing causes it to be and to act in a particular way—is no less 'physicalist' than efficient causality, and final causality—the way in which the goal toward which a thing strives influences its behaviour—is associated with vitalist, dualist, and supernaturalist accounts of the world, accounts that most emergentists would prefer to avoid. Formal causality—the influence of the form, structure, or function of an object on its activities—is thus probably the most fruitful of these Aristotelian options. Several authors have begun formulating a broader theory of causal influence, including Terrence Deacon (Ch. 5),[2] although much work remains to be done.

2. THE PREHISTORY OF THE EMERGENCE CONCEPT

By most accounts, George Henry Lewes was the scholar whose use of the term 'emergence' was responsible for the explosion of emergence theories in the

---

[2] See also Rom Harré and E. H. Madden (1975), John Dupré (1993), and Robert N. Brandon (1996).

early twentieth century (see Lewes, 1875). Yet precursors to the concept can be traced back in the history of Western philosophy at least as far as Aristotle. Aristotle's biological research led him to posit a principle of growth within organisms that was responsible for the qualities or form that would later emerge. Aristotle called this principle the *entelechy*, the internal principle of growth and perfection that directed the organism to actualize the qualities that it contained in a merely potential state. According to his doctrine of 'potencies', the adult form of the human or animal emerges out of its youthful form. (Unlike contemporary emergence theories, however, he held that the complete form is already present in the organism from the beginning, like a seed; it just needs to be transformed from its potential state to its actual state.) As noted, Aristotle's explanation of emergence included 'formal' causes, which operate through the form internal to the organism, and 'final' causes, which pull the organism (so to speak) toward its final telos or 'perfection'.

The influence of Aristotle on the Hellenistic, medieval, and early modern periods cannot be overstated. His conception of change and growth was formative for the development of Islamic thought in the Middle Ages and, especially after being baptized at the hands of Thomas Aquinas, it became foundational for Christian theology as well. In many respects biology was still under the influence of something very much like the Aristotelian paradigm when Darwin began his work.

A second precursor to emergence theory might be found in the doctrine of *emanation* as presented by Plotinus in the third century CE[3] and then further developed by the Neoplatonic thinkers who followed him. On Plotinus's view, the entire hierarchy of being emerges out of the One through a process of emanation. This expansion was balanced by a movement of (at least some) finite things back up the ladder of derivation toward their ultimate source. The Neoplatonic model thus involved both a *downward* movement of differentiation and causality and an *upward* movement of increasing perfection, diminishing distance from the Source, and (in principle) a final mystical reunification with the One. (The claim that new species or structural forms arise only 'top down', as it were, and never in a bottom-up manner represents an important point of contrast with most twentieth-century emergence theories.) Unlike static models of the world, emanation models allowed for a gradual process of becoming. Although the later Neoplatonic traditions generally focused on the downward emanation that gave rise to the intellectual, psychological, and physical spheres (respectively *nous*, *psyche*, and *physika* or *kosmos* in Plotinus), their notion of emanation did allow for the emergence of new species as well. In those cases where the

---

[3] More detail is available in Clayton (2000), chapter 3.

emanation was understood in a temporal sense, as with Plotinus, the emanation doctrine provides an important antecedent to doctrines of biological or universal evolution.[4]

When science was still natural philosophy, emergence played a productive heuristic role. After 1850, however, emergence theories were several times imposed unscientifically as a metaphysical framework in a way that blocked empirical work. Key examples include the neo-vitalists (e.g. H. Driesch's theory of entelechies) and neo-idealist theories of the interconnections of all living things (e.g. Bradley's theory of internal relations) around the turn of the century, as well as the speculations of the British Emergentists in the 1920s concerning the origin of mind, to whom we turn in a moment.

Arguably, the philosopher who should count as the great modern advocate of emergence theory is Hegel. In place of the notion of static being or substance, Hegel offered a temporalized ontology, a philosophy of universal becoming. The first triad in his System moves from Being, as the first postulation, to Nothing, its negation. If these two stand in blunt opposition, there can be no development in reality. But the opposition between the two is overcome by the category of Becoming. This triad is both the first step in the System and an expression of its fundamental principle. Always, in the universal flow of 'Spirit coming to itself', oppositions arise and are overcome by a new level of emergence.

As an idealist, Hegel did not begin with the natural or the physical world; he began with the world of ideas. According to his system, at some point ideas gave rise to the natural world, and in Spirit the two are re-integrated. His massive *Phenomenology of Spirit* represents an epic of emergence written on a grand scale. The variety of 'philosophies of process' that followed Hegel shared his commitment to the 'temporalization of ontology', construing reality itself as fundamentally in process. Henri Bergson, William James, and especially Alfred North Whitehead reconstructed the emergence of more and more complex objects, structures, institutions, forms of experience, and cultural ideas. Their work in mathematical physics (Whitehead) and psychology (James) gave their work a more concrete and empirical orientation than one finds in the great German and Anglo-American Idealist systems. Whitehead in particular provided a rigorous metaphysical system of 'emergent evolution' in his *magnum opus, Process and Reality* (1978, e.g. p. 229). Although on Whitehead's view *experience* is present from the beginning and does not emerge at some point in cosmic evolution, nevertheless subjectivity,

---

[4] Note however that Plotinian emanation entails emergence from the top down, as it were, whereas most contemporary emergence theories speak of higher-order objects emerging out of the lower-level objects and forces that precede them in natural history.

consciousness, and even the 'consequent nature' of God are emergent products of evolution: 'For Kant, the world emerges from the subject; for the philosophy of organism, the subject emerges from the world' (p. 88).

Before a close collaboration could arise between science and the conceptual world of emergence, it was necessary that the rationalist and idealist excesses of the Hegelian tradition be corrected. The 'inversion' of Hegel by Ludwig Feuerbach and Karl Marx, which replaced Hegel's idealism with a radically materialist starting point, provided the first step. Feuerbach's *Essence of Christianity* traced the development of spiritual ideas beginning with the human species in its concrete physical and social reality ('species-being'). In Marx's early writing the laws of development were still necessary and triadic (dialectical) in Hegel's sense (e.g. Marx, 1983, pp. 87–90). But Marx eventually completed the inversion by anchoring the dialectic in the means of production. Now economic history, the study of the development of economic structures, became the fundamental level and ideas were relagated to a 'superstructure', the ideological after-effects or *ex post facto* justifications of economic structures.

The birth of sociology (or, more generally, social science) in the nineteenth century is closely tied to this development. Auguste Comte, the so-called father of sociology, provided his own ladder of evolution. But now science crowned the hierarchy, being the rightful heir to the Age of Religion and the Age of Philosophy. The work of Comte and his followers (especially Durkheim), with their insistence that higher-order human ideas arose out of simpler antecedents, helped establish an emergentist understanding of human society. Henceforth studies of the human person would have to begin not with the realm of ideas or Platonic forms but with the elementary processes of the physical and social worlds.

3. WEAK AND STRONG EMERGENCE

Although the particular labels and formulations vary widely, commentators generally agree that twentieth-century emergence theories fall into two broad categories. These are best described as 'weak' and 'strong' emergence—with the emphatic insistence that these adjectives refer to the degree of emergence and not to the argumentative quality of the position in question (Bedau, 1997, pp. 375–99). Strong emergentists maintain that genuinely new causal agents or causal processes come into existence over the course of evolutionary history. By contrast, weak emergentists insist that, as new patterns emerge, the fundamental causal processes remain, ultimately, physical. It may be more convenient for *us* to explain causal processes using emergent categories such as protein synthesis, hunger, kin selection, or the desire to be loved; indeed, there may even be permanent blocks to reconstructing the fundamental causal history. Yet however great the role of emergent patterns and explanations, ultimately the causal work is done at the microphysical level (see Jaegwon Kim's essay, below).

Weak emergentists grant that different sorts of causal interactions may *appear* to dominate 'higher' levels of reality. But our inability to recognize in these emerging patterns new manifestations of the same fundamental processes is due primarily to the currently limited state of our knowledge. For this reason weak emergence is sometimes called 'epistemological emergence', in contrast to strong or 'ontological' emergence. Michael Silberstein and John McGreever nicely define the contrast between these two terms:

A property of an object or system is epistemologically emergent if the property is reducible to or determined by the intrinsic properties of the ultimate constituents of the object or system, while at the same time it is very difficult for us to explain, predict or derive the property on the basis of the ultimate constituents. Epistemologically emergent properties are novel only at a level of description. . . . Ontologically emergent features are neither reducible to nor determined by more basic features. Ontologically emergent features are features of systems or wholes that possess causal capacities not reducible to any of the intrinsic causal capacities of the parts nor to any of the (reducible) relations between the parts. (Silberstein and McGreever, 1999, p. 186)[5]

It is not difficult to provide a formal definition of emergence in this weak sense: 'F is an emergent property of S iff (a) there is a law to the effect that all systems with this micro-structure have F; but (b) F cannot, even in theory, be deduced from the most complete knowledge of the basic properties of the components $C_1, \ldots, C_n$' of the system (Beckermann, 1992, p. 104).

Unquestionably, the weak causal theory dominated presentations of emergence in the philosophy of science and metaphysics from the end of the heyday of British Emergentism in the early 1930s until the final decade of the century. The gap between weak and strong theories of emergence is vast, including both the interests that motivate them and the arguments they employ; at times it leads to the appearance of incommensurability between them. And yet the issues that divide the two camps remain the most important in the entire field of emergence studies, and the debate between them is the red thread that connects almost all the chapters that follow. In the following pages I sketch the origins of and major positions in this debate in the twentieth century.

---

[5] The same distinction between epistemological and ontological, or weak and strong, emergence lies at the centre of Jaegwon Kim's important 'Making Sense of Emergence' (1999).

4. STRONG EMERGENCE: C. D. BROAD

We begin with perhaps the best known work in the field, C. D. Broad's *The Mind and Its Place in Nature*. Broad's position is clearly *anti*-dualist; he insists that emergence theory is compatible with a fundamental monism about the physical world. He contrasts this emergentist monism with what he calls 'Mechanism' and with weak emergence:

On the emergent theory we have to reconcile ourselves to much less unity in the external world and a much less intimate connexion between the various sciences. At best the external world and the various sciences that deal with it will form a kind of hierarchy. We might, if we liked, keep the view that there is only one fundamental kind of stuff. *But we should have to recognise aggregates of various orders.* (Broad, 1925, p. 77)

Emergence, Broad argues, can be expressed in terms of laws ('trans-ordinal laws') that link the emergent characteristics with the lower-level parts and the structure or patterns that occur at the emergent level. But emergent laws do not meet the deducibility requirements of, for example, Hempel's 'covering law' model;[6] they are not metaphysically necessary. Moreover, they have another strange feature: 'the only peculiarity of [an emergent law] is that we must wait till we meet with an actual instance of an object of the higher order before we can discover such a law; and ... we cannot possibly deduce it beforehand from any combination of laws which we have discovered by observing aggregates of a lower order' (Broad, 1925, p. 79).

These comments alone would not be sufficient to mark Broad as a strong rather than weak emergentist. Nor do his comments on biology do so. He accepts teleology in nature, but defines it in a weak enough sense that no automatic inference to a cosmic Designer is possible. Broad also attacks the theory of entelechies (p. 86) and what he calls 'Substantial Vitalism', by which he clearly means the work of Hans Dietsch. Broad rejects Biological Mechanism because 'organisms are not machines but are systems whose characteristic behaviour is emergent and not mechanistically explicable' (p. 92). He thus accepts 'Emergent Vitalism', while insisting that this watered-down version of Vitalism is an implication of emergence and not its motivation: 'What must be assumed is not a special tendency of matter to fall into the kind of arrangement which has vital characteristics, but a general tendency for complexes of one order to combine with each other under suitable conditions to form complexes of the next order' (p. 93). Emergentism is consistent with theism but does not entail it (p. 94).

[6] On the covering law model, see classically Carl Hempel and Paul Oppenheim (1948); see also Ernst Nagel (1961).

It is in Broad's extended treatment of the mind–body problem that one sees most clearly why the stages of emergence leading to mind actually entail the strong interpretation. Mental events, he argues, represent another distinct emergent level. But they cannot be explained in terms of their interrelations alone. Some sort of 'Central Theory' is required, that is, a theory that postulates a mental 'Centre' that unifies the various mental events as 'mind' (pp. 584 ff.). Indeed, just as Broad had earlier argued that the notion of a material event requires the notion of material substance, so now he argues that the idea of mental events requires the notion of mental substance (pp. 598 ff.). Broad remains an emergentist in so far as the 'enduring whole', which he calls 'mind' or 'mental particle', 'is analogous, not to a body, but to a material particle' (p. 600). (Dualists, by contrast, would proceed from the postulation of mental substance to the definition of individual mental events.) The resulting strong emergentist position lies between dualism and weak emergence. Broad derives his concept of substance from *events* of a particular type (in this case, mental events), rather than presupposing it as ultimate. Yet he underscores the emergent reality of each unique level by speaking of actual objects or specific emergent substances (with their own specific causal powers) at that level.

Broad concludes *The Mind and Its Place in Nature* by presenting seventeen metaphysical positions concerning the place of mind in nature and boiling them down ultimately to his preference for 'emergent materialism' over the other options. It is a materialism, however, far removed from most, if not all, of the materialist and physicalist positions of the second half of the twentieth century. For example, 'Idealism is not incompatible with materialism' as he defines it (p. 654)—something that one cannot say of most materialisms today. Broad's (redefined) materialism is also not incompatible, as we have already seen, with theism.

5. EMERGENT EVOLUTION: C. L. MORGAN

Conway Lloyd Morgan became perhaps the most influential of the British Emergentists of the 1920s. I reconstruct the four major tenets of his emergentist philosophy before turning to an initial evaluation of its success.

First, Morgan could not accept what we might call Darwin's *continuity principle*. A gradualist, Darwin was methodologically committed to removing any 'jumps' in nature. On Morgan's view, by contrast, emergence is all about the recognition that evolution is 'punctuated': even a full reconstruction of evolution would not remove the basic stages or levels that are revealed in the evolutionary process.

In this regard, Morgan stood closer to Alfred Russel Wallace than to Darwin. Wallace's work focused in particular on qualitative novelty in the evolutionary process. Famously, Wallace turned to divine intervention as the explanation for each new stage or level in evolution. Morgan recognized that such an appeal would lead sooner or later to the problems faced by any 'God of the gaps' strategy. In the conviction that it must be possible to recognize emergent levels without shutting down the process of scientific inquiry, Morgan sided against Wallace and with 'evolutionary naturalism' in the appendix to *Emergent Evolution* (Morgan, 1931). He endorsed emergence not as a means for preserving some causal influence *ad extra*, but because he believed scientific research points to a series of discrete steps as basic in natural history.

Secondly, Morgan sought a philosophy of biology that would grant adequate place to the emergence of radically new life forms and behaviours. Interestingly, after Samuel Alexander, Henri Bergson is one of the most cited authors in *Emergent Evolution*. Morgan resisted Bergson's conclusions ('widely as our conclusions differ from those to which M. Bergson has been led', p. 116), and for many of the same reasons that he resisted Wallace: Bergson introduced the *élan vital* or vital energy as a force from outside nature.[7] Thus Bergson's *Creative Evolution* (1983), originally published in 1911, combines a Cartesian view of non-material forces with the pervasively temporal perspective of late nineteenth-century evolutionary theory. By contrast, the underlying forces for Morgan are thoroughly immanent in the natural process. Still, Morgan stands closer to Bergson than this contrast might suggest. For him also, 'creative evolution' produces continually novel types of phenomena. As Rudolf Metz noted, 'It was through Bergson's idea of creative evolution that the doctrine of novelty [became] widely known and made its way into England, where, thanks to a similar reaction against the mechanistic evolution theory, Alexander and Morgan became its most influential champions. Emergent evolution is a new, important and specifically British variation of Bergson's creative evolution' (Metz, 1938, as quoted in Blitz, 1992, p. 86).[8]

Thirdly, Morgan argued powerfully for the notion of levels of reality. He continually emphasized a study of the natural world that looks for novel properties at the level of a system taken as whole, properties that are not present in the parts of the system. Morgan summarizes his position by arguing that the theory of

[7] I thus agree with David Blitz that Morgan's work is more than an English translation of Bergson.

[8] Blitz's work is an invaluable resource on the early influences on Morgan's thought.

levels or orders of reality…does, however, imply (1) that there is increasing complexity in integral systems as new kinds of relatedness are successively supervenient;
(2) that reality is, in this sense, in process of development; (3) that there is an
ascending scale of what we may speak of as richness in reality; and (4) that the richest
reality that we know lies at the apex of the pyramid of emergent evolution up to date.
(Morgan, 1931, p. 203)

The notion of levels of reality harkens back to the philosophy of Neoplatonic
philosophy of Plotinus, mentioned above, who held that all things emanate
outward from the One in a series of distinct levels of reality (nous, psyche,
individual minds, persons, animals, etc.). In the present case, however, the
motivation for the position is not in the first place metaphysical but scientific:
the empirical study of the world itself suggests that reality manifests itself as a
series of emerging levels rather than as permutations of matter understood as
the fundamental building blocks for all things.

Finally, Morgan interpreted the emergent objects at these various levels in the
sense of strong emergence. As his work makes clear, there are stronger and
weaker ways of introducing the idea of levels of reality. His strong interpretation
of the levels, according to Blitz, was influenced by a basic philosophy text by
Walter Marvin. The text had argued that reality is analysable into a series of
'logical strata', with each new stratum consisting of a smaller number of more
specialized types of entities: 'To sum up: The picture of reality just outlined is
logically built up of strata. The logical and mathematical are fundamental and
universal. The physical comes next and though less extensive is still practically, if
not quite, universal. Next come the biological, extensive but vastly less extensive
than the chemical. Finally, comes the mental and especially the human and the
social, far less extensive' (Marvin, 1912, as quoted in Blitz, 1992, p. 90).

Emergence is interesting to scientifically minded thinkers only to the extent
that it accepts the principle of parsimony, introducing no more metaphysical
superstructure than is required by the data themselves. The data, Morgan
argued, require the strong interpretation of emergence. They support the
conclusions that there are major discontinuities in evolution; that these
discontinuities result in the multiple levels at which phenomena are manifested in the natural world; that objects at these levels evidence a unity and
integrity, which require us to treat them as wholes or objects or agents in their
own right; and that, as such, they exercise their own causal powers on other
agents (horizontal causality) and on the parts of which they are composed
(downward causation). Contrasting his view to 'weaker' approaches to ontology, Morgan treats the levels of reality as *substantially* different:

There is increasing richness in stuff *and in substance* throughout the stages of
evolutionary advance; there is redirection of the course of events at each level; this

redirection is so marked at certain critical turning-points as to present 'the apparent paradox' that the emergently new is incompatible in 'substance' with the previous course of events before the turning-point was reached. All this seems to be given in the evidence. (Morgan, 1931, p. 207, italics added)

Introducing emergent levels as producing new substances means attributing the strongest possible ontological status to wholes in relation to their parts. Blitz traces Morgan's understanding of the whole–part relation back to E. G. Spaulding. Spaulding had argued that 'in the physical world (and elsewhere) it is an established empirical fact that parts as non-additively organized form a whole which has characteristics that are qualitatively different from the characteristics of the parts' (Spaulding, 1918, as quoted in Blitz, p. 88). Significantly, Spaulding drew most of his examples from chemistry. If emergence theories can point to emergent wholes only at the level of mind, they quickly fall into a crypto-dualism (or perhaps a not-so-crypto one!); and if they locate emergent wholes only at the level of life, they run the risk of sliding into vitalism. Conversely, if significant whole–part influences can be established already within physical chemistry, they demonstrate that emergence is not identical with either vitalism or dualism.

How are we to evaluate Morgan's *Emergent Evolution*? The strategy of arguing for emergent substances clashes with the monism that I defended above, and a fortiori with all physicalist emergence theories. Morgan's strategy is even more regrettable in that it was unnecessary; his own theory of *relations* would actually have done the same work without recourse to the substance notion. He writes, 'There is perhaps no topic which is more cardinal to our interpretation ... than that which centres round what I shall call relatedness' (p. 67). In fact, relation forms the core of his ontology, as it does of Whitehead's: 'It is as an integral whole of relatedness that any individual entity, or any concrete situation, is a bit of reality' (p. 69; note the close connection to contemporary interpretations of quantum physics).

Since the relations at each emergent level are unique, complexes of relations are adequately individuated: 'May one say that in each such family group there is not only an incremental resultant, but also a specific kind of integral relatedness of which the constitutive characters of each member of the group is an emergent expression? If so, we have here an illustration of what is meant by emergent evolution' (Morgan, 1931, p. 7). Or, more succinctly: 'If it be asked: What is it that you claim to be emergent?—the brief reply is: Some new kind of relation', for 'at each ascending step there is a new entity in virtue of some new kind of relation, or set of relations, within it' (p. 64). As long as each relational complex evidences unique features and causal powers, one does not need to lean on the questionable concept of substance in order to describe it.

Let's call those theories of emergence 'very strong' which not only (a) individuate relational complexes, (b) ascribe reality to them through an ontology of relations, and (c) ascribe causal powers and activity to them, but also (d) treat them as individual substances in their own right. The recent defence of 'emergent dualism' by William Hasker in *The Emergent Self* provides an analogous example: 'So it is not enough to say that there are emergent properties here; what is needed is an *emergent individual*, a new individual entity which comes into existence as a result of a certain functional configuration of the material constituents of the brain and nervous system' (Hasker, 1999, p. 190). The connection with a theory of substantival entities becomes explicit when Hasker quotes with approval an adaptation of Thomas Aquinas by Brian Leftow: 'the human fetus becomes able to host the human soul... This happens in so lawlike a way as to count as a form of natural supervenience. So if we leave God out of the picture, the Thomist soul is an "emergent individual"' (Leftow, conference comment, quoted in Hasker, pp. 195–6).

Clearly, emergence theories cover a wide spectrum of ontological commitments. According to some the emergents are no more than patterns, with no causal powers of their own; for others they are substances in their own right, almost as distinct from their origins as Cartesian mind is from body. An emergence theory that is to be useful in the philosophy of science will have to accept some form of the law of parsimony: emergent entities and levels should not be multiplied without need. From a scientific perspective it is preferable to explain mental causation by appealing only to mental properties and the components of the central nervous system, rather than by introducing mental 'things' such as minds and spirits. I have argued that Morgan's robust theory of emergent relations would have done justice to emergent levels in natural history, and even to downward causation, without the addition of emerging substances. Morgan, in his attempt to avoid the outright dualism of Wallace and Bergson, would have been better advised to do without them.

6. STRONG EMERGENCE SINCE 1970

Emergence theory in general, and strong emergence in particular, began to disappear off the radar screens during the mid 1930s and did not reappear for some decades. Individual philosophers such as Michael Polanyi may still have advocated emergence positions. Generally, however, the criticisms of the British Emergentists—for instance, by Stephen Pepper in 1926, W. T. Stace in 1939, and Arthur Pap in 1952—were taken to be sufficient. Stace argued, for example, that, although evolution produces novelty, there is nothing philosophically significant to say about it; neither indeterminism nor emergence can make novelty philosophically productive.

In 1973, Pylyshyn noted that a new cognitive paradigm had 'recently exploded' into fashion (Pylyshyn, 1973, p. 1). Whatever one's own particular position on the developments, it's clear that by the end of the century emergence theories were again major topics of discussion in the sciences and philosophy (and the media). Now one must proceed with caution in interpreting more recent philosophy, since histories of the present are inevitably part of what they seek to describe. The authors of the following chapters provide a better picture of the pros and cons of emergence than any single author could. Nonetheless, it's useful to consider the immediate prehistory of strong views in contemporary emergence theory. Two figures in particular played key roles in the re-emergence of interest in strong emergence: Michael Polanyi and Roger Sperry.

i. Michael Polanyi

Writing in the heyday of the reductionist period, midway between the British Emergentists of the 1920s and the rebirth of the emergence movement in the 1990s, Michael Polanyi was a sort of lone voice crying in the wilderness. He's perhaps best known for his defence of tacit knowledge and the irreducibility of the category of personhood, views that were in fact integrally linked to his defence of emergence. In his theory of tacit knowing, for instance, Polanyi recognized that thought was motivated by the anticipation of discovery: 'all the time we are guided by sensing the presence of a hidden reality toward which our clues are pointing' (Polanyi, *Tacit Dimension* (*TD*), 1967, p. 24). Tacit knowing thus presupposes at least two levels of reality: the particulars, and their 'comprehensive meaning' (*TD* 34). Gradually Polanyi extended this 'levels of reality' insight to a variety of fields, beginning with his own field, physical chemistry, and then moving on to the biological sciences and to the problem of consciousness (Polanyi, *Knowing and Being* (*KB*), 1969, Part 4). In his view even physical randomness was understood as an emergent phenomenon (*Personal Knowledge* (*PK*) 390–1); all living things, or what he called 'living mechanisms', were classed with machines as systems controlled by their functions, which exercise a downward causation on the biological parts (e.g. *KB* 226–7; *PK* 359ff.). Processes such as the composition of a text serve as clear signs that human goals and intentions are downward causal forces that play a central role in explaining the behaviour of *homo sapiens*. Polanyi combined these various argumentative steps together into an overarching philosophy of emergence:

The first emergence, by which life comes into existence, is the prototype of all subsequent stages of evolution, by which rising forms of life, with their higher principles, emerge into existence.... The spectacle of rising stages of emergence confirms this generalization by bringing forth at the highest level of evolutionary emergence those mental powers in which we had first recognized our faculty of tacit knowing. (*TD* 49)

Several aspects of Polanyi's position are reflected in contemporary emergence theories and served to influence the development of the field; I mention just three:

(1) *Active and passive boundary conditions.*[9] Polanyi recognized two types of boundaries: natural processes controlled by boundaries; and machines, which function actively to bring about effects. He characterized his distinction in two different ways: as foreground and background interest, and as active and passive constraint. Regarding the former distinction, he argued, a test tube constrains the chemical reaction taking place within it; but when we observe it, 'we are studying the reaction, not the test tube' (*KB* 226). In watching a chess game, by contrast, our interest 'lies in the boundaries': we are interested in the chess master's strategy, in *why* he makes the moves and what he hopes to achieve by them, rather than in the rule-governed nature of the moves themselves.

More important than the backgrounding and foregrounding of interest, Polanyi recognized that the 'causal role' of the test tube is a passive constraint, whereas intentions *actively* shape the outcome in a top-down manner: 'when a sculptor shapes a stone or a painter composes a painting, our interest lies in the boundaries imposed on a material and not in the material itself' (*KB* 226). Messages from the central nervous system cause hormone release in a much more active top-down fashion than does the physical structure of microtubules in the brain. Microtubule structure is still a constraining boundary condition, but it is one of a different type, namely a passive one.[10]

(2) *The 'from–at' transition and 'focal' attention.* Already in the Terry Lectures, Polanyi noticed that the comprehension of meaning involved a movement from 'the proximal'—that is, the particulars that are presented— to the 'distal', which is their comprehensive meaning (*TD* 34). By 1968 he had developed this notion into the notion of 'from–at' conceptions. Understanding meaning involves turning our attention from the words to their meaning; 'we are looking *from* them *at* their meaning' (*KB* 235, emphasis added).

---

[9] I am grateful to Walter Gulick for his clarifications of Polanyi's position and criticisms of an earlier draft of this argument. See Gulick (2003).

[10] Gulick argues (see previous note) that Polanyi is not actually this clear in his usage of the terms; if so, these comments should be taken as a rational reconstruction of his view.

Polanyi built from these reflections to a more general theory of the 'from–to' structure of consciousness. Mind is a 'from–to experience'; the bodily mechanisms of neurobiology are merely 'the subsidiaries' of this experience (*KB* 238). Or, more forcibly, 'mind is the meaning of certain bodily mechanisms; it is lost from view when we look *at* them focally'.[11]

Note, by the way, that there are parallels to Polanyi's notion of mind as focal intention in the theory of consciousness advanced by the quantum physicist Henry Stapp, especially in his *Mind, Matter, and Quantum Mechanics* (2004). These parallels help to explain why Stapp is best characterized as a strong emergentist, if not actually a dualist.[12] Both thinkers believe that mind is best construed as the function of 'exercising discrimination' (*PK* 403n1). If Polanyi and Stapp are right, this represents good news for the downward causation of ideas, since it means that no energy needs to be added to a system by mental activity, thereby preserving the law of the conservation of energy, which is basic to all physical calculations.

(3) *The theory of structure and information.* Like many emergence theorists, Polanyi recognized that structure is an emergent phenomenon. But he also preserved a place for downward causation in the theory of structure, arguing that 'the structure and functioning of an organism is determined, like that of a machine, by constructional and operational principles that control boundary conditions left open by physics and chemistry' (*KB* 219). Structure is not simply a matter of complexity. The structure of a crystal represents a complex order without great informational content (*KB* 228); crystals have a maximum of stability that corresponds to a minimum of potential energy. Contrast crystals with DNA. The structure of a DNA molecule represents a high level of chemical improbability, since the nucleotide sequence is not determined by the underlying chemical structure. While the crystal does not function as a code, the DNA molecule can do so because it is very high in informational content relative to the background probabilities of its formation.

Polanyi's treatment of structure lies very close to contemporary work in information biology.[13] Terrence Deacon for example argues that 'it is essential

---

[11] Ibid.; cf. 214. Polanyi writes later, 'We lose the meaning of the subsidiaries in their role of pointing to the focal' (*KB* 219). For more on Polanyi's theory of meaning, see Polanyi and Prosch (1975).

[12] Stapp's use of the von Newmann interpretation of the role of the observer in quantum mechanics represents a very intriguing form of dualism, since it introduces consciousness not for metaphysical reasons but for physical ones. But for this very reason it stands rather far from classical emergence theory, in which natural history as a narrative of (and source for) the biological sciences plays the central role.

[13] See Hubert Yockey (1992), Werner Loewenstein (1999), Holcombe and Paton (1998), Susan Oyama (2000), and Baddeley, Hancock, and Földiák (2000).

to recognize that biology is not merely a physical science, it is a semiotic science; a science where significance and representation are essential elements.... [Evolutionary biology] stands at the border between physical and semiotic science'.[14] Perhaps other elements in Polanyi's work could contribute to the conceptual side of contemporary work in information biology.

At the same time that emergence theory has profited from Polanyi, it has also moved beyond his work in some respects. I briefly indicate two such areas:

(1) *Polanyi was wrong on morphogenesis.* He was very attracted by the work of Hans Driesch, which seemed to support the existence of organismic forces and causes (*TD* 42–3, *PK* 390, *KB* 232). Following Driesch, Polanyi held that the morphogenetic field pulls the evolving cell or organism toward itself. He was also ready to argue that the coordination of muscles, as well as the recuperation of the central nervous system after injury, was 'unformalizable ... in terms of any fixed anatomical machinery' (*PK* 398). While admitting that the science had not yet been established, he hitched his horse to its future success: 'once ... emergence was fully established, it would be clear that it represented the achievement of a new way of life, induced in the germ plasm by a field based on the gradient of phylogenetic achievement' (*PK* 402). He even cites an anticipation of the stem cell research that has been receiving so much attention of late: the early work by Paul Weiss, which showed that embryonic cells will grow 'when lumped together into a fragment of the organ from which they were isolated' (*KB* 232). But we now know that it is not necessary to postulate that the growth of the embryo 'is controlled by the gradient of potential shapes', and we don't need to postulate a 'field' to guide this development (ibid.). Stem cell research shows that the cell nucleus contains the core information necessary for the cell's development.

(2) *Polanyi's sympathy for Aristotle and vitalism clashes with core assumptions of contemporary biology.* Aristotle is famous for the doctrine of *entelechy*, whereby the future state of an organism (say, in the case of an acorn, the full-grown oak) pulls the developing organism toward itself. In a section on the functions of living beings, Polanyi spoke of the causal role of 'intimations of the potential coherence of hitherto unrelated things', arguing that 'their solution establishes a new comprehensive entity, be it a new poem, a new kind of machine, or a new knowledge of nature' (*TD* 44). The causal powers of non-existent (or at least not-yet-existent) objects make for suspicious enough philosophy; they make for even worse science. Worse from the standpoint of biology was Polanyi's advocacy of Bergson's *élan vital* (*TD* 46), which led him to declare the affinity of his position with that of Teilhard de Chardin.

---

[14] Terrence Deacon (2003), p. 6; also see his essay in Ch. 5.

The doctrine of vitalism that Polanyi took over from Driesch meant, in fact, a wholesale break with the neo-Darwinian synthesis, on which all actual empirical work in biology today is based. Beyond structural features and mechanical forces, Polanyi wanted to add a broader 'field of forces' that would be 'the gradient of a potentiality: a gradient arising from the proximity of a possible achievement' (*PK* 398). He wanted something analogous to 'the agency of a centre seeking satisfaction in the light of its own standards' (ibid.). What we do find in biology is the real-world striving that is caused by the appetites and behavioural dispositions of sufficiently complex organisms. The operation of appetites cannot be fully explained by a Dawkinsian reduction to the 'selfish gene', since their development and expression are often the result of finely tuned interactions with the environment. Combinations of genes can code for appetites, and the environment can select for or against them, without however needing to introduce mysterious forces into biology.

In the end, Polanyi went too far, opting for 'finalistic' causes in biology (*PK* 399). It is one thing to say that the evolutionary process 'manifested itself in the novel organism', but quite another to argue that 'the maturation of the germ plasm is *guided* by the potentialities that are open to it through its possible germination into new individuals' (*PK* 400). It is one thing to say that the evolutionary process has given rise to individuals who can exercise rational and responsible choices, but it breaks with all empirical biology to argue that 'we should take this active component into account likewise down to the lowest levels' (*PK* 402–3). This move would make all of biology a manifestation of an inner vitalistic drive, and that claim is inconsistent with the practice of empirical biology.

ii. Roger Sperry

In the 1960s, at a time when such views were not only unpopular but even anathema, Roger Sperry began defending an emergentist view of mental properties. As a neuroscientist, Sperry would not be satisfied with any explanation that ignored or underplayed the role of neural processes. At the same time, he realized that consciousness is not a mere epiphenomenon of the brain; instead, conscious thoughts and decisions *do something* in brain functioning. Sperry was willing to countenance neither a dualist, separationist account of mind, nor any account that would dispense with mind altogether. As early as 1964, by his own account, he had formulated the core principles of his view (Sperry, 1980, pp. 195–206, cf. p. 196). By 1969 emergence had come to serve as the central orienting concept of his position:

The subjective mental phenomena are conceived to influence and govern the flow of nerve impulse traffic by virtue of their encompassing emergent properties. Individual nerve impulses and other excitatory components of a cerebral activity pattern are simply carried along or shunted this way and that by the prevailing overall dynamics of the whole active process (in principle—just as drops of water are carried along by a local eddy in a stream or the way the molecules and atoms of a wheel are carried along when it rolls downhill, regardless of whether the individual molecules and atoms happen to like it or not). Obviously, it also works the other way around, that is, the conscious properties of cerebral patterns are directly dependent on the action of the component neural elements. Thus, a mutual interdependence is recognized between the sustaining physico-chemical processes and the enveloping conscious qualities. The neurophysiology, in other words, controls the mental effects, and the mental properties in turn control the neurophysiology. (Sperry, 1969, pp. 532–6)

Sperry is sometimes interpreted to hold only that mental language is a re-description of brain activity as a whole. But he clearly does assert that mental properties have causal force: 'The conscious subjective properties in our present view are interpreted to have causal potency in regulating the course of brain events; that is, the mental forces or properties exert a regulative control influence in brain physiology' (Sperry, 1976, p. 165).[15]

Sperry initially selected the term 'interactionism' as a result of his work with split-brain patients. Because these patients' *corpora callosa* had been severed, no neurophysiological account could be given of the unified consciousness that they still manifested. Thus, Sperry reasoned, there must be interactions at the emergent level of consciousness, whereby conscious states exercise a direct causal influence on subsequent brain states (perhaps alongside other causal factors).

Sperry referred to this position as 'emergent interactionism'. He also conceded that the term 'interaction' is not exactly the appropriate term: 'Mental phenomena are described as primarily *supervening* rather than intervening, in the physiological process....Mind is conceived to move matter in the brain and to govern, rule, and direct neural and chemical events without interacting with the components at the component level, just as an organism may move and govern the time-space course of its atoms and tissues without interacting with them' (Sperry, 1987). Sperry is right to avoid the term 'interaction' if it is understood to imply a causal story in which higher-level influences are interpreted as specific (efficient) causal activities that push and pull the lower-level components of the system. As Jaegwon Kim has shown, if one conceives downward causation in that manner, it would be simpler to tell the whole story in terms of the efficient causal history of the component parts themselves.

---

[15] See also Sperry (1987), pp. 164–6.

Sperry was not philosophically sophisticated, and he never elaborated his view in a systematic fashion. But he did effectively chronicle the neuroscientific evidence that supports some form of downward or conscious causation, and he dropped hints of the sort of philosophical account that must be given: a theory of downward causation understood as whole–part influence. Thus Emmeche, Køppe, and Stjernfelt are right to develop Sperry's position using the concepts of part and whole. On their interpretation, the higher level (say, consciousness) constrains the outcome of lower-level processes. Yet it does so in a manner that qualifies as causal influence: 'The entities at various levels may enter part–whole relations (e.g., mental phenomena control their component neural and biophysical sub-elements), in which the control of the part by the whole can be seen as a kind of functional (teleological) causation, which is based on efficient, material as well as formal causation in a multinested system of constraints' (Emmeche, Køppe, and Stjernfelt, 2000, p. 25). Sperry's approach to the neuroscientific data (and the phenomenology of consciousness or *qualia*), combined with a more sophisticated theory of part–whole relations and an updated account of mental causation (see, e.g. the chapters by Silberstein, Murphy, Ellis, and Peacocke below), represents one important strategy for developing a rigorous theory of strong emergence today.

7. WEAK EMERGENCE: SAMUEL ALEXANDER

We turn now to what has undoubtedly been the more popular position among professional philosophers, weak emergence. Recall that weak emergence grants that evolution produces new structures and organizational patterns. We may *speak* of these structures as things in their own right; they may serve as irreducible components of our best explanations; and they may seem to function as causal agents. But the real or ultimate causal work is done at a lower level, presumably that of microphysics. Our inability to recognize in these emerging patterns new manifestations of the same fundamental processes is due primarily to our ignorance and should not be taken as a guide to ontology. The first major advocate of this view, and its classic representative, is Samuel Alexander.

Samuel Alexander's *Space, Time, and Deity* presents a weak emergentist answer to the mind–body problem and then extends his theory into a systematic metaphysical position. Alexander's goal was to develop a philosophical conception in which evolution and history had a real place. He presupposed both as givens: there really are bodies in the universe, and there really exist mental properties or mental experience. The problem is to relate them. Alexander resolutely rejected classical dualism and any idealist view that would make the mental pole primary (e.g. Leibniz, and British Idealists such as F. H. Bradley), yet he would not countenance physicalist views that question the existence of mind. Thus, he argued, mind must emerge in some sense from the physical.

Spinoza's work provided a major inspiration for Alexander. At any given level of reality, Spinoza held, there is only one (type of) activity. Thus in the mind–body case there cannot be both mental causes and physical causes; there can be only one causal system with one type of activity. Alexander argued in a similar manner: 'It seems at first blush paradoxical to hold that our minds enjoy their own causality in following an external causal sequence, and still more that in it [sc. the mind] influencing the course of our thinking we contemplate causal sequence in the objects' (Alexander, 1920, 2:152).[16] As a result, although minds may 'contemplate' and 'enjoy', they cannot be said to *cause*.

Recall that the contrast between strong and weak emergence turns on the strength of the claim made on behalf of mental causation (or, for others, the role of the active subject or mental pole). As Alexander is one of the major defenders of the 'weak' view of the emergence of the mental, his view pushes strongly toward the physical pole. The real causality in nature seems to come from events in the external world. Some causal strings are actual; others are only imagined: 'Plato in my dreams tells me his message as he would in reality' (2:154). For example, suppose you think of the city Dresden and of a painting by Raphael located there. 'When thinking of Dresden makes me think of Raphael, so that I feel my own causality, Dresden is not indeed contemplated as the cause of Raphael, but Dresden and Raphael are contemplated as connected by some causal relation *in the situation which is then* [that is, then becomes] *my perspective of things*' (2:154).

Alexander then extends this account from sensations to a universal theory of mind. Our motor sensors sense movement of objects in the world; we are aware of our limbs moving. Our eyes detect movement external to us in the world. Thus, 'My object in the sensation of hunger or thirst is the living process or movement of depletion, such as I observe outside me in purely physiological form in the parched and thirsting condition of the leaves of a plant'. It's a mistake to think that 'the unpleasantness of hunger is ... psychical' or to treat hunger 'as a state of mind' (2:171). Here Alexander's position stands closest to the 'non-reductive physicalist' view in contemporary philosophy of mind: 'It is no wonder then that we should suppose such a condition to be something mental which is as it were presented to a mind

---

[16] Subsequent references to this work appear in the text, preceded by volume number.

which looks on at it; and that we should go on to apply the same notion to colours and tastes and sounds and regard these as mental in character' (ibid).

In order to generalize this position into a global metaphysical position, Alexander uses 'mind' in a much broader sense than as consciousness alone. More generally, the 'body' aspect of anything stands for the constituent factors into which it can be analysed, and the 'mind' aspect always represents the new quality manifested by a group of bodies when they function as a whole.[17] This generalization allows him to extend his answer to the mind–body problem to all of nature, producing a metaphysics of emergence. As he defines the concept, 'Within the all-embracing stuff of Space-Time, the universe exhibits an emergence in Time of successive levels of finite existence, each with its characteristic empirical quality. The highest of these empirical qualities known to us is mind or consciousness. Deity is the next higher empirical quality to the highest we know' (2:345). The result is a ladder of emergence of universal proportions. I reconstruct the steps of this ladder in eight steps, noting the points at which Alexander did not actually differentiate steps but should have done:[18]

(1) At the base of the ladder lies Space-Time. Time is 'mind' and space is 'body'; hence time is 'the mind of space'. Space-Time is composed of 'point-instants'. Already the early commentators on Alexander found this theory hard to stomach. It has not improved with age.

(2) There must be a principle of development, something that drives the whole process, if there is to be an ongoing process of emergence. Thus Alexander posited that 'there is a nisus in Space-Time which, as it has borne its creatures forward through matter and life to mind, will bear them forward to some higher level of existence' (2:346).

(3) Thanks to the nisus, Space-Time becomes differentiated by 'motions'. Certain organized patterns of motions (today we would call them energies) are bearers of the qualities we can material. So, *contra* Aristotle, matter itself is emergent. (Quantum field theory has since offered some support for this conception. For example, in *Veiled Reality* Bernard d'Espagnat describes atomic particles as products of the quantum field, hence as derivatives of it (d'Espagnat, 1995)).

(4) Organizations of matter are bearers of macrophysical qualities and chemical properties. This constitutes emergence at the molecular level.

(5) When matter reaches a certain level of complexity, molecules become the bearers of life. (This response is consistent with contemporary work on

[17] See Dorothy Emmet's introduction to *Space, Time, and Deity* (Alexander, 1920), p. xv. The concept is reminiscent of Whitehead's well-known claim that mind is 'the spearhead of novelty'.
[18] Again, see Dorothy Emmet's excellent introduction to *Space, Time, and Deity*, on which I have drawn in this reconstruction.

the origins of life, which postulates a gradual transition from complex molecules to living cells.)

(6) Alexander didn't adequately cover the evolution of sentience but should have done. Thus he could have covered the evolution of simple volition (e.g. the choice of where to move), symbiosis (reciprocal systems of organisms), sociality, and primitive brain processing as extensions of the same framework of bodies and their emergent holistic properties, which he called 'mind'.

(7) Some living structures then come to be the bearers of the quality of mind or consciousness proper, 'the highest empirical quality known to us'.

(8) At a certain level mind may be productive of a new emergent quality, which Alexander called 'Deity'. We know of Deity only that it is the next emergent property, that it is a holistic property composed of parts or 'bodies,' and that it results from an increased level of complexity.

To be consistent, Alexander had to postulate that Deity is to minds as our mind is to (the parts of) our bodies. It follows that Deity's 'body' must be the minds in the universe:

One part of the god's mind will be of such complexity and refinement as mind, as to be fitted to carry the new quality of deity. . . . As our mind represents and gathers up into itself its whole body, so does the finite god represent or gather up into its divine part its whole body' [namely, minds]. . . . For such a being its specially differentiated mind takes the place of the brain or central nervous system with us. (2:355)

Alexander also ascribed certain moral properties to Deity. But beyond this, one can say nothing more of its nature:

That the universe is pregnant with such a quality we are speculatively assured. What that quality is we cannot know; for we can neither enjoy nor still less contemplate it. Our human altars still are raised to the unknown God. If we could know what deity is, how it feels to be divine, we should first have to have become as gods. What we know of it is but its relation to the other empirical qualities which precede it in time. Its nature we cannot penetrate. (2:247)

One might have supposed that only a strong emergentist could introduce language of Deity. Yet here we have a case of theological language interpreted in the sense of weak emergence: Alexander introduces this predicate in a manner (largely) consistent with his physicalism.[19] For example, he consistently refuses to talk of the actual existence of a spiritual being, God; all that actually exists is the physical universe:

---

[19] Interestingly, the Gifford lectures by the neuroscientist Michael Arbib almost 70 years later make a similar move: schemas can be extended upward to include God-language, yet no commitment is made to the metaphysical existence of a god. See Arbib and Hesse (1986).

As actual, God does not possess the quality of deity but *is the universe as tending to that quality.* . . . Thus there is no actual infinite being with the quality of deity; but there is an actual infinite, the whole universe, with a nisus toward deity; and this is the God of the religious consciousness, though that consciousness habitually forecasts the divinity of its object as actually realised in an individual form. . . . The actual reality which has deity is the world of empiricals filling up all Space-Time and tending towards a higher quality. Deity is a nisus and not an accomplishment. (2:361–2, 364)

Alexander's view remains a classic expression of the weak emergentist position. No new entities are postulated; his physicalism remains robust. Timothy O'Connor, who also interprets Alexander as a weak emergentist (without using the term), cites the crucial text: 'The [emergent] quality and the constellation to which it belongs are at once new and expressible without residue in terms of the processes proper to the level from which they emerge' (2:45; cf. O'Connor and Wong, 2002). The *properties* of things become more mental or spiritual as one moves up the ladder of emergence, but the constituents and the causes remain part of the one physical world. Like Spinoza's famous view (in *Ethics*, Book 2)—bodies form wholes, which themselves become bodies within a larger whole—Alexander nowhere introduces separate mental or spiritual entities. There is no ghost in the machine, even though the machine (if it's complicated enough) may manifest ghost-like properties. In its highly complex forms the universe may become fairly mysterious, even divine; but the appearance of mystery is only what one would expect from a universe that is 'infinite in all directions' (see Dyson, 1988).

Although largely consistent, Alexander's position fails to answer many of the most burning questions one would like to ask of it. If time is the 'mind of space,' time itself is directional or purposive. But such teleology is rather foreign to the spirit of modern physics and biology. Nor does Alexander's notion of *nisus* relieve the obscurity. Nisus stands for the creative tendency in Space-Time: 'There is a nisus in Space-Time which, as it has borne its creatures forward through matter and life to mind, will bear them forward to some higher level of existence' (2:346). Yet creative advance does not belong to the furniture of physics. If time is 'the advance into novelty', then there is an 'arrow' to time. But what is the source of this arrow in a purely physical conception? Isn't it more consistent for a physicalist to say that time consists of a (potentially) infinite whole divided into point-instants?

In the mind–body debate, one wants to know what consciousness is and what causal powers, if any, pertain to it and it alone. Alexander is not helpful here. Of course, neuroscience scarcely existed in the 1910s. What he did say about minds and brains is hardly helpful today: 'consciousness is situated at the synapsis of juncture between neurones' (2:129). But if Alexander offers nothing substantive on the mind–brain relation, how are contemporary philosophers to build on his work? At first blush it looks as if the only thing left of his position after the indefensible elements are removed is a purely formal specification: for any given level L, 'mind' is whatever whole is formed out of the parts or 'bodies' that constitute L. But a purely formal emergentism will not be sufficient to address the critical reservations that have been raised against it.

Strong emergentists will add a further reservation: that Alexander does not adequately conceptualize the newness of emergent levels, even though his rhetoric repeatedly stresses the importance of novelty. If life and mind are genuinely emergent, then living things and mental things must play some sort of causal role; they must exercise causal powers of their own, as in the doctrine of downward causation. According to Alexander, a mental response is not separable into parts but is a whole (2:129). For the strong emergentist, however, it's not enough to say that mind is the brain taken as a whole; a mental event is the whole composed out of individual neural events and states, *and something more.*

8. CONCLUSION

Without a doubt, more philosophers in the second half of the twentieth century advocated a position similar to Alexander's than to Broad's or Morgan's. The same is true of neuroscientists: they will often speak of consciousness in commonsense terms, implying that it is something and does something. But, they usually add, to give a neuroscientific account of consciousness *just is* to explain conscious phenomena in terms of neuro-physiological causes.

The preponderance of the weak emergence position is reflected in the great popularity of the supervenience debate, which flourished in the 1980s and '90s. Standard notions of supervenience accept the causal closure of the world and a nomological (i.e. law-based), or even necessary, relationship between supervenient and subvenient levels. In its most popular form, non-reductive physicalism, supervenience for a time seemed to preserve both the dependence of mental phenomena on brain states and the non-reducibility of the former to the latter. Yet these are precisely the goals that weak emergence theorists such as Samuel Alexander sought to achieve.[20]

---

[20] For standard criticisms of supervenience in the guise of non-reductive physicalism see Jaegwon Kim (1993b; 2000; 2002).

A number of the authors in this book argue that one should prefer those answers to the mind–body problem which preserve the causal closure of the world and seek to relate mental phenomena in a law-like way to states of the central nervous system. Only if these two assumptions are made, they argue, will it be possible to develop a (natural) science of consciousness. And isn't one better advised to wager on the possibility of scientific advances in some field than arbitrarily to rule out that possibility in advance? Indeed, if one is a physicalist, then one will have even greater reason to wager on this side. That is, if one holds that causal-explanatory accounts ultimately depend on the exercise of microphysical causal influences, then one will have to (seek to) explicate each *apparent* higher-order causal relationship as in the end a manifestation of fundamental physical particles and forces.

I think it is important to acknowledge in advance that weak emergence is the starting position for most natural scientists. Many of us may start with intuitions that are in conflict with weak emergence; indeed, the man or woman in the street would find the denial of mental causation highly counter-intuitive. But when one engages the dialogue from the standpoint of contemporary natural science—or contemporary Anglo-American philosophy, for that matter—one enters a playing field on which the physicalists and weak emergentists have the upper hand. Many of the essays in this volume help to explain why this is the case.

Nonetheless, strong emergence has received increasingly sophisticated formulations in recent years, and several of the authors in this text (including Ellis, Silberstein, Peacocke, Gregersen, the present author, and perhaps others) argue that it is a no less viable response to the mind–body problem. Strong emergence—that is, emergence with downward causation—has the merit of preserving commonsense intuitions and corresponding to our everyday experience as agents in the world. *If* it can respond successfully to the criticisms raised by its critics, it may represent one of the most significant philosophical developments of the late twentieth century. Also, for those who are idealists of a variety of stripes, and for theists who maintain that God as a spiritual being exercises some causal influence in the natural world, defending strong emergence may be a *sine qua non* for their position.

The chapters that follow offer a systematic overview of the re-emergence of emergence theories in contemporary thought. In the conviction that emergence must be anchored in the sciences of the natural world if it is to command serious attention, we have included in-depth reflections on emergence across the natural sciences: from cosmology and quantum physics, through the biological sciences (from biophysics through cell biology to primate evolution), and on to contemporary debates concerning neuroscience, consciousness, and religion. The volume includes defences of both weak and strong emergence, as well as probing questions about the entire concept of emergence, by some of the leading figures in the field today.

We have not been shy about extending the discussion all the way to the level of religious belief. For those with interests in the philosophy of religion or theology, the light that emergence sheds on religion may represent its most crucial feature. But those who appeal to the concept should beware: emergence is no silent ally, and it may require certain modifications to traditional versions of theism and to traditional theologies (as the articles by Peacocke and Gregersen in particular make clear). Even for those without explicitly religious interests, the application of emergence to religion offers an intriguing test case or thought experiment, one which may increase or decrease one's sense of the viability of this notion for explaining more inner-worldly phenomena such as consciousness.

The net result of the entire discussion, we hope, will be a fuller understanding not only of the strengths of this concept that is receiving so much attention today, but also of the key criticisms that it faces. The volume includes essays on both sides of the debate and should help to clarify the core questions concerning this concept: What precisely is meant by emergence? How is the term used differently in different fields? What data support it and what theoretical roles does it play? And what significance might emergence have for understanding phenomena as diverse as evolution, consciousness, and the nature of religious belief?

9. REFERENCES

Agazzi, Evandro (ed.) (1991), *The Problem of Reductionism in Science*, *Episteme*, 18 (Dordrecht: Kluwer Academic Publishers).

Alexander, Samuel (1920), *Space, Time, and Deity*, the Gifford Lectures for 1916–18, 2 vols. (London: MacMillan).

Arbib, Michael, and Mary B. Hesse (1986), *The Construction of Reality* (Cambridge: Cambridge University Press).

Baddeley, Roland, Peter Hancock, and Peter Földiák (eds.) (2000), *Information Theory and the Brain* (Cambridge: Cambridge University Press).

Beckermann, Ansgar, Hans Flohr, and Jaegwon Kim (eds.) (1992), *Emergence or Reduction?: Essays on the Prospects of Nonreductive Physicalism* (New York: W. de Gruyter).

Bedau, Mark (1997), 'Weak Emergence', *Philosophical Perspectives*, 11 ('Mind, Causation, and World').

Bergson, Henri (1983), *Creative Evolution*, authorized translation by Arthur Mitchell (Lanham, MD: University Press of America).

Blitz, David (1992), *Emergent Evolution: Qualitative Novelty and the Levels of Reality*, *Episteme*, 19 (Dordrecht: Kluwer Academic Publishers).

Brandon, Robert N. (1996), 'Reductionism versus Wholism versus Mechanism', in R. N. Brandon (ed.), *Concepts and Methods in Evolutionary Biology* (Cambridge: Cambridge University Press), 179–204.

Broad, C. D. (1925), *The Mind and Its Place in Nature* (London: Routledge and Kegan Paul).

Brown, Terrance, and Leslie Smith (eds.) (2003), *Reduction and the Development of Knowledge* (Mahwah, N.J.: L. Erlbaum).

Clark, Austen (1980), *Psychological Models and Neural Mechanisms: An Examination of Reductionism in Psychology* (Oxford: Clarendon Press).

Clayton, Philip (2000), *The Problem of God in Modern Thought* (Grand Rapids, MI.: Eerdmans Press).

Deacon, Terrence (2003), 'The Hierarchic Logic of Emergence: Untangling the Interdependence of Evolution and Self-Organization', in Bruce H. Weber and David J. Depew (eds.), *Evolution and Learning: The Baldwin Effect Reconsidered* (Cambridge, Mass.: MIT Press).

d'Espagnat, Bernard (1995), *Veiled Reality: An Analysis of Present-day Quantum Mechanical Concepts* (Reading, MA.: Addison-Wesley).

Dupré, John (1993), *The Disorder of Things: Metaphysical Foundations of the Disunity of Science* (Cambridge, MA.: Harvard University Press).

Dyson, Freeman (1988), *Infinite in All Directions*, the 1985 Gifford Lectures (New York: Harper and Row).

el-Hani, Charbel Nino, and Antonio Marcos Pereira (2000), 'Higher-level Descriptions: Why Should We Preserve Them?' in Peter Bøgh Andersen, Claus Emmeche, Niels Ole Finnemann, and Peder Voetmann Christiansen (eds.), *Downward*

Causation: Minds, Bodies and Matter (Aarhus, Denmark: Aarhus University Press), pp. 118–42.

Emmeche, Claus, Simo Køppe, and Frederik Stjernfelt (2000), 'Levels, Emergence, and Three Versions of Downward Causation', in Peter Bøgh Andersen, Claus Emmeche, Niels Ole Finnemann, and Peder Voetmann Christiansen (eds.), *Downward Causation: Minds, Bodies and Matter* (Aarhus, Denmark: Aarhus University Press), 13–34.

Gillett, Carl, and Barry Loewer (eds.) (2001), *Physicalism and Its Discontents* (New York: Cambridge University Press).

Gulick, Walter (2003), 'Response to Clayton: Taxonomy of the Types and Orders of Emergence', *Tradition and Discovery: The Polanyi Society Periodical*, 29/3: 32–47.

Harré, Rom, and E. H. Madden (1975), *Causal Powers: A Theory of Natural Necessity* (Oxford: Blackwell).

Hasker, William (1999), *The Emergent Self* (Ithaca, NY: Cornell University Press).

Hempel, Carl, and Paul Oppenheim (1948), 'Studies in the Logic of Explanation', *Philosophy of Science*, 15, 135–75.

Holcombe, Mike, and Ray Paton (eds.) (1998), *Information Processing in Cells and Tissues* (New York: Plenum Press).

Kim, Jaegwon (1993), *Supervenience and Mind: Selected Philosophical Essays* (Cambridge: Cambridge University Press).

—— (1999), 'Making Sense of Emergence', *Philosophical Studies*, 95: 3–36.

—— (2000), *Mind in a Physical World: An Essay on the Mind–Body Problem and Mental Causation* (Cambridge, Mass.: MIT Press).

—— (ed.) (2002), *Supervenience* (Aldershot, England: Ashgate).

Lewes, G. H. (1875), *Problems of Life and Mind*, 2 vols. (London: Kegan Paul, Trench, Turbner, and Co.).

Loewenstein, Werner (1999), *The Touchstone of Life: Molecular Information, Cell Communication, and the Foundations of Life* (New York: Oxford University Press).

Marvin, Walter (1912), *A First Book in Metaphysics* (New York: MacMillan).

Marx, Karl (1983), *The Portable Karl Marx*, ed. Eugene Kamenka (New York: Penguin Books).

Metz, Rudolf (1938), *A Hundred Years of British Philosophy*, ed. by J. H. Muirhead (London: G. Allen and Unwin).

Morgan, C. Lloyd (1931), *Emergent Evolution*, the 1922 Gifford Lectures (New York: Henry Holt).

Morowitz, Harold (2002), *The Emergence of Everything: How the World Became Complex* (New York: Oxford University Press).

Nagel, Ernest (1961), *The Structure of Science: Problems in the Logic of Scientific Explanation* (London: Routledge and Kegan Paul).

O'Connor, Timothy (1994), 'Emergent Properties', *American Philosophical Quarterly*, 31: 97–8.

—— and Hong Yu-Wong (2002), 'Emergent Properties', in Edward N. Zalta (ed.), *Stanford Encyclopedia of Philosophy* (Winter 2002 Edition), <http://plato.stanford.edu/entries/properties-emergent/>.

Oyama, Susan (2000), *The Ontogeny of Information: Developmental Systems and Evolution*, 2nd edition (Durham: Duke University Press).

Pap, Arthur (1952), 'The Concept of Absolute Emergence', *The British Journal for the Philosophy of Science*, 2, 302–11.

Pepper, Stephen (1926), 'Emergence', *Journal of Philosophy*, 23, 241–5.

Polanyi, Michael (1962), *Personal Knowledge: Towards a Post-critical Philosophy* (London: Routledge & Kegan Paul).

—— (1967), *The Tacit Dimension* (Garden City, NY: Doubleday Anchor Books).

—— (1969), *Knowing and Being: Essays*, ed. by Marjorie Grene (London: Routledge and Kegan Paul).

—— and Harry Prosch (1975), *Meaning* (Chicago: University of Chicago Press).

Primas, Hans (1983), *Chemistry, Quantum Mechanics and Reductionism: Perspectives in Theoretical Chemistry*, 2nd corrected edition (Berlin: Springer-Verlag).

Pylyshyn, Z. W. (1973), 'What the Mind's Eye Tells the Mind's Brain: A Critique of Mental Imagery', *Psychological Bulletin*, 80, 1–24.

Silberstein, M., and J. McGeever (1999), 'The Search for Ontological Emergence', *The Philosophical Quarterly*, 49: 182–200.

Spaulding, E. G. (1918), *The New Rationalism* (New York: Henry Holt and Co.).

Sperry, Roger (1969), 'A Modified Concept of Consciousness', *Psychological Review*, 76, 532–6.

—— (1976), 'Mental Phenomena as Causal Determinants in Brain Function', in Gordon G. Globus, Grover Maxwell, and Irwin Savodnik (eds.), *Consciousness and the Brain: A Scientific and Philosophical Inquiry* (New York: Plenum Press).

—— (1980), 'Mind–Brain Interaction: Mentalism, Yes; Dualism, No', *Neuroscience*, 5, 195–206.

—— (1987), 'Consciousness and Causality', in R. L. Gregory (ed.), *The Oxford Companion to the Mind* (Oxford: Oxford University Press).

Stace, W. T. (1939), 'Novelty, Indeterminism, and Emergence', *The Philosophical Review*, 48, 296–310.

Stapp, Henry P. (2004), *Mind, Matter, and Quantum Mechanics* (Berlin and New York: Springer).

Wimsatt, William C. (1994), 'The Ontology of Complex Systems: Levels of Organization, Perspectives, and Causal Thickets', *Canadian Journal of Philosophy*, Supplementary vol. 20.

Whitehead, Alfred North (1978), *Process and Reality: An Essay in Cosmology*, corrected edition, ed. by David Ray Griffin and Donald W. Sherburne (New York: the Free Press).

Yockey, Hubert (1992), *Information Theory and Molecular Biology* (Cambridge: Cambridge University Press).

Part I

The Physical Sciences

2

The Physics of Downward Causation

Paul C. W. Davies

1. REDUCTION AS NOTHING-BUTTERY

By tradition, physics is a strongly reductionist science. Treating physical systems as made up of components, and studying those components in detail, has produced huge strides in understanding. The jewel in the crown of reductionist science is subatomic particle physics, with its recent extension into superstring theory and M theory (see, for example, Greene, 1998). Few would deny the efficacy of the reductionist method of investigation. The behaviour of gases, for example, would lack a satisfactory explanation without taking into account their underlying molecular basis. If no reference were made to atoms, chemistry would amount to little more than a complicated set of ad hoc rules, while radioactivity would remain a complete mystery.

Whilst the foregoing is not contentious, differences arise concerning whether the reductionist account of nature is merely a fruitful methodology, or *whether it is the whole story.* Many physicists are self-confessed out-and-out reductionists. They believe that once the final buildings blocks of matter and the rules that govern them have been identified, then all of nature will, in effect, have been explained. Obviously such a *final theory* would not in practice provide a very useful account of much that we observe in the world. A final reductionist theory along the lines of, say, the much-touted superstring theory, would not explain the origin of life, nor have much to say about the nature of consciousness. But the committed reductionist believes such inadequacies are mere technicalities, and that the *fundamental core* of explanation is captured—completely—by the reductionist theory.

A minority of physicists challenge this account of nature. Whilst conceding the power of reduction as a methodology, they nevertheless deny that the putative final theory would yield a complete explanation of the world. The anti-reductionist resists the claim that, for example, a living cell is *nothing but* a collection of atoms, or a human being is *nothing but* a collection of cells. This, they say, is to commit the fallacy of 'nothing-buttery'. Physicists who espouse anti-reductionism usually work in fields like condensed matter physics, where reduction often fails even as a methodology. These workers are impressed by the powerful organizational abilities of complex multi-component systems acting collectively, which sometimes lead to novel and surprising forms of behaviour.

All physicists concede that at each level of complexity new physical qualities, and laws that govern them, *emerge*. These qualities and laws are either absent at the level below, or are simply meaningless at that level. Thus the concept of wetness makes sense for a droplet of water, but not for a single molecule of H_2O. The entrainment of a collection of harmonic oscillators such as in an electrical network makes no sense for a single oscillator. The Pauli exclusion principle severely restricts the behaviour of a collection of electrons, but not of a single electron. Ohm's law finds no application to just one atom. Such examples are legion. The question we must confront, however, is *so what*? What, exactly, is it that the anti-reductionist is claiming *emerges* at each level of complexity?

In some cases the novel behaviour of a complex system may be traced in part to the fact that it is an open system. The claim that a reductive account is complete applies only to closed systems. For example, the motion of the planets in the solar system is described very precisely by Newton's laws, and even better by Einstein's theory of relativity, because the solar system is effectively isolated. Contrast this situation with, say, the motion of a hurricane, or of the great red spot of Jupiter. In these cases the swirling fluids are continuously exchanging matter and energy with their environment, and this leads to novel and unexpected behaviours; indeed, it may lead to random or unpredictable behaviour (the skittishness of hurricanes is notorious). It would not be possible to give an accurate account of these systems by restricting the analysis to the fluid components alone. However, there is no implication that the vortex has been seized by new forces or influences not already present in both the vortex itself and the wider environment. In principle, a satisfactory reductive account could be given by appealing to the components of the total system. But because nature abounds with chaotic systems, such a project would most likely soon become impracticable, since it is a characteristic feature of deterministic chaos that the 'domain of influence' rapidly balloons to encompass a vast region—even the entire universe.

Another example where limited reduction fails is quantum mechanics. A quantum superposition is famously fragile, and will tend to be rapidly degraded—decohered to use the jargon—by interactions with the environment. This is the project pursued by Zurek (e.g. 1991, 2002) and reported in this volume by Erich Joos. To illustrate this point, consider the simple case of an electron that scatters from a target with a fifty per cent chance each of rebounding left or right. This process may be described by a wave packet that, on its encounter with the target, splits into two blobs, one left-moving, the other right-moving. In general, there will be some overlap between the two blobs, and because the wave packet spreads as it goes, this overlap will remain as the system evolves. In practice, the electron is not isolated from its environment, and the effect of its interactions with a vast number of sur-rounding particles is to scramble the phases of the wave function, which results in the overlap of the blobs being driven rapidly to zero. In effect, the wave packet 'collapses' into two disconnected blobs, each representing one of the two possible outcomes of the experiment (left-moving electron and right-moving electron). In this manner, the ghostly superposition of quantum mechanics gets replaced by the classical notion of distinct states present with a fifty-fifty probability. In the early days of quantum mechanics, this 'collapse of the wave packet' was considered a mysterious additional process that was not captured by the rules of quantum mechanics applied to the electron and target alone. The system's decoherence and classicalization is an emergent property, and it was thought by some that this required new rules that were not part of quantum mechanics, but would come in at a higher level. What level? While some thought it was when the system was massive enough, others sought the rule-change at a higher level of complexity (e.g. if there was a device elaborate enough to perform a measurement of the electron's position). Some even suggested that a full understanding of the 'collapse' demanded appeal to the mind of the observer. But in fact, as Zurek, Joos, and others have amply demonstrated, decoherence and wave packet collapse are well explained by appealing to the quantum interactions with the wider environment, suit-ably averaged over time and distance. So, in this aspect of quantum mechanics at least, there is no longer any need to invoke mysterious extra ingredients, or rules that emerge at the 'measurement level', even though the 'collapse of the wave packet' is legitimately an emergent phenomenon.

What the two foregoing examples illustrate is that emergent behaviour need not imply emergent forces or laws, merely a clear understanding of the distinction between open and closed systems. And we see that language about 'the vortex' or 'the right-moving electron' is indeed merely a convenient *façon de parler* and not a reason to invoke fundamentally new forms of interaction or laws of physics. Both of these examples, whilst affirming the meaningful-ness of emergence as a phenomenon, nevertheless illustrate that a reductive account of that phenomenon is still adequate, so long as the environment is included within the system. The term 'weak emergence' is sometimes used to denote those systems for which the micro-level laws in principle capture the entire physics of the system, but for which nothing less than inspection of the real system, or simulation, would reveal its behaviour.

So we are confronted with the key question: is it *ever* the case that an emergent phenomenon cannot be given a satisfactory reductive account, even in principle? Systems for which more is needed, not just as a convenience, but as a necessity, are called strongly emergent. Do there exist *any* strongly emergent systems? If the answer is yes, then we come to the next key question: in what way, precisely, does the value-added emergent 'law' or 'behaviour' affect the system? A survey of the literature shows lots of flabby, vague, qualitative statements about higher-level descriptions and influences springing into play at thresholds of complexity, without one ever being told specifically how these emergent laws affect the individual particle 'on the ground'— the humble foot soldier of physics—in a manner that involves a fundamentally new force or law. Thus we are told that in the Bénard instability, where fluids spontaneously form convection cells, the molecules organize themselves into an elaborate and orderly pattern of flow, which may extend over macroscopic dimensions, even though individual molecules merely push and pull on their near neighbours (see, for example, Coveney and Highfield, 1995). This carries the hint that there is a sort of global choreographer, an emergent demon, marshalling the molecules into a coherent, cooperative dance, the better to fulfil the global project of convective flow. Naturally that is absurd. The onset of convection certainly represents novel emergent behaviour, but the normal inter-molecular forces are not in competition with, or over-ridden by, novel global forces. The global system 'harnesses' the local forces, but at no stage is there a need for *an extra type of force* to act on an individual molecule to make it comply with a 'convective master plan'.

The fact that we need to make reference to the global circumstances to give a satisfactory account of the local circumstances is an important feature of many physical systems. It is instructive to recast this feature in the language of causation. We can ask, what *caused* a given water molecule to follow such-and-such a path within a given convection cell? The short answer is: the inter-molecular forces from near neighbours. But we must appeal to the *global* pattern of flow to provide a complete answer, because those near neighbours are also caught up in the overall convection. However, and this is the central point, we do not need to discuss *two sorts of forces*—near-neighbour and global forces—even though we do need to invoke two aspects in the causation story. The molecule's motion is caused by the push and pull of neighbours, *in the context of* their own global, systematic motion. Thus a full account of causation demands appeal to (i) local forces, and (ii) *contextual information* about the global circumstances. Typically the latter will enter the solution of the problem in the form of constraints or boundary conditions.

Some emergent phenomena are so striking that it is tempting to explain them by encapsulating (ii) as a separate causal category. The term 'downward causation' has been used in this context (Campbell, 1974). The question then arises whether this is just another descriptive convenience (as in the case of weak emergence), or whether downward causation ever involves new sorts of forces or influences (as is the case with strong emergence, for example, and with most versions of biological vitalism). In the cases cited above, the answer is surely no, but what about more dramatic examples, such as the mind–body interaction? Could we ever explain in all cases how brain cells fire without taking into account the mental state of the subject? If minds make a difference in the physical world (as they surely do), then does this demand additional, genuinely new, causes (forces?) operating at the neuronal level, or will all such 'mental causation' eventually be explained, as in the case of vortex motion, in terms of the openness of the brain to its environment and the action of coherent boundary conditions (i.e. (ii) above)?

For the physicist, the only causes that matter are, to paraphrase Thomas Jefferson, the ones that kick. Wishy-washy talk of global cooperation is no substitute for observing a real, honest-to-goodness force that moves matter at a specific place. And if the movement is due to just the good old forces we already know about, simply re-packaged for convenience of discussion, the response is likely to be a monumental 'so what?' For emergence to become more than just a way of organizing the subject matter of physics, there has to be a clear-cut example of a new type of force, or at any rate a new causative relation, and not just the same old forces at work in novel ways. Unless, that is, those forces are being subordinated in turn to some other, new, forces.

When it is put this bluntly, I doubt if many physicists would hold their hands on their hearts and say they believed that any such forces exist. The history of science is littered with failed forces or causative agencies (the ether, the *élan vital*, psi forces...) that try to explain some form of emergent behaviour on the cheap. In what follows I shall try to sharpen the idea of downward causation and ask just what it would take for a hard-headed physicist to be convinced that emergence demands any new causes, forces, or principles beyond the routine (though possibly technically difficult) consideration of the global situation.

2. WHAT IS DOWNWARD CAUSATION?

For the physicist, the concept of causality carries certain specific implications. Chief among these is *locality*. All existing theories of causation involve forces acting at a point in space. At a fundamental level, theories of force are expressed in terms of *local fields*, which is to say that the force acting on a particle at a point is determined by the nature of the field at that point. For example, an electron may accelerate as a result of an electric field, and the magnitude of the force causing the acceleration is proportional to the intensity of the electric field at the point in space the electron occupies at that moment.

When discussing the interaction between spatially separated particles, we have the concept of action at a distance, which has a non-local ring to it. The sun exerts a gravitational pull on the Earth across 150 million kilometres of space. The phenomenon may be recast in terms of local forces, however, by positing the existence of a gravitational field created by the sun. It is the action of this field on the Earth, at the point in space that the Earth happens to occupy, which creates the force that accelerates the Earth along its curved path. There is a long history of attempts to eliminate the field concept and replace it with direct non-local inter-particle action (e.g. the Wheeler–Feynman theory of electrodynamics (Davies, 1995)), but these theories run into problems with physical effects propagating backward in time and other oddities. Overwhelmingly, physicists prefer local field theories of causation.

This fundamental locality is softened somewhat when quantum mechanics is taken into account. For example, two electrons may interact and move a large distance apart. Theory suggests, and experiment confirms, that subtle correlations exist in their behaviour (see, for example, Brown and Davies, 1986; Aczel, 2002). However, it has been determined to most physicists' satisfaction that the existence of such non-local correlations does not imply a causative link between the separated particles. (A lot of popular articles convey the misconception that separated quantum particles in an entangled state can communicate information faster than light. These claims stem from confusion between correlation and communication.)

The problem of downward causation from the physicist's point of view is: How can wholes act causatively on parts if all interactions are local? Indeed, from the viewpoint of a local theory, what is a 'whole' anyway other than the sum of the parts?

Let me distinguish between two types of downward causation. The first is whole–part causation, in which the behaviour of a part can be understood only by reference to the whole. The second I call level-entanglement (no connection intended with quantum entanglement, a very different phenomenon), and has to do with higher conceptual levels having causal efficacy over lower conceptual levels.

3. WHOLE–PART CAUSATION

Sometimes physicists use the language of whole–part causation for ease of description. For example, a ball rolling down a hill implies that each of the ball's atoms is accelerated according to the state of the ball as a whole. But it would be an abuse of language to say that the rotating ball *caused* a specific atom to move the way it did; after all, the ball *is* the sum of its atoms. What makes the concept 'ball' meaningful in this case is the existence of (non-local) constraints that lock the many degrees of freedom together, so that the atoms of the ball move as a coherent whole and not independently. But the forces that implement these constraints are themselves local fields, so in this case whole–part causation is effectively trivial in nature. Similar remarks apply to other examples where 'wholes' enjoy well-defined quasi-autonomy, such as whirlpools and electric circuits.

The situation is different again in the case of spontaneous self-organization, such as the Bénard instability, or the laser, where atomic oscillators are dragooned into lockstep with a coherent beam of light. But even here the essential phenomenon can be accounted for entirely in terms of local inter-actions plus non-local constraints.

There are a few examples of clear-cut attempts at explicit whole–part causation theories in physics. One of these is Mach's principle, according to which the force of inertia, experienced locally by a particle, derives from the particle's gravitational interaction with all the matter in the universe. There is currently no very satisfactory formulation of Mach's principle within accepted physical theory, although the attempt to construct one is by no means considered worthless, and once occupied the attention of Einstein himself. Another somewhat ambiguous example is the second law of thermodynamics, which states that the total entropy of a closed system cannot go down. However, 'closed system' here is a global concept. There are situations where the entropy goes down in one place (e.g. inside the refrigerator), only to go up somewhere else (the kitchen). As far as I know this law would not forbid entropy going down on Earth and up on Mars at the same instant, though one needs a relativistic theory of thermodynamics to discuss this. In quantum field theory there can be regions of negative energy that could cause a local entropy decrease, with the positive energy flowing away to another region to raise the entropy. I am not suggesting that there is an additional whole–part causation to make the respective regions 'behave themselves', only that implicit in the second law is some sort of global constraint (or compul-sion) on what happens locally.

Other examples where global restrictions affect local physics are cosmic censorship (an event horizon preventing a naked singularity) and closed timelike lines (time travel into the past) constrained by causal self-consistency. A less exotic example is Pauli's exclusion principle, where the laws governing two or more electrons together are completely different from the laws governing a single electron. It is an interesting question whether a sufficiently long list of global restrictions would so constrain local physics as to define a local theory completely. Thus a final unifying theory of physics might be specifiable in terms of one or more global principles. However, it is important to remember that global principles do not have causal efficacy over local physics; rather, local physics operates in such a manner as to comply with global principles. For example, we would not say that the law of conservation of energy causes a dropped ball to accelerate to the ground. The ball accelerates because gravity acts on it, but in such a way that the total kinetic and potential energy is conserved. It seems reasonable to suppose that in a final theory, all whole–part causation will reduce to a local physics that happens to comply with certain overarching global principles. In a sense, global principles may be said to *emerge* from local physics, but most physicists see things the other way round, preferring to regard global principles as somehow more fundamental.

4. LEVEL-ENTANGLEMENT

Let me now turn to the other sense of downward causation: the relationship between different conceptual levels describing the same physical system. In common discourse we often refer to higher levels exercising causal efficacy over lower. Think, for example, of mind–brain interaction: 'I felt like moving my arm, so I did.' Here the mental realm of feelings and volitions is expressed as exercising causal efficacy over flesh. Another example is hardware versus software in computing. Consider the statement: 'The program is designed to find the smallest prime number greater than one trillion and print out the answer.' In this case the higher-level concept 'program' appears to call the shots over what an electronic gizmo and printer and paper do. Many examples may be found in the realm of human affairs, such as economics. Pronouncements such as 'stock market volatility made investors nervous' conveys the impression that the higher-level entity 'the stock market' in part determines how individual agents behave.

In the latter two examples at least no physicist would claim that there are any mysterious new physical forces acting 'down' from the software onto the electronic circuitry, or from the stock market onto investors. Software talk and reference to 'market forces' in economics do not imply the deployment of additional *physical* forces at the component level. The existing inventory of physical forces suffices to account for the detailed behaviour of the components. Once again, the best way to think about downward causation in these examples is that the global system harnesses existing local forces. The mind–brain example is much harder because of the complexity and openness of the system. A more dramatic example of mind–brain causation comes from the field of neurophysiology. Recent work by Max Bennett (Bennett and Barden, 2001) in Australia has determined that neurones continually put out little tendrils that can link up with others and effectively rewire the brain on a time scale of twenty minutes! This seems to serve the function of adapting the neuro-circuitry to operate more effectively in the light of various mental experiences (e.g. learning to play a video game). To the physicist this looks deeply puzzling. How can a higher-level phenomenon like 'experience', which is also a global concept, have causal control over microscopic regions at the sub-neuronal level? The tendrils will be pushed and pulled by local forces (presumably good old electromagnetic ones). So how does a force at a point in space (the end of a tendril) 'know about', say, the thrill of a game?

Twenty years ago I conceived of a device to illustrate downward causation in a straightforward way (Davies, 1986). Consider a computer that controls a microprocessor connected to a robot arm. The arm is free to move in any direction according to the program in the computer. Now imagine a program that instructs the arm to reach inside the computer's own circuitry and rearrange it, for example, by throwing a switch or removing a circuit board. This is software–hardware feedback, where software brings about a change in the very hardware that supports it. In a less crude and brutal formulation of this scenario we might imagine the evolution of the computer/arm to be quite complex, as the continually rearranged circuitry changed the instructions to the arm, which, in turn, changed the circuitry.

Although it is hard to think of this example in terms other than software acting on hardware, there presumably exists a complete hardware description of events in terms of local interactions. In other words, there are no new forces or principles involved here. Use of terms like software and arm are simply linguistic and conceptual conveniences and not causal categories.

5. WHICH WAY DO THE ARROWS OF CAUSATION POINT?

An interesting example of downward causation is natural selection in evolution. Here the fate of an organism, maybe an entire species, depends on the

circumstances in the wider ecology. To take a specific example, consider the
case of convergent evolution, where similar ecological niches become filled by
similar organisms, even though genetically these organisms might be very far
apart. The eye has evolved in at least forty independent ways in insects, birds,
fish, mammals, and so on; although the starting points were very different, the
end products fulfil very similar functions. Now the morphology of an organism is determined by its DNA, specifically by the exact sequence of base pairs
in this molecule. Thus one might be tempted to ask, how does the biosphere
act downwards on molecules of DNA to bring about species convergence? But
this is clearly the wrong question. There is no mystery about convergence in
Darwinian evolution. Random mutations alter the base-pair sequences of
DNA and natural selection acts as a sieve to remove the less fit organisms.
Selection takes place at the level of organisms, but it is the genes (or base-pair
sequences) that get selected.

Darwinism provides a novel form of causation inasmuch as the causal
chain runs counter to the normal descriptive sequence. Chronologically,
what happens is that first a mutation is caused by a local physical interaction,
for example, the impact of a cosmic ray at a specific location with an atom in a
DNA molecule. Later, possibly many years later, the environment 'selects' the
mutant by permitting the organism to reproduce more efficiently. In terms of
physics, selection involves vast numbers of local forces acting over long
periods of time, the net result of which is to bring about a long-term change
in the genome of the organism's lineage. It is the original atomic event in
combination with the subsequent complicated events that together give a full
causative account of the evolutionary story. Yet biologists would be hard-
pressed to tell this story in those local physical terms. Instead, natural
selection is described as having causal powers, even though it is causatively
neutral—a sieve. In this respect, natural selection is better thought of as a
constraint, albeit one that may change with time.

6. INFORMATION AND LEVEL-ENTANGLEMENT

There is one place in mainstream physics where two conceptual levels seem to
become inextricably entangled in our description of events, and that is
quantum mechanics. (Recall that I am not using the word entanglement
here in the conventional sense of an entangled quantum state.) The much-
vaunted wave–particle duality of quantum mechanics conceals a subtlety
concerning the meaning of the terms. Particle talk refers to hardware: physical
stuff such as electrons. By contrast, the wave function that attaches to an

electron encodes *what we know* about the system. The wave is not a wave of 'stuff', it is an information wave. Since information and 'stuff' refer to two different conceptual levels, quantum mechanics seems to imply a duality of levels akin to mind–brain duality.

When an observation is made of a quantum system such as an electron, the wave function typically jumps discontinuously as our information about the electron changes. For example, we may measure its position which was previously uncertain. Thereafter the wave evolves differently because of the jump. This implies that the particle is likely to be found subsequently moving differently from the manner in which it might have been expected to move had the measurement not been made. Quantum mechanics appears to mix together information and matter in a bewildering way.

What I have been describing is really an aspect of the famous measurement problem of quantum mechanics, which is how we should understand the 'jump' referred to above. The work of Zurek and others (Zurek, 1982) attempts to eliminate the appearance of a discontinuity and the intervention of an observer by tracing the changes to the electron's wave function to a decohering environment. However, even if the wave function is seen to evolve smoothly, it must still be regarded as referring to knowledge or information about the quantum system, and information is meaningful only in the context of a system (e.g. a human observer) that can interpret it. Wheeler has stressed the level-entanglement involved in quantum mechanics in his famous 'meaning circuit', in which 'observership' underpins the laws of physics (for a recent review see Barrow, Davies, and Harper, 2003). We can trace a causal chain from atom through measuring apparatus to observer to a community of physicists able to interpret the result of the measurement. In Wheeler's view there must be a 'return portion' of this 'circuit' from observers back down to atom.

Information enters into science in several distinct ways. So far, I have been discussing the wave function in quantum mechanics. Information also forms the statistical basis for the concept of entropy, and thus underpins the second law of thermodynamics (information should not come into existence in a closed system). In biology, genes are regarded as repositories of information—genetic databanks. In this case the information is semantic; it contains coded instructions for the implementation of an algorithm. So in molecular biology we have the informational level of description, full of language about constructing proteins according to a blueprint, and the hardware level in terms of molecules of specific atomic sequences and shapes. Biologists flip between these two modes of description without addressing the issue how information controls hardware (e.g. in 'gene silencing' or transcription-inhibition)—a classic case of downward causation. Finally, there is a fourth use of information in physics, entering via the theory of relativity. This principle says that information shouldn't travel faster than light.

Recently there have been ambitious attempts to ground all of physics in information; in other words, to treat the universe as a gigantic informational or computational process (Frieden, 1998). An early project of this type is Wheeler's 'It from bit' proposal (Barrow, Davies, and Harper, 2003). We might call this 'level inversion' since information is normally regarded as a higher-level concept than, say, particles.

7. EMERGENCE AND THE CAUSAL STRAIGHTJACKET

The problem about strong emergence is that there is simply no 'room at the bottom' for the deployment of additional 'downwardly mobile' forces if the physical system is already causally closed. Thus a typical closed and isolated Newtonian system is already completely determined in its evolution once the initial conditions are specified. To start adding top-down forces would make the system over-determined. However, this causal straightjacket presupposes the orthodox idealized view of the nature of physical law, in which the dynamical evolution of a physical system is determined by a set of differential equations in which the mathematical operations (e.g. differentiation) are in principle implementable in nature. In turn, this supposes that space-time is continuous and at least twice differentiable, that real numbers map one-to-one onto physical states, and so on. Most physicists regard the laws of physics Platonically, that is, as existing in some idealized mathematical realm, and take for granted that the mathematical operations captured in the description of the physical laws may actually be carried out (by nature) to infinite precision. This idealization, in which the laws of physics, expressed as perfect immutable mathematical relationships, enjoy a transcendent ontological status, is one of the founding assumptions of science as we know it. The duality between timeless, given, eternal laws and changing, contingent, physical states reflects the theological roots of physics, in which a timeless, eternal Lawgiver created an evolving world. But this idealized view of the laws of physics has been challenged, most famously by John Wheeler (1984) and Rolf Landauer (1967, 1986), who seek to invert the relationship between laws, matter, and information by making information the foundation stone for physics. According to this viewpoint, information stands at the base of the explanatory scheme, while matter is a concept derived from information, and laws are properties of matter that *emerge*, both conceptually and temporally, as the universe congeals from the big bang. It is a relationship pithily summarized by Wheeler's dictum 'It from bit'.

Landauer adopts the position that it is illegitimate to apply a mathematical operation to a law-like description of a physical phenomenon if that operation could not, even in principle, be implemented in the real universe, given its finite age and computational resources. Thus the laws of physics do not, on this view, enjoy an independent, transcendent, absolute ontological status. This philosophy is well described by Bruckner and Zeilinger (2003): 'The laws we discover about Nature do not already exist as "Laws of Nature" in the outside world.' Landauer invites us to envisage the universe as a gigantic computer, and the question then arises just what are the limitations to its computational power. Seth Lloyd (2002) has estimated the maximum number of bits of information that have ever been processed by the volume of the universe we currently observe to be 10^{120} bits. Now 10^{120} bits buys you a lot of mathematics, but there are some phenomena, most notably complex systems, which scale exponentially (or worse) rather than linearly in key properties, for which the foregoing finite number represents a severe limitation. For example, in molecular biology, the number of possible sequences of amino acids in a peptide chain rises exponentially in step with the chain length, and one immediately finds that a chain the size of a small protein has more combinations than it would be within the computational power of the universe to store, let alone process (Davies, 2004). Taking Landauer seriously, one would predict that new, higher-level organizational laws of complexity (even 'biological laws') might emerge in peptide chains that exceed this critical threshold of complexity.

Similar calculations may be done to determine the emergence of classicality from complex quantum states, and (at least in principle) the emergence of autonomous mental systems from networks of neurones. For example, consider a quantum system consisting of n two-state objects, such as particles with two spin states, labelled 0 and 1 for 'down' and 'up' respectively. Classically such a system may be described by a sequence of n digits, e.g. 001010110110...010110. But a quantum superposition requires 2^n digits to specify all the components of the wave function needed to define the state uniquely. The exponentially greater resource base of quantum mechanics makes it vulnerable to the Lloyd bound when $2^n \sim 10^{120}$, or $n \sim 400$. Thus, if one accepts the Landauer ontology of the laws of physics, by the time one reaches the level of several hundred particles it becomes impossible, even in principle, to specify—let alone determine—the evolution of an entangled quantum state. It is tempting to suppose that it is at this level of complexity that the classical world emerges from the quantum world. The so-called 'collapse of the wave function' could come about under these circumstances without coming into conflict with the linear, unitary evolution of the components. Note that this lassitude in the laws of quantum physics has nothing to do with Heisenberg's uncertainty principle. Rather, it represents an ambiguity in the operation of the unitary evolution itself.

8. WHERE DO WE GO FROM HERE?

Most physicists are sceptical of downward causation, because they believe there is no room in existing theories of causation for additional forces. Certainly the idealized model of a physical system—a physically closed, deterministic, dynamical system obeying local second order differential equations—is causally closed too. Sometimes quantum mechanics, with its inherent indeterminism, is seen as opening a chink through which additional forces or organizational influences might enter. This is the reasoning behind some attempts to root consciousness and free will in quantum fuzziness (see, for example, Penrose, 1989; Hodgson, 1991). However, standard quantum mechanics is really a deterministic theory in its dynamics, even though its predictions are statistical. Slipping in extra forces by 'loading the quantum dice' is an unappealing prospect. For one reason, the 'loading forces' would by definition lie outside the scope of quantum mechanics, leading to a dualistic description of nature in which quantum and non-quantum forces acted in combination. But quantum mechanics makes no sense if it is not a universal theory. If control could be gained over the 'loading forces' they could, for example, be used to violate the uncertainty principle.

Another way to escape the strictures of causal closure is to appeal to the openness of some physical systems. As I have already stressed, top-down talk refers not to vitalistic augmentation of known forces, but rather to the system harnessing existing forces for its own ends. The problem is to understand how this harnessing happens, not at the level of individual intermolecular interactions, but overall—as a coherent project. It appears that once a system is sufficiently complex, then new top-down rules of causation *emerge*. Physicists would like to know whether these rules can ultimately be derived from the underlying laws of physics or must augment them. Thus a living cell commandeers chemical pathways and intermolecular organization to implement the plan encoded in its genome. The cell has room for this supra-molecular coordination because it is an open system, so its dynamical behaviour is not determined from within the system. But openness to the environment merely explains *why* there may be room for top-down causation; it tells us nothing about *how* that causation works.

Let me offer a few speculations about how. In spite of the existence of level-entanglement in quantum physics and elsewhere, none of the examples cited above amounts to the deployment of specific local forces under the command of a global system, or subject to emergent rules at higher levels of description. However, we must be aware of the fact that physics is not a completed discipline, and top-down causation may be something that would not show up using current methods of enquiry. There is no logical impediment to constructing a whole–part dynamics in which local forces are subject to global rules. For example, my foregoing suggestion that the classicalization of quantum systems might involve a complexity threshold would entail such a dynamics (Davies, 1987; Leggett, 1994). Since complexity is another higher-level concept and another global variable, this would introduce explicit downward causation into physics. There have been attempts to introduce non-linearity into quantum mechanics to explain the 'collapse of the wave function', but as far as I know there is no mathematical model of system complexity entering the dynamics of a complex system to bring about this step. My proposal evades the problems associated by the 'loading forces' suggestion discussed above, because it operates at the interface between the quantum and classical realms. It is easier to imagine downward causation acting at that interface rather than mingling with quantum processes deep within the quantum realm.

9. SOME EXPLICIT EXAMPLES

Any attempt to introduce explicitly global variables into local physics would necessarily come into conflict with existing purely local theories of causation, with all sorts of ramifications. First would be consistency with experimentation. If downward causation were limited to complexity as a variable, then effects would most likely be restricted to complex systems, where there is plenty of room for surprises. For example, in the case of the living cell it is doubtful whether additional 'organizational' forces related to a global complexity variable acting at the molecular level would have been detected by techniques used so far. Similar remarks apply to mind–brain causation. Secondly, global principles such as the second law of thermodynamics might be affected by downward causation. For example, a cellular automaton in which the dynamical rules depend in certain ways on the complexity of the state might develop entropy-lowering behaviour, and thus be ruled out of court.

Finally, let me discuss a different mechanism of downward causation that avoids the problem of coming into conflict with existing local theories. As remarked already, many authors have suggested that the universe should be regarded as a gigantic computer or information-processing system, and that perhaps information is more primitive than matter, underpinning the laws of physics. As I discussed in Section 7, the information-processing power of the universe is limited by its resources, specifically, by the number of degrees of freedom contained within the particle horizon (the causal limit of the universe imposed by the finite speed of light). As the universe ages, so the particle horizon expands, and more and more particles come into causal contact. So the universe begins with very limited information-processing power, but its capability grows with time. As remarked, the maximum amount of information that the universe has been able to process since the big bang comes out to be about 10^{120} bits. Now this number 10^{120} is very familiar. It turns out to be the same factor by which the so-called cosmological constant is smaller than its 'natural' value as determined on dimensional grounds. (The cosmological constant refers to a type of anti-gravitational force that seems to be accelerating the rate of expansion of the universe.) This vast mismatch between the observed and actual values of the cosmological constant was described by Stephen Hawking as 'the biggest failure of theory known to science'. The mismatch is known as 'the cosmological constant problem'.

A possible solution of the cosmological constant problem comes from top-down causation. Suppose this quantity, normally denoted Λ, is not a constant at all, but a function of the total amount of information that the universe has processed since the beginning. Lloyd points out (Lloyd, 2002) that the processed information increases as the square of the age of the universe, t^2. Then I hypothesize.

$$\Lambda(t) = \Lambda_{\text{Planck}}(t_{\text{Planck}}/t)^2$$

where 'Planck' refers to the Planck time, 10^{-43} s, at which the universe contains just one bit of information. It can be seen from the above equation that Λ starts out very large, then decays with time, dropping to its present value and declining still further in the future. If my hypothesis is correct, evidence will show up in the astronomical data currently being gathered about Λ. This, then, is a theory where a basic force of nature derives (via a mechanism that I have not attempted to explicate) from the higher-level quantity 'processed information', in a manner that leads to directly observable consequences.

Finally let me consider an even more radical notion. Reductionist local causation has been a feature of physics since Newton made the fundamental separation between dynamical states and laws. Attempts to include explicit whole–part causative processes would introduce a fundamental change in theoretical physics by entangling law and state in a novel manner. Whether this complication would be welcomed by physicists is another matter.

Many emergentists would not welcome it either. The conventional emergentist position, if one may be said to exist, is to eschew the deployment of new forces in favour of a description in which existing forces merely act in surprising and cooperative new ways when a system becomes sufficiently complex. In such a framework, downward causation remains a shadowy notion, on the fringe of physics, descriptive rather than predictive. My suggestion is to take downward causation seriously as a causal category. But it comes at the expense of introducing either explicit top-down physical forces or changing the fundamental categories of causation from that of local forces to a higher-level concept such as information.

10. REFERENCES

Aczel, Amir (2002), *Entanglement* (New York: Four Walls Eight Windows).

Barrow, John, Paul Davies, and Charles Harper (eds.) (2003), *Science and Ultimate Reality* (Cambridge: Cambridge University Press).

Bennett, C., and R. Landauer (1985), 'The Fundamental Physical Limits of Computation', *Scientific American*, July 1985, 48–56.

Bennett, M. R., and M. R. Barden (2001), 'Ionotropic (P2X) Receptor Dynamics at Single Autonomic Varicosities', *NeuroReport*, 12: A91–A97.

Brown, Julian, and Paul Davies (1986), *The Ghost in the Atom* (Cambridge: Cambridge University Press).

Bruckner, C., and A. Zeilinger (2003), 'Information and Fundamental Elements of the Structure of Quantum Theory,' in L. Castell and O. Ischebek (eds.), *Time, Quantum, and Information* (Springer).

Campbell, D. T. (1974), '"Downward Causation" in Hierarchically Organized Biological Systems', in F. J. Ayala and T. Dobzhansky (eds.), *Studies in the Philosophy of Biology* (London: Macmillan), 179–86.

Coveney, Peter, and Roger Highfield (1995), *Frontiers of Complexity* (New York, Ballantine Books), ch. 6.

Davies, Paul (1986), 'Time Asymmetry and Quantum Mechanics', in Raymond Flood and Michael Lockwood (eds.), *The Nature of Time* (Oxford: Blackwell), ch. 7.

—— (1987), *The Cosmic Blueprint* (New York: Simon and Schuster).

—— (1995), *About Time* (New York: Simon and Schuster), ch. 9.

—— (2004), 'Emergent Biological Principles and the Computational Properties of the Universe', *Complexity* 10(2), 1 (2004).

Frieden, B. Roy (1998), *Physics from Fisher Information* (Cambridge: Cambridge University Press).

Greene, Brian (1998), *The Elegant Universe* (New York: Norton).

Hodgson, David (1991), *The Mind Matters* (Oxford: Oxford University Press).

Landauer, R. (1967), 'Wanted: A Physically Possible Theory of Physics', *IEEE Spectrum*, 4: 105–9.

—— (1986), 'Computation and Physics: Wheeler's Meaning Circuit?', *Foundations of Physics*, 16: 551–64.

Leggett, A. J. (1994), *Problems of Physics* (Oxford: Oxford University Press).

Lloyd, Seth (2002), 'Computational Capacity of the Universe', *Physical Review Letters*, 88: 237901.

Penrose, Roger (1989), *The Emperor's New Mind* (Oxford: Oxford University Press).

Wheeler, J. A. (1984), in A. Giovanni, F. Mancini and M. Marinaro (eds.), *Problems in Theoretical Physics* (Salerno: University of Salerno Press).

Zurek, W. H. (1982), 'Environment-Induced Superselection Rules', *Phys. Rev.* D26: 1862.

—— (1991), 'Decoherence and the Transition from Quantum to Classical', *Physics Today*, 44/10 (1991), 36–44.

—— (2002), 'Decoherence and the Transition from Quantum to Classical—Revisited', *Los Alamos Science*, 27 (2002).

3

The Emergence of Classicality from Quantum Theory

Erich Joos

A thoroughgoing and consistent application of quantum theory shows that the connection between classical and quantum physics is very different from what can be found in standard textbooks. In the last two decades it has been shown that the elements of classical physics emerge through an irreversible quantum process called 'decoherence'. According to decoherence theories, quantum objects acquire classical properties only through interactions with their natural environment as a consequence of the holistic features of quantum theory. In view of the interpretation problem of quantum theory, only two directions out of the host of proposals suggested in the course of time appear to remain consistent solutions.

1. CLASSICAL AND QUANTUM PHYSICS

The relation between classical and quantum physics has been at the centre of dispute since the beginnings of quantum theory. Does quantum theory simply contain classical physics as a limiting case, similar to relativistic mechanics, which reduces to Newton's theory in the limit case in which the velocities are much smaller than the velocity of light? Or do we need classical physics from the outset to deal with quantum theory at all? How do these two theories fit together?

Essential progress has been made on these questions in the last two decades.[1] On the basis of the new results, many are now claiming that we

---

[1] A lucid account of the present situation was written by Max Tegmark and John Wheeler (2001), '100 Years of Quantum Mysteries'. The various aspects of decoherence are described in depth in E. Joos, H. D. Zeh, C. Kiefer, D. Giulini, J. Kupsch, and I. O. Stamatescu (2003), *Decoherence and the Appearance of a Classical World in Quantum Theory*.

no longer need to take classical notions as our starting point. These can be *derived* from quantum concepts. Classical physics is not a 'built in' feature of quantum theory, however. Only through certain (irreversible) quantum processes—now called decoherence—does the world of classical physics dynamically emerge from the quantum world. The disturbing dichotomy between quantum and classical notions was only a delusion.

The theory of decoherence originated from the desire to achieve a better understanding of the quantum–classical relation, in particular of the quantum measurement process. The orthodoxy of the Copenhagen school overshadowed these questions for a long time. The so-called Copenhagen interpretation, born out of despair in the 1920s, was, from a pragmatic point of view, extremely successful. Yet the inner contradictions of this view were only experienced as dissatisfying by a few, amongst them the co-founders of quantum theory, Einstein and Schrödinger. Quantum theory essentially started with Bohr's atomic theory, although its range of application was later rapidly extended. Obviously quantum theory does describe some fundamental properties of nature and is much more than a preliminary theory, soon to be replaced by something better. Hence it needs to be taken with extreme seriousness. Experimental physicists can now increasingly test the critical transition region between 'microscopic' and 'macroscopic'. Exploring this intermediate range makes it questionable and more and more meaningless to discriminate between 'microscopic' and 'macroscopic'. Therefore it is of utmost importance to formulate a unique, consistent theory. From what we know today, this can only be some sort of quantum theory. Now, what picture of nature does quantum theory provide, and how can we find in this theory the classical world of our everyday experience?

2. KINEMATICS: HOW DO WE DESCRIBE OBJECTS?

To appreciate better the problems that arise when we inquire into the relation between classical and quantum physics, it is a good idea to take a step back and recall how a physical theory is usually built.

The first component in a theory of nature is a conceptual scheme to describe the things we want to talk about. These may be raindrops, the trees in my garden, the moons of Jupiter, or the electrons in a computer screen. The mathematical notions that we use comprise the kinematic foundation of our theory. As a first step, then, let us compare the mathematical description of objects in classical and quantum physics.

A simple example is a mass point—the centre of gravity of a dust particle, say. A complete specification in classical physics requires defining the position

x and momentum (or velocity) p. In quantum theory, the description looks completely different. Instead of particle coordinates the concept of a wave function is used. This wave function is no longer concentrated at a single point x in space, but rather extended over some region. The most important feature is this: wave functions can be superposed. Given two states (wave functions), Ψ and Φ, one can 'add' these and the result is a new wave function describing a physical state with completely different properties. In fact, all the 'strange' features of quantum theory originate from this superposition principle.

This superposition of wave functions has its classical analogue in well-known wave phenomena, such as waves in a pond or radio waves. In these cases one can observe interference phenomena typical for waves. These are also found for quantum objects. But the superposition principle of quantum theory is much more general. It allows superposing *any* two physical states. For example, a superposition of states with different particle numbers is allowed. Such states are important for a correct description of laser fields. How do particles and waves fit together? This is an old question. In the microscopic domain we are now quite sure that a description in terms of particles (that is, as objects localized in space) is untenable, while such a picture in fact works quite well in the macroscopic world.

At first sight the situation seems hopeless. How could classical notions ever emerge from the radically different structures imposed by quantum theory? (See Table 3.1.)

3. DYNAMICS: HOW THINGS CHANGE WITH TIME

The second part of a theory has to specify how the objects previously defined evolve in time. Again, there is a big difference between the classical and the quantum case, since the laws of motion in the two cases look quite dissimilar.

Table 3.1. Comparing the kinematical notions in classical and quantum physics. There is no obvious or superficial connection between the right and the left part of this table.

Classical physics Galileo, Newton,...	Quantum physics Schrödinger
mass points:, $\vec{x}, \vec{p}$	wave function $\Psi(\vec{x})$
fields $\vec{E}(\vec{x})$, $\vec{B}(\vec{x})$	superposition principle: $\Psi, \Phi \longrightarrow \Psi + \Phi$

In classical mechanics, mass points move according to Newton's law $\vec{F} = m\vec{a}$ (or, expressed in a more sophisticated manner, they follow Hamilton's equations of motion). This fundamental law specifies the time development of position and momentum. The analogous primary law of evolution in quantum physics is Schrödinger's equation, governing the time dependence of wave functions. But here we stumble on a very strange (in fact, unsolved) problem: it appears that Schrödinger's equation is not always valid. When a measurement is made it is replaced by another law of motion, substituting for the wave function another one with a certain probability (the so-called collapse of the wave function). After every measurement the wave function is thereby 'updated' according to the measurement result. Strictly speaking, such a theory is inconsistent, or at least ill-defined, since it has two laws of motion. Of course, every physicist knows when to apply one law or the other. Schrödinger's equation is valid for isolated systems; the 'collapse' occurs when a measurement is made. (See Table 3.2.) But what is a measurement?

Obviously, we have some trouble clearly seeing the connection between classical and quantum physics. It is therefore not surprising that the same questions are asked again and again when physicists think about the interpretation of quantum theory. The questions include, for example:

- What is the meaning of the wave function Ψ?
- What is the meaning of the collapse of the wave function?
- What precisely is the connection between classical and quantum physics? Do we need classical and quantum notions at the same time?

For more than seventy-five years we have had at our disposal an extremely successful quantum theory. Shouldn't one expect to find the answer to all these questions in standard textbooks by now? If we examine a contemporary textbook, however, what do we find?

Table 3.2. Comparison of laws of motion in classical and quantum physics. In the quantum case, the Schrödinger equation appears as fundamental, but is sometimes replaced by the collapse of the wave function.

Classical physics Newton/Hamilton	Quantum physics Schrödinger
$\vec{F} = m\vec{a}$ or $\dot{\chi}_i = \frac{\partial H}{\partial p_i}$ $\dot{P}_i = -\frac{\partial H}{\partial x_i}$ Maxwell's equations for $\vec{E}(\vec{x})$, $\vec{B}(\vec{x})$	Two (!) laws of motion 1. Schrödinger's equation $i\hbar \frac{d}{dt}\Psi = H\Psi$ 2. Collapse of the wave function $\Psi = \sum_n c_n \Psi_n \longrightarrow \Psi_k$ with probability $|c_k|^2$

4. THE TALE OF THE CLASSICAL LIMIT

Landau and Lifschitz wrote a well-known textbook series on Theoretical Physics. The volume on quantum mechanics contains the following statements: 'Quantum mechanics contains classical mechanics as a limiting case... The transition from quantum mechanics to classical mechanics [is] analogous to the transition from wave optics to ray optics... Then the claim can be made that in the semiclassical case a wave packet is moving along its classical orbit of a particle.' (Landau and Lifschitz)

Assertions of this kind can be found in nearly all textbooks on quantum mechanics. The usual arguments are, for example, that the well-known spreading of the wave packet does not play any role for massive objects, since it would be extremely slow. Other mathematical arguments rely on the so-called Ehrenfest theorems, which show that mean values approximately follow classical orbits. For the calculation of molecular properties one uses approximation schemes (going back to Born and Oppenheimer) that lead to classical-looking states. That is, molecular wave functions are constructed where atoms or groups of atoms show a well-defined spatial orientation—like the pictures we are all used to from chemistry books. A point to remember is that all these approximation schemes start from the Schrödinger equation. So far everything seems fine.

5. WHAT'S WRONG: PART 1

The above-mentioned superposition principle is the most important characterizing property of quantum theory. Starting from two arbitrary states of a system one can construct new states by linear combination (superposition). If Ψ_1 and Ψ_2 are two solutions of the Schrödinger equation, then any state of the form

$$\Psi = c_1\Psi_1 + c_2\Psi_2$$

is automatically also a solution, for any (complex) coefficients c_1 and c_2. There obviously exist a great many possibilities for constructing such combinations by varying the coefficients. The big problem is this: if Ψ_1 and Ψ_2 describe 'classical states' (such as spatially localized objects or dead and alive cats), most of the above combinations are totally 'non-classical'. This means that most states that are allowed by quantum theory are never observed! We only see dead or alive cats or the moon at a definite position, and we don't have any idea what such a linear combination ('both dead *and* alive at the same time') should mean.[2]

One way out of this dilemma could perhaps be the idea that such strange states simply never occur, since all macro-objects were created from the beginning in special classical states. Unfortunately this argument does not help, since in measurement-like situations a microscopic superposition is necessarily amplified into the macroscopic domain, such that the occurrence of these states becomes unavoidable. (This is in essence Schrödinger's cat argument of 1935, where uncertainty in nuclear decay is transferred to the poor cat via a Geiger counter.)

The above argument is not new; it can also be found in an interesting exchange of letters between Max Born and Albert Einstein. Let me quote from a letter of Einstein's to Born, dated 1 January 1954:

> Your opinion is quite untenable. It is in conflict with the principles of quantum theory to require that the Ψ-function of a 'macro'-system be 'narrow' with respect to the macro-coordinates and momenta. Such a demand is at variance with the superposition principle for Ψ-functions. . . . Narrowness with regard to macro-coordinates is a requirement which is not only *independent* of the principles of quantum mechanics, but is, moreover, *incompatible* with them. (Born, 1955)

Any attempt to establish some kind of 'classical physics' from a quantum framework has to explain why we see only very special states, the ones that we then call 'classical'. Special states are common not only in regions that appear as obviously 'macroscopic'. Even a single sugar molecule is 'classical' in the sense that it is found only in a right- or left-handed configuration, never in a superposition state, as is common in atomic physics. The term 'macroscopic' has nothing to do with 'size' in the first place; there are also well-known (and well-understood) 'big' macroscopic quantum states, such as superconductors.

6. WHAT'S WRONG: PART 2

The second point I want to emphasize derives from a quite simple yet important observation: macroscopic objects are never isolated from their natural environment. To convince oneself that this is true, one simply has to open one's eyes. The fact that we can see things in our surroundings means

---

[2] The widespread view—that the cat is either dead or alive and we just don't yet know which—turns out to be untenable. Superpositions have completely different properties compared with their components, that is, they describe 'new' states.

that they scatter light. The scattering of light off an object implies that it cannot be thought of as isolated. Furthermore, this interaction has properties similar to a measurement. After scattering, the light contains 'information'[3] about the position of the object it was scattered from. In quantum theory, measurement is an often disputed and highly nontrivial subject. A measurement usually destroys the typical quantum behaviour, the possibility of interference. If such measurements happen repeatedly, interferences can never show up. (See Fig. 3.1.)

This could explain why we never see a superposition of a dead and an alive cat or a superposition of the moon at different places. If this interaction is strong enough (more on that below), it follows that there can be no Schrödinger equation for macro-objects. And all the above-mentioned quantum textbook derivations are obsolete for this simple reason.

Hence, what kind of equation replaces the Schrödinger equation? Unfortunately, there is no simple answer to this question, since the consequences of the interaction of a system with its environment vary to a large degree. There is no other way than to look at simple situations and apply the Schrödinger equation as the fundamental law. Of special importance is the fact that for macroscopic objects the environment acts in a manner similar to a measurement device. Therefore it is appropriate to start with a look at the quantum theory of measurement.

Fig. 3.1. Macroscopic objects are always under 'continuous observation' through their natural environment. They scatter light and molecules, even in the vacuum of outer space. Their position becomes classical in this way.

---

[3] I was hesitant to use the term 'information' at all in this text. There is at present so much confusion about 'quantum information' in the literature. In our case, the phrase 'the environment gains information about position' simply means that its state after interaction *depends on* (varies with) the location of the object.

7. SUPERPOSITIONS, INTERFERENCE, DENSITY MATRICES, AND THE LIKE

There is a useful tool for giving a compact description of all predictions of quantum theory: the so-called density matrix. It is constructed from wave functions and can be used to calculate all probabilities for the occurrence of certain states in certain measurements.

The simplest quantum system is a two-state system, such as might be realized, for example, by polarizing electron spin or light. Recently the concept of a 'quantum bit' has become quite common. The most general state allowed by quantum theory is a superposition of two basis states $|1\rangle$ and $|2\rangle$ of the form[4]

$$|\Psi\rangle = a|1\rangle + b|2\rangle.$$

The density matrix corresponding to this state shows four peaks (see Fig. 3.2). Two of these just represent the probability to find $|1\rangle$ or $|2\rangle$ when a measurement is made (therefore the height of these peaks is given by the probabilities $|a|^2$ and $|b|^2$, respectively). The other two peaks show that we have here a coherent quantum superposition. These additional peaks are responsible for all interference effects which may occur in appropriate situations.

Fig. 3.2. Density matrix of a superposition of two basis states $|1\rangle$ and $|2\rangle$. The height of the two peaks along the main diagonal gives the probability for finding one of these states in a measurement. The two additional interference terms show that *both* components are present, the state should therefore be characterized by $|1\rangle$ *and* $|2\rangle$.

---

[4] I will mainly use Dirac's 'kets' to describe quantum states. This is a very useful and compact notation, in particular for the general arguments of this paper. A quantum state can then be characterized in a simple way by 'quantum numbers' or just by words, as in $|\text{dead cat}\rangle$.

Now imagine that we want to describe an ensemble of $|1\rangle$ or $|2\rangle$ that represents the particular situation after a measurement has been made (where either $|1\rangle$ *or* $|2\rangle$ will be found). Here the density matrix simply describes a probability distribution. In this case it has only two contributing factors, since members of an ensemble clearly cannot interfere with one another (see Fig. 3.3).

Figure 3.3 resembles the standard black-box situation: there 'is' a certain state, but we may not know what it is before taking a look. Therefore, as an important criterion for knowing whether a particular physical behaviour is classical we will have to look for the presence or absence of interference terms in the density matrix. If there are none, we can at least say that the system behaves *as if* it is in the state where *either* $|1\rangle$ *or* $|2\rangle$ obtains.

A well-known analogy to the above two situations is the interference of two radio stations. If both are on air at the same frequency, they can interfere, since their signals can add coherently. This phenomenon is parallel to the density matrix in Fig. 3.2. If only one radio station is on air (even if we do not know which one) clearly there can be no interference (Fig. 3.3). Similar arguments can be applied to a double-slit experiment, which can only show an interference pattern if both partial waves (through each slit) are present.

8. THE QUANTUM THEORY OF MEASUREMENT

In physical terms, a measurement device is nothing more than a certain system whose state after an interaction with a 'measured object' contains information about the latter. The state of the device then tells something about the object.

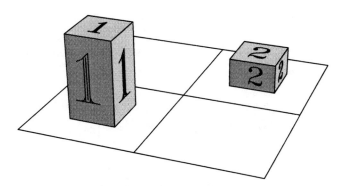

Fig. 3.3. Density matrix of an ensemble of two states $|1\rangle$ and $|2\rangle$. Since only $|1\rangle$ *or* $|2\rangle$ is present (with a certain probability), there are no interference terms.

The application of the quantum formalism to such a situation is straightforward. John von Neumann first showed this in his 1932 treatise 'Mathematical Foundations of Quantum Mechanics'. (See Fig. 3.4.)

Suppose the device is constructed in such a way that it discriminates between a set of possible states $|1\rangle, |2\rangle, \ldots, |n\rangle$. In the special case of a so-called ideal measurement (the only one I consider here), nothing happens to the object; only the state of the device changes from an initial state $|\Phi_0\rangle$ to $|\Phi_n\rangle$, for example

$$|1\rangle|\Phi_0\rangle \xrightarrow{t} |1\rangle|\Phi_1\rangle,$$

or

$$|2\rangle|\Phi_0\rangle \xrightarrow{t} |2\rangle|\Phi_2\rangle,$$

and so on, depending on the initial state of the object. So far this scheme follows classical expectations of what should happen during a measurement. Here's where the superposition principle leads to problems. For an arbitrary initial state $a|1\rangle + b|2\rangle$ we can combine the two equations from above and immediately write down a new solution to Schrödinger's equation,

$$(a|1\rangle + b|2\rangle)|\Phi_0\rangle \xrightarrow{t} a|1\rangle|\Phi_1\rangle + b|2\rangle|\Phi_2\rangle.$$

What we get, however, is no longer a single measurement result but a superposition of all possible pointer positions (which is 'quantum correlated to' the corresponding object states). The important point to note here is that after this interaction both parts (object + apparatus) now have only a common wave function. We have here a so-called 'entangled state'. States of this kind display 'quantum nonlocality', for example, by violating Bell's inequalities, which means that correlations between distant events are stronger than could be expected if these were created by local causes.

If after the measurement the usual rules for calculating probabilities are applied to the apparatus or the measured system (for example, by calculating

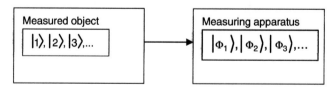

Fig. 3.4. Von Neumann scheme for a measurement process. Information about the state $|n\rangle$ of the object is transferred to a 'pointer', displaying the value n after the measurement; that is, its state is described by a pointer state $|\Phi_n\rangle$.

the respective density matrices), one can see that the interferences have disappeared. This corresponds to the well-known feature of quantum theory that measurements destroy interference, since only one of the possible alternative outcomes is found in a measurement. The above state is, however, perfectly coherent. The interference terms still exist, but they can only be found through measurements on the *combined* system. This is the reason why it is so difficult to find interference effects for 'large' systems, since in general one must have access to all degrees of freedom.

This disappearance of interference for a subsystem of a larger system is now usually called decoherence. It is an immediate consequence of quantum non-locality, which is what's responsible for all the 'strange' properties of entangled states. Since coherence (interference) is a property only of the whole system, it seems to vanish in our observations of subsystems, though it never 'really' disappears.

As emphasized above, macroscopic objects (this of course includes measuring instruments!) are strongly interacting with their natural environment. Therefore von Neumann's model needs to be extended by including the surroundings. This can be done quite easily—at least schematically.

9. THE EMERGENCE OF CLASSICAL PROPERTIES

Since the environment itself works similarly to a measurement device, we can apply the above scheme also to the interaction with the environment, thus simply extending the scheme of the previous section.

If the measurement device shows $|\Phi_1\rangle$, for example, the natural environment E will very rapidly take notice (see Fig. 3.5), so the complete chain now reads

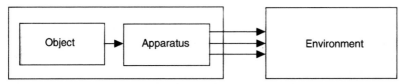

Fig. 3.5. Realistic extension of von Neumann's measurement model. Information about the state of the measured object is transferred to the measuring apparatus. The environment very rapidly recognizes the pointer position of the apparatus. As a consequence, interferences are destroyed irreversibly at the local system object+ apparatus, leading to classical behaviour. This 'back-reaction' is a consequence of quantum non-locality: After the interaction only a common wave function exists.

$$|1\rangle|\Phi_0\rangle|E_0\rangle \longrightarrow |1\rangle|\Phi_1\rangle|E_0\rangle \longrightarrow |1\rangle|\Phi_1\rangle|E_1\rangle.$$

The meaning of $|E_1\rangle$ is that the 'rest of the world' has 'seen' the (macroscopic) measuring apparatus displaying the result $|\Phi_1\rangle$. Consequently the quantum mechanical description for the locally accessible system (object+apparatus) changes: as expected, the interference effects are gone. In formal language, the corresponding terms in the density matrix (the non-diagonal elements) have disappeared, as in Fig. 3.3. The selected (interference-free) states are now stable against decoherence. Only the irreversible interaction with the environment defines what is a possible candidate for a 'classical state'. This dynamical stability of certain states seems to be the central feature of classical objects in a quantum world. In a nutshell: *the macro-system 'apparatus' behaves classically because it is permanently 'measured' itself.*

Is the apparatus now truly classical? This is a delicate question, and I return to it at the end of this chapter. As far as the observable behaviour is concerned (as described by the density matrix), all results are independent of the chosen interpretation of quantum theory. For this reason all physicists agree on the phenomenological meaning of decoherence—on what we actually observe— but not on its interpretation.

10. SPATIAL LOCALIZATION

Macroscopic objects always appear well-localized in ordinary space (though not in momentum space). This fact cannot be understood by considering these objects alone. By contrast, microscopic objects are usually found in very different sorts of states, which we call *energy eigenstates*. An energy eigenstate for a free mass point, for example, would be represented by an extended (plane) wave—just the opposite of a well-localized object!

A realistic assessment of macroscopic objects shows that scattering processes are extremely important (compare Fig. 3.1). The state of the scattered object (a photon or a molecule, for example) depends on the *position* of the scattering centre, that is, the position of the macroscopic object. In this sense, the scattered particle 'measures' the position x of the object. The formal quantum description then looks like

|Object at position x⟩|incoming particle⟩

$\longrightarrow$ |Object at position x⟩|particle scattered off x⟩

According to the quantum theory of measurement, as outlined above, one can expect that such processes destroy interferences over large distances—or, more precisely, over the distances that the environment can 'discriminate'. As is known from optics, for example, the resolution of a microscope is largely determined by the wavelength of the light used. In the quantum case the fact that a great many scattering processes usually happen in a short time interval also plays an enormous role. The typical distance over which coherence can survive may be called 'coherence length' l. Then one could say that, in a double-slit experiment, no interference pattern can be observed any longer if the distance between the slits is larger than l.

In a simple model for scattering processes it turns out that the coherence length l roughly falls off according to the formula

$$l(t) = \frac{1}{\sqrt{\Lambda t}}.$$

The numerical value for the constant Λ (which may be appropriately called the 'localization rate') depends on the concrete situation and can be very large. If we consider a dust particle of radius 10^{-5} cm interacting only with the cosmic background radiation, we obtain $\Lambda = 10^{-6} cm^{-2} s^{-1}$; thermal radiation at room temperature gives $\Lambda = 10^{12} cm^{-2} s^{-1}$; the scattering of air molecules yields $\Lambda = 10^{32} cm^{-2} s^{-1}$.

This means that any initial coherence over considerable distances is destroyed very rapidly—at least for 'large' objects such as dust particles (see Figs 3.6 and 3.7). On the other hand, interference can be observed for small objects, such as electrons or neutrons. Recently, beautiful interference (double-slit) experiments were performed for C_{60} and C_{70} (fullerene) molecules. Whether or not an object shows interference effects is thus a *quantitative* question.

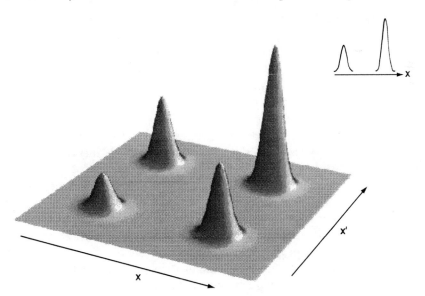

Fig. 3.6. Density matrix of a superposition of an object at two places. The non-diagonal terms show the presence of coherence between the two parts of the wave function (shown in the insert); compare this with Fig. 3.2.

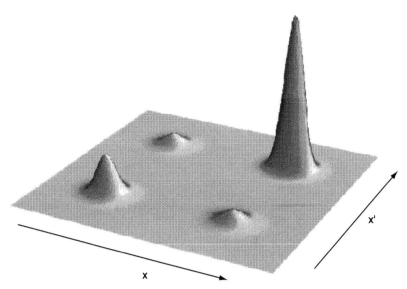

Fig. 3.7. The interaction with the environment damps coherence. The density matrix now looks similar to Fig. 3.3.

To complete the dynamical description of a mass point, one has to include the internal dynamics. The latter leads to the well-known spreading of the wave packet as described in all quantum mechanics textbooks. If we wish to incorporate the scattering processes, we have to use a different equation. In the next step, the no-recoil approximation can be relaxed, leading to another modification of the dynamics. It turns out that, for macroscopic objects, coherence is always destroyed very rapidly and the remaining coherence length is very small—indeed, on the order of the so-called thermal de Broglie wavelength $\lambda = h/\sqrt{mk_BT}$ of the macro-object. This is a very small quantity. For the dust particle mentioned above it is of the order of $10^{-14}\,cm$.

The highly effective resolution of scattering processes has another consequence. It means that the spatial structure of molecules becomes well defined (except for very small ones, such as ammonia, where complete quantum behaviour is still observed). All the pictures one finds in chemistry books are thus well founded, but only after properly taking into account that large molecules are not isolated. It is as if the environment continuously 'observes' the spatial structure of these large molecules. From the viewpoint of quantum mechanics it has been a non-trivial question.

Consider as an example a pyramidal molecule as sketched in Fig. 3.8. If the four ligands were different, this would be an optically active molecule, always found in either right-handed or left-handed form (like sugar and many other molecules). A 'racemate' would simply be a mixture (not a superposition!) of both versions.

The transition between the right- and left-handed version can be described, in simple terms, as a tunnelling of atom #1 through a potential barrier as sketched in Fig. 3.9. For symmetry reasons we describe the ground state of the molecule by a wave function that is distributed over *both* minima of the potential (as in the case of Schrödinger's cat). In most cases the probability for quantum tunnelling is extremely small, so the molecules almost always remain in an oriented state if they are already there. But this alone does not explain what discriminates the classical configurations from the general superpositions (such as the ground state).

Given decoherence caused by the scattering of photons and by other molecules, one can now easily understand why most molecules appear to have a shape. The only exceptions are very small molecules, such as ammonia, which show complete quantum behaviour. This difference can be understood in detail when the relevant timescales are calculated.

The property 'to have a shape' thus emerges through the interaction with the natural environment. This is easy to understand. When we look at objects, we see their form because the scattered light contains the necessary information. Left alone, molecules (and also larger objects) would not have a shape.

Another point deserves to be mentioned here. It seems plausible to identify the scattering processes discussed above with the phenomenon of Brownian motion. Indeed, the situation in the two cases is quite similar. Many 'small' objects are scattered off a 'large' one. Decoherence, however, is a truly quantum

Fig. 3.8. Most molecules show a well-defined orientation of atoms or groups of atoms. Many optically active molecules come in two versions that are mirror images of each other. From a quantum viewpoint a superposition of these two states is to be expected, but never observed.

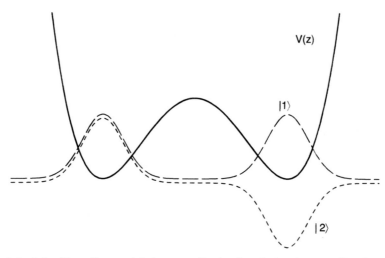

Fig. 3.9. A double well potential gives a qualitative description for tunnelling between the two classical configurations (with wave function concentrated in one minimum of the potential) of Fig. 3.8. The quantum mechanical ground state $|1\rangle$ and the first excited state $|2\rangle$ are both represented by wave functions which are smeared out over both minima. They cannot be given a pictorial representation.

phenomenon. The reason is related to the fact that decoherence is a consequence of quantum entanglement as described in Section 8. Decoherence does not (yet) include dynamical effects such as recoil. This means that we can have decoherence without changing the state of the object. This difference can also be seen in the equations when the quantum analogue of Brownian motion is considered.

When we compare the equations of motion in the two cases, we see that the theory of quantum Brownian motion includes a further term for friction, described by an additional friction parameter γ. (In the simplest model the relation to the decoherence constant Λ is given as $\Lambda = m\gamma k_B T/\hbar^2$; here T is the temperature of the environment, k_B, Boltzmann's constant and m the mass of the considered object.) A comparison of decoherence and friction terms for a certain distance Δx shows that their ratio is roughly given by

$$\frac{\text{decoherence}}{\text{friction}} = \frac{mk_B T}{\hbar^2}(\Delta x)^2 = \left(\frac{\Delta x}{\lambda_{th}}\right)^2 \longrightarrow 10^{40}.$$

Here again T is the temperature of the environment, m the mass of the considered object, and λ_{th} the thermal de Broglie wavelength. Simply inserting typical macroscopic values in this equation, for example, 1 g for the mass and 1 cm for the distance, a large number, of the order of 10^{40}, results! This shows clearly that decoherence is much more important than friction for macroscopic objects.

The onset of decoherence has been tested by beautiful experiments in the microscopic realm. For truly macroscopic objects this is a rather hopeless enterprise, since decoherence is 'already there' because of its high effectiveness. Superpositions of several photons have been produced and the loss of coherence can be manipulated to a certain extent by changing the coupling to the environment. Although this is still more or less microphysics, these states are often called 'Schrödinger cat states'. These 'cats' live for only a few microseconds. Of course, for real cats decoherence times would be many orders of magnitude smaller (in particular, much smaller than the lifetime of a cat), so that such objects will always appear to be in a classical state. This also means that the infamous 'quantum jumps' are not jumps at all, but only a consequence of smooth processes, albeit with a very small decoherence time.

The transition from quantum to classical behaviour can be summarized as in Table 3.3.

11. SPACE-TIME STRUCTURE

Similar ideas can be applied to gravity. All experiments so far support the view that the structure of space-time is classical and well defined down to distances of the order of 10^{-15} cm. According to the theory of General Relativity, space, time, and gravity are intimately intertwined. If gravity also obeys quantum laws (which consistency seems to demand), the superposition principle will then allow arbitrarily many combinations of different gravitational fields (different space-times). Remember that space-time is coupled to matter; hence the latter 'measures' the former. The mechanisms described above can also be put to use here.

Table 3.3. The transition from quantum to classical behaviour

Decoherence in space	
Theory	Experiment
Superposition of different positions	Double-slit experiments
⇓	⇓
Ensemble of different positions	'Particles'
Decoherence in time	
Theory	Experiment
Superposition of different decay times	'Collapse and revival' experiments
⇓	⇓
Ensemble of different decay times	Quantum jumps

A simple example is shown in Fig. 3.10. Molecules traversing a certain volume measure the value g of acceleration, since their trajectory clearly depends on the value of g. A simple calculation shows that any superposition of different values of g is rapidly destroyed.

To go beyond this toy model requires a full-fledged theory of quantum gravity—which unfortunately does not yet exist. One approach is the so-called Wheeler–de Witt equation, which has the form of a time-independent Schrödinger equation,

$$H|\Psi\rangle = 0.$$

The wave function Ψ contains matter as well as gravitational (space-time) degrees of freedom. There are many technical problems to solve, and the interpretation is even trickier than in ordinary quantum theory. Where is time? Where is the observer, if $|\Psi\rangle$ describes everything? Quite independently of these problems, in simple models one can study the consequences of the coupling between matter and space-time structure. Entanglement with matter leads to a destruction of interferences for the metric of space-time in normal situations (that is, far from the big bang). For example, the solution of the model for a quantized Friedmann universe yields a superposition of an expanding and a contracting universe (just think of a gigantic Schrödinger cat!). The interference between these two components is, however, damped because of the coupling to matter by the extremely small factor

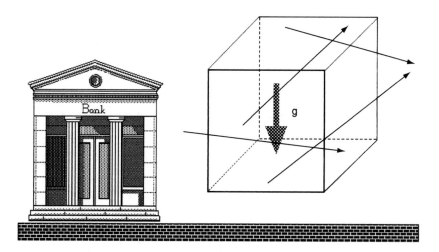

Fig. 3.10. Molecules travelling through a gravitational field act like a measurement apparatus for acceleration.

$$\exp\left(-\frac{\pi m H_0^2 a^3}{128}\right) \approx \exp\left(-10^{43}\right) <<< 1.$$

(Here H_0 is Hubble's constant, $a \approx 1/H_0$ the current size of our universe, m a typical particle mass, and here $\hbar = c = 1$.)

12. MORALS TO BE DRAWN

What conclusions can we draw? Clearly, the strong dynamical coupling of macro-objects to their natural environment cannot simply be ignored.[5] Because of the non-local properties of quantum states, a consistent description of some phenomenon in quantum terms must finally include the entire universe. Similar arguments can be put forward in classical physics, where it has been known for a long time that most systems are severely influenced by the rest of the world. However, the new holistic properties of entangled states require one to consider matters from another viewpoint, that of quantum physics.

The properties of the 'ordinary' objects of our experience—precisely those that we call macroscopic—are now seen not to be inherent in these objects. Instead, they emerge from, or are *created* by, irreversible interactions with the environment. In this way the local classical properties with which we are so familiar have their origin in the nonlocality of (entangled) quantum states. The properties of the interaction decide which properties become classical. For example, objects appear localized in *space,* since these interactions typically depend on *position.*

It should be evident by now that classical properties can be seen to emerge from the quantum world *only after* decoherence has properly been taken into account. No classical notions are needed at a fundamental level. The robustness of certain quantum states—those that survive under the influence of the environment—defines what we typically call 'classical'.

Can decoherence solve all problems related to the quantum–classical transition? Is there really a classical world out there? Up to this point we have appealed only to the established rules of quantum theory. Now let's take a closer look.

---

[5] From a historical perspective it appears surprising that decoherence has been overlooked for such a long time. One reason is certainly that according to the orthodox Copenhagen interpretation of quantum theory an application of quantum concepts in the macroscopic domain was unjustified from the start.

13. WHAT IS AN OBSERVER?

Most of what was detailed above had one big advantage: all the results are independent of any specific interpretation of quantum theory, and any disagreement among the experts concerns technical details only. Constructing a consistent picture of nature is a much more demanding task, however. Therefore a critical analysis of what we have achieved so far is in order. The widely used density matrices, for example, are merely a tool to calculate measurement results. But what is a measurement? Both laws of quantum evolution—the deterministic Schrödinger equation and the stochastic collapse of the wave function—are contained in the density matrix. Everyone agrees that quantum theory is empirically well founded. What does this mean? As is often emphasized, the last and final evidence comes in the form of perceptions made by some observer. This aspect played a role from the very beginning of quantum theory. Heisenberg, for example, recalls in his auto-biography a discussion with Einstein on how to construct new physical theories:

'One cannot observe the orbits of electrons in an atom' [I said]. 'Seriously, you can't believe', Einstein replied, 'that a physical theory can be based only on observable quantities'.... 'But I thought that precisely that idea was essential for your theory of relativity?' 'Perhaps I used this kind of philosophy', Einstein answered, 'but it is nonsense nevertheless.... It may be of heuristic value to recall what one really observes. But as a matter of principle it is quite wrong to insist on founding a theory on observed quantities alone. In reality just the opposite is true. The theory alone decides about what can be observed.... Along [the] entire long path from a process up to our conscious perception we need to know how Nature is working in order to claim that we have observed anything at all.' (Heisenberg, 1973)

Subjective perception is obviously related to certain brain functions. Can we apply quantum theory also there?

14. DECOHERENCE IN THE BRAIN

There are many models for describing the communication of neurons in the brain. Nearly all of them are classical in the sense that the neurons are described by a classical state, which changes according to certain rules. As already emphasized, quantum theory allows many non-classical states. Most of these cannot be easily related to what we perceive.

For example, consider the superposition

$$|\Psi\rangle = |\text{Neuron is firing}\rangle + |\text{Neuron is not firing}\rangle.$$

This is a perfectly legal state in the framework of quantum theory, but what could it mean with respect to subjective experience? Recently there have been investigations showing that quantum coherence does not play a role in such a state.[6] It turns out that the environment can very rapidly distinguish both alternatives, thereby destroying coherence and producing a 'classical' state (see Fig. 3.11). Some of the estimated timescales are as small as $10^{-20}s$. This means that we have no chance to have 'strange' experiences corresponding to such non-classical states, since they are far too short-lived.

This result is relevant to the discussion of mind and emergence that takes place in later chapters. It turns out that the entire classical level related to brain functions such as language, communication between individuals, and so on can be seen to emerge from the quantum level as I have described. In

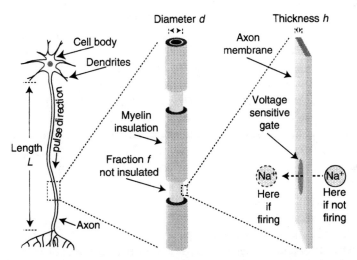

Fig. 3.11. Neurons communicate with each other by sending electrical pulses along axons. The difference between 'firing' and 'not-firing' in essence consists in about 10^6 sodium or potassium ions being on one or the other side of a membrane. The environment rapidly recognizes this difference. (Illustration from M. Tegmark, Phys. Rev. E61, 4194)

---

[6] There have been suggestions (by Penrose and others) that certain parts of the brain act coherently like a 'quantum computer'. Even if such regions were to be found, it is hard to see what would be gained in understanding consciousness. It rather appears that the physical states which can be related to consciousness acquire their objective meaning through decoherence.

fact, the very existence of life as we know it depends on decoherence. The stability of biological structures such as DNA, for example, is a result of the same process. Without decoherence we could not exist as 'quasi-stable' beings, communicating with each other and reading books.

There is also an intimate connection to the second law of thermodynamics. Indeed, in the classical domain, decoherence is the most effective irreversible process, thereby defining a fundamental arrow of time. Even classical chaos (which has no strict analogue in the quantum world) emerges to a very good approximation via decoherence.

15. SERIOUS QUANTUM THEORY

There are good reasons, then, to take the quantum description of physical reality at face value. And we have seen that decoherence theory can be viewed as a direct consequence of taking quantum theory seriously. I want therefore to close this contribution with some remarks concerning the possible interpretations of quantum theory and the alternatives to it. As an introduction, let me add some very brief comments about some interpretations that are frequently advanced but in my view are either misleading or inconsistent.

First, there is a widespread opinion that quantum theory is simply some sort of 'statistical' theory. In this case the collapse of the wave function would not be very surprising, since it would only describe a certain increase of information in the observer. Unfortunately, things are not that simple, as a wave function cannot be viewed as an ensemble of other wave functions. To make the statistical interpretation work, one would have to invent a theory beyond quantum theory. (Theories with additional parameters, such as Bohm's theory, do not seem to be of much help.)

One other—and perhaps the most prevalent—method for sweeping the interpretive problems under the carpet is simply to assume, or rather postulate, that quantum theory is only a theory of micro-objects, whereas in the macroscopic realm per decree (or should I say wishful thinking?) a classical description has to be valid. Such an approach leads to the endlessly discussed paradoxes of quantum theory. These paradoxes arise only because this particular approach is conceptually inconsistent, and it remains inconsistent even when its advocates appeal to notions such as 'dualism' and 'complementarity' to help with the difficulties. In addition, micro- and macro-objects are so strongly dynamically coupled that we do not even know where the boundary between the two supposed realms could possibly be found. For these reasons it seems obvious that there is no boundary. Classical concepts must emerge dynamically, then, from the quantum level via decoherence.

If one seeks a unified description in quantum terms, only two choices appear plausible.

16. FIRST CHOICE: COLLAPSE

After a measurement we are always aware of one concrete result. The Schrödinger equation as a universal law, however, typically yields a superposition of all alternatives because of its linearity. Thus all 'wrong' components of the wave function Ψ must finally disappear, except the one that describes the 'correct' perception, for example in the famous cat experiment,

$$|\Psi\rangle = |\text{atom not decayed}\rangle |\text{cat is alive}\rangle |\text{environment sees living cat}\rangle$$
$$|\text{observer sees living cat}\rangle$$
$$+ |\text{atom decayed}\rangle |\text{cat is killed}\rangle |\text{environment sees dead cat}\rangle$$
$$|\text{observer sees dead cat}\rangle$$
$$\xrightarrow{collapse} |\text{atom decayed}\rangle |\text{cat is killed}\rangle |\text{environment sees dead cat}\rangle$$
$$|\text{observer sees dead cat}\rangle$$

This implies an explicit change in the Schrödinger equation. Obviously it must not happen too early, since otherwise it would have been observed in at least some experiments. It has to occur, however, before subjective perception comes into play. Many suggestions have been made as to where and how the change could occur. Even von Neumann connected the collapse with consciousness, an idea that was later reconsidered by Wigner and others. Models that explicitly change the Schrödinger equation have been suggested by Penrose (who claims that gravity may trigger a collapse) and, in a rather detailed form, by Ghirardi, Rimini, and Weber (1986, p. 470). Up to now there are no hints showing that the Schrödinger equation loses its validity in any experiment.

17. SECOND CHOICE: EVERETT

If Schrödinger's equation is valid without exception, then all components of the wave function remain in existence. The following equation shows another possibility. A superposition of 'classical' alternatives would arise if a 'quantum jump' leading to the possible death of the cat at a certain time t were described as

$$|\Psi\rangle = \sum_t |\text{atom decays at time t}\rangle |\text{Geiger counter fires at time t}\rangle$$
$$|\text{environment sees dead cat at time t}\rangle$$
$$|\text{observer sees dead cat at time t}\rangle$$

Since every component of this wave function contains an observer state, more and more different versions of this observer emerge in the course of time, with different perceptions and different (but consistent) memories of what he has seen. The factors involved in such a model are thus copious, if not, as John Bell once put it, 'extravagant'. And yet all this follows automatically from the simple dynamics of the Schrödinger equation.

18. THE BURDEN OF CHOICE

Which of these two possibilities should be given preference? Both have their promises and weaknesses. But it should be clear by now that, whichever interpretation one prefers, the classical world view has been ruled out.

Collapse models need to specify at what point the deviation from the Schrödinger equation should happen. There are only a few precise models. What triggers a collapse? Consciousness? Or does it happen earlier, in the physical realm? Perhaps gravity might be the reason; after all, the inclusion of gravity into the quantum framework is still one of the big unsolved problems. The attractiveness of collapse models results from the fact that subjective perception can be directly connected to physical states of the brain, as in classical physics. In the Everett interpretation, by contrast, we have to relate subjective perception to certain *components* (parts) of the wave function. One important outcome of Everett's model is the parallel existence of many different versions of every observer, each of them having different experiences. This consequence seems intimidating to many. It should be emphasized, however, that this result seems unavoidable if the Schrödinger equation is really a fundamental law of nature.

A frequently asked question is where the probabilities in quantum theory come from. In collapse models these are simply put in by hand. This means that these theories contain an additional mechanism which 'throws dice'. There need not be any 'reason' for one or another outcome. In Everett-like interpretations, by contrast, all possibilities are realized simultaneously. There is still some controversy as to whether or not one needs additional axioms to obtain the same numerical values of the probabilities that are predicted by standard quantum theory.

Some collapse theories lead to conflicts with relativity. This is not surprising, because a collapse changes an extended wave function everywhere at once. Still, this is not a problem for all the theories in this category. Conversely, in Everett-like theories relativity does not pose a difficulty at all, since all interactions, and thus the dynamics, are local.

Physics is an empirical science, and so we should like to have an experimental test to discriminate between these two very different approaches. Unfortunately this is rather difficult to achieve, although the two theories indeed give different predictions. To test collapse theories one would like to see deviations from the Schrödinger equation. The trouble is, the effects of decoherence just *look like* a collapse. To discriminate between decoherence and the posited collapse is extremely difficult. On the other hand, the Everett interpretation claims that all components always exist, since a collapse never happens. This means that the superposition of dead cat and alive cat is never destroyed. Yet coherence between these two components can never be observed by local measurements—because of decoherence.

Whatever solution is preferred, the message of decoherence remains the same: we do not need classical notions as the starting point for physics. Instead, these emerge through the dynamical process of decoherence from the quantum substrate.

19. REFERENCES

Born, M. (1955), *Albert Einstein, Hedwig und Max Born, Briefwechsel 1916–1955* (München: Nymphenburger Verlagshandlung).

Ghirardi, G. C., A. Rimini, and T. Weber (1986), 'Unified Dynamics for Microscopic and Macroscopic Systems', *Phys. Rev.*, D34, 470.

Heisenberg, W. (1973), *Der Teil und das Ganze* (Munich: Deutscher Taschenbuchverlag).

Joos, E., H. D. Zeh, C. Kiefer, D. Giulini, J. Kupsch, and I. O. Stamatescu (2003), *Decoherence and the Appearance of a Classical World in Quantum Theory*, 2nd edn. (Berlin: Springer).

Landau, L. D. and E. M. Lifschitz, *Lehrbuch der Theoretischen Physik*, Vol. 3 (Berlin: Akademie Verlag).

Tegmark, Max, and John Wheeler (2001), '100 Years of Quantum Mysteries', *Scientific American* 284: 54.

Further information about decoherence can be found on <www.decoherence.de>.

4

On the Nature of Emergent Reality

George F. R. Ellis[1]

If the human [soul] is anything, it must be of unimaginable complexity and diversity [...] I can only gaze with wonder and awe at the depth and heights of our psychic nature. Its non-spatial universe conceals an untold abundance of images which have accumulated over millions of years of living development and become fixed in the organism. My consciousness is like an eye that penetrates to the most distant spaces, yet it is the psychic non-ego that fills them with nonspatial images. And these images are not pale shadows, but tremendously powerful psychic factors... Beside this picture I would like to place the spectacle of the starry heavens at night, for the only equivalent of the universe within is the universe without; and just as I reach this world through the medium of the body, so I reach that world through the medium of the psyche. (C. G. Jung, *Freud and Psychoanalysis, Collected Works of C. G. Jung,* 4, p. 331)[2]

1. BROAD THESES ON EMERGENT REALITY

How does this amazing structure emerge from its basis in physics? The following sections aim to give a basic understanding of how complexity emerges at higher levels of the hierarchy of structure on the basis of the underlying physics, leading to emergent behaviours that cannot be reduced to a description at any lower level. To start with, a number of theses are put forward that encapsulate the understanding proposed; these are then followed in the remainder of the article by a more detailed discussion of various issues that arise.

i. The Hierarchy of Physical Structure and Causation.

The emergence of complex structures, including conscious life, from simpler physical structures is based on tightly structured non-linear relations between

---

[1] I thank Chuck Harper and Evelyn Fox-Keller for useful references, and Philip Clayton for useful discussions.
[2] From <http://www.JourneyintoWholeness.org/news/nl/v11n3/index.shtm>.

Table 4.1. The hierarchy of structure and causation for living systems, characterized in terms of the corresponding academic subjects.

The hierarchy of structure
Sociology/Politics/Economics
Animal Behaviour/Psychology
Botany/Zoology/Physiology
Cell Biology
Biochemistry/Molecular Biology
Molecular Chemistry
Atomic Physics
Nuclear Physics
Particle physics

components, designed to produce specific higher-level functioning. This emergence of higher-level structuring is captured in the structural and causal hierarchy (Peacocke, 1983; Campbell, 1991; Murphy and Ellis, 1995; Scott, 1995) shown in Table 4.1.

Each higher level, created by structured combinations of lower-level elements, has different properties from the underlying lower levels. The entities at each level show behaviours characteristic of that level. One finds a vast variety of existences at each higher level in the hierarchy (very large numbers of possible organic macromolecules, very many species of animals, etc.) but fewer kinds of entities at the lower levels (atoms are made just of protons, neutrons, and electrons), so complex objects with complex behaviour are made by highly structured combinations of simpler objects with simpler behaviour. Each level underlies what happens at the next higher level in terms of physical causation. The existence of higher-level complex behaviour, which does not occur at the lower levels, then emerges from the lower-level properties both structurally and functionally (at each moment) and in evolutionary and developmental terms (over time).

ii. Theses on Emergence

I first make some broad observations on the nature of emergence in this section and then elaborate on some of them in the following sections.

1. *Emergence is different in different contexts.* It is useful to look at the variety of complex systems (Ellis, 2002) to see its different aspects: (a) *natural objects* (non-living), (b) *living beings* (including conscious beings) (Campbell,

1991; Scott, 1995), (c) *manufactured objects* (artefacts), particularly computer systems (Tannenbaum, 1990).

The different kinds of emergence corresponding are discussed in Section 5 below. This paper mainly concentrates on the highest level of emergence—self-conscious human beings.

2. *Emergence is characterized by hierarchical structures with different levels of order and descriptive languages (levels of phenomenology), plus a relational hierarchy at each level of the structural hierarchy.* The structural hierarchy is indicated in Table 4.1. Note that one can't even describe higher levels in terms of lower-level languages; a different phenomenological description of causation is at work at the higher levels, which may be described in terms of different causal entities.[3] The different levels of language are particularly clear in the case of computers and the genetic information coded in DNA.

One can't understand relations between the vast variety of objects at each higher level without using a hierarchical characterization of properties at that level, for example,

'animal – mammal – domestic animal – dog – guard dog – Doberman – Fred';
'machine – transport vehicle – automobile – sedan – Toyota – CA687-455'.

The characterization used here may be based on (i) appearance, (ii) structure, (iii) function, (iv) location and/or history (e.g. evolutionary history), or (v) an arbitrarily assigned labelling (e.g. alphabetic or numeric order). Note that these categorizations go from the very generic to the individual/specific.

3. *These hierarchical structures are modular; they are made up of structural combinations of semi-autonomous components with their own internal state variables, each carrying out specific functions.* It is useful here to look at the case of computer systems (Tannebaum, 1990) and object-oriented languages (Booch, 1994) for the principles, such as abstraction and inheritance, that underlie modularity. In general, many lower-level states correspond to a single higher-level state, because a higher-level state description is arrived at by averaging over lower-level states and throwing away a vast amount of lower-level information ('coarse graining'). The number of lower-level states corresponding to a single higher-level state determines the entropy of that state. This is lower-level information that is hidden in the higher-level view. In life, the crucial module is the cell (Morowitz, 2001).

---

[3] In terms of physics, we have macroscopic *effective theories* occurring (Hartmann 2001) that are the result of averaging over lower-level causal relations and that differ from the microscopic relations. For example, in electromagnetism we have the difference between the electromagnetic field governing microphysics and the induction field governing macrophysics, related by the polarization tensor—which is a measurable physical quantity.

George F. R. Ellis

Table 4.2. The different timescales associated with evolution, development, and functioning. In the 'natural system' row, 'function' refers to events such as volcanoes, earthquakes, typhoons, etc. In the 'biological systems' row, it refers for example to typical brain operations, while in the 'artificial systems' row it refers to a typical modern computer and its micro-operations.

	Timescales			
Kind of system	Long term evolution	Short term evolution	Development	Function
Natural	10^9 yrs	10^5 yrs	10^5 yrs	hours–days
Biological	10^9 yrs	10^5 yrs	20 yrs	1 msec
Artificial	10^4 yrs	10^2 yrs	10 yrs	1 μsec

Binding is tighter and speeds of interaction and energies are higher at the lower levels of the hierarchy; combinations of many high-frequency lower-level interactions result in lower-frequency higher-level actions. For example, a computer microchip may perform millions of operations per second, but the user still has to wait for the computer to do what she wants at the macro level.

4. *Emergence occurs in at least three different ways: (a) the evolution of species or type, (b) the development or creation of each individual object or being, and (c) the functioning of individual objects and beings, each occurring within very different timescales.* As life emerges, in each case there is a dramatic change from matter without complex functionality to living material. The relevant timescales (Table 4.2) are related both to physical size and to degree of tightness of coupling. At the topmost level, each type of emergence is characterized by adaptive selection in interaction with the physical and social environment, which are the boundary conditions for the system.

5. *Emergence is enabled by the simultaneous operation of (a) bottom-up, (b) same-level, and (c) top-down action,* the latter two occurring by coordinating lower-level actions according to the system structure and boundary conditions. Reliable higher-level laws—the key requirement for meaningful higher-level behaviour—result when the variety of lower-level states corresponding to a particular higher-level state all lead to the same higher-level action. Then the lower-level actions may be coordinated by the higher-level ones, so that top-down action occurs and effects same-level action. This affects the nature of causality in an important way, because same-level and inter-level negative and positive feedback loops become possible (Fig. 4.1).

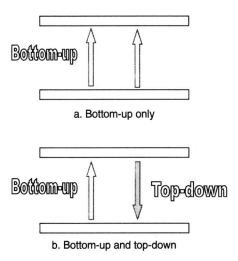

Fig 4.1. Bottom-up and top-down action. The fundamental importance of top-down action is that it changes the overall causal relation between upper and lower levels in the hierarchy of structure and organisation, cf. the difference between a and b.

Causality in coherent complex systems has all these dimensions: bottom-up, same-level, and top-down. For example (cf. Ackoff, 1999), the question: 'Why does an aircraft fly?' can be answered:

- In *bottom-up terms*: because air molecules impinge against the wing with slower-moving molecules below, creating a higher pressure than the pressure caused by faster-moving molecules above, leading to Bernoulli's law, and so on, in short: physics underlies higher-level functioning;
- In terms of a *same-level explanation*: because the pilot is flying it, and she is doing so because the airline's timetable dictates that there will be a flight today from Madrid at 16.35 to Granada at 17.40;
- In terms of a *top-down explanation*: because it is designed and manufactured to fly! The designing was done by a team of highly trained engineers, in a historical context that includes the development of metallurgy, combustion, lubrication, aeronautics, control systems, computer aided design, and so on, and in the economic context of a society with a need for transportation and with complex industrial organizations able to mobilize all the necessary resources for design and manufacture. It also occurred because individuals had the passion to make it happen.

These are all true explanations *that are simultaneously applicable*. The higher-level explanations rely on the existence of the lower-level explanations in order that they can succeed, but they are of a quite different nature from the lower-level ones; they are neither reducible to them nor dependent on their specific nature. The system cannot exist and function unless *all* these levels of causation are effective.

6. *Living systems are structured as (a) feedback control systems (b) that can learn (c) by capturing, storing, recalling, and analysing information.* This involves *(d) pattern recognition and (at the conscious levels) (e) implementation of predictive models based on (f) abstraction and symbolic representation and manipulation.* It is these capacities that make the difference between complicated systems and systems that are complex in the technical sense of this term (Ellis, 2002a). These capacities enable strongly emergent phenomena such as the functioning of cells (Morowitz, 2001), recognizing voices and faces, the existence of the rules of chess and the resulting strategies of chess players, as well as social institutions such as money and exchange rates.

There is no implication here as to how the information is stored; it might for example be encoded in particular atomic or molecular energy levels, in sequences of building block molecules, in synaptic connection patterns, in books, or in computer memories. Higher-level behaviour is based on throwing away vast amounts of information, selecting what is relevant from a vast flow of incoming information, storing it, analysing it in a broad existential context, differentially amplifying it, and utilizing it in feedback control systems. Feedback control systems in particular give higher-level behaviour its teleological nature, since in effect they comprise causal models of the system and its environment in relation to some set of desired goals.

In emergent phenomena we see non-material features such as concepts, information, and goals having causal effects in the material world of forces and particles, which means they have an ontological reality. We must assign a reality to all features that demonstrably causally affect the world of matter and particles. These include human conceptual schemes, plans, intentions, and emotions, as well as socially constructed features such as prices and chess rules. It must be emphasized here that *a concept is not the same as any physical configuration or entity.* Rather, it is an abstract entity that can be characterized as a socially realized equivalence class of physical representations, without being identical to any particular physical representation in this class. A jumbo jet, for instance, can be represented in a photograph, in speech, in written text, in a computer digital image, in CAD files, in a brain state, and so on; the concept is the same, but the representation varies.

7. *Emergence takes place in, and partly enables, a context of multiple forms of existence.* These include (a) particles and fields (the material world), (b) possibility landscapes characterizing possible existence and changes of state (controlled by the laws of physics), (c) human ideas, goals and intentions, emotions, and social constructions, and (d) platonic math-

ematical properties and objects (Popper and Eccles, 1977; Penrose, 1997; Ellis, 2003). In the analysis of emergence one assigns a reality to any feature that can be demonstrated to have a causal effect in the material world of particles, carefully distinguishing between epistemology (knowledge) and ontology (existence). The structural relations that enable complex functionality must be assigned an ontological status, as well as the particles and forces that underlie them.

In philosophical terms, the outcome of emergent phenomena is *emergentist pluralism:* many levels of reality emerge in the natural world, and the objects at the various levels have their own types of reality (Clayton, 2004, e.g. pp. 62, 148). What is not obvious is *whether true emergence is ever possible:* that is, the creation through physical and biological processes of completely new types of structure and information without any kind of precursor—the creation of a completely new kind of order—or whether emergence in the physical world (which undoubtedly happens) is rather just the realization of pre-existing potential and hence not a truly creative event. Complex objects are certainly preceded by the possibility of their existence, that is, their pre-image exists before them in a possibility space delimiting what is physically possible in the real universe;[4] otherwise they could not come into existence (see Ellis, 2002b). The philosophical implications are unclear.

We now turn to look at specific aspects in more detail.

2. HIERARCHY AND TOP-DOWN ACTION

The first key to handling complexity is *hierarchical physical structuring and function* (Simon, 1962; Flood and Carson, 1990; Peacocke, 1983). Such functioning involves the combination of *bottom-up* and *top-down action* (Campbell, 1974) in the hierarchy of structure.

i. The Nature of Hierarchy and Modularity

A hierarchy represents a decomposition of a problem into constituent parts and of processes into sub-processes to handle each of these sub-problems, each sub-process requiring less data and more restricted operations than the problem as a whole (Simon, 1962; Simon, 1982). The levels of a hierarchy represent *different levels of abstraction,* each built upon the other and each

---

[4] For example, energy and momentum conservation cannot be violated in real physical systems.

understandable by itself. *Emergent order* results: the behaviour of the whole is greater than the sum of its parts and cannot even be described in terms of the language that applies to the parts.

The success of hierarchical structuring depends on implementing modules to handle lower-level processes and on integrating these modules into a higher-level structure (for example, atoms comprise molecules and cells comprise a living being). Complex structures are made of modular units that evidence abstraction, encapsulation, and inheritance (Booch, 1994 and references therein). This structuring enables the modification of modules and their reuse for other purposes. *An abstraction* denotes the essential characteristics of an object that distinguishes it from all other kinds of objects. It focuses on the outside view of the object and so serves to separate its essential behaviour from its implementation; it emphasizes some of the system's details or properties while suppressing many others. Information is thrown away by the billions of bits all the time, because not all the micro-alternatives can be either examined or controlled. The high-frequency dynamics of the internal structures of components (relating internal variables) contrasts with the low-frequency dynamics of interactions amongst components (relating external variables). *Encapsulation* takes place when the internal workings are hidden from the outside, such that internal procedures can be treated as black-box abstractions. A key point is that no part of any complex system should depend on the internal details of any other part; system functionality only specifies each component's function, leaving it to the object to decide how to do it.

Inheritance occurs when specialized modules (forming a sub-class) preserve most or all of the functions of the super-class, but with extra specialization or further properties built in. This corresponds to fine-tuning the modules to handle more specialized problems (e.g. generalized cells specialize to form neurons).

A key feature is that *compound objects (combinations of modules) can be named and treated as units by appropriate labelling.* This leads to the power of abstract symbolism and symbolic computation.

ii. Coherent Higher-Level Action

In general, many lower-level states correspond to a single higher-level state, because a higher-level description H_I is arrived at by ignoring the micro-differences between many lower-level states L_i, therefore throwing away a vast amount of lower-level information (*coarse graining*). For example, numerous micro-states of particle positions and velocities correspond to a single macro-

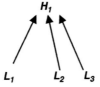

Fig 4.2. Lower level states all corresponding to the same higher level state.

Fig 4.3. Specifying a higher level state specifies a whole family of lower level states.

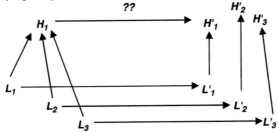

Fig 4.4. First case: the lower level dynamics do not lead to coherent higher level dynamics.

state of nitrogen gas with a pressure of one bar and temperature of 20°C in a volume of 1 litre (see Fig. 4.2).

The number of lower-level states corresponding to a single higher-level state determines the entropy of that state. This is lower-level information that is hidden in that higher-level view. For this reason, specifying a higher-level state H_1 determines a family of lower-level states L_i, any one of which may be implemented to obtain the higher-level state (see Fig. 4.3).

The specification of higher-level structure may be broad (attainable in a very large number of ways, e.g. the state of a gas) or detailed (defining a very precise structure, e.g. the currents in a VLSI chip in a computer). In the latter case both description and implementation require far more information than in the former.

The system dynamics (causal interactions due to physical interactions between the components) acts on each lower-level state L_i to produce a new lower-level state L_i'. Two major cases arise:

(a) Different lower-level realizations of the same higher-level initial state result, through microphysical action, in different higher-level final states (see Fig. 4.4).

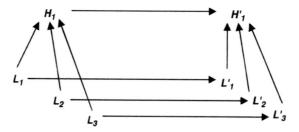

Fig. 4.5. Second case: the lower level dynamics leads to coherent higher level dynamics

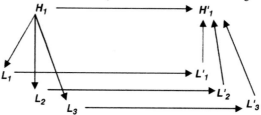

Fig. 4.6. Top-down action resulting in reliable output from a higher level initial state.

Here there is no coherent higher-level action generated by the lower-level actions; the higher-level result is unpredictable. Chaotic systems (with highly sensitive dependence on initial conditions) are examples.

(b) Different lower-level realizations of the same higher-level initial state result, through microphysical action, in the same higher-level final state, up to the accuracy of the higher-level description utilized (see Fig. 4.5).

A coherent higher-level action results from the lower-level action (perhaps in a statistical sense). An example is a gas in a container that is initially hot in one region and cooler elsewhere; diffusion will result in a final state of uniform temperature. Both the initial and final states can be realized through numerous micro-states. It is possible that $H_1 = H_1'$; in this case we have an equilibrium state of the system (in the case of the gas, this will occur if the initial state is one of uniform temperature).

iii. Top-Down Action Underlying Coherent Higher-Level Properties

Top-down action occurs when the higher levels of the hierarchy causally effect what happens at the lower levels in a coordinated way. Micro-causation occurs in the context of the structure given, and it can happen that each lower-level state corresponding to a specific initial higher-level state results in the same final upper-level state, so that every lower-level implementation of the initial higher-level state gives the same higher-level outcome (see Fig. 4.6).

$H_1 \xrightarrow{\hspace{4cm}} H'_1$

Fig. 4.7. The resultant higher level action regarded in its own right; it can be analysed without knowledge of the underlying lower-level interations.

In such cases consistent behaviour occurs at the higher level, regarded as a causal system in its own right; there is now effective higher-level autonomy of action, enabled by coordinated lower-level action (see Fig. 4.7). An example is pressing a key on a computer (H_1 is the computer with the key pressed), resulting in a letter being displayed on the screen (H'_1 is the computer with the key pressed and the letter displayed on the screen). The higher-level action is the same whatever detailed (lower-level) electron motions result in the computer circuits. The lower-level action and resultant final higher-level state would be different if the higher-level state were different (e.g. if a different key were pressed).

Boundary effects as well as structural relations effect top-down action. The higher-level action is effective by coordinating actions at the lower levels. Whether this reliably happens may depend on the particular coarse graining (i.e. higher-level description) chosen. Describing the higher-level change at the lower level is not desirable because it is not illuminating and may not even be possible. For example, the statement, '10^{24} nuclei and the associated electrons moved simultaneously in a coordinated manner so as to decrease the volume available to 10^{23} gas molecules', which requires about 10^{36} bits of information for a full description, actually describes the phenomenon 'the piston moved and compressed the gas'. Indeed, this is the reason that we develop and use higher-level language and mathematical descriptions in the first place. These may be employed whether or not we understand the lower-level causation.

Multiple top-down action as well as bottom-up action *enables the self-organization of complex systems*, in so far as it enables higher levels to coordinate action at lower levels which otherwise would not have occurred; it thereby contributes to the resulting organization and to the causal effectiveness of the lower-level processes. Top-down action is prevalent in the real physical world and in biology, because no real physical or biological system is isolated; through this process, information flows from the higher to the lower levels. Consider these seven examples:

(a) A gas in a cylinder with a piston. The cylinder walls together with the piston's position determine the gas pressure and temperature. Both are macro-concepts which make no sense at the micro level.

(b) Nucleosynthesis in the early universe. The creation of light elements in the early universe is controlled by nuclear reaction rates and the slow decay

rate of the neutron, together with the expansion rate of the universe. The latter is determined by cosmology through the Friedmann equation. The light element production is different if the universe expands differently, and the expansion rate depends on the kinds of matter present then in-bulk; consequently, we can use the light element abundances to determine the amount of baryons in the universe (Rees, 2001).

(c) Local physics experiments. Top-down action occurs in the quantum measurement process, because the experimenter determines the range of possible outcomes of the experiment by her choice of apparatus set-up. Also, top-down action from the universe itself determines the local arrow of time in all local physics, and hence in chemistry and biology. The arrow of time is not determined by the fundamental physical laws (Ellis, 2003); it is determined by the boundary conditions at the start and end of the universe, which select which solutions of the fundamental physical laws are accepted as physically allowed solutions. These boundary conditions reject all the time-reversed solutions that are otherwise legitimate solutions of the physical equations.

(d) Determination of DNA codings through evolution. The development of DNA codings (the particular sequence of bases in the DNA) through an evolutionary process, which results in adaptation of an organism to its ecological niche, is a top-down process proceeding from the environment to the DNA (Campbell, 1991). For example, a polar bear has genes that cause its fur to turn white, reflecting its adaptation to the Antarctic, as opposed to the gene sequence in Canadian bears that turns them brown because they have adapted to the Canadian forest. This is a classical case of top-down action from the environment to detailed biological microstructure: through the process of adaptation, the environment (along with other causal factors) fixes the specific DNA coding. There is no way one could ever predict this coding on the basis of biochemistry or microphysics alone.

(e) Biological development through the reading of DNA codings. The central process of developmental biology, whereby positional information determines which genes get switched on and which do not in each cell, thereby determining their developmental fate (Gilbert, 1991; Wolpert, 1998) is a top-down process from the developing organism to the cell, largely based on the existence of gradients of positional indicators in the body. These essentially tell each cell where it is in the developing body and hence what kind of cell it should be (forming blood, bone, hair, neurons, etc).

Without this feature, the development of organisms in a structured fashion would not be possible. Thus the functioning of the crucial cellular mechanism determining the type of each cell in a body is controlled in an explicitly top-down way. The gene does not function as an automaton following a fixed program (Fox-Keller, 2000); the body has its own structural regularities and programs in addition to those determined by genes.

(*f*) *Mind on body.* Top-down action occurs from the mind to the body and thence into the physical world. The movement of a hand is an example of many millions of atoms moving in response to a decision made, which is conveyed to the specific muscle structure by the central nervous system (Guyton, 1977; Rhoades and Pflanzer, 1989). Top-down action by the mind on health occurs through neurotransmitters acting on the immune system (Sternberg, 2000).

(*g*) *The effect of human intentions.* When a human being has a plan in mind (say, a proposal for building a bridge) and this plan is implemented, enormous numbers of micro-particles are moved around as a consequence of this plan and in conformity with it. The same kind of top-down action occurs in the making of aircraft and in the detonation of a nuclear bomb.

Social constructions such as chess rules are socially embodied and are causally effective. Imagine a computer or alien analysing a large set of chess games and deducing the rules of chess (i.e. what moves are allowed and what not). It would know that these are inviolable rules but would have no concept of their origins, that is, whether they are implied by some modification of Newton's laws, whether some type of potential fields constrain the motion of the chess pieces, or whether a social agreement that might be embodied in computer algorithms restricts the pieces' movements. Note that the chess rules are not just mind states—they exist independently of any particular mind or physical representation. Other examples include an economy and its associated exchange rates. Money is a physical embodiment of this order, while the exchange rates are socially embodied; yet they are also embodied in

Table 4.3. Hierarchy of causal relations. The hierarchy of physical relations (Table 4.1) extended to a branching hierarchy of causal relations. The right hand branch involves goals and conscious choices, which are causally effective; no such effects occur in the left hand branch.

Hierarchical structure: 2		
Cosmology		Ethics
Astronomy		Sociology
Geology		Psychology
Materials		Physiology
		Biochemistry
	Chemistry	
	Physics	

ink on newspaper pages and in computer programs stored in computer memories and utilized by banks.

Thus in the real world, the detailed micro-configurations of many objects—which electrons and protons go where—is in fact to a major degree determined by the macro-plans that humans have for what will happen. This means the structural hierarchy, interpreted as a causal hierarchy (Murphy and Ellis, 1995), bifurcates, as shown in Table 4.3.

The right-hand side deals with the choice of goals that lead to actions. Ethics is the high-level subject that deals with the choice of appropriate goals. Because it constrains the lower-level goals chosen, and thence the resulting actions, ethics is causally effective in the real physical world. For example, a prison may or may not have present on its premises the physical apparatus of an execution chamber; whether or not this is so depends on the ethics of the country in which the prison is situated.

3. FEEDBACK CONTROL AND INFORMATION

The second key to the emergence of truly complex properties is the role of hierarchically structured information in setting goals via *feedback control systems*. Such systems are implemented through their highly coordinated physical structure as, for example, in human physiology (Guyton, 1977; Rhoades and Pflanzer, 1989).

i. Feedback Control

The central feature of organized action in complex systems is *feedback control* (Beer, 1966; Milsum, 1966), whereby the setting of goals results in specific actions taking place that aim to achieve those goals. A comparator compares the system state with the goals; if needed, it then sends an error message to the

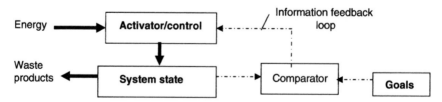

Fig. 4.8. The basic feedback control process. The goals determine the final state of the system, rather than the initial conditions—indeed the system is designed precisely so as to damp out the effect of initial conditions.

system controller to correct the state by making it a better approximation to the goals (Fig. 4.8). Classic examples are controlling the direction of an automobile, the heat of a shower, or the speed of a steam engine. One should note that the linkages to the comparator and thence to the controller are *information linkages* rather than power and/or material linkages, like that from the activator to the system. (The information flow will use a little power, but only the amount needed to get the message to where it is utilized.)

Thus it is here that the *key role of information* is seen: *information is the basis of goal choice in living systems* (and in artefacts that embody feedback control). The crucial issue is, what determines the goals? Where do they come from? Two major cases need to be distinguished.

ii. Homeostasis

There are numerous feedback control systems at all structural levels in all living cells, plants, and animals (Milsum, 1966) that automatically (i.e. without conscious guidance) maintain homeostasis. These systems keep the structures in equilibrium through multiple feedback loops that function to fight intruders (as in the immune system), control energy and material flows, and influence breathing, heart functions, body temperature and pressure, and so on. They are effected through numerous enzymes, anti-bodies, and regulatory circuits of all kinds (e.g. those that maintain body temperature and blood pressure). Indeed, Guyton suggests that all the major human physiological systems can be viewed as homeostasis systems (Guyton, 1977).

The innate goals that guide these activities are implicit rather than explicit. For example, the temperature of the human body is maintained at 98.4 F with great accuracy but without that figure being explicitly pre-set in some control apparatus; nevertheless this temperature goal is identifiable and very efficiently attained. In living systems, feedback control systems have developed over the course of time through the processes of evolution and hence are historically determined in a particular environmental context. In manufactured artefacts, the goal may be explicitly stated and controllable (e.g. the temperature setting of a thermostat).

It is important to realize that *not only are the feedback control systems themselves emergent systems,* but also *the implied goals are emergent properties that guide numerous physical, chemical, and biochemical interactions in a teleological way.*[5] They represent distilled information about the behaviour

---

[5] The system itself is emergent in that it embodies the organization that enables the resultant homeostasis.

of the environment in relation to the needs of life; hence they represent implicit information processing by the organism. Information storage and recognition occurs and allows adaptive responses already at the level of supra-molecular chemistry (Lehn, 1995). Neurons are specifically structured to process information (Rhoades and Pflanzer, 1989) and underlie the instinct-ive (inbuilt) behaviour of animals and humans.

iii. Goal Seeking

At higher levels in animals and humans, important new features come into play: one now detects explicit behavioural goals that are either learnt or are consciously chosen. *It is in the choice of these goals that explicit information processing plays a vital role.* Information arrives from the senses; it is then sorted and either discarded or stored in long-term and short-term memory, representing past situations and causal patterns. Conscious and unconscious processing of this information in the context of the current environmental and social situation sets up a goal hierarchy which then controls purposeful action through feedback control loops in the human body. These feedback loops are hierarchically structured, with a maximum decentralization of control from the higher to the lower levels, as is required both in order to handle requisite variety and the associated information loads (Beer, 1972) and for maximal local efficiency (i.e. the ability to respond to local conditions). A similar structuring is evident in the societal feedback loops that underlie welfare in society (Ellis, 1984; Ellis, 1985). Consider just three examples:

(a) Memory and learning. Memory allows both the long-term past and the immediate environmental context to be taken into account in choosing goals; it provides historical information that is used to shape these goals in conjunction with present data (e.g. remembering that an individual let us down in important ways years ago). *Learning* allows particular responses to develop into an auto-matic skill, in particular allowing responses to become inherited and therefore able to be rapidly deployed (e.g. walking, driving a car, sports moves, and so on).

(b) Analysis and prediction. The brain is continually capturing, storing, recalling, and analysing information. These functions involve, *inter alia*, pattern recognition and selection of what is important, discarding most of the rest, and using the information retained to implement predictive models. In the process one is guided by expectations of what is 'normal' in a given context, modelling in particular how other people may be expected to behave (Donald, 2001).

A key issue here is how context influences behaviour, in so far as one must continually choose which predictive model to use in a given context. This choice is guided by higher-level analysis. Implicit or explicit goals guide all of this mental activity, producing and informing the strategies chosen to reach the goals.

(c) Symbols and social behaviour. At the highest level, the process of analysis and understanding is driven by the power of images (Boulding, 1961) and symbolic abstractions (Deacon, 1997) that are codified into language. Language embodies both syntax and semantics, along with other social creations such as the monetary system and various specialized roles in society, together with higher-level abstractions such as mathematics, physical models, and philosophy. The brain co-evolves with culture, which largely shapes the brain according to distributed symbolic systems (Donald, 1991); these systems enable shared experience and understanding to be causally effective. Human brains do not develop and function in isolation; the causative whole is a entire social network (Donald, 2001), without which language and symbolism could not evolve.

How context influences behaviour is guided and constrained by a system of ethics based on an overall world-view associated with meaning. This world-view will itself be encoded in language and symbols. The point here is that our minds function by implementing a hierarchy of goals, and these goals are clearly causally effective. They have effects on the physical world, resulting in physical products from cakes to jumbo jets to skyscrapers. What count as acceptable goals is constrained by our ethical stances: shall I kill the competitor who is also bidding to build the skyscraper? Will we allow the death penalty in our State? Thus ethics is causally effective precisely because it constrains the shape of the set of goals that are implemented in the real world.

iv. Information Origin and Use

Responsive behaviour thus depends on the purposeful use of information—its storage, transmission, recall, and assessment—to control physical functions in accord with higher-level goals. Current information received from the senses is filtered against a relevance pattern; the irrelevant information is discarded; significant information is stored in compressed form; and the important information is selectively amplified and used in association with current expectations to assess and revise immediate goals. Recall of past events (long-term memory) allows for a temporally non-local kind of causation, which enables present and future behaviours to be based on interpretations of long-past events. Expectations are based on contextually based causal models, which are grounded in past experience and are constantly revised on the basis of newer experience and information. Thus feedback control systems based on sophisticated interpretations of present and past data enable purposeful (teleological) behaviour. This is the way that the hierarchy of goals is causally effective in the physical world: they are effected through the nervous system. The whole process is based on a symbolic representation of reality.

The goals, symbols, and expectations are all strongly emergent phenomena that are causally effective but are certainly not derivative from physics or chemistry. There can be no direct connection between micro-physics and choice of these goals and strategies—they are determined at higher causal levels. They exist as non-material effective entities, created and maintained through social interaction and teaching, and are codified in books and sometimes in legislation. Thus while they may be represented and understood in individual brains, their existence is not contained in any individual brain. They certainly are not equivalent to brain states, which are just one of many possible forms of embodiment of these features.

v. The Full Depth of Humanity

The emergent qualities envisaged must entail the full depth of humanity, precisely because we do indeed know that these qualities exist. Key features are characterized by Rescher (1990) as

1. *Intelligence* (assessing information and holding beliefs about the world and one's place in it),
2. *Affective* (evaluating developments as good or bad and driven by ideals),
3. *Agency* (autonomous agents pursuing goals proceeding from within their own thought),
4. *Rationality* (acting in a reasoned manner),
5. *Self-understanding* (conceiving of oneself as an intelligent free agent),
6. *Self-esteem* (valuing oneself), and
7. *Mutual recognizance* (acknowledging other persons and valuing them).

They extend to the best literature and art in the world—Shakespeare, Dostoevsky, Michelangelo, Rembrandt, and so on—as well as to the heights of generosity, love, and self-sacrificial (kenotic) moral endeavour, as in the lives of Ghandi, Martin Luther King, Desmond Tutu, and others (cf. Murphy and Ellis, 1995). All these higher qualities emerge from their physical foundations through the mind and are in turn determined largely by its social interactions (Siegel, 2001).

Both these qualities and the interactions that lead to them are thus causally effective, and any theory of emergence must recognize this and take it into account. This requirement strongly contradicts the attitude that anything which does not fit into a restrictive strong reductionist framework must be either denied existence or declared to have no value (see Donald, 2001 for an analysis and refutation of views denying the causal effectiveness of consciousness).

4. EVOLUTION AND DEVELOPMENTAL PROCESSES

The development of complexity in living systems requires both evolutionary processes acting over very long time periods and developmental processes acting over much shorter times.

i. Darwinian Evolution and Developmental Processes

The historical rise of these complex emergent features on a planet that came into existence in the expanding universe has occurred through the spontaneous self-organization of structures (Morowitz, 2002). In this process gravitational attraction has produced planets (Rees, 2001), molecular and chemical evolution have led to living cells and life, and then a Darwinian process of natural selection has acted on living systems to create high-level functionality (Campbell, 1991). This process has developed and stored genetic information in the form of a sequence of bases in DNA and RNA, characterizing the nature of the biological family involved. The information stored is selected on the basis of evolutionary adaptation to specific environmental niches. The process can be regarded as the selective amplification of favourable lower-level causal processes (Murphy 2003; Murphy and Brown, forthcoming).

As mentioned above, the embodiment of this complexity in living individuals, as they develop from a single cell to multi-cellular organisms with as many as 10^{13} cells, occurs through a developmental process which uses positional information to control the reading of this genetic information and thereby to determine the fate of each cell. Morphogen gradients and environmental information structure the developing organism (Gilbert, 1991; Wolpert, 1998). Information from the external and internal environment is crucial in this process of cell development (Harold, 2001).

ii. The Brain: Both Combined

While the body utilizes genetic information in each individual for brain development, principles of Darwinian natural selection also apply in the developmental process (cf. the 'neural Darwinism' of Edelmann, 1989), controlling detailed neural connections of each brain. This is necessary both because the stored information is far too little to control brain development by itself—the Human Genome Project tells us there are about 45,000 genes in each human cell, but there are 10^{13} cells and 10^{11} neurons in a human being, with about 10^{14} synaptic connections—and because this process allows the brain to adapt optimally to its local environment.

In essence, neuronal connections are established on a broadly structured basis that is largely random at a detailed level: those connections that are useful are strengthened, while those of little value are allowed to decay, and those of negative value are killed off. The key issue then is what provides the *fitness characterization* that determines whether particular connections are strengthened or not (the 'value system', Edelmann and Tononi, 2001). The most plausible answer to the question of fitness characterization involves the *signals provided by the set of primitive emotional functions,* each characterized by specific neurotransmitters such as dopamine. Panksepp (1998) describes the mechanism:

> The neurobiological systems that mediate the basic emotions...appear to be constituted of genetically coded, but experientially refined executive circuits situated in subcortical areas of the brain which can coordinate the behavioural, physiological and psychological processes that need to be recruited to cope with a variety of survival needs (i.e., they signal evolutionary fitness issues).... The various emotional circuits are coordinated by different neuropeptides, and the arousal of each system may generate distinct affective/neurodynamic states.

The proposal here is that emotions also help govern the microstructure of neural connections by emitting neurotransmitters (Ellis and Toronchuk, 2004).

This answer makes explicit the way in which emotions can guide the emergence of intellect through identified physical processes. They provide the evaluation functions by which the processes of neural Darwinism determine whether some particular set of neural connections are fit to survive or not. The basic emotional systems active in this way are the following:

1. general motivation: seeking/expectancy and associated satisfaction/dissatisfaction
2. rage/anger
3. fear/anxiety
4. lust/sexuality
5. care/nurturance
6. panic/separation
7. play/joy
8. rank/dominance/status/attachment
9. disgust

The first seven are clearly identified by Panksepp (1998), who also lists the associated key brain areas and neurotransmitters; the last two are plausible extras. In particular, the foundation for learning on the basis of the success or failure of one's endeavours is provided by the signals from the seeking system.

This mechanism provides the basis for brain–culture co-evolution (Deacon, 1997), the top-down view of which is described by Berger and Luckmann (1967) and the same-level view by Donald (2001).

5. TYPES OF EMERGENCE

Different levels of emergence have been suggested by Terrence Deacon (in Chapter 5; see also Deacon, 2003; Murphy, 2003). The following is a different proposal for characterizing such levels, based on the analysis of complex systems given above:

Level 1 Emergence: *Bottom-up action leads to higher-level generic properties but not to higher-level complex structures or functions.* This type of emergence determines the generic properties of gases, liquids, and solids and is involved in the gas law, conductivity, heat capacity, and so on. (Goodstein, 1985). At this level statistical physics applies, and entropy represents hidden information due to coarse graining. This kind of emergence leads to coherent upper-level action, and reduction is in principle possible. However, reduction fails in practice, not just because of (i) the inability to derive by reductionist means the full complexity of the behaviour of substances as simple as water, but also because (ii) the arrow of time (the entropy problem) remains unresolved (Zeh, 1989; Halliwell et al, 1994), (iii) quantum measurement issues are unresolved (Penrose, 1989), and (iv) divergences and incorrect predictions of the value of the cosmological constant mean that we do not properly understand quantum field theory. Reduction is also fundamentally challenged by R. B. Laughlin's claim (v) that all elementary particle properties may be emergent (Laughlin, 1999).

Level 2 Emergence: *Bottom-up action plus boundary conditions lead to interesting higher-level structures not directly implied by the boundary conditions*—as for example in (i) sand piles, (ii) the reaction diffusion equation, (iii) magnetic domains, (iv) convection patterns, (v) cellular automata, (vi) gravitational structure formational in the expanding universe, and (vii) inorganic and organic molecules. This kind of emergence increases the level of complexity above what was entered into the system, and so leads to the emergence of structures that are not reducible. Nevertheless, despite the immense combinatorial possibilities (Scott, 1995), such structures are not truly complex, since they do not have the key element of goal-seeking that characterizes living systems. However, they may sometimes be an important initial step on the way toward the evolution of genuinely complex systems (such as in processes in developmental biology). Standard statistical physics does not apply here; one needs to goes beyond it to critical phenomena

(Binney et al., 1993; Bak, 1997), chaos theory (Bai-Lin, 1984; Thompson and Stewart, 1987), kinetic self-organization (Peacocke, 1983), and basic chemical structure (Atkins and Jones, 2002). Yet these interactions are not yet directed by information or goals.

Level 3 Emergence: *Bottom-up action in highly structured systems leads to existence of feedback control systems at various levels* and hence to coordinated responses that allow for meaningful top-down action. The result is *coherent non-reducible upper-level action directed by implicit innate goals*. These systems enable an element of teleonomy—of goal-seeking—and thus represent an effective physical effect of information. However the inherited goals guiding these feedback systems are independent of individual life history, being pre-determined by the evolutionary history of the species—no learning occurs. They thus allow for adaptive behaviour, but only based on pre-set rules. Examples are processes in all living cells (Harold, 2001) and in plants (Bidwell, 1979). This information-based functioning starts at the supra-molecular level (Lehn, 1995).

Level 4 Emergence: Here, in addition to the emergence evident in Level 3, *there exist feedback control systems directed by explicit goals related to memory, i.e. influenced by specific events in the individual's history*. Learning occurs based on individual experience and some form of stored memory, allowing adaptive behaviour that responds to historical events. This kind of emergence is presumably always related to some form of consciousness, leading to goal choice related to the remembered past. It occurs in animals (Slater, 1999) when, for example, a dog responds to its feeding bowl or leash based on the integrated complexity of its hierarchy of control systems and support systems (Randall, 2002). Emergent phenomena of this type extend to complex social interactions as in much animal behaviour (Slater, 1999), including significant forms of communication.

Level 5 Emergence: In addition to level 4, *some goals are explicitly expressed in language systems and/or are determined by symbolic understanding or complex modelling of the physical and social environment*. Here, in addition to individual consciousness, what is crucial is the capacity to handle *symbolic systems* with both syntax and semantics (Deacon, 1997). Presumably this ability arises in conjunction with the capacity for self-conscious reflection and (integral to this) with the feature of *distributed consciousness*, with the development of brains and culture occurring in interaction with each other (Berger and Luckmann, 1967; Donald, 1991; Donald 2001). On earth, this only occurs in the case of humans, enabled by the structure of the human brain (Kingsley, 1996) and all its supporting mechanisms (Rhoades and Pflanzer, 1989). Level-5 emergence enables the creation of artefacts (conscious design) and the transcendence of specific given conditions by changing the environment or the context of action. Note that in this chapter I am presuming the effectiveness of consciousness, as discussed by Donald (2001).

6. THE CHALLENGE TO PHYSICS

Emergent effects are determined by a combination of chance (historical contingency) and necessity (physical laws), but there is additionally a role of conscious choice in level-4 and level-5 emergence. This is a key feature in our analyses of the world around us, for without conscious choice the attempt to understand does not make sense. We can only believe the outcome of our arguments and analyses if we have the ability to relate them to evidence, logic, and coherence. Consciousness is a high-level emergent activity by which we are able to weigh the evidence and make a choice; if we cannot make a choice, we cannot weigh the evidence. Thus free will is necessary for scientific activity (or, for that matter, for any decision-making) to occur, and I am assuming that it exists. Any total reductionism that denies consciousness and/or free will also denies the ability to reason logically and arrive at a valid conclusion, and so undermines science itself (see Zeilinger, 2003).

The issue facing scientists is, are we trying to construct a causally complete theory of interactions that affect events in the physical world? If so, then humans must be included in the causal system (since, for example, physicists carry out experiments), and the emergence of all the higher-order phenomena mentioned above must be taken into account. If not, we will necessarily have a causally incomplete theory, and we must not pretend it can satisfactorily link human behaviour to physics and chemistry.

The challenge to physics is that the higher levels are demonstrably causally effective, and, in particular, consciousness is causally effective; but conscious plans and intentions and emotions are not describable in present-day physical terms. Thus physics has two choices: either

1. to extend its scope of description to encapsulate such higher-level causal effects, for example including new higher-level variables representing thoughts and intentions, in the effort to model the effects of consciousness and its ability to be causally effective in the real physical world,

or

2. to decide that these kinds of issues are outside the province of physics, which properly deals only with inanimate objects and their interactions. In

that case physics must give up the claim to give a causally complete description of interactions that affect the real physical world.[6]

Whichever option is adopted, the idea of a 'theory of everything' as usually understood by physicists (a unified theory of fundamental forces and interactions such as String Theory; see, e.g. Greene, 1999) is in trouble. One must now acknowledge that we do not have the concept of a complete account of all causally effective aspects of the physical world, which includes the biological world. At minimum, physics has to be related somehow to the world of thoughts and feelings before it can make any claim to provide causal completeness—which presumably a true 'theory of everything' should do.

The key point is that human intentions and goals are not just convenient auxiliary variables that summarize physical microstates; rather they are essential variables in many causal processes. Without them we cannot adequately model causation involving human beings (e.g. we cannot predict whether a pair of spectacles or a jumbo jet will be likely to emerge from a given mental process). Human intentions and goals are irreducible higher-level quantities that are clearly causally effective in the physical world.

Additionally, there is a major question to be answered by physics, whether or not the answer is based on a unified theory of interactions, namely, why does it allow the complexity examined in this chapter to come into being (Ellis, 2003)? Why does it satisfy the well-known series of anthropic constraints that allow life as we know it to exist (Rees, 2003; Tegmark, 2003)? Most such unified theories would not be able physically to underpin the complexity we observe in the real world. Thus there is a double relation of fundamental physical theory to the existence of intelligent life that needs clarification.

7. CONCLUSION

In these pages I have defended a view of emergent complex systems that includes structuring relations and triggering relations, as well as environmental influences and internal variables. This view is summarized in Fig. 4.9.

---

[6] For example, statements such as 'the function of the brain is based on electromagnetic interactions between particles in neurons' are true, but they have zero predictive power in terms of higher-level brain function. Such statements are analogous to replying, in response to a request for a weather forecast, with the true statement, 'the behaviour of the atmosphere is determined by energy and momentum conservation for fluids.' The public, which pays for weather forecasting services, will not be impressed.

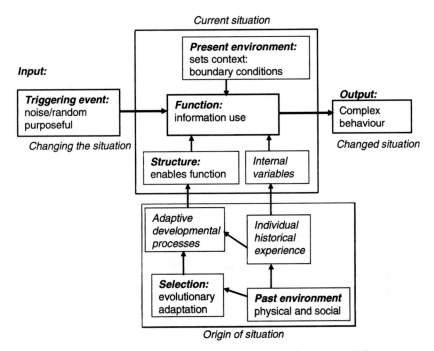

Fig. 4.9. The system and its situation: contextual and triggering influences.

On this view, function takes place in the context of a social and physical situation that, together with the values of internal variables, is the current operating environment. Triggering events, which are varying causal quantities, operate in a given situation and provide the input. Structure is constant on the relevant timescale; it enables the input to have a predictable result. Thus function follows structure. The environment sets the boundary conditions, and the internal variables (memory and learnt behaviour patterns) result from past experience. Noise or chance represents the effects of detailed features that we do not know because they are subsumed in the coarse graining that leads to higher-level descriptions of either the system or the environment. The system structure is determined by developmental processes that use genetic information, though the genetic information is read in the context of the system–environment interactions that occur in the organism's history. For example, genes develop a brain capacity to learn language, but in the actual process of language acquisition the brain is adapted to that specific language. The genetic heritage that leads to this result itself came into being through evolutionary adaptation to the past environment over very long timescales. Language then forms the basis for complex symbolic modelling and associated understanding; these take place in particular social contexts and in turn guide future actions. Thus human understandings of events and their meanings govern human actions, which then change the situation around them. Symbolic systems are causally effective.

Strong reductionist claims, usually characterized by the phrase 'nothing but' and focusing only on physical existence, simply do not take into account the depth of causation in the real world as indicated above, nor the inability of physics on its own to comprehend these interactions and effects. Reductionist claims represent a typical fundamentalist position, claiming a partial truth (based on some subset of causation) to be the whole truth and ignoring the overall rich causal matrix while usually focusing on purely physical elements of causation. They do not and cannot be an adequate basis of explanation or understanding in the real world. Consequently they do not represent an adequate basis for making ontological claims.

This chapter has outlined a view of emergent reality in which it is clear that non-physical quantities such as information and goals can have physical effect in the world of particles and forces and hence must be recognized as having a real existence (Ellis, 2003). Associated with this view is a richer ontology than simple physicalism, which omits important causal agencies from its vision. That view does not deal adequately with the real world.

8. REFERENCES

Ackoff, Russell (1999), *Ackoff's Best: His Classic Writings in Management* (New York: Wiley and Sons).

Atkins, P. and L. Jones (2002), *Chemical Principles: The Quest for Insight* (New York: W. H. Freeman and Co.).

Bai-lin, H. (1994), *Chaos* (River Edge, N.J.: World Scientific).

Bak, P. (1997), *How Nature Works: The Science of Self-Organised Criticality* (Oxford: Oxford University Press).

Beer, Stafford (1966), *Decision and Control* (New York: Wiley and Sons).

—— (1972), *Brain of the Firm* (New York: Wiley and Sons).

Berger, Peter L. and Thomas Luckmann (1967), *The Social Construction of Reality: A Treatise in the Sociology of Knowledge* (New York: Anchor Books).

Bidwell, R. G. S. (1979), *Plant Physiology* (Basingstoke: Collier/MacMillan).

Binney, J. J., N. J. Dowrick, A. J. Fisher, and M. E. J. Newman (1993), *The Theory of Critical Phenomena: An Introduction to the Renormalisation Group* (Oxford: Oxford University Press).

Booch, Grady (1994), *Object Oriented Analysis and Design with Applications* (Reading, Mass.: Addison-Wesley).

Boulding, Kenneth E. (1961), *The Image: Knowledge in Life and Society* (Ann Arbor, MI: Ann Arbor Paperbacks).

Campbell, D. T. (1974), 'Downward Causation', in F. J. Ayala and T. Dobhzansky (eds.), *Studies in the Philosophy of Biology: Reduction and Related Problems*, (Berkeley, CA: University of California Press).

Campbell, Neil A. (1991), *Biology* (Menlo Park, CA.: Benjamin/Cummings).

Clayton, Philip (2004), *Mind and Emergence: From Quantum to Consciousness* (Oxford: Oxford University Press).

Deacon, Terrence (1997), *The Symbolic Species: The Co-Evolution of Language and the Human Brain* (New York: Penguin Books).

—— (2003), 'The Hierarchic Logic of Emergence: Untangling the Interdependence of Evolution and Self-Organization', in Bruce H. Weber and David J. Depew (eds.), *Evolution and Learning: The Baldwin Effect Reconsidered* (Cambridge, MA.: MIT Press).

Donald, Merlin (1991), *Origins of the Modern Mind: Three Stages in the Evolution of Culture and Cognition* (Cambridge: Harvard University Press).

—— (2001), *A Mind So Rare: the Evolution of Human Consciousness* (New York: WW Norton).

Edelman, Gerald (1989), *Neural Darwinianism* (Oxford: Oxford University Press).

—— and G. Tononi (2001), *Consciousness: How Matter Becomes Imagination.* (New York: Penguin).

Ellis, G. F. R. (1984), 'The Dimensions of Poverty', *Social Indicators Research* 15, 229–53.

Ellis, G. F. R. (1985), 'An Overall Framework for Quality of Life Evaluation Schemes, With Application to the Ciskei (South Africa)', in J. G. M. Hilhorst and M. Klatter (eds.), *Social Development and the Third World* (London: Croom Helm), 63–90.

—— (2002a), 'The Universe Around Us: an Integrative View of Science and Cosmology', <http://www.mth.uct.ac.za/~webpages/ellis/cos0.html>.

—— (2002b), 'Natures of Existence (Temporal and Eternal)', in G. F. R. Ellis (ed.), *The Far Future Universe* (Philadelphia, PA: Templeton Foundation Press).

—— (2003), 'True Complexity and its Associated Ontology', in J. D. Barrow, P. C. W. Davies, and C. L. Harper (eds.), *Science and Ultimate Reality: From Quantum to Cosmos* (Cambridge: Cambridge University Press).

—— and Judith Toronchuk (2004) 'Neural Development: Affective and Immune System Influences', *Consciousness and Emotion* (2004).

Flood, Robert L. and Ewart R. Carson (1990), *Dealing with Complexity* (New York: Plenum Press).

Fox-Keller, Evelyn (2000), *The Century of the Gene* (Cambridge: Harvard University Press).

Gilbert, Scott F. (1991), *Developmental Biology* (Sunderland, MA: Sinauer).

Goodstein, David L. (1985), *States of Matter* (New York: Dover).

Greene, Brian (1999), *The Elegant Universe* (London: Johnathan Cape).

Guyton, Arthur C. (1977), *Basic Human Physiology* (Philadelphia: W. B. Saunders).

Halliwell, J. J., J. Perez-Mercader, and W. H. Zurek (1994), *Physical Origins of Time Asymmetry* (Cambridge: Cambridge University Press).

Harold, Franklin (2001), *The Way of the Cell: Molecules, Organisms, and the Order of Life* (Oxford: Oxford University Press).

Hartmann, Stephan (2001), 'Effective Field Theories, Reductionism, and Scientific Explanation', *Stud. Hist. Phil. Mod. Phys.* 32: 267–304.

Kingsley, R. E. (1996), *Concise Text of Neuroscience* (Philadelphia: Lippincott, Williams, and Wilkins).

Laughlin, Robert B. (1999), *Rev. Mod. Phys.* 71: 863.

Lehn, Jean Marie (1995), *Supramolecular Chemistry* (Berlin: Springer-Verlag).

Milsum, John H. (1966), *Biological Control Systems Analysis* (Columbus, OH: McGraw Hill).

Morowitz, Harold (2002), *The Emergence of Everything* (Oxford: Oxford University Press).

Murphy, Nancey (2003), Unpublished Notes on Emergence.

—— and Warren S. Brown (forthcoming), *Did My Neurons Make Me Do It? Philosophical and Neurobiological Perspectives on Moral Responsibility and Free Will.*

—— and Ellis, G. F. R. (1995), *On the Moral Nature of the Universe* (Minneapolis, MN: Fortress Press).

Panksepp, Jaak (1998), *Affective Neuroscience* (Oxford: Oxford University Press).

Peacocke, Arthur (1983), *An Introduction to the Physical Chemistry of Biological Organisation* (Oxford: Oxford University Press).

Penrose, Roger (1989), *The Emperor's New Mind* (Oxford: Oxford University Press).

—— (1997), *The Large, The Small, and the Human Mind* (Cambridge: Cambridge University Press).

Popper, Karl, and John Eccles (1977), *The Self and its Brain: An Argument for Interactionism* (Berlin: Springer-Verlag).

Randall, D., W. Burgren, and K. French (2002), *Animal Physiology: Mechanisms and Adaptations* (New York: W. H. Freeman and Co.).

Rescher, Nicholas (1990), *Human Interests: Reflections on Philosophical Anthropology* (Palo Alto, CA: Stanford University Press).

Rhoades, Rodney, and Richard Pflanzer (1989), *Human Physiology* (Philadelphia: Saunders College Publishing).

Scott, Alwyn (1995), *Stairway to the Mind* (Berlin: Springer-Verlag).

Siegel, Daniel J. (2001), *The Developing Mind: How Relationships and the Brain Interact to Shape Who We Are* (New York: Guilford Press).

Simon, Herbert A (1962), 'The Architecture of Complexity', *Proc. Am. Phil. Soc.* 106.

—— (1982), *The Sciences of the Artificial* (Cambridge, MA: MIT Press).

Slater, P. J. B. (1999), *Essentials of Animal Behaviour* (Cambridge: Cambridge University Press).

Sternberg, Esther (2000), *The Balance Within: The Science Connecting Health and Emotions* (New York: W. H. Freeman and Co.).

Tannebaum, A. S. (1990), *Structured Computer Organisation* (Englewood Cliffs, NJ: Prentice Hall).

Thompson, J. M. T., and H. B. Stewart (1987), *Nonlinear Dynamics and Chaos* (New York: Wiley and Sons).

Wolpert, Lewis (1998), *Principles of Development* (Oxford: Oxford University Press).

Zeh, H. Dieter (1989), *The physical basis of the direction of time* (Berlin: Springer-Verlag).

Zeilinger, Anton (2003), 'Why the Quantum? "It" from "Bit"? A Participatory Universe?', in John Barrow, Paul Davies, and Charles Harper (eds.), *Science and Ultimate Reality* (Cambridge: Cambridge University Press).

Part II

The Biological Sciences

5

Emergence: The Hole at the Wheel's Hub[1]

Terrence W. Deacon

1. MIND OVER MESS

Consider the famous Latin pronouncement: '*Ex nihilo nihil fit*' (from nothing, nothing comes). It suggests that whatever exists now must have been preceded by something equally substantial and that only material and energetic processes can have substantial consequences. It is the precursor to the first law of thermodynamics, which states that energy (recognized as matter-energy after Einstein) can neither be created nor destroyed. In other words, it assumes that existing structures, patterns, and forces are just shuffled versions of others that came before. It suggests that absolute novelty is likely a fiction, and that there is nothing truly new under the sun.

The assumption expressed in this classic proposition has been tested to quite precise values by modern science. It is implicit in the conservation laws of physics. It's what keeps the cosmic books balanced. All of modern physics and chemistry are erected on this reliable foundation (except for that one tiny exception, the Big Bang, which created the whole of the visible universe—but that's another story). It's also just common sense. Magic is trickery. Things don't simply vanish or appear from nowhere. It takes something to make something. And so on.

There is a corollary to this as well, when it comes to processes that produce new structures: the more rare, complicated, or 'well-designed' something appears, the less likely that it could have 'just happened'. It tends to take more effort and care to construct something that doesn't tend to form on its own, especially if it's composed of many complicated parts. And even 'found' objects often require effort, when 'good fit' is required. In general, when things work well despite the many ways they could potentially fail, when

---

[1] Significant parts of this chapter have previously appeared in modified form in a chapter titled 'The Hierarchic Logic of Emergence: Untangling the Interdependence of Evolution and Self-Organization', in B. Weber and D. Depew, *Evolution and Learning: The Baldwin Effect Reconsidered* (2003), pp. 273–308.

they exhibit sophisticated functional matching to their context, especially where this matching is highly contingent, then such 'fittedness' tends to be a product of both extensive effort and intelligent planning. So the type of thing that 'just happens' (or so bumper-stickers will tell you) is generally unattractive, undesirable, and inappropriate. Good luck is rare, bad luck is the norm, and most problems left unattended don't improve on their own.

This tendency of things to fall effortlessly into messiness—the inevitable increase in entropy—is the essence of the second law of thermodynamics. All other things being equal, and without outside interference (or, more specifically, in a hypothetically closed physical system in which energy neither enters nor leaves), entropy will inevitably tend to increase. There is a simple reason for this, as Gregory Bateson once explained to his daughter.[2] There are so many more possible arrangements of things that are messy (i.e. aren't regular) than those that are ordered—usually vastly more. Nature, being unbiased, tends to shuffle through all the possibilities with respect to their relative probabilities of occurrence, and so the very miniscule domain of arrangements of things that are highly regular (or that we judge to be so) is often never sampled spontaneously and tends to become progressively more improbable over time.

So, when spontaneous processes like the complex adaptive functions of living bodies tend to produce increasing orderliness, complex interdependencies, and designs that are precisely correlated and matched to one another and the world, we can be excused for being just a little mystified. And when introspection confronts us with the everyday experience of living in a world of representations, anticipations, and efforts to mobilize energy to alter future conditions, we can perhaps be forgiven for treating this as magic, imported from another non-material realm. There is the dead, uncaring world and its rules, and the living feeling world and its rules, and the two seem to be quite contradictory.

On their surface, the first and second laws of thermodynamics appear to exclude the possibility of true teleological processes, such as functional design, representation, and intentional initiation of action. The notion that something absent, like a represented object or a possible future state, could be a cause of physical change appears a bit like something coming from nothing, and the possibility that functional design could arise other than by preserved accident seems to violate the very logic of physical causality. It has become common for contemporary science to treat all teleological phenomena as

---

[2] See the 'Metalogue: Why do Things Get in a Muddle', in Gregory Bateson's *Steps to an Ecology of Mind* (1972), pp. 3–8.

purposive in name only—teleonomic[3]—and to assume that true teleology is illusory and that the supposed role of representation and the experience of intentionality even in human actions must ultimately be epiphenomenal.

There is something unsatisfying about this denial, however. We are aware, for example, of some quite stark reversals of causal logic as certain transitions are crossed. The same atoms that constitute your body now once comprised merely inanimate bits of matter when they were scattered about the galaxy some billions of years ago. They will doubtless resume this passive existence again as they move on to comprise dust or air. Nevertheless, together in your living body they now share in a mode of existence that is quite distinctive and discontinuous from their separated inanimate existences. Together they are alive; apart they are not. And when they are together in this form, a curious and atypical inversion of thermodynamic tendencies seems to characterize the whole collection. What besides being-in-proximity makes the difference? Even if such dichotomies are illusory and there is unbroken causal continuity across the threshold from non-life to life, machine to mind, we nevertheless require an explanation for why causal architecture changes so abruptly at these transitions and why it is so difficult to follow the logic linking human teleological experience with its physical basis.

2. *TELOS EX MACHINA*[4]

The most sophisticated early recognition of a corresponding distinction among modes of causality comes from Aristotle. In fact, he considered the problem to be even more complicated than this. He distinguished four modes of causality: material, efficient, formal, and final. If we use the example of carpentry, material cause is what determines the structural stability of a house, efficient cause is the carpenter's modifications of materials to create this structure, formal cause is the plan followed in this construction process, and final cause is the aim of the process, that is, producing a space protected from the elements. A final cause is that 'for the sake of which' something is done. For Aristotle these were different and complementary ways of understanding how and why change occurs. There has been an erosion of this plural understanding of causality since Aristotle that, although an important

---

[3] The term was coined by C. S. Pittendrigh (1958, p. 394) and often is used to describe the behaviour of mechanisms which act as though they had an aim, such as a thermostat, but which can be completely described in purely mechanical terms.

[4] Apologies for the cross-linguistic play on words.

contribution to the unity of knowledge, may in part contribute to our present intellectual (and indeed spiritual) dilemma.

By the Renaissance, final causality was in question. Seminal thinkers like Bacon, Descartes, Spinoza, and others progressively chipped away at any role final causality might play in physical processes. Bacon argued that teleological explanations were effectively redundant and thus superfluous additions to physical explanations of things. Descartes considered animate processes in animal bodies to be completely understandable in mechanical (i.e. efficient) terms, while mental processes comprised a separate extensionless domain. Spinoza questioned the coherence of the literal sense of final causality, since it was nonsensical to think of future states producing present states. Appealing to intentions as physical causes accomplishes little more than pointing to an unopened black box. Even positing purposes for actions still requires a physical account of their implementation. And inside that black box? Well, a further appeal to purposive agency only leads to vicious regress. Accordingly, it was held, purpose and intention are intrinsically incomplete notions. They require replacement with something more substantial. A purpose, conceived as the 'pull' of some future possibility, must be illusory, lacking the materiality to affect anything. As exemplified by the early explanations of the power of vacuums and buoyancy, only 'pushes' seem allowable as determinants of the efficacy and direction of physical changes.

This heritage of modern science has guided a relentless effort to replace the black boxes and their end-directed explanations of function, design, or purposive action with mechanistic accounts. This effort has yielded astounding success. Perhaps the greatest triumph of this enterprise came with the elucidation of the mechanism of natural selection. It showed, in principle, that through accidentally produced variations, competition for resources, and selective reproduction or preservation of lineages, living mechanisms with apparent purposiveness and fittedness to local conditions could have evolved. Where the natural theology of Paley had concluded that observing functional organization, complexity, and perfection of design in an object (e.g. a watch) implied the operation of prior intelligence to fashion it, Darwin and subsequent researchers could suggest ways that the organization could be the result of preserved chance variation. The assumption that end-directedness was needed to explain the origin of these features was unnecessary. For Darwin, organisms were mechanisms like watches, but their adaptive organization could have arisen serendipitously by matching accidentally formed mechanisms with conditions favouring their persistence.

The metaphor of the world as an immense machine full of smaller machines is however deeply infected with the special assumptions of human artefact design. Hence when Richard Dawkins caricatures evolution as a 'blind watchmaker' he still characterizes organisms as machines, and machines are assembled to do something for some end. Though we typically think of organisms as analogous to engineered artefacts performing some designed task, the analogy can provide quite misleading expectations. Design is a function of imposed order that derives from outside. The integration of parts in a machine is the result of the careful selection of materials, shaping of parts, and systematic assembly, all of which occurs with respect to an anticipated set of physical behaviours and ends to be achieved. Although living processes are at least as precisely integrated with parts which are as interdependent in function as in any machine yet conceived, there is little else that makes them like anything that could have been engineered. Whole organisms are not assembled by bringing together disparate parts but by having their parts differentiate from one another. Organisms are not built or assembled. Although they grow by the multiplication of cells, these divide and differentiate from prior, less differentiated precursors. Both in development and in phylogeny, wholes precede parts, integration is not imposed, and design is a *post hoc* attribute. The machine metaphor is too limited. Indeed, many embryological processes and regulatory mechanisms resemble micro natural selection processes (e.g. between cell lineages) more than pre-programmed construction. Because of this engineering preconception, however, caricatures of natural selection often fall into the trap of replacing the absent designer with amazing accidents producing lucky coincidences and 'hopeful monsters' that are preserved like serendipitous inventions because of their novel usefulness.

This tacit importation of a human artefact view of the world, with its implicit design logic, into a materialist metaphysics that restricts the introduction of anything like final causal relationships, creates the logical necessity of a *telos ex machina* universe. In such a world we appear as accidental robots blindly running randomly generated programs. But there is an implicit contradiction in this conception, though it is not due to the exclusion of *telos* as much as to the limitations of the machine metaphor. Machines are intentional simplifications of the causal world. Abstractly conceived, a machine is finite and all its features and future states are fully describable. They are essentially closed off from all physical variations except those that are consistent with a given externally determined function. Thus the whole notion of machine causality is predicated on the very logic of causality that is excluded from consideration. Perhaps it would make more sense to expand beyond the watch metaphor altogether than to argue over whether it is necessary to include or exclude a watchmaker. Paying attention to the broader range of processes that share some but not all features with the logic of ends-determining-means is a good place to start the search for a middle ground.

The processes I have in mind are those that appear on the surface to violate the spirit if not the law of increasing entropy: processes in which orderliness appears to increase spontaneously rather than decrease as one might normally expect.

In the moment-to-moment processes of cellular metabolism and in the grand sweep of evolution there are myriad examples of spontaneous processes that produce an increase in order. They are harnessed with such subtle biasing as to seem almost inevitable—until we consider how curious and improbable they are in the context of physical processes in general. The molecular processes that constitute metabolism in a living cell manage to produce chemical reactions that defy the odds by many orders of magnitude. The production of selected molecules can be billions of times more likely to occur in a cell than could take place in a test tube, even if one adds all the right ingredients in the right proportion in the proper sequence. This makes it appear as though cells can micromanage individual chemical reactions in ways that would exceed the wildest Machiavellian dreams of any CEO. Yet, as molecular biologists have looked into these processes more closely, it has become increasingly clear that the outcome is *not* accomplished by precise control of every detail, as if in some chemical processing factory where everything is carefully measured and mixed. Rather it is accomplished by a remarkably prescient system of mediating molecular relationships (catalytic relationships) which bias and constrain other molecular interactions so that they occur with vastly greater or lesser probability than if unmediated. At the molecular level, evolution appears to have made the nearly impossible all but inevitable.

Unlike the logic of machine design, however, in which things must be forced to occur, pushed into place, and restricted in their deviant tendencies, the logic of organism 'design' instead depends on recruiting the spontaneous intrinsic tendencies of molecular substrates and structural geometries. A superficial interpretation of the evolutionary process might suggest that the introduction of new ordering principles in organism design derives solely from lucky accidents achieving serendipitous functions. Yet an analysis of intracellular molecular processes and of the morphogenetic mechanisms of development suggests that a significant fraction of the order-generating processes of life are instead due to self-organizing dynamics, which are intrinsic to molecular geometries and cell–cell communications. Indeed, the majority of macromolecular structures in cells tend to self-assemble, and the majority of critical chemical reactions occur within self-reinforcing cycles of reactions. Machines need to be built with extrinsic means, but organisms must develop themselves. Where there is no external means for the generation of order, order must arise from tendencies already present.

So, even if the mechanistic gambit seems on the verge of succeeding, there is some reason to be cautious about its eventual completeness, at least as modelled on the image of human artefacts. There clearly is a sense in which our descriptions of living functions and mental representations are *nothing but* glosses of incompletely described mechanisms. But the machine metaphor is implicitly incomplete itself, resting as it does on the assumption that the design logic of real machines can be bracketed out of consideration without changing the very meaning of mechanism. To the extent that organisms don't resemble machines in the spontaneous logic of their component processes, we should question the core assumptions of the eliminative enterprise, according to which all 'pulls' are merely illusory. Is there some way to identify a real and substantial sense of the 'pull' of future possibilities in terms of 'pushes' from the past?

3. BACK TO THE FUTURE

Spontaneous order-production is deeply counterintuitive, like magic or something coming out of nothing, and so it demands a special explanation. The general tendency of things to degrade according to the second law of thermodynamics makes these apparently contrary phenomena stand out and appear enigmatic and intriguing. Orderly arrangements should spontaneously degrade, and they shouldn't gain complexity with time. When highly regular and complicated patterning appears spontaneously, or when future states of organization appear to be the drivers of antecedent processes, they demand a special explanation, because they give the impression of *time running backwards*.

This superficial appearance of time-reversal is the original motive for describing functional and purposive processes in terms of final causality. Of course, even Aristotle was clear that this could not be a literal ends-causing-the-means process, but rather something about the organization of living systems that made it appear as though this were the case. This time-reversed appearance is a common attribute of living processes, albeit in slightly different forms, at all levels of function. The highly ordered interactions of cellular chemistry succeed in maintaining living systems in far-from-equilibrium states, thus resisting the increase of internal entropy, as though thermodynamic time were stopped. The increasing complexity of organism structures and processes that characterizes the grand sweep of evolution thus seems to be running counter to the trend of increasing mess and decreasing intercorrelations, as though thermodynamic time were running in reverse. Furthermore, mental processes recruit energy and organize their implementation with regard to the potential of achieving some future state that does not yet exist, thus seeming to use even thermodynamics against itself. Viewed introspectively, intentional action seems time-reversed in a particularly convoluted way. One detects both the generation of ordered behaviour without a more ordered antecedent state causing it and a currently nonexistent future state that initiates and regulates this time-reversed decrease in entropy. Of course, despite superficial appearances, time is not stopped nor running backwards in any of these processes. Moreover, thermodynamic processes are proceeding uninterrupted. Future states of things are not directly causing present events to occur. So what *is* responsible for these appearances? To answer this we must look beyond life and mind.

Though the epitome of this reversal of causal logic is found in living and thinking beings, the roots of the time-reversed character of these processes can be traced to inanimate processes. Less enigmatic apparent deviations from thermodynamic expectation are found in many non-biological phenomena, though they are fewer and fleeting in comparison with those in life. They are not processes that suggest any final causal logic either, because there is no end or function implied. Final causal organization, whatever it entails, is more complex. Yet many physical processes share in common with their biological and mental counterparts at least one aspect of this time-reversal character: order developing from disorder. Understanding the dynamics of this intermediate inversion of the logic of the second law offers hints that can be carried forward into our explorations of the causality behind life and mind.

In these processes we glimpse a backdoor in the second law of thermodynamics that allows—even promotes—the spontaneous increase of order, correlated regularities, and functional complexity under certain conditions. Curiously, these conditions inevitably include a reliable and relentless increase of entropy. In many nonliving processes—especially when subject to a steady influx of energy or materials—self-organizing features may become manifest. These spontaneous ordering features are dependent on the flow of energy provided by increasing entropy because they are not so much *regularities of structure* as they are *regularities in the dynamics of a process*, though it may also leave a structural trace. Among these processes are simple dynamical regularities like eddies and convection cells, coherence-amplifying dynamics like the conversion of incoherent white light into monochromatic coherent light within a laser, structural pattern-generation processes like snow crystal formation, and complex chemical dynamics like autocatalysis (all of which will be discussed in more detail below). Even computational toy versions of this logic, such as are found in cellular automata and a variety of recursive nonlinear computational processes, exemplify the need for constant throughput of change and energy as well as a recycling of constraints and biases.

4. ABSENCE IS NOT NOTHING

What is common to all these seeming reversals of causality-as-usual is that on the surface they seem to exhibit something like a violation of the *ex nihilo nihil fit* dictum. Since time *isn't* running backwards in these cases, it appears as though the appropriate antecedent conditions aren't actually present to produce these consequences. Order should not spontaneously appear within a previously chaotic system. When it does, it gives the equally counterintuitive impression that these things must have happened due to uncaused causes. Indeed, that is the impression that our own introspection provides us when it comes to our intentional actions. We experience ourselves as originating points for action, not as mere consequences of previous states. It is as though the cause of my thoughts and behaviours, while influenced by my past states, is not determined by them and, to the extent that it is separable from these states, this intervening source—me—becomes something akin to a self-caused cause. Creating something from nothing cannot be what it appears, of course. Nor can the appearance of time-reversed causal sequences really reflect a correspondingly reversed physical causal architecture. But what convoluted causal relationships could make it appear as though something—order—is appearing out of nothing, that is, out of the absence of prior order?

Perhaps we are thinking about something and 'nothing' in the wrong way. Let me contrast the *ex nihilo* perspective with a quite different view presented in one of the oldest written texts in history, the *Tao Te Ching*, produced by the 'ancient sage', Lao-tzu:

Thirty spokes converge at the wheel's hub to an empty space that makes it useful. Clay is shaped into a vessel, to take advantage of the emptiness it surrounds. Doors and windows are cut into walls of a room so that it can serve some function. Though we must work with what is there, use comes from what is not there.[5]

This is a very different sense of nothing from that offered by medieval Western scholars as quoted at the top of this chapter—a *specific absence* rather than, well, just nothing. I think it is more applicable to the present problem than

---

[5] From verse number 11 of the *Tao Te Ching*. My favourite source for this text is Robert Henrick's (1989) combined translation and translator's notes on a recently discovered ancient version of the text because of the new comparisons it offers. Many others are excellent. My paraphrase will be considered quite deviant from the original by all scholars of the material, because it is far from a literal translation. I can only defend it as a gloss offered by a dilettante trying to find English phrasing that is slightly less cryptic than literal translations of a millennia-distant text written in a very different language.

one might otherwise have imagined. That which is empty or unfilled in these examples creates possibilities. Each case involves a highly selective absence that leaves space for something else. What was there is taken out of the way, so to speak, to make room for that something else. It is not so much the absence itself that is critical, but how it affects what is left and how this may relate to other things. The Western mind sees causality primarily in the presence of something, in the pushes and resistance that things offer. Here we are confronted with a different sense of causality, in the form of an 'affordance': a specifically constrained range of possibilities, a potential that is created by virtue of something missing.[6]

What I want to show, using a number of examples, is that the processes of self-organizing dynamics all involve taking advantage of an affordance logic, in the sense just defined. Consider a whirlpool, stably spinning behind a boulder in a stream. As moving water enters this location it is compensated for by a corresponding outflow. The presence of an obstruction imparts a lateral momentum to the molecules in the flow. The previous momentum is replaced by introducing a reverse momentum imparted to the water as it flows past the obstruction and rushes to fill the comparatively vacated region behind the rock. So not only must excess water move out of the local vicinity at a constant rate; these vectors of perturbed momentum must also be dissipated locally so that energy and water doesn't build up. The spontaneous instabilities that result when an obstruction is introduced will effectively induce irregular patterns of build-up and dissipation of flow that 'explore' new possibilities, and the resulting dynamics tends toward the minimization of the constantly building instabilities. This 'exploration' is essentially the result of chaotic dynamics that are constantly self-undermining. To the extent that characteristics of component interactions or boundary conditions allow any degree of regularity to develop (e.g. circulation within a trailing eddy), these will come to dominate, because there are only a few causal architectures that are not self-undermining. This is also the case for semi-regular patterns (e.g. patterns of eddies that repeatedly form and disappear over time), which are just less self-undermining than other configurations. In the jargon of complexity theory, such patterns are called 'attractors', as though they exerted a 'pull' toward this form. This term captures a non-mechanical sense that is implicit in this causal logic. The flow is not forced to form into a whirlpool. This dynamical geometry is not 'pushed' into existence, so to speak, by

---

[6] Just for fun consider the implications of combining this Taoist conception of the role of what's not there with the medieval scholars' insight about the barrenness of nothing. Putting them together one can draw a somewhat less bleak conclusion: if nothing *can* come from nothing then there ought to be an unlimited source of new usefulness available.

specially designed barriers and guides to the flow. Rather the system as a whole will tend to spend more time in this semi-regular behaviour because the dynamical geometry of the whirlpool affords one of the few ways that the constant instabilities can most consistently compensate for one another.

5. EMERGENCE

The term that is most often used by scientists to describe the spontaneous appearance of unprecedented orderliness in nature is 'emergence'. This special use of the term has been around for over a century.[7] It still owes much of its relevance to the fact that it is applied to the same troublesome explanatory 'gaps' as it was over a century ago: the unprecedented nature of life and of mind with respect to other physical processes. The term 'emergence' connotes the image of something coming out of hiding, coming into view for the first time—something without precedent and perhaps a bit surprising. Emergence used in this context is intended to convey the something-from-nothing impression that is produced when unprecedented properties are produced spontaneously without the intervention of external modifications of a system.

Additionally, most uses of the emergence concept implicitly assume an effect that is manifested at ascending levels of scale. Natural phenomena that are described as emergent tend to be mostly compositional in some sense. An early precursor to this idea can be found in discussions of the unprecedented properties of chemical compounds in comparison with those of the elements that comprise them. Thus, John Stuart Mill found the poisonous character of pure sodium and pure chlorine surprising in comparison with the dietary necessity of their compound, table salt.[8] Though most contemporary scientists prefer to reserve the term 'emergence' for describing more systemic phenomena, this sense of discontinuity due to compositional effects remains a persistent refrain. Scale is of special importance to the problem of emergence because an increase in numbers of components increases iterative interaction possibilities. With every iterated interaction, relational properties are multiplied with respect to each other, so an increase in numbers of

---

[7] The first apparent use of the term for this purpose probably comes from Lewes's *Problems of Life and Mind*, but an earlier fairly explicit use of this concept is at least traceable to John Stuart Mill's *System of Logic*.

[8] John Stuart Mill described this radical modification of properties due to chemical combination (via formation of covalent bonds) as transformation. Although he did not use the term 'emergence' this related notion of transformation was discussed in book 5 of his *A System of Logic: Ratiocinative and Inductive*, 8th edn. (London: Longman, Green, and Co.).

elements and chances for interactions increases the relative importance of interaction parameters and related contextual variables. Consequently, a somewhat more extensive definition of emergence might be something like: *unprecedented global regularity generated within a composite system by virtue of the higher-order consequences of the interactions of composite parts.*

Over the past few decades, this compositional usage has become more and more prominent as scientists in different fields have encountered similar transitional patterns in systems as diverse as liquid convection patterns and the appearance of unprecedented social dynamics. In non-technical discussions the phrase 'the whole is more than the sum of the parts' is often quoted to convey this sense of novelty generated via ascent in scale. This phrase originates with Aristotle and captures two aspects of the emergence concept: the distinction between a merely quantitative difference and a qualitative one, and effects involving the combination of elements whose patterns of interaction contribute to global properties that are not evident in the components themselves. There is something a bit misleading about this way of phrasing the relationship that harkens back to a something-from-nothing conception. Exactly what 'more' is being appealed to, if not the parts and their relationships, is seldom made explicit.

This additive conception has often led to the expectation that new classes of physical laws come into existence with increases in scale and the interaction effects that result. This conception of emergence is often described as 'strong emergence' because it implies a dissociation from the physics relevant to the parts and their relationships. It is contrasted with 'weak emergence' that does not entail introduction of any new physical principles. The latter is often seen merely as a redescriptive variant of standard reductionistic causality, and thus as emergence only with respect to human observers and their limited analytic tools. In this essay I will argue that we can still understand the emergence of novel forms of causality without attributing it to the introduction of unprecedented physical laws. Indeed, I will argue that only to the extent that an unbroken chain of causal principles links such higher-order phenomena as consciousness to more basic physical processes will we have an adequate theory of emergence.

In the last decades of the twentieth century the concept of emergence has taken on a merely descriptive function in many fields. It is applied to any case of the spontaneous production of complex dynamical patterns from uncorrelated interactions of component parts. This shift from a largely philosophical to this more descriptive usage of the term emergence has been strongly influenced by the increasing use of computational simulations to study complex systems. Some of the more elaborate examples of these phenomena have been the topics of so-called chaos and complexity theories, and have become commonplace in computational models of dynamical systems, cellular automata, and simulations of non-equilibrium thermodynamic processes. This more general conception of emergence has been adopted by many other fields where complex interaction effects may be relevant, such as in the social sciences. Evolutionary and mental processes are also treated as producing emergent effects, though the complexity of evolution, not to mention cognition compared with dynamical systems, suggests that more subtle distinction between kinds of emergence may be necessary (see below). Because of this terminological promiscuity there is likely to be no common underlying causal principle that ties all these uses together. Nevertheless, I think that with care a technical usage tied to a well-characterized class of empirical exemplars can be articulated for which a clear theory of emergent processes can be formulated.

The exemplars of emergent phenomena that serve as guides for this analysis occupy a middle position in the taxonomy of different emergent dynamics that I describe below. They represent a well-understood set of physical and computational systems that all share a form-amplifying, form-propagating, form-replicating feature. This feature is exhibited irrespective of whether they are physical or computational phenomena. These phenomena are often called *self-organizing*, because their regularities are not externally imposed but generated by iterative interaction processes occurring in the media that comprise them. They serve as a useful starting point because they allow us to extrapolate both upward to more complex living phenomena and downward to simpler, merely mechanistic phenomena.

I decry using emergence as an anti-reductionistic code word in holistic criticisms of standard explanations. In this use, the concept of emergence is a place holder, indicating points where standard reductionistic accounts seem to be incomplete in explaining apparent discontinuities. In this negative usage, emergence serves only as a philosophically motivated promissory note for a missing explanation that, critics argue, is needed to fill in a gap. In contrast, the purpose of the present essay is to outline a technical sense of emergence that explicitly describes a specific class of causal topologies (i.e. self-constituting causal structures) and then attempts to show how this may help to explain many of the attributes that have motivated the emergence concept. This approach avoids engaging the pointless semantic debates about the completeness of reductionism or dealing with metaphysical questions about the ontological status of emergence. The term will only be applied to well-understood empirical processes, and yet I will argue that it does indeed mark the transition to unprecedented and indecomposable causal architectures.

It may be wondered, then, what more besides a taxonomic exercise is provided by identifying the emergent architectural features of known physical processes? By providing an explicit account of how apparent reversals of causal logic come about, how variant forms of these processes are related to one another, and what aspects of their dynamic organization are most critical to the development of these attributes, we can gain critical perspective on the apparent discontinuities between simple mechanistic and teleological models of causality.

6. OUROBOROS

The image of a snake biting its own tail (ouroboros) is an ancient sign for the mysterious. Circularity is also the key to unlocking the mystery of the apparent time-reversed causality of self-organizing and teleological processes. The principal hypothesis of this essay is that *emergent phenomena grow out of an amplification dynamic that can spontaneously develop in very large ensembles of interacting elements by virtue of the continuing circulation of interaction constraints and biases, which become expressed as system-wide characteristics.* In other words, these emergent forms of causality are due to a curious type of circular connectivity of causal dynamics, not a special form of causality. This circularity enables certain distributional and configurational regularities of constituents to reinforce one another iteratively throughout an entire system.

The relative autonomy of higher-order 'holistic' properties of complex systems is largely a function of this recycling of constraints and biases. It is also the means by which apparent 'top-down' effects from global system attributes may come to influence the properties and dynamics of constituents. By virtue of an amplification dynamic, higher-order causal properties can be generated that effectively 'drag along' component constituent dynamics, even though these higher-order regularities are constituted by lower-order interactions. By means of these circles, nature tangles its causal chains into complex knots in such a way that the global effects can come to resemble a reversal of time. Discerning the major topological variants of these 'knots' of causal organization and identifying the conditions under which they form is the primary aim of this theory of emergence.

Wherever it occurs in nature, amplification is accomplished by a repetitive superimposition of similar forms. It can be achieved by mathematical recursion in a computation, by the recycling of a signal that reinforces itself and cancels the uncorrelated background noise in an electronic circuit, or by repetitively sampling from the same biased set of phenomena in a statistical analysis. In each case, a reciprocal relationship between interaction (or sampling) regularities and form regularities serves as the basis for amplification. Amplification depends on redundancy of form and on a process that enables a repeated reinforcement of these redundancies while damping non-redundant variations. In this way, certain minor or even incidental aspects of a process can come to be the source of its dominant features.

Coupling these two factors—a stochastic amplification logic and reciprocally reinforcing patterns of bias and interaction constraint—serves as the basis for the present account of emergent dynamics. Additionally, by distinguishing progressively higher-order nested forms of this circularity we will be able to differentiate between mere order-from-chaos forms of emergence (e.g. self-organization) and teleological processes.[9] Historically, theoretical discussions of complexity and emergence have regularly cited examples with this causal architecture—whether in terms of non-linear dynamics or computational recursion—but to date I know of no effort to formalize this intuition or to use it as a general analytic tool.

Perhaps the simplest and best known example of 'circular causality' is embodied in a thermostatic control system. By connecting a heating device to a temperature-sensitive switch located in the space being heated, the coupled devices can be configured to change one another's states reciprocally. This creates a self-undermining pattern of cause and effect—so-called negative feedback—which tends to produce behavioural oscillation around some set-point. If this causal linkage is reversed, so that deviation away from the set-point activates mechanisms to cause the environmental temperature to deviate yet further, a very different and unstable behaviour results—so-called positive feedback. This latter runaway effect is checked only by outside constraints. Even simple deterministic engineering devices where a number of such feedback control devices are coupled together can produce highly complex quasi-periodic behaviours or even deterministic chaos as the time-lags in effects interact.

Though emergent effects arise from an analogous logic of nonlinear interactions, and in part derive their causal indirectness from it, emergent dynamics differ from simple feedback dynamics by virtue of the contribution of massively stochastic features. Recursive causal interactions that develop up-scale in large stochastic systems exhibit progressive amplification of feedback-like effects between different dynamical levels. As distributional and configurational features of components and their interactions become differentially damped and amplified by virtue of their circulating influences, their global characteristics can further bias these component interaction patterns. Both runaway and self-regulating effects can in this way be manifested at a higher-order system level. In more colloquial terms, one might describe it as

[9] It might be more accurate to use the metaphor of 'spiral' causality rather than circular causality; however, I prefer the terms 'circular' and 'recursive' because they make it easier to visualize more complex convoluted architectures.

'compound interest' of form across adjacent levels of scale—such that global attributes alter component attributes alter global attributes, and so on.

Three general categories of emergent dynamics can be derived in this way, and they are distinguished from one another by the way recurrent causal architectures can be embedded in one another across levels of scale. This embedded relationship can be described as *non-recurrent, simple recurrent,* and *hyper-recurrent* causal architectures (in the latter, simple recurrent causal architectures are embedded in a yet higher-order recurrent architecture). These produce phenomena that I will correspondingly call *first-, second-,* and *third-order emergence,* respectively. In the discussion that follows I will argue that many *thermodynamic effects* correspond to first-order emergent relationships; that self-organizing phenomena (the prototypical exemplars of emergence in most current discussions) correspond to second-order emergent relationships (a mode of causality I will call *morphodynamics*); and that life, evolution, and mind all correspond to third-order emergent relationships (a mode of causality I will call *teleodynamics*).

7. THE SUPERVENIENCE OF SIMPLE THERMODYNAMICS

The most basic class of emergent phenomena, exhibiting what I have called *first-order emergence,* are higher-order thermodynamic phenomena. This sense of the term emergence is often applied to descriptively 'simple' higher-order properties of stochastic systems. Some commonly cited examples are liquid properties. Laminar flow, surface tension, viscosity, and so forth are all first-order emergent properties in this sense. Statistical dynamics and quantum theory have provided a remarkably complete theory of how the properties of molecules can produce liquid properties under appropriate conditions. Thus in one sense they are considered to be fully reducible to relational molecular properties. But such relational properties, as opposed to intrinsic molecular properties (e.g. mass, charge, configuration of electron shells, etc.), are not symmetric across levels of description. Precisely because they are relational, these higher-order properties are not applicable to descriptions of, for example, water molecules in isolation.

More importantly, interaction relationships *between* molecules are what become amplified and summed to produce aggregate behaviours that emerge as liquid properties with ascent in scale. This is why a highly diverse class of molecular species are capable of exhibiting similar liquid behaviours in appropriate conditions. Philosophers of science often refer to the dependence of higher-order properties on lower-order properties as 'supervenience'.

Liquid properties supervene on these lower-order properties, including their interaction effects, and are therefore entirely determined by them. And yet we require a separate explanation for the fact that these properties are also to some extent independently converged upon despite a diversity of substrates. Liquid properties reveal an independence from the details of matter and energy with ascent in scale, even though these details contribute to the particular values of liquid behaviour parameters (e.g. viscosity). This fact suggests an interesting reducibility issue that has been periodically noticed. Knowing all the details of the liquid parameters does not allow us to predict such component details as the molecular structure of components or the many microscopic peculiarities of their interaction features, except in a statistical sense, because the stochastic features of interactions reflect combinatorial relationships between the various parameters. So there are many possible ways that different micro-details of structure and interaction can converge to produce the same higher-order properties. A given higher-order liquid property 'supervenes' on specific lower-order interactions to the extent that the former always entails the latter, but the vast iterative dynamics of these interactions also has a variety-cancelling effect that converges to similar results across a wide range of substrates and modes of interaction.

Before continuing, it is worth reflecting on a parallel that will become more relevant later in this essay. This many-to-one mapping is analogous to a related mapping issue in the philosophy of mind, which has been cited extensively in comparisons of mental processes to computing. This asymmetric many-to-one relationship between substrate and higher-order properties is analogous to the core assumption of a paradigm called 'functionalism'. Functionalism is basically the view that it is the form of a process, not its substance or its energetics, that determines its intentional (read: mentalistic) properties, and that the same form embodied in different media (read: same algorithm on different computing platforms) is functionally the same. Forgetting the mentalistic implications for a moment, notice that calling a multitude of molecular systems 'liquids' effectively exemplifies this logic, that is, that a collection of entities is expressible as a single functional state. Of course, the fact that this hierarchic re-description is a quite generic feature of compositional entities (such as liquid water) suggests that it is not likely, by itself, to provide key insights into the emergent features of mind, any more than it changes what we think of water.

Liquid water properties 'supervene' on the properties of water molecules (see Fig. 5.1) primarily because of *relational* features. In repeated microscopic interactions the specific unique features of individual molecules (e.g. their charge, geometry, orientation, momentum, internal vibration, etc.) distribute in such a way as to cancel one another in aggregate, thus leading to a higher ordered state.

These astronomically many details cancel out, except for the average effect expressed globally via the relative linearity of the summed stochastic processes.

The net result is a reduction in complexity and increase in regularity that correlates with ascent in scale, and in the whole system with continuation in time (e.g. an increase in entropy). Only attributes that are additive and non-cancelling are relevant. This selective cancellation and amplification of inter-action parameters is, I suggest, the key to emergence—even if in simple thermodynamic systems the result is a direct extrapolation from micro to macro. In the real world, with vastly many parameters that can interact in any process, it is almost inevitable that their non-correlations and non-coherence will result in a cancelling dynamic.

So why consider these higher-order relationships emergent? The answer is that they are what I would call stochastic dispositional properties (for want of a more compact description). These properties and the trends they exhibit (i.e. expressions of the second law of thermodynamics) are not merely the results of Newton's laws. Their aggregate character requires a statistical account because of the additional critical role played by distributional fea-tures. In a very general way, as will shortly be made more evident, the lesson of emergence is that 'shape' matters. By shape, I mean something quite gen-eral—including ultimately the geometry, topology, form, and so on of com-ponents, their distributional characteristics, their interaction possibilities, and their boundary conditions in general. Shape matters because it introduces dimensional biases, and these can sometimes uniquely amplify instead of

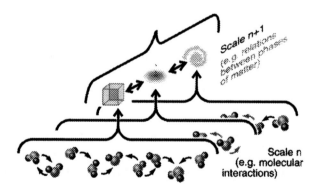

Fig. 5.1. First-order (thermodynamic) 'emergence': Cartoon depiction of causal inter-actions in first-order dynamics. The example of a phase shift in water shows that the shift can still produce discontinuities when aggregate values of interaction parameters reach certain threshold values. A key feature is that shifts in higher-order supervenient properties (e.g. phase changes) do not have any additional effect that changes the nature of molecular interactions. In other words, there are no 'top-down' effects.

cancelling with scale. Typical thermodynamic conditions are, all other things being equal, cases where shape-specificity can be ignored.

The cancelling dynamic of a *simple* thermodynamic system dominates because there are no special features caused by the influence of shape at the component level that could constitute a process of reciprocal amplification via iteration of interactions. For this reason there is also no way for large-scale regularities (e.g. macroscopic interactions, distribution asymmetries, etc.) to reinforce or amplify complementary biases in microscopic interactions. Hence large-scale patterns of distribution and interaction ultimately dominate, making this a standard case of simple supervenience. The result is a causal transparency from micro to macro of the sort that makes reductive analysis possible.

Phase changes represent a special case, though ultimately they are an exception that proves the rule. Change of phase is a higher-order property, one that can have a macro-to-micro biasing effect. In supercooled water, for example, the seeding of crystallization can produce a rapid chain reaction that is accelerated the more molecules become bound to the growing lattice. The seed for crystallization is an external factor; by virtue of shape effects, it then initiates a process of microscopic interaction that rapidly propagates throughout the system. In such cases, the propagated shape-effect—alignment into the crystal lattice—also has a cancelling effect that is evened out throughout the system. Crystallization is intrinsically a shape-determined dynamic. There are conditions where this dynamic can produce amplified biases that affect macroscopic properties which in turn can reinforce these microscopic biases even further. Such a runaway amplification is exhibited by snow crystal growth, which is discussed below as an exemplar of a second-order emergent dynamic.

Philosophical and scientific discussions of the mind–brain mystery often invoke some notion of supervenience to model the presumed relationship between higher-order mental phenomena and the lower-order cellular-molecular processes on which they depend. But it is clear that the functionalist analogy with simple thermodynamic properties isn't nearly adequate. One major factor glossed over in such direct comparisons is development across time. In thermodynamically simple systems the features of each individual component (say, a molecule) are uncorrelated with those of others. Consequently, the properties of the constituents do not cause any consistent biasing effects over large numbers of interactions; the temporal development increasingly tends to cancel deviations from the normal distribution. Another way to think about the inexorable trend to increasing entropy in simple thermodynamic systems is that the simple, non-interactive state is the unbiased condition—unbiased by external perturbations and unbiased by internal form relationships. By contrast, as we will see, very different trends can develop if biased conditions prevail, whether they are due to extrinsic or intrinsic influences. In these cases, the very same interaction dynamics that normally 'cancel out' perturbations can, in fact, come to amplify them.

8. MORPHODYNAMICS: EMERGENCE IN SELF-ORGANIZING SYSTEMS

The thermodynamic simplification processes that I have so far described— including the second law—must be understood as something more than mere mechanism. Classical thermodynamics assumed Newtonian mechanics but required something more as well: an account of parameters affecting the pattern of the average interaction (i.e. shape factors). Thus thermodynamic properties might better be understood as *physical dispositions* of material systems, because they depend critically on formal, distributional, and con- figurational contributions to change. Simple thermodynamic dispositions (e.g. the tendency for entropy of a system to increase) can be characterized as processes of system change that are unbiased by any structural or temporal regularities. These are dispositions in which configuration variables and regularities of system perturbation are uncorrelated, and so cannot introduce reinforcible biases because they reciprocally cancel. In any system of components with even a modestly high dimensionality of potentially variable properties non-correlation is the overwhelmingly likely condition.

But there are conditions where this is not the case—conditions that produce (more or less) chaotic dynamics or self-organized behaviours. Under chaotic conditions, for example, certain higher-order regularities become unstable, resulting in unpredictable global dynamics. This unpredict- ability of chaotic systems derives from the fact that the interaction dynamics at lower levels become strongly affected by regularities emerging at higher levels of organization. This can produce a deviation-amplifying dynamic that propagates throughout the system. If perturbations of this type are incessant, bias comes to dominate over distributive tendencies.

A classic simple example is the formation of Bénard cells in a heated liquid. These are regularly spaced hexagonal convection cells of hot-rising and cool- descending liquid that form spontaneously if there is relatively uniform depth and an even heating from below (see Fig. 5.2). This phenomenon depends on thermodynamic tendencies settling into higher-order stable states; it is also the product of the constant perturbation of these regularities by continuous heating. As heat is conveyed out of the liquid by moving molecules, others must take their place in such a way that there is no persistent local accumu- lation of heat due to uneven convection. The hexagonal regularity forms

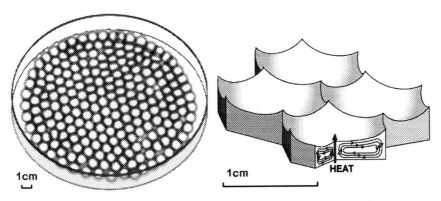

Fig. 5.2. Bénard cell dynamics. Left: A tracing of a photo of Bénard cells forming in a heated dish, showing their approximate hexagonal symmetry (though distorted by the constraints of the circular edge of the dish). Right: A diagram of the convection current pattern for a single Bénard cell in stable dynamical configuration.

because hexagonal close-packing is geometrically the most even and dense distribution of regions of constant size on a surface. In Bénard cells, the precise regularity of dynamical organization emerges out of a more or less disorganized state as the various unstable patterns of convection mutually cancel. The system eventually settles into this hexagonal tessellation of columns of rapidly circulating liquid because this close-packing pattern most uniformly distributes dissipation of heat by moving liquid.

This well-understood example is relevant because it also reveals how, despite the tendency toward equilibrium, continuous imbalance of the system can unmask the self-reinforcing effects of regular geometry. This particular shape bias is a result of dynamical regularity, not any intrinsic or extrinsic imposition of hexagonal symmetry. The shape properties of Bénard cell dynamics arise solely from geometric properties of close-packing on a plane. This pattern is self-amplified with respect to others, because it most evenly distributes the countervailing flows of water. It is the thermodynamic instability of all the other regular and irregular patterns of convection that generates this effect. Thus, the operation of the second law of thermodynamics is essential to the amplification of this regularity. The amplification of this persistent pattern is a function of what *wasn't* able to persist: in a sense, all the unstable dynamics 'pushed' the system towards increasing dynamical order. One might draw a (metaphorical) comparison to the logic of natural selection: it is as though all the other forms were selected against by the tendency toward increasing entropy.

If the geometric constraint on close packing is to express itself, so to speak, a variety of factors must be present, including uniformity in depth, uniformity of heating, a large surface to volume ratio, and limited asymmetry of the

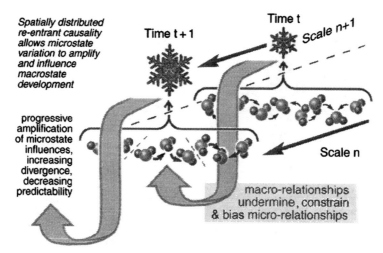

Fig. 5.3. Second-order (morphodynamic) emergence: Cartoon diagram indicating the introduction of a top-down influence (constraints of prior crystal geometry, expressed by the large grey arrows) on molecular interactions (binding patterns in a crystal lattice) in a growing snow crystal. Second-order emergence is a function of this cross-scale amplification occurring by virtue of the concordances of micro and macro geometries.

sides of the container. Their effects are contributed by virtue of what they don't do: they don't introduce countervailing biases or asymmetries. So the role played by symmetry constraints in 'attracting' the dynamics of convection to converge to a regular hexagonal pattern is generic. In other cases, however, the symmetry constraints may come from the components. Consider for example the amplification of form constraints in growth processes, where constant instability is introduced by continually adding similar components, as is the case in snow crystal formation.[10] The structure of an individual snow crystal reflects the interaction of three factors: (1) the hexagonal micro-structural biases of ice crystal lattice growth, inherited from water molecule symmetry, (2) the radial symmetry of heat dissipation, and (3) the unique history of changing temperature, pressure, and humidity regimes as a developing crystal falls through the air.

Snow crystal growth occurs across time in diverse regions in a variable atmosphere, the history of temperature and humidity differences it encounters is captured and expressed in the variants of crystal structure at successive diameters. In this way, the crystal is effectively a record of the conditions of its

---

[10] I will ignore many more subtle and poorly understood aspects of snow crystal growth (e.g. the physics of the quasi-liquid processes on the surface); however, I believe these do not substantially alter what is relevant to this account.

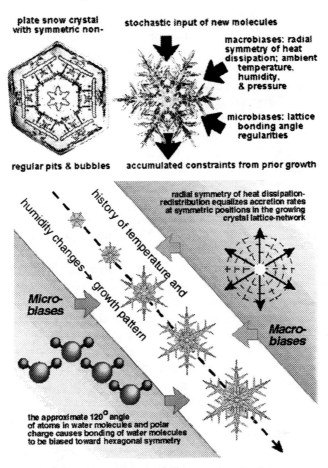

Fig. 5.4. Morphodynamics (form-propagating processes) of snow crystal growth. Top: Snow crystal variation and symmetries (after Bentley). Bottom: Diagram depicting the factors affecting snow crystal growth.

development. But snow crystals are more than merely a historical record of these conditions because of a 'compound interest' effect in which prior stages of crystal growth progressively constrain subsequent stages. So even identical conditions of pressure, temperature, and humidity, which otherwise produce identical lattice growth, can produce different patterns depending on the prior growth history of the crystal. The global configuration of this tiny developing system plays a critical causal role in its microscopic dynamics; it excludes the vast majority of possible molecular accretions and growth points and strongly predisposes accretion and growth at certain other sites (see Figs. 5.3 and 5.4).

Snow crystals are self-organizing. Reciprocally-reinforcing biases of molecular configuration and the contingencies of crystal growth together determine their macroscopic patterning. Contingent events in the growth history of the crystal also play an important role in determining the final configuration. For example, as partially formed crystals or water droplets randomly collide and freeze onto the growing crystal lattice they unbalance its temperature and bias subsequent growth, as the temperature asymmetry propagates throughout the developing crystal to influence the probability of subsequent accretions. As growth continues, the increasingly complex crystalline form leads to progressive constraint on the potential growth options.[11] In this sense, snow crystal growth also includes the unpredictable influence of these random accretions and incorporates them into the complex symmetry of the crystal. This includes even the effects of melting and refreezing, resulting in symmetric semi-regular shapes as well. This is what contributes to the proverbial individuality of each crystal.

Laser physics provides another example of a shape-mediated amplification effect that is manifested in temporal regularity. Lasers produce intense beams of monochromatic light where all the waves are in precise phase alignment (see Fig. 5.5). Light with these precisely correlated features is called coherent light; it is generated from white light, which contains mixed wavelengths aligned in every possible phase. The conversion of white light to coherent light is accomplished by virtue of the recurrent emission and reabsorption of light by atoms whose emission features correlate with their excitation features. When the energy of out-of-phase polychromatic light is absorbed into the electron shells of the atoms of the laser material, it is incorporated into a system with very specific energetic regularities. When the polychromatic light energy is re-emitted as the atom reverts to a lower energy state, the light it emits carries a discrete amount of energy and is thus in a specific frequency. If the lasing material is uniform, the excitation results in uniform colour output. Amplification of the features of this light is achieved by causing the emitted light to re-enter the laser by virtue of partially silvered mirrors. Thanks to the character of the light-absorbing-and-emitting atoms and the frequencies intrinsic to their structure, light at this emission frequency is most likely to induce an energized atom to emit its excess energy as light, and in a phase that is precisely correlated with the exciting light. Repeated charging with white light and recycling of emitted light thus amplifies this pattern by many orders

---

[11] Note that growth is not an essential factor, since this same dynamic also obtains if during certain phases of snow crystal development there is periodic partial melting, which is a common occurrence. The melting is similarly historically constrained and can lead to elaborately shaped entrapped bubbles and pits with smooth curved edges; see the left crystal in Fig. 5.4.

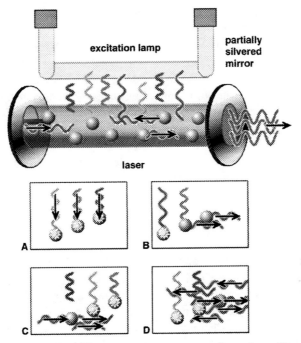

Fig. 5.5. Laser light form amplification. Top: Basic configuration of laser operation, showing excitation by polychromatic mixed phase light from an excitation lamp, absorbance and emission of light within the laser material; and partial reflection by partially silvered mirrors. Light emitted from the laser (right) is monochromatic, has high amplitude, and is entrained to the same phase. Bottom: Stages in the process of amplifying amplitude and coherence: (a) the absorbance of polychromatic light excites atoms; (b) atoms spontaneously drop back to an unexcited state by emitting light energy at a specific frequency; (c) light reflected from mirrors re-enters and induces emission from excited atoms at the same frequency and phase; (d) the repeated recycling of emitted light progressively amplifies the coherence (phase-locking) and amplitude of light at the emission frequency.

of magnitude. To return to my previous analogy, this recurrent emission and reabsorption results in a 'compound interest' of both frequency and phase.

Consider one final example of a second-order emergent phenomenon, albeit one that is more indirectly determined by shape: autocatalytic reactions. In snow crystal dynamics the micro-configuration of each molecule is the same, producing symmetric interactions and strongly constrained structural consequences. When a system is composed of different types of components it can also exhibit a more distributed interactional reflexivity. In *autocatalysis* the interaction of a set of different molecules is constrained both by the configurational properties of the whole collection, as above, *and* by the configuration symmetries and asymmetries that exist between the micro-configurations of the different classes of its components.

For example, molecules that interact in a highly allosteric fashion—that is, they weakly bond selectively with some but not other types of molecules—can constitute interaction sets with more elaborate self-organizing features. Both the configurations of the different classes of individual interactions and the configuration of the whole set of possible interactions become critical organizing influences. This can occur in a chemical 'soup' that contains enough different types of molecules. Among all these types there is a subset in which each type of molecule can catalyze the formation of some other member in the set, thus constituting a closed loop of catalyzed syntheses. So long as sufficient energy and other raw materials are available to keep reactions going (i.e. it must be an open system), the set will continue to be 'autocatalytic'.

A functioning autocatalytic set will play an inordinate role in determining both what chemical reactions can take place and how the soup as a whole will be constituted. It is this higher-order distributed ordering and reordering of the interactions of the different classes of constituents that matters. Such a system can generate far more complex micro- and macro-dynamics than if the interactions were symmetric. Chemical reactions with these features were well-described by Prigogine and colleagues a generation ago;[12] they have since become the basis for extensive research with both real and simulated chemical systems. Ultimately, the metabolic dynamics that constitute living cells depends on numerous fully and partially autocatalytic sets of molecules. Together, these sets constitute a system dynamics that is 'autopoietic' (literally, 'self-making').

What do these examples of second-order emergent phenomena have in common? In each case we find a tangled hierarchy of causality, where micro-configurational particularities can be amplified to determine macro-configurational regularities and where these in turn further constrain and/or amplify subsequent micro-configurational regularities. In such cases, it is more appropriate to call the aggregate a 'system' rather than a mere collection, since the specific reflexive regularities and the recurrent causal architecture are paramount. Although these systems must be open to the flow of energy and components—which is what enables their growth and/or development—they additionally include a closure as well. These material flows carry structural constraints inherited from past states of the system which constrain the future behaviours of its components. As material and energy flows in, through, and out again, *form* also recirculates and becomes amplified. In one sense this form

---

[12] See for example discussions and references in Prigogine and Stengers, *Order out of Chaos* (1984).

is nothing more than a set of restrictions upon and biases toward possible future material and energetic events; in another sense, it is what defines and bounds the higher-order unity that we identify as the system. This centrality of form-begetting-form is what justifies calling these processes *morphodynamic.*

9. TELEODYNAMICS: EVOLUTION AND SEMIOSIS

We find a further difference, however, between merely chaotic or self-organizing emergent phenomena, like snow crystal growth, and evolving emergent phenomena, such as living organisms. The latter, in addition to the effects mediated by second-order processes discussed above, also involve some form of *information* or *memory* (as represented in nucleic acids, for example) that is not seen in second-order systems. The result is that specific historical moments—either of higher-order regularity or of unique micro-causal configurations—can additionally exert a cumulative influence over the entire causal future of the system. In other words, thanks to memory, constraints derived from specific past higher-order states can get repeatedly re-entered into the lower-order dynamics which lead to future states. This is what makes the evolution of life both chaotically unpredictable on the one hand, and yet on the other hand also historically organized, with an unfolding quasi-directionality.

For these kinds of phenomena we must introduce a third order—one that recognizes an additional loop of recursive causality that transcends and encloses the second-order recursive causality of self-organized systems. *Third-order emergence* inevitably exhibits a developmental and/or evolutionary character. It occurs where there is not only an amplification of the global influences on parts, but also a redundant 'sampling' of these influences which reintroduces them into different realizations of the system over time. The result is, in effect, a higher-order stochastic process extending across time that—like the limited stochastic processes of thermodynamics and morphodynamics—is capable of both cancelling and amplifying biases. Under these conditions, there can be extensive amplification of lower-order relationships (both supervenient and self-organizing relationships) due to the fact that historical residues of such processes repeatedly get re-entered into the system.

Third-order emergence is to morphodynamic processes as second-order emergence is to thermodynamic processes. It occurs when there is a recursive stochastic amplification of complementary morphodynamic relationships. In other words, it is a function of one non-equilibrium process that tends to converge to a stable pattern which is then reciprocally reinforced by another. But whereas second-order emergent phenomena involve amplification effects among energetically coupled thermodynamic regularities, third-order emergent phenomena involve the amplification of reciprocally reinforcing morphodynamic relationships *despite vast spatial, temporal, and energetic separation.*

Third-order emergence is the basis for the selection logic of evolution (see Fig. 5.6). Its reciprocity of form and production creates a dynamic that can be called *self-similarity maintenance.* This is the basis for the existence of discrete individuals and lineages that are linked by unbroken continuity of changing structures and relationships. It is also the basis of what we mean by memory. This maintenance of a discrete unit through the correlation of form and dynamics is a necessary condition for evolution. We might thus describe natural selection as a stochastic 'exploration' of variant morphodynamic relationships of reciprocity with respect to environmental regularities. For such exploration to take place, morphodynamic processes must be reliably reproducible.

Third-order emergent phenomena can thus be considered as a form of the self-organization of self-organizing dynamics. As morphodynamic processes

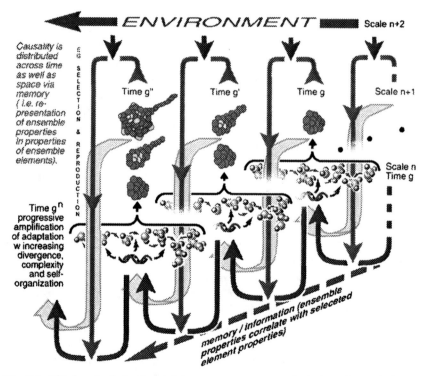

Fig. 5.6. Third-order (teleodynamic) emergence: cartoon depiction of causal circuits in third-order emergence, which is here expressed as a caricature of an evolutionary sequence.

become increasingly synergistically interdependent over the course of evolution, the amplification of complexity and of self-organizational dynamics can become enormously complex. This is because memory allows every prior morphodynamic relationship itself to become a potentially amplifiable initial condition contributing to any later relationship. Through the amplification of size and time constraints alone, the stochastic amplification capacity is vastly greater than what can occur within a morphodynamic process. Second-order emergent, that is, morphodynamic, processes depend on *energetic* continuity, but third-order processes require *morphodynamic* continuities, and these, as we have seen, are to some extent substrate independent. This linkage by form, rather than by shared specific material or energetic substrate, allows for a much vaster domain of amplification. Distant separation in time and the disruption of energetic continuity are not barriers. Moreover, because there is a remembered trace of each prior 'self' state contributing to the dynamics of future states, such systems develop not merely with respect to the immediately prior state of the whole, but also with respect to their own remembered past states. This contributes to the characteristic differentiation and divergence from, and the convergence back toward, some 'reference' state, which organisms standardly exhibit.

In order to describe the relationship of representation that is implicit in third-order emergent phenomena, we need to employ a combination of multi-scale, historical, and semiotic analyses (analyses based on the relationships between signs). This is why living and cognitive processes require us to introduce concepts such as representation, adaptation, information, and function in order to capture the logic of the most salient emergent phenomena. It is what makes the study of living forms qualitatively different from other physical sciences. It makes no sense to ask about the function of granite, or the purpose of a galaxy. Though the atoms composing a neurotransmitter molecule or a heart muscle fibre have no function in themselves, the particular configurations of the neurotransmitter molecule or the heart and its cell types do additionally beg for some type of teleological assessment, some function. They do something *for* something. Organisms evolve and regulate the production of multiple second-order emergent phenomena with respect to some third-order phenomenon. Only a third-order emergent process has such an intrinsic identity.

So life, even in its simplest forms, can't be fully understood apart from either history or representational relationships. Indeed, it may be that any third-order emergent system must be considered 'alive' in some sense. This suggests that third-order emergence may be something like a definition of life. If this is so, then the origins of life on earth must also be the initial emergence of third-order emergent phenomena on the earth. More generally, emergence of this type constitutes the origination of information, semiosis, and teleology in the world. Its embedded circular architecture of circular architectures definitely marks the boundary of a unit of causal self-reference that is extended both in space and time. It is the creation of an 'epistemic cut', to use Howard Pattee's felicitous reuse of a classic phrase: the point where physical causality acquires (or rather constitutes) significance.

Any of the components of an organism—say, a haemoglobin molecule—can be given an arbitrarily complete and precise description in the language of atomic physics or chemistry, and yet this description will miss something that is nevertheless materially relevant to its structure and its very existence. Specifically, it will provide no hint of why this highly improbable molecular configuration is so prevalent, as compared with the astronomical number of molecular forms that are not present. Haemoglobin, and indeed any complex structure within an organism, has the structure and properties it does because it is embedded in a vast elaborate evolutionary web. This evolutionary disposition is the third-order analogue to the increase in entropy.

Comparing haemoglobin to a molecular form of even vastly less complexity —for instance, a diamond—reveals the comparative incompleteness of describing haemoglobin merely in terms of its structure and physical properties. Knowing the atomic structure of the carbon atom gives us a considerable ability to predict the probability that a diamond crystal will form. In contrast, knowing the atomic structure of haemoglobin provides almost no information about its probability of formation, its prevalence in certain environments, why it is found in context with certain other molecules, and why a normal distribution of related molecular forms is nowhere to be found.

Every atom in a haemoglobin molecule has a determinate physical history. Specific converging tributaries of 'pushes' from one molecular event to another over vast stretches of time helped to determine how each of the thousands of atoms (created in perhaps dozens of distant supernovae) came together to form a given haemoglobin molecule. But this is almost irrelevant. The more important causal story is told by what is *not* around, what did not end up as part of the molecule. Haemoglobin's existence must be seen against a backdrop of vastly more numerous molecular forms that were eliminated via natural selection, leaving haemoglobin as the one representative of the set. And this is so for every complex biomolecule as well as for their dynamical relationships to one another within each organism.

Almost every feature that biologists find interesting about haemoglobin has to do with how it fits with other things in the living context in which it has long been embedded. This fit was not created by the 'push' of specific antecedent molecular events, but by the evolutionary cancelling dynamic of natural selection that pushed alternative forms out of existence. Haemoglobin occupies the space of possibilities that was left. The 'function' that haemoglobin provides is thus vaguely analogous to an 'attractor' in a self-organizing dynamic. Haemoglobin is what is left after the self-cancelling consequences of not-fitting-well have cleared away potentially competing similar configurations. So in physical terms what haemoglobin *is*, is a result of what it is *not.*

Molecules like haemoglobin exist, then, because of a process that historically 'captures' and interlinks many self-organizing processes. In a functional sense, the dynamical forms of these self-organizing processes are the equivalents of the spokes and rim of the wheel in the Taoist verse. They determine a constitutive absence with respect to the conditions they require in order to persist. The historical process that stabilizes these dynamical forms with respect to each other and the available resources is of course evolution. Looked at in this way, however, we can see that evolution must involve the self-organization of self-organizing processes, and so must be a higher-order relationship emergent from morphodynamic relationships. But how can self-organizing processes self-organize? The answer is that certain relationships among morphodynamic processes must be capable of producing the necessary and sufficient conditions for evolution.

Elsewhere I have described in some detail a simple example of a system of self-organizing processes that together spontaneously bring an evolutionary (i.e. teleodynamic) process into existence from morphodynamic precursors (Deacon, forthcoming). It is a simple molecular system called an autocell; its basic logic is depicted in Fig. 5.7. It is comprised of two interlocking self-organizing (i.e. morphodynamic) processes: an autocatalytic process and a self-assembly process. Autocatalysis occurs when the catalyst that aids the formation of one molecule is itself (either directly, or indirectly by the intermediary of other catalysts) a catalyst that aids the formation of the first. This produces a circle of catalytic reactions that becomes self-amplifying. Self-assembly is essentially a form of crystallization in which duplicate molecules tend to accrete into larger aggregates with specific geometric forms. In life these are typically tubes, sheets, and polygons. Autocellularity occurs when one catalyst in an autocatalytic set is also able to self-assemble into a structure that can contain other catalysts. Thus, autocatalysis will generate molecules that tend to enclose regions of space that are likely to include the catalysts of the very set that creates such enclosures. This makes autocells self-repairing if they are broken open; moreover, they are potentially self-reproducing if broken open in the vicinity of sufficient raw materials to support many additional cycles of autocatalysis.

The transition from self-reproduction to selection dynamics occurs as an autocell lineage happens also to enclose one or more additional molecules that get caught up in the autocatalysis and increase, in some manner, the reproductive capacity (e.g. by increasing rate, reliability, or matching to more plentiful substrates in the environment). In this way autocells can spontaneously evolve, even though they are not in any typical sense alive.

The point of introducing this example is that autocells embody a definite potential as well as the tendency to achieve this potential. They manifest a definite

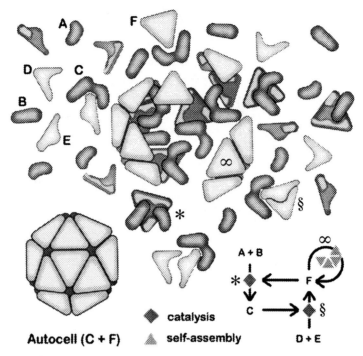

Fig. 5.7. Idealized cartoon depiction of autocell dynamical relationships based on a minimal number of catalytic components ($N=2$). Dark and light objects are intended to represent molecules with distinct geometries that determine their interaction properties. A, B, D, and E represent substrate molecules, assumed to pre-exist in the surrounding medium. C and F represent synthesized catalysts produced from covalently bonded substrates (as depicted by various states of molecular attachment and fusion). F is also shown as able to self-assemble into an icosahedral shell (lower left; the many other possible polyhedral forms are not depicted for simplicity) containing a number of C catalysts (not visible). The letter and arrow diagram at the bottom right schematizes the catalytic relationships depicted in the cartoon. Although a two-component autocell may be easiest to achieve in the laboratory, it is not obvious that such a minimal configuration would be the most likely to arise spontaneously in naturalistic conditions.

self–other relationship; their parts can be said to have functions with respect to this potential; and their evolutionary 'adaptations' can be seen as embodying information about the environment. These are teleodynamic features not evident in simpler systems or in any isolated components. Finally, one does not have to postulate in advance any particular assumptions about information or take as given the existence of information-bearing molecules like DNA in order to understand these teleodynamic features. The autocell's teleodynamic features are emergent: they are embodied and instantiated in the dynamical topology that is constituted by the interdependency of morphodynamic processes.

This self-reproducing 'potential' may be viewed as a higher-order constitutive absence. It is what defines the autocell as distinct from a mere colocation of self-organizing processes. One can interpret the further emergent potential to evolve, and thus to generate additional new 'aboutness' relationships as, in effect, a capacity to generate constitutive absence. The locus of this capacity is physical and material; and yet with each replication the thread that ties this potential together is only its complex causal topology passed down through the generations—and even this can become further augmented and differentiated over time. Such could be the precursor of life.

In the case of autocells, the embodied potential is also a tendency to achieve that potential. Specifically, it is the tendency to reconstitute the morphodynamic and thermodynamic resources that are required. As described, it is a self-realizing potential—or, to put the point differently, a constitutive absence that tends to fill itself.

10. TELEOLOGICAL CAUSALITY

In this way, the adaptations of organisms are like the wheel or the vessel in the Taoist verse quoted above. Organism adaptations, and the processes they include, are materially bounded structures and processes; and yet, in a curious way, they are defined by a fundamental *incompleteness*. Third-order emergent dynamics are thus intrinsically organized around specific absences. This physical disposition to develop toward some target state of order merely by persisting and replicating better than neighbouring alternatives is what justifies calling this class of physical processes *teleodynamic*, even if it is not directly and literally a 'pull' from the future.

All three of the dynamics we have discussed have one general logic in common: they can all be described as processes in which the most salient feature is a 'least-discordant-remainder'. In other words, it's not so much what *was* determined to happen that is most relevant for future states of the system, but rather what *was not* cancelled or eliminated. It is the negative aspect that becomes most prominent. This is the most general sense of *constitutive absence*: something that is produced by virtue of determinate processes that eliminate most or all of the alternative forms. It is this, more than anything else, which accounts for the curious 'time-reversed' appearance of such phenomena. This logic itself becomes self-reinforcing in teleodynamic processes, because they are the result of a least-discordant-remainder *dynamic* operating on a least-discordant-remainder *substrate*—higher order constitutive absences *based on lower order* constitutive absences.

This is, of course, also the essence of representation, or intentionality: something whose existence is conditional upon something it is not. It is this feature of mental phenomena that has most mystified scholars for millennia: their 'aboutness'. The implication of the present analysis is that the 'constitutive absences' characteristic of both life and mind are the sources of this apparent 'pull of yet unrealized possibility' that constitutes function in biology and purposive action in psychology. The point is that absent form can indeed be efficacious, in the very real sense that it can serve as an organizer of thermodynamic processes. We are now in a position to explain more precisely how the specific absence of something can itself do work, that is, how a possibility can constitute a locus of thermodynamic 'push'.

What this three-level analysis suggests is that a constitutive absence derives its efficacy by virtue of a series of thermodynamic and evolutionary reversals (a combined 'double reversal') which each results in a least-discordant-remainder dynamics. These reversals are the consequence of distributed dynamical interactions that stochastically cancel each other out, leaving serendipitously non-discordant tendencies in their stead. Through the progressive layering of what are essentially negative determination processes, the organizing capacity of these constitutive absences is amplified until, at the level of human mental causation, it appears that a very large fraction of all material and energetic processes in the body are entrained by what is no more concrete than the 'conceivably possible'. Let's try to break these double-reversals down into their component steps.

The first reversal occurs via morphodynamics: self-organizing processes that generate regularity by virtue of the spontaneous reciprocal cancelling of non-reinforcing forms of dynamical interactions. Morphodynamics can be caricatured as a process of falling toward regularity through the mutual cancellation of pushes occurring in most alternative configurations. The dynamic form that 'survives' and persists is in this sense 'left over' after others have taken themselves out of the way. Although the stable forms that arise and are eventually amplified in morphodynamic processes are perhaps best viewed as reliable side-effects of the underlying thermodynamics, this thermodynamic basis remains a necessary condition. Ultimately, this necessary coupling carries over into the higher-order relationships among the morphodynamic processes that constitute life and evolution.

The second reversal occurs via teleodynamics: the amplification of morphodynamic synergies due to the differential preservation of more contextually fitted variants. Evolution is the paradigm exemplar of this second reversal. As in the previous case, Darwinian selection processes can also be caricatured as a 'falling toward' or 'backing into' regularity. In this case, however, the relationships *between* morphodynamic processes are what are pitted against one another; they are the units that use up resources for self-replication. But when morphodynamic processes themselves fall into recipro-cally reinforcing relationships—as they do in life—they do so only to the extent that they maintain mutually reinforcing thermodynamic conditions at the same time. This interdependence of form and dynamics constitutes the condition for selection, because it allows alternative form–form relationships to be 'sampled' by virtue of their thermodynamic correlates (i.e. the relative 'cost' of the morphodynamics that produced them). The form–form relation-ships that tend to persist and propagate in evolution are those generated by morphodynamic linkages that minimize chaotic dissipation by 'falling into' dynamical short-cuts between dynamical forms. This is the essence of 'fitted-ness' in a biological sense. It is both a formal and an energetic relationship, one that is continually reconstituted and updated by virtue of mutually reinforcing least-discordant-remainder processes at work across levels of scale.

Darwinian selection processes, like morphodynamic processes, are the expres-sion of indirect and mutually cancelling 'pushes'. But what is doing the 'pushing' if the morphodynamic processes that constitute organisms are themselves a reflec-tion of the space of least resistance in a context where all other pushes cancel? Since the mutually reinforcing morphodynamic processes that define 'organism' are essentially a linked set of convergent tendencies due to non-resistance, it might seem that they would be unable to provide any source of resistance themselves. Yet, it turns out, the self-similarity maintenance that results from a series of morphodynamic processes can itself determine a locus of resistance. The com-ponent morphodynamic dispositions of an organism reflect an underlying non-equilibrium thermodynamics; hence the reciprocal relationships between the various morphodynamic processes that allow organisms to remain self-similar over time must be organized so that they maintain the self-similarity of these non-equilibrium dynamics as well. The competition on which natural selection is based arises from these thermodynamic 'requirements', culling morphody-namic relationships with respect to their relative thermodynamic consequences. Again, the *work* is done by thermodynamic processes. But this work is harnessed to create formal and thermodynamic conditions that are not immediately present, driven by the tendency to resist deviation from a target form that incessantly reconstitutes itself. This is what ultimately licenses *functional* terminology in biology: component processes and structures are indeed organ-ized 'for the sake of' achieving future target states of least discord or best fit.

Like the reciprocal form-reinforcing relationships that constitute morphody-namic processes and produce a higher-order appearance of thermodynamic time-reversal, teleodynamic processes produce a yet higher-order appearance of morphodynamic time-reversal. In morphodynamic processes, order can spon-taneously arise without a similarly ordered antecedent state. In teleodynamic processes, specific order can arise spontaneously because of its specific absence in an antecedent state. In this way, absent order can in effect bring itself into being.

This is only the beginning of an analysis of teleological causality. It offers no more than a demonstration of plausibility, albeit one that has long been needed and missing. There are many embeddings of these processes that must be considered just to get to biological systems as they are currently understood, and many many more above the level of biological functionality before we can approach anything like what is involved in mental processes. Within this analysis I think we can nevertheless discern a modus operandi for ascending the hierarchy of processes. The key additional ingredient can be found by noticing that the three-step hierarchic embedding required to achieve this simplest level of teleology—function—is itself susceptible to recursive embedding. Embryological processes, neural development, and (I predict) neural signal processing itself represent progressively embedded teleodynamic processes within teleodynamic processes. With each progressive embedding, the achieved adaptations and functions of lower domains become the ground for subordinate higher-order teleodynamic processes; one might think of it as evolutionary dynamics 'for the sake of' evolutionary possibilities. In this way, by backing into possibility level upon level via least-discordant-remainder dynamics, teleological causality has grown. The thermodynamic constraint on which forms of constitutive absences can come to affect which forms of physical processes has, correspondingly, been radically reduced.

11. SUMMARY AND CONCLUSIONS

In this essay I have defined three subcategories of emergent phenomena that can be arranged into a hierarchy of increasing topological complexity, each growing out of and dependent on emergent processes at the level below (see Fig. 5.8). Thus third-order emergent processes (teleodynamics) require self-amplifying second-order emergent processes (morphodynamics) to create their necessary conditions, which in turn require self-amplifying (non-equilibrium) first-order emergent processes (thermodynamics) to create their necessary conditions. Conversely, teleodynamics is a special limiting case of morphodynamics, which is a special limiting case of thermodynamics. The three categories are distinguished by their causal *topology* in the sense that the circularity of their dynamics creates a certain 'closure'. This closure helps to explain both the discontinuities that they evidence with respect to one another and the reversal in dispositions as one ascends from one to the others.

As a result, while it is technically correct to say that life and mind supervene on chemical processes, it is misleading to say that they are 'merely' or 'nothing but' chemical processes. Moreover, because higher-order emergent phenomena are dependent on and constituted by lower-order emergent phenomena,

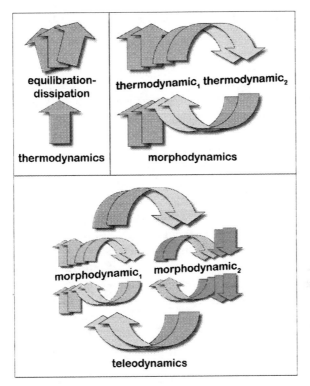

Fig. 5.8. Three panels schematizing the hierarchic levels of the recursive causal logic constituting the three levels of dynamics described. As in earlier figures, arrows abstractly represent directions of physical change from an antecedent to a consequent condition, but also (in the case of morpho- and teleodynamics) changes in conditons that reciprocally promote the repeated production of specific thermodynamic or morphodynamic processes (indicated by cyclic arrows). This depicts the way higher-order modes of dynamics are composed of and dependent on lower order modes.

their probability of formation is substantially lower. There is a vastly higher probability of the spontaneous formation of simple thermodynamic phenomena than morphodynamic phenomena, and a vastly higher probability of the spontaneous formation of morphodynamic phenomena than teleodynamic phenomena. But whereas it is almost astronomically improbable that teleodynamic systems might form spontaneously, whenever they do their self-similarity-maintaining dynamic results in a powerful disposition further to reinforce their persistence, which we call evolution. As such a system evolves, it becomes able to expand vastly the self-reinforcing interconnections of this organizational pattern in which underlying morphodynamic and thermodynamic relationships are (or are made to be) mutually complementary. Spontaneously generated morphodynamic phenomena are transient and unstable, however, so the vast majority of morphodynamic processes in the world occur within organisms. This tail-wagging-the-dog effect reflects the higher-order disposition of teleodynamic relationships to self-replicate, thereby replicating their constitutive morphodynamic features.

We are now in the position to give a more precise formulation to the insistent criticisms that systems theorists have made both of genetic reductionism in evolutionary theory and of computational reductionism in cognitive theory. Life and mind cannot be adequately described in terms that treat them as merely supervenient because this collapses the complex levels of emergent relationships that stand in between. More critically, supervenience analyses entirely overlook the defining dispositional reversals that occur within these higher-order transitions. As a result, these analogies miss the most salient and descriptively important dynamics of these phenomena, which are precisely what make them emergent in the sense discussed above.

In many ways, I see this analysis of causal topologies as a modern reaffirmation of the original Aristotelian insight about categories of causality. Whereas Aristotle simply treated his four modes of causality as categorically independent, however, I have tried to demonstrate how at least three of them—efficient (thermodynamic), formal (morphodynamic), and final (teleodynamic) causality—are hierarchically and internally related to one another by virtue of their nested topological forms. Of course there is so much else to distinguish this analysis from that of Aristotle (including ignoring his material causes) that the reader would be justified in seeing this as little more than a loose analogy. The similarities are nonetheless striking, especially considering that it was not the intention to revive Aristotelian physics.

There is a sense in which all is 'reducible' to thermodynamics (efficient causality), though only to the limited extent that the higher-order forms assume lower-order forms in their constitution. But the topological closure created by the circular relationships at each succeeding level makes each of the two higher-order dispositional dynamics irreducible to mere combinations of the lower-order forms. Ignoring these topological transitions, as reductionistic analyses do, also obscures the source of the higher-order reversals of disposition, which is what distinguishes the formal and the final causal levels from simple efficient mechanisms.

So what are the implications for the efficacy of human desires, reasons, and intentions? Of course, the elaboration of this dynamic in neurological processes, which produces that peculiarly convoluted version that we call thought, does not yield to any simple solution. Our brains are constituted of hundreds of billions of densely interacting cells, each of which is itself a vast third-order emergent dynamo. In a sense, each nerve cell is sentient in some small way by virtue of its necessary functional organization and incompleteness. This fact creates, among the linked neurons, an affordance to one another that involves them in first-, second-, and third-order processes of a higher rank than that which is internally regulated within each alone.

In addition, a symbolic species such as *Homo sapiens* has further entangled the causal architecture of its billions of minds in a vast higher-order emergent semiotic web. This web is characterized by symbolic self-organizing and by evolutionary processes that are quite different from those at lower levels. In addition to the least-dissonant-remainder effects of the various underlying levels of genetic teleodynamic processes (including neurological, embryological, and evolutionary processes), the further distributive power of symbolic communication itself provides a multi-stage dissociation from specific thermodynamic factors. A symbolizing mind has perhaps the widest possible locus of causal influence of anything on earth. Minds that have become deeply immersed in the evolving symbolic ecosystem of culture—as are all modern human minds—may have an effective causal locus that extends across continents and back millennia, and which grows out of a locally least-discordant-remainder dynamic involving hundreds of thousands of individual communications and actions. Each symbolically mediated thought is the emergence of a specific 'constitutive absence'; each is a specific variant instance of an evolved adaptation within this vast spatially and temporally distributed ecology. This immense convergence of causal determination is coupled with an equally vast capacity for selective amplification via the teleodynamics of neural processing. With so many levels of amplification and causal inversion mediating between brain chemistry, conscious cognition, and symbolic evolution, it is no wonder that we experience symbolically mediated causality as almost completely disconnected from thermodynamic causality, even though its very efficacy is founded upon it.

Human consciousness—with its features of autonomous causal locus, self-origination, and implicit 'aboutness'—epitomises the logic of emergence in its very form. Like something coming out of nothing, the subjective self is, in effect, a constitutive absence for the sake of which new constitutive absence is being incessantly evolved. In this sense, there is some legitimacy to the eliminativist claim that there is no 'thing' that it is. Indeed this must be so. The locus of self is, effectively, a negative mode of existence, that can act as an unmoved mover of sorts: a non-thing that nonetheless is the locus of a form of inertia—a resistance to change—with respect to which other physical processes can be recruited and organized. Consciousness is not exactly something from nothing. It merely appears this way because of the misdirection provided by the double-negative logic of the least-dissonant-remainder processes involved. It is, nevertheless, a form of being that is constituted by what it is not, and yet remains a locus of physical influence. It is the hole at the wheel's hub.

12. REFERENCES

Bateson, Gregory (1972), *Steps to an Ecology of Mind* (New York: Ballantine Books).

Deacon, Terrence (2003), 'The Hierarchic Logic of Emergence: Untangling the Interdependence of Evolution and Self-Organization', in B. Weber and D. Depew (eds.), *Evolution and Learning: The Baldwin Effect Reconsidered* (Cambridge, MA: MIT Press), 273–308.

—— (Forthcoming), 'Reciprocal Linkage Between Self-organizing Processes is Sufficient for Self-reproduction and Evolvability', *Biological Theory.*

—— (Forthcoming), *Homunculus* (New York: W. W. Norton & Co.)

Henrick, Robert (1989), *Lao Tzu's Tao-Te Ching* (New York: Ballantine Books).

Lewes, George Henry (1874–9), *Problems of Life and Mind,* 5 vols. (New York: Houghton Mifflin).

Mill, John Stuart (1843), *A System of Logic: Ratiocinative and Inductive,* 8th edn., (London: Longman, Green, and Co., 1925).

Pittendrigh, C. S. (1958), 'Adaptation, Natural Selection and Behavior', in A. Roe and G. G. Simpson (eds.), *Behavior and Evolution* (New Haven: Yale University Press), 390–416.

Prigogine, Ilya, and Isabelle Stengers (1984), *Order out of Chaos* (New York: Bantam Books).

6

The Role of Emergence in Biology

Lynn J. Rothschild[1]

1. SUMMARY

What is emergence in biology? The question seems odd to most practicing biologists, but an inversion produces startling familiarity. Is emergence—in the philosophical sense—nothing more than a denial of reductionism? If so, to acknowledge emergence is to assail the approach that is so prevalent in biology today, the perception that with an increasing knowledge of chemistry and molecular biology (and to some extent, cellular biology) we will be able to explain all of biology. What started as a methodological simplification has turned into a faith that, by means of reductions of higher-order phenomena, all biological questions will be answered.

Here I argue by contrast that there are a vast number of examples of form and function in biology that may, and probably *should*, be analysed from the perspective of emergence. These include, 'What is life?', 'Are evolutionary innovations emergent?', 'What are the properties of higher-level individuals, such as species, that are meaningless at lower hierarchical levels?' The reasons for the great interest in emergence in biology are the peculiarities of higher ordered biological systems, including the prevalence of feedback loops and downward causation. Some cases presented will be viewed by the philosopher as 'weak emergence', some as 'strong emergence'. But the most important contribution emergence theory can make to biology is what is termed here *pragmatic emergence*, that is, treating biological situations as emergent is a valid research strategy regardless of its philosophical underpinnings.

[1] I am indebted to Paul Davies and the Templeton Foundation for inviting me to participate in the fascinating workshops on emergence, and for their unfailing encouragement to explore emergence in the context of biology. Ernan McMullin kindly guided me into this field and critiqued this paper at its early stages. I am enormously grateful to Philip Clayton for his encouragement and excellent suggestions during the preparation of this chapter.

2. INTRODUCTION

Is biology really anything but physics elaborated through chemistry? Or are gene or protein sequences the sole key to unravelling life's mysteries? If so, this essay is complete: emergence is absent from biology.

But here I argue that there *is* more, much more. The riches of the biological world contain a multitude of examples and types of emergence, perhaps greater than found elsewhere in nature. It is this prevalence of emergence that led Mayr (1982, pp. 58–9) to identify emergence as one of the six reasons that prediction is so difficult in the biological sciences.[2] Yet the word 'emergence', in the philosophical sense,[3] is heard only sporadically among practicing biologists, as in 'Is fitness an emergent property of species?' In contrast, the philosophical literature regularly examines examples from biology, such as whether consciousness is an emergent property. While the discussions in Mayr (1976, 1982), Salthe (1985), and Gould (2002) provide an invaluable foundation for examining biological emergence, a general study and analysis of emergence in biology is lacking.

What follows is a fresh look at the question of emergence in biology, from the origin of life to evolution and ecology. The perspective is that of an evolutionary biologist, rather than a philosopher, so the emphasis will be on providing new material for philosophical inquiry. In the process I will consider potential examples of emergence and whether innovations in structure or process can be considered emergent. Of greatest value is the concluding discussion regarding whether such an inquiry has any practical implications for biology, either philosophically or methodologically.

3. WHAT IS EMERGENCE IN BIOLOGY?

Here I use a definition of emergence that I will call the 'salt test', a commonly used criterion by whatever name.[4] 'Salt' here refers to table salt, a compound composed simply of one atom of sodium and one of chlorine.

---

[2] The other five are the facts that (1) biology is historical; (2) events are random with respect to their significance, as in mutations; (3) the properties of a unique event or entity cannot be predicted; (4) the interactions of unique individuals with a variable and changing environment are crucial; and (5) the complexity of living organisms introduces new and perhaps irreducible factors.

[3] The word 'emergence' does appear sporadically in biology in other contexts. For example, in botany an emergence is an outgrowth coming from the tissue beneath the epidermis, as, for example, a rose thorn. In zoology, an emergence is the appearance of the adult form (imago) of an insect on the completion of the change (metamorphosis) from the larval stage. Such uses of 'emergence' are not discussed further.

[4] A similar argument could be made for water or a myriad of other compounds.

Sodium is a soft, bright, silvery metal. It can float on water and, when doing so, decomposes with the production of hydrogen and the formation of hydroxide. Sodium may ignite spontaneously on water, depending on the amount of oxide and metal exposed to the water. It normally does not ignite in air at temperatures below 115° C.

Chlorine is a greenish-yellow gas that is a respiratory irritant. As little as 3.5 p.p.m. (parts per million) can be detected as an odour, and 1000 p.p.m. is likely to be fatal after a only few deep breaths. Chlorine is so toxic it was used in gas warfare in 1915.

From this information it is impossible to predict that sodium chloride should be the benign compound that makes the oceans salty and is an essential compound for life, not to mention potato chips and margaritas. It is possible that a knowledgeable chemist could make this prediction—not today, but perhaps sometime in the future—but at this point 'salt' appears as an emergent property of sodium and chlorine. In contrast, combining sand and water will make a predictable mess.

The first potential problem that arises in such an assessment is the possibility that even the 'salt test' is emergent because of the current state of knowledge. There was a time that microbes were seen as an emergent property of soiled cloth and water, something that Louis Pasteur disproved categorically. Perhaps chemical modelling will achieve the ability to predict the properties of sodium chloride in the future—perhaps not. Nonetheless, this potential predictability is somewhat problematic for a more complete articulation of emergence.

The above problematic has led to the separation of emergence into two philosophical types:

1. *Strong emergence:* knowledge of higher-level processes cannot *in principle* be derived from knowledge of lower-level processes.
2. *Weak emergence:* properties of the higher level are not expected based on knowledge of lower-level components. We might suspect that the property is strongly emergent, but we cannot prove it *at this point.* This may be due to an inadequate state of scientific knowledge, or to insufficient funds, computer power, or other experimental tools needed to understand the higher levels of a system with a reductionist approach.

Secondly, the 'salt test' implies that a formal hierarchy must exist between the product and its components. We can distinguish two types of hierarchies in biology. *Simultaneous hierarchies* occur at the same point in time, but they are spatially distinct. For example, a gene resides in a cell. *Sequential hierarchies* are separated temporally. There are hierarchies that occur during development and evolution. In some cases the two may blend. An organism belongs to a species which may exist while the individual exists, as well as before and after. Two types of hierarchies, a nested and a top-down hierarchy, are shown diagrammatically in Fig. 6.1.

There are numerous examples of hierarchies in biology (Table 6.1). For example, the structure of a cell is composed of organelles, membranes, and cytoplasm, which themselves are made of molecules (chemicals), which, in turn, are manifestations of physics. Moving in the other direction, the cells themselves may be parts of tissues, organs, and organisms. There are also

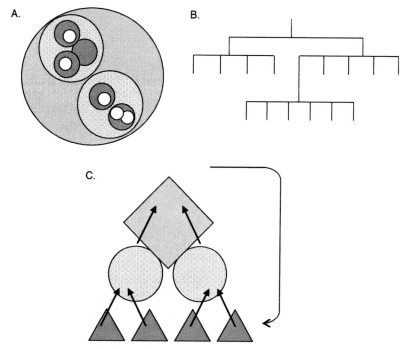

Fig. 6.1. Diagrammatic representations of (A) a nested or compositional hierarchy, (B) a top-down hierarchy, and (C) an interactional hierarchy. Salthe (1985) refers to (B) as a control hierarchy, but note that it is strikingly similar to diagrammatic representations of evolutionary trees, and thus is also an example of a nested evolutionary hierarchy. Example (C) can be thought of as simply a food chain or control circuit. However, as discussed in the text, feedback loops are common in biology from the biochemical to the ecological levels, and are alluded to with the arrow. (A) and (B) are after Salthe (1985).

hierarchies of function, such as the initiation and elongation reactions which are components of protein synthesis.

Even more convoluted, there are hierarchies where the lower levels differ in kind; for example, sexual reproduction has a behavioural as well as a biochemical basis:

Sex

Behaviour

Physiological prerequisites

Biochemistry

Genetics

Figure 6.1 is an attempt to show this diagrammatically.

Once a hierarchy exists, can the properties at one level be predicted with sufficient knowledge of the lower levels? If so, the property is not normally considered emergent, and, furthermore, can be considered as functionally reducible.

This questioning might seem odd to the practicing biologist, but an inversion produces startling familiarity: is emergence nothing more than a denial of reductionism? And, if so, are we now open to charges of being sloppy in our thinking or methodology—or, worse, the charge of being vitalists? By suggesting the possibility of emergence, we are attacking the approach of functional reductionism that is so prevalent in biology today, the idea that with increasing knowledge of molecular (and to some extent, cell) biology we will be able to explain all of biology. But matters are much more complicated than this. What started as a methodological simplification in biology has turned into a faith that, through such reductions, all biological questions will be answered. The pragmatics of reductionism has given way to an outright

Table 6.1. Examples of hierarchies in biology

	Lowest level	Intermediate levels	Highest level
Structural	Molecules	Macromolecular complexes, subcellular components	Cells*
Biochemical	DNA	RNA	Proteins, including enzymes
Physiological	Individual chemical reactions	Metabolic pathway	
Ecological	Primary producers	Herbivores	Carnivores
Evolutionary	Genotype	Individual organism, populations	Species

*In the case of multicellular organisms, the hierarchy would continue to tissues, organs, organ systems, and the individual organism.

theory of reductionism. This is seen in those who believe that gene or protein sequences hold the key to unravelling life's mysteries.[5]

Thus, the question of emergence goes from being a philosophical curiosity to an issue that strikes at the core of methodology in the biological sciences. For, *if emergence exists, absolute reductionism fails.*

Other evidence gleaned from biology further problematizes the issue. Causality within biological hierarchies may be bi-directional. In other words, there is both upwards and downwards causation. Four examples help to illustrate this point:

- In feedback loops, the product of pathway A regulates (induces or inhibits) pathway A. At the biochemical level, the enzyme that catalyzes the first step in a biosynthetic pathway is usually inhibited by the final product, a process called *feedback inhibition.* Examples include the biosynthesis of purine nucleotides and the amino acid isoleucine in *Escherichia coli.* On a macroscopic level, the production of children may inhibit further production.
- Sexual recombination determines the raw material for evolution, but evolution shapes sexual recombination. The nature of sexual encounters, the genetics of recombination, the biochemistry of the recombination process—all are subject to broader evolutionary processes that are not fully conditioned by lower causal processes.
- Sexual behaviour, which may be induced by such emergent (or social) concepts as beauty and love, ultimately influences gene sequences of offspring, which in turn influence sexual behaviour.
- In evolution, species-level changes influence all levels. If a species changes, all individuals must change to remain part of the gene pool. Changes must invariably include gene sequence changes. There will be pre- and possibly post-mating anti-hybridization mechanisms. Species-level changes will also change higher-level interactions with other species, thus changing the ecosystem as a whole. All of these changes will feed back to affect species evolution further.

In fact, one cannot understand biology without understanding feedback loops. They effectively form the constitutive basis for 'top-down' and 'bottom-up' causality, as well as providing the dynamism that is empirically evident in biological systems.

---

[5] Of course, that approach could be extended beyond the realm of biology by insisting that biochemistry can be explained by organic chemistry, which reduces to quantum mechanics and the properties of electrons and atomic nuclei, on down to quantum fields.

To dispense with the vitalist charge, Mayr (1982, pp. 64) points out that while some of the nineteenth- and early twentieth-century emergentists were vitalists, modern emergentists are not. Today's emergentists accept the fact that living organisms can be reduced to their material constituents and nothing more (monism). Thus, they do not postulate a 'vital force' within the material body.

The charge of sloppiness would be appropriate only against those who do not believe that there is any point in studying biology except as a whole, for example a whole organism. Certainly no practicing biologist today would take such an extreme 'holist' stand. Rather, contemporary emergentists exploit reductionism when appropriate but acknowledge that there are phenomena that can be understood today—or perhaps forever—only when they are treated as emergent.

If emergence is the opposite of reductionism, then a brief discussion of the types of reductionism is warranted. It is standard to divide reductionism into two categories. *Ontological reductionism* states that, in principle, objects and processes at a higher level (e.g. biology) reduce to a lower level (e.g. chemistry). In contrast, *epistemic reductionism* states that the properties of one level must be ideally explained as the effects of the processes at the next level down. More helpfully, Mayr (1982, pp. 60–3) identifies three kinds of reductionism:

1. *Constitutive reductionism.* The material composition of organisms is drawn solely from the inorganic world. There is no vital force; constitutive reductionists are not vitalists. Virtually all biologists are constitutive reductionists.
2. *Explanatory reductionism.* One cannot understand the whole until one understands the constituent parts. Thus, one cannot fully understand biology without understanding its molecular basis. This is a very popular attitude today, but it fails because of the fact that function can be independent of composition in biology, and because it does not take into account the interactions of components. I would add that the historical nature of living organisms also makes extreme reductionism impossible. For example, our work (Rothschild, 1994; Cockell and Rothschild, 1998) has shown that studying photosynthetic rates in response to a particular light level is meaningless without taking into account the history of the organism, such as its previous exposure history and nutrition.
3. *Theory reductionism.* Theories in biology are simply special cases of the theories and laws of physics and chemistry. In Mayr's view, theory reductionism is 'a fallacy because it confuses *processes* and *concepts*'. For example, biological processes such as meiosis are also chemical and physical processes. But the concepts biologists use in their theories are distinctively

biological concepts, not chemical or physical. Further, a biological concept may have entirely different meanings in different biological contexts, something a physical or chemical concept would be blind to.

Again if we assume that there is an inverse relationship between reduction and emergence, how would these types of reductionisms translate into categories of emergentism? I suggest the following:

1. *Constitutive emergentism.* The material composition of organisms is drawn solely from the inorganic world. Thus, on a physical basis, there is no emergence. The stuff of physics is the stuff of biology. Clearly this is simply the same as constitutive reductionism.
2. *Explanatory emergentism.* One cannot understand the whole until one understands the constituent parts. Because function can be independent of composition in biology, and because components interact and living organisms are historical entities, some part of explanation in biology must be based on emergence.
3. *Theory emergentism.* If theories in biology are simply special cases of the theories and laws of physics and chemistry, then biology (and chemistry) would be taught in physics departments. But, as Mayr points out, biological processes are different from biological concepts, and the latter may be context dependent. Thus, biological theory must be based on emergence.

4. EXAMPLES OF EMERGENCE IN BIOLOGY

In order to elucidate the general thesis of biological emergence, in the sense of these latter two categories, I include here a number of examples of emergence in biology. There are an almost infinite number of potential examples. Taken together, they show that form and function in biology can be analysed from the perspective of emergence, ranging from the origin of self-replication to emergent fitness. For the purpose of discussion, I will focus on three major types of examples:

Emergence based on statistical probability. One of the sources of complexity in biology is that its success is based on statistics. For example, barring unforeseen disasters, there will be humans inhabiting the Earth in 1000 years. Yet we cannot predict which people alive today will be the ancestors of these people. An outcome that is based on statistical probability may be emergent in that complete knowledge of even every individual human alive today will not allow predictive accuracy 1000 years into the future. Our predictive capacities are stifled by pure statistical variability. Thus one must

consider the underlying biological complexity as a cause for, and as constitutive of, emergence. Still, what are emergent are the particular outcomes of
evolution, rather than the statistically based predictions that particular events
will or will not happen.

What is life? This question is not only of philosophical interest; it is also
critical to religious, biomedical, and astrobiological discussions.

One aspect of this question involves identifying the time that an individual
life begins from either non-living components or from living components of
the parental organism. The second aspect is how to identify an entity as alive.
Having such a definition may someday be of the utmost importance, for
example, when we find life elsewhere in the universe, or when an entity that
we had previously classified as non-living (e.g. a computer) demands clas-
sification as a living being.

Thirdly, to answer the question we must be able to identify when life ceases.
Is there anything different about lower-level structures or activities, such as
genes or gene function, that would allow one to determine that the higher-level
entity, the organism, is dead? We know that unless death occurs by freezing the
entire body quickly, by boiling, or some such event, biochemical reactions, and
even organ functions, can continue beyond what we consider death. In contrast, there are organisms such as nematode worms and frogs that can freeze
solid, ceasing biochemical activity, and yet are alive upon defrosting (reviewed
in Rothschild and Mancinelli, 2001). Similarly, many organisms can undergo
desiccation. Organisms that are in a state of extreme desiccation enter anhy-
drobiosis, a state characterized by little intracellular water and no metabolic
activity (Rothschild and Mancinelli, 2001). Even the loss of parts such as a limb
does not necessarily result in death. Thus, one has the suspicion that it is
impossible unambiguously to determine death in a reductionist way.

This discussion supports the philosophical view that life, and consequently
death, are emergent phenomena, not in principle reducible to a known suite
of underlying biochemical processes.

A related phenomenon, extinction, appears emergent, though this one can
be interpreted both ways. The death of individuals is expected. So are non-
reproducing members. But if all individual members of a species die without
leaving offspring, we are left with a predictable but species-level phenomenon.
In this case, extinction is not emergent. But the *cause* of extinction may be
emergent, that is, each individual has died *because it is part of a group;* in many
cases, the cause of death could not be predicted only by examining lower
levels. Thus, while the case is made in this chapter for emergence in biological
phenomena, emergence is most emphatically not universal.

Levels of selection. During the last several decades there has been an
enrichment of the traditional Darwinian view of natural selection. While

the traditional view holds that natural selection acts on the individual organism, even early Darwinians such as August Weismann and Hugo de Vries
suggested that selection could operate on other levels. More recently, Michael
Ghiselin (1974; 1987) renewed the debate by suggesting that species be
considered individuals rather than classes. Even more passionate has been
the debate by George Williams and Richard Dawkins over whether the gene
might best be considered the proper locus of natural selection (reviewed in
Gould, 2003). Thus evolutionary individuals could very well include the
individual gene, organism, deme, and species (e.g. Brosius and Gould, 1992;
Gould and Lloyd, 1999). Indeed, one could argue for even more levels, such as
the level of a tissue or subcellular organelle.

Particularly confusing are examples of partial genetic identity among
potentially separate individuals. Is a bee or an ant colony an individual,
since it represents a single genetic future? What about members of a colonial
whole, such as grass blades or hydrozoan colonies?

Each level can be thought of as an individual or, more neutrally, as an
interactor. Interactors interact with their environment, whereas *replicators*
(genetic units, per Dawkins, 1976) are said not to—which is what Gould
thought was the fallacy of gene selection (Gould, 2002). Further, the function,
appearance, and behaviour of an organism cannot be foretold based only on a
knowledge of its genes. Genes create organisms in a non-additive and non-
linear fashion; otherwise identical twins would be identical in all respects,
including thoughts and behaviour. I am particularly sympathetic to the
notion that an 'interactor' is the phenotypic manifestation of the genotype
and its environment, and is thus the level of selection that is most important
in the end. If so, this suggests that interactors—an emergent feature—are *the*
primary unit of selection.

Gould and Lloyd (1999) introduce three criteria for recognizing a Darwinian
individual:

1. It must be a biological individual with a distinct birthpoint, distinct
   deathpoint, and sufficient stability in between.
2. These individuals generate offspring, and those offspring must be more
   like them than other members of the parental generation, owing to some
   type of heredity.
3. These individuals must interact with the physical and biological environment.

Clearly, this definition leaves an opening for higher-level Darwinian individuals, such as populations or species.

At least two types of emergence can thus arise from evolution: *emergent
function* and *emergent fitness* (see Gould, 2002, for background). Emergent
function occurs when the properties of an organism—such as look, smell,

thought, and behaviour—cannot be predicted from knowing the entire gene sequence. Often we cannot predict function from lower-level analysis even if we add intervening levels such as supermolecular complexes, organelles, and the like. But can we ever? If not, is this a case of strong or weak emergence (or simply ignorance)? Similarly, emergent fitness maintains that the fitness of a species is different from the sum of its parts. For example, fitness could depend on its ecological interactions or other environmental factors, which cannot be deduced from lower levels. The dinosaurs were ultimately unfit in light of the impact of an asteroid, whereas minutes before it struck they were remarkably fit.

5. CAN EVOLUTIONARY INNOVATIONS BE CONSIDERED EMERGENT?

Evolutionary innovations are critical to evolution, since evolution requires change. Are evolutionary innovations ever (or even: always) emergent?

The preceding discussion has noted that for emergence to occur there must be hierarchy and the inability to predict a higher-level function based on its components. Evolutionary innovations may satisfy these criteria. For example, multicellularity is an innovation based on either the coming together of cells in a population, such as in the slime mould *Dictyostelium*, or a failure of progeny cells to separate, as in animals and plants. Thanks to increasingly detailed comparisons of unicellular and multicellular organisms, more prerequisites for multicellularity are now known, including cellular communication. Still, is a sponge or *Dictyostelium*—much less a whale—predictable on the basis of its cellular composition? Hardly.

Another type of evolutionary innovation is *exaptation*. Exaptation was originally defined by Gould and Vrba (1982) as occurring when a structure or function that evolved in response to one evolutionary pressure is co-opted to quite another function. Since, as François Jacob (1977) pointed out, evolution is a tinkerer, working with the raw materials that are present rather than designing future generations as an engineer would, one would expect that exaptation should be extensive. For example, feathers are thought to have originally evolved for thermoregulation but were later exapted for use in flight. Similarly, the bacterium *Deinococcus radiodurans* is superbly resistant to radiation, to levels far in excess of what would be encountered on the Earth. Current thinking is that such radiation resistance is a by-product of the evolutionary adaptation to desiccation resistance (Battista, 1997). Similarly, the human brain evolved in response to predation and an unpredictable environment. Yet today this same brain is used for a variety of functions from architecture to music. Moreover, activities such as communication and building shelters are critical to human survival, and thus evolved under obvious selection pressure, but the specific forms that they take today are exaptations.

Can exaptation be considered emergent? On the gene level, whereas the DNA sequence may be similar in the ancestral and descendent genes, the new function is not always predictable from the previous one. If it is not, emergence has occurred.

Gould and Lewontin (1979; Gould 1997) have identified another form of novelty that does not fit a strict definition of adaptation. Spandrels—named from the features in the cathedral at San Marco—are biological forms (structures or behaviours) that do not directly confer a selective advantage in a given environment, though they arise as the by-products of other forms that were under selection in that environment. Spandrels are emergent properties if we view evolutionary history as following from one adaptation to the next. If, however, we view organisms with the impartial scrutiny of an engineer, it is possible that we would recognize spandrels as completely predictable.

A more complex example than the spandrels is the carbon fixation enzyme, ribulose-1,5-bisphosphate carboxylase/oxygenase (RuBisCO). RuBisCO is the most prevalent protein in nature as it is responsible for fixing (adding) carbon to ribulose during the process of photosynthesis. Yet it is also an oxygenase, capable of adding oxygen to ribulose, which results in the breakdown of ribulose rather that the production of organic carbon. Structurally, these two antithetical functions can be explained as a simple by-product of the binding site, but from a functional point of view, the process is an exaptation of a paradoxical sort. Likewise, some enzymes are used in both DNA damage repair and sexual recombination, and one is hard-pressed to predict one function from the other. Hence, whether something is emergent or not depends on the context and the complex historical lineage associated with each locus of emergence.

6. WHAT ARE THE PRACTICAL IMPLICATIONS OF EMERGENCE FOR BIOLOGY?

There is a suspicion among biologists that the philosophy of science is irrelevant to the advancement of science. But emergence, because of its inverse relationship to reductionism, has the potential to extend beyond philosophical inquiries to a more practical application.

For biology to progress, I suggest that a third type of emergence should be recognized, in addition to strong emergence and weak emergence. We might call it *pragmatic emergence*. While the philosopher might view this as the most feeble example of emergence, pragmatic emergence could be the most useful for biology as a discipline. There are a multitude of cases where we know that a reductionist approach will lead to useful results. But sometimes this approach may be too expensive, time consuming, or otherwise infeasible. In this case, a higher-level approach, which acts *as if the characteristic were emergent*, may lead more quickly to results. For example, treating extinction as an emergent property of species, or treating chemical interactions (e.g. allelopathy) as organismal-level interactions, will lead to more rapid results.

Perhaps the most important candidate for pragmatic emergence is the study of life itself. It is possible that life is no more than the sum of its chemical reactions—a position all too familiar in biochemistry classes. Certainly on the material level it is. But progress in the biomedical sciences would slow dramatically if every question were approached solely on the biochemical level. Biology depends on treating many properties as emergent simply because today such questions are far more tractable that way. In any case, the meaning of life is completely different from the individual chemical reactions, which suggests that life can never be truly understood from only a reductionist perspective.

Another example where pragmatic emergence is indicated is consciousness. A few years ago the National Institute of Mental Health in the United States held a symposium, 'Scientific Approaches to Consciousness: Reductionism Debated', which brought together four of the leading researchers—two scientists and two philosophers—in the field of consciousness. They explored whether our sense of consciousness could ever be reduced to a set of nerve cells and chemical interactions in the brain. The participants differed in their views, but a summary of the discussion (Wein, 2000) suggests that they all agreed that the reductionist approach has made enormous progress and should be continued. Whether it will ultimately explain everything about consciousness, thereby establishing that consciousness is not an emergent property, is, in my view, unlikely.

On an even more speculative note, I would suggest that many, if not most, of the large, unanswered questions in biology remain such because they are emergent. The following list is not complete, but certainly illustrative of the exciting examples available:

- Origin of self-replication
- Origin of metabolic pathways
- Origin of life
- Origin and nature of sex
- Origin of eukaryotic cell

- Origin of multicellularity
- Levels of selection (includes extinction)
- Exaptation (e.g. origin of flight, radiation resistance, carbon fixation)
- Emergent function
- Behaviour
- Emergent fitness

Perhaps it is no surprise that such critical evolutionary innovations are potentially emergent. Lower-level building blocks are used to create something that has a new biological meaning and usage, and thus could not be predicted from a structural or mechanistic knowledge of the lower-level building blocks. For example, the biochemical pathways that go into making an organism are cast in a completely new role when placed in the context of life rather than isolated reactions. Further, organismal structure only takes on meaning, including having a level of fitness, when viewed in the context of its physical and biological environment and its history. Thus, when reductionists focus on individual components, the interactive aspects—and, more important, the system level significance of the resulting process—are missed.

In summary, I contend that the question of emergence is of great importance for modern biology. It guides us in determining whether a strict reductionist approach will suffice for solving questions of life. Biology is opaque without an understanding of interactions, feedback loops, history, statistics, and other such biologically characteristic phenomena. Even as simple a concept as density can change the nature of the biological world. Emergence is critical to the examination of the most fundamental question of biology: what is life? Although every case in biology that is treated as emergent may not be so in the strict philosophical sense, pragmatic emergence can be the most direct path to scientific enlightenment.

7. REFERENCES

Battista, J. R. (1997), 'Against all Odds: the Survival Strategies of *Deinococcus radiodurans*', *Ann. Rev. Microbiol.* 51: 203–24.

Brosius, J., and S. J. Gould (1992), 'On "Genomenclature" A Comprehensive (and respectful) Taxonomy for Pseudogenes and Other "junk DNA" ', *Proc. Natl. Acad. Sci. USA* 89: 10706–10.

Dawkins, R. (1976), *The Selfish Gene* (New York: Oxford University Press).

Ghiselin, M. T. (1974), 'A Radical Solution to the Species Problem', *Syst. Zool.*, 23: 536–44.

—— (1987), 'Species Concepts, Individuality, and Objectivity', *Biol. Philos.*, 2:127–44.

Gould, S. J. (1997), 'The Exaptive Excellence of Spandrels as a Term and Prototype', *Proc. Natl. Acad. Sci. USA* 94: 10750–5.

—— (2002), *The Structure of Evolutionary Theory* (Cambridge: Belknap Press).

—— and R. C. Lewontin (1979), 'The Spandrels of San Marco and the Panglossian Paradigm: a Critique of the Adaptationist Programme', *Proc. Royal Soc. London* B 205: 581–98.

—— and E. A. Lloyd (1999), 'Individuality and Adaptation Across Levels of Selection: How Shall we Name and Generalize the Unit of Darwinism?', *Proc. Natl. Acad. Sci. USA* 96: 11904–9.

—— and E. Vrba (1982), 'Exaptation—A Missing Term in the Science of Form', *Paleobiology* 8: 4–15.

Jacob, F. (1977), 'Evolution and Tinkering', *Science* 196, 1161–6.

Mayr, E. (1976), *Evolution and the Diversity of Life* (Cambridge: Belknap Press).

—— (1982), *The Growth of Biological Thought* (Cambridge: Belknap Press), 58–64.

Rothschild, L. J. (1994), 'Elevated CO_2: Impact on Diurnal patterns of Photosynthesis in Natural Microbial Ecosystems', *Adv. Space Res.* 14 (11): 285–9.

—— and R. L. Mancinelli (2001), 'Life in Extreme Environments', *Nature* (London) 409: 1092–1101.

Salthe, S. N. (1985), *Evolving Hierarchical Systems* (New York: Columbia University Press).

Wein, H. (2000), 'Of Chemistry and Consciousness', NIH record 6/27/2000.

7

Emergence in Social Evolution: A Great Ape Example

Barbara Smuts

1. INTRODUCTION

Arguably, human societies are a paradigmatic instance of 'strong' or 'third-order' emergence (Clayton, Ch. 1; Deacon, Ch. 5; respectively). Clearly, human groups possess properties not present in human individuals. Equally obviously, the properties of social groups influence their parts. In this case, societies exert influence on lower-level social units, such as individuals, in a top-down fashion, often called 'downward causation' by philosophers (see Murphy, Ch. 10; and Silberstein, Ch. 9). Likewise, individuals and lower-level units obviously exert bottom-up influences on higher levels in a never-ending, recursive fashion. Finally, human societies exhibit functional properties (e.g. group defence, economic exchange networks, culture, etc.) that both influence and are influenced by the goals and behaviours of individuals.

These emergent properties and downward causal influences also apply to many non-human animal societies, both in terms of how their societies work and how they evolved. In this chapter, I use the evolution of bonobo society—and specifically, how it came to develop some radical differences from chimpanzee society—to illustrate the role of emergence in social evolution. Why bonobos? Attempts to reconstruct the social evolution of any species are of necessity based mainly on the comparative method,[1] which uses comparisons of social behaviours in living species (a) to infer social behaviours of ancestral

---

[1] The only other evidence we can currently use to reconstruct social evolution is that derived from fossils, which can provide only a few hints (e.g. if fossil evidence indicates that males were much larger than females, we can assume that the mating system was not monogamous). In any case, no fossils have yet been found that would tell us what the recent common ancestor of bonobos and chimpanzees was like, and no fossils exist of chimpanzee or bonobo ancestors since these two lineages split about 2.5 million years ago.

species, and (b) to infer the processes by which the behaviour of living species came to diverge from that of their ancestors.[2] Reconstruction of bonobo social evolution involves comparisons with other great apes and, in particular, with their closest relatives, chimpanzees.

The bonobo–chimpanzee comparison is especially interesting and useful for several reasons. First, these two species are our closest-living relatives,[3] so better understanding of their societies helps shed light on human social evolution. Secondly, both species have been studied intensively in the wild and in captivity, providing abundant information for comparison. Thirdly, bonobos and chimpanzees split from their common ancestor relatively recently (about 2.5 million years ago), and they retain many features in common. Since these features were most likely also present in their common ancestor, we have a pretty good idea of what that progenitor species was like. Finally, several lines of evidence suggest that the modern-day chimpanzee social system resembles that of the common ancestor more closely than does the bonobo social system (Stanyon et al., 1986; Wrangham and Peterson, 1996; but see also Parish and de Waal, 2000, for a different view). In other words, the bonobo system appears to be more divergent. Taken together, this evidence allow us to formulate the question as follows: how did bonobos come to diverge socially from a chimpanzee-like common ancestor? The account provided here is not the last word on this subject, but it is firmly rooted in the available evidence. I hope that describing in detail one example of how social changes may have come about will serve to illustrate the kinds of emergent processes involved in primate social evolution, as well as to stimulate others to investigate how such processes might apply to other species.

Furthermore, as mentioned above, chimpanzees and bonobos are our closest living relatives. Because of this extremely close phylogenetic relationship, they have been central to scientific attempts to understand human evolution. Chimpanzees were studied intensively in the wild a couple of decades before bonobo studies began, and until recently they played a much more important role in accounts of human evolution than did bonobos.

---

[2] In recent years evidence from DNA is also often included in these comparisons. To date, such evidence has been used mainly to estimate more accurately the time at which different species diverged (i.e. last shared a common ancestor), which, in turn, produces a phylogenetic tree for a given clade, such as great apes and humans (Wildman et al., 2003).

[3] Recent work estimates that humans and chimpanzees/bonobos shared a common ancestor 4–5 million years ago (Gagneux et al., 1999). The chimpanzee–bonobo–human lineage split from the lineage leading to gorillas about 8 million years ago, which means that not only are chimpanzees and bonobos our closest living relatives, but we, not gorillas, are their closest relatives.

Chimpanzee society bears many striking similarities to that of humans: male–
male alliances are central; males are extremely status-oriented and form
hierarchical relationships; males dominate females; and males from one
community conduct what has been described as a form of primitive warfare
against neighbouring communities (Mitani et al., 2002). Thus, the nature of
chimpanzee society seemed to confirm the very deep roots—and perhaps
even the inevitability—of some of the less appealing aspects of our own social
behaviour.

But then, as research on wild bonobos grew, it became increasingly clear
that their society differs radically from that of chimpanzees. As detailed
further below, female bonobos usually dominate males, and, compared with
chimpanzee society, bonobo society is more peaceful and less hierarchical
(although by no means completely egalitarian). Furthermore, these differences appear to be the result of female political strategies. Since the two
species are equally closely related to humans, these surprising discoveries
were of great import. They suggested that very different characteristics
might have emerged in human societies if our species had taken an evolutionary path more like that of bonobos than like that of chimpanzees (Wrangham and Peterson, 1986).

The path bonobos took, and why they might have taken this path, are
explored below.

2. THE EVOLUTION OF BONOBO SOCIETY

A few million years ago, an ape resembling today's chimpanzees roamed the
forests of central Africa. Today, those forests boast two different kinds of
chimpanzees: the 'common' chimpanzee (usually shortened to 'chimpanzee')
and the bonobo.

In terms of physical traits, life histories, and social structure, the two apes
show many similarities, presumably inherited from their common ancestor.
They barely diverge physically (they look so alike that they were not distinguished as different species until the 1930s), and both species rely on ripe fruit
for the bulk of their diet. In both, individuals reach sexual maturity in their
teens, and individuals can live as long as fifty years in the wild. Adult male
chimpanzees are slightly larger than chimpanzee females, and bonobos show
similar sexual dimorphism.

Similarities also exist in social structure. Both species live in 'fission–fusion'
communities, characterized by the formation of temporary sub-groups

(termed 'parties') among individuals who share a common home range. In both species, males remain in their natal communities, but females, at adolescence, typically transfer to a new community where they will most likely remain. Neither species forms pair bonds, and typically females mate with several different males during each oestrous cycle. In neither species do males recognize or care for their own offspring, but, in both, males are very tolerant of younger community members (Goodall, 1986; Kano, 1982).

When we shift to the level of social relationships, however, we find radical differences. Among chimpanzees, all adult males have a higher status than any adult female, and males frequently threaten and attack females (Goodall, 1986). But female bonobos, unlike female chimpanzees, routinely form alliances against males (Kano, 1982; Parish, 1996; Vervaecke et al., 1999), and adult females often rank above adult males (Hohmann and Fruth, 1993; Parish and de Waal, 2000; Parish, 1996; Vervaecke et al., 2000a; Sannen et al., 2004). For example, in seven out of seven captive bonobo groups studied, female bonobos held the top-ranking position (Vervaecke et al., 2000a). Male aggression against females is rare (Kano, 1992; Hohmann and Fruth, 2003), and when a male does charge or threaten a female, she may ignore him (Vervaecke et al., 2000a) or other females will come to her defence (Kano, 1992; Vervaecke et al,. 2000b). Females usually have priority of access to the best foods (Furuichi, 1989; Kano, 1992; Parish, 1996; Hohmann and Fruth, 1993; Vervaecke et al., 2000a). Relationships in general are less aggressive and competitive among bonobos than among chimpanzees, and bonobo society is generally considered more egalitarian and less hierarchical (Kano, 1982; de Waal, 1987; Vervaecke et al., 2000a; Sannen et al., 2004; but see Hohmann and Fruth, 2003). In addition, bonobos exhibit oestrous cycles much more often than do chimpanzees, and bonobo females consequently copulate much more often than female chimpanzees (reviewed in Wrangham, 1993). In addition, female bonobos often engage in sexual interactions with each other ('genito-genital' or G-G rubbing; Kuroda, 1980; cf. de Waal, 1987; Kano, 1992), a behaviour not reported for wild female chimpanzees.

So why the seemingly radical differences in social structure? Primatologist Richard Wrangham, who has studied wild chimpanzees for over thirty years, attempted to reconstruct the process by which the societies of chimpanzees and bonobos diverged so dramatically. Although we shall never know for certain if his account is correct in every detail, it unites a diverse array of facts and, in my view, provides the best explanation we currently have for why two species that differ little physically show such striking differences in their social relationships (Wrangham, 1986; Wrangham and Peterson, 1996).

Today, chimpanzees and bonobos in central Africa are separated by the Zaire River, which neither species can cross. The forests on both sides of the river are similar, but with one key difference: chimpanzees share their habitat with gorillas, while bonobos do not. It is thought that, at some point before chimps and bonobos began to diverge, gorillas inhabited both sides of the river. Then a prolonged cold, dry spell reduced suitable gorilla habitat to a few mountaintops that retained enough moisture to sustain the young herbs and shoots so critical to their survival (Vrba, 1988). North of the Zaire River the ancestors of today's gorillas survived in these high places, later recolonizing the lowlands when the climate got wetter and the rainforests expanded. But no mountains existed south of the river and there gorillas disappeared for good, consistent with the 1,000 km gap in their distribution across central Africa. But how can the absence of gorillas possibly explain the transformation of a chimpanzee-like creature into a bonobo? Wrangham's answer is a nice example of how an unpredictable and seemingly minor change can exert effects that amplify through a system over time and at several levels, resulting in the emergence of novel patterned relationships, and, in this case, distinct species-specific behaviours (in the sense of 'weak emergence' (Clayton, Ch. 1)).

Although chimpanzees live in large groups or 'communities' that share a common, defended territory, they typically split into small parties when foraging because the fruits on which they depend usually occur in clumps too small to feed many chimps at once (reviewed in Wrangham et al., 1996). Female chimpanzees are especially likely to forage alone (with their dependent young) to avoid feeding competition from males (Wrangham and Smuts, 1980). The gorilla diet, in contrast, includes a lot of herbs and young shoots (terrestrial herbal vegetation or 'THV') that, unlike fruits, tend to be fairly abundant and evenly dispersed. This means less feeding competition in gorillas compared with chimps, allowing gorillas to live and forage in permanent groups considerably larger than typical chimpanzee foraging parties.

Wrangham hypothesizes that the disappearance of gorillas left a lot more THV for proto-bonobos to eat. Indeed, when today's bonobos deplete a fruiting grove, they travel for a while on the ground, munching on THV. This rich supplement allows them to forage in larger parties than chimpanzees, who, on the other side of the river, must compete with gorillas for THV.[4] The importance of THV in the bonobo diet is further supported by the fact that bonobo teeth have longer shearing edges than those of chimpanzees, which has been interpreted as an adaptation for eating herbs (Kinzey, 1984).

---

[4] Bonobos may also be able to forage in larger parties due to other differences between their habitat and that of chimpanzees, including larger fruiting patches (White and Wrangham, 1988) and less seasonal variation in food abundance (Malenky and Wrangham, 1994).

So, Wrangham argues, proto-bonobos began to forage in larger parties because they could afford to do so. (Larger groups can offer many benefits, including better defence against predators.) These larger parties meant that females could spend much more time together. Apparently, simply being together more often created a novel opportunity for female bonobos to band together to reduce male aggression against them and their infants. In contrast, male chimpanzees show considerable aggression against females, including sexual coercion (Goodall, 1986; Smuts and Smuts, 1992). Several chimpanzee study sites also report male killing of infants they are unlikely to have sired (Mitani et al., 2002). Male aggression against females is extremely rare in bonobos, despite the fact that males are larger, and infanticide has never been observed (see below for further details). It thus appears that female bonobos would have reaped considerable reproductive benefits from cooperating against males (Smuts and Smuts, 1993; Parish, 1993; Wrangham, 1993). If so, once larger foraging parties provided an opportunity for such alliances to occur, natural selection would likely have favoured genetic changes or social behaviours that enhanced female–female cooperation.

One of these potential genetic changes involved shifts in female sexual proclivities. In the wild, female–female sex is very common—more common than female–male sex. For example, in the Lomako forest, out of 484 genital contacts observed, 464 involved two females, 15 involved a male and female, and 2 involved two males (Hohmann and Fruth, 2000). G-G rubbing occurs in the ventro-ventral position, with one female lying on her back on a surface while the second female wraps her arms around the first, sometimes lifting part of her body off the ground. In this position, the females rub their genitals together rapidly using sideways (not up and down) movements. G-G rubbing typically includes mutual eye-gazing and apparent mutual orgasm (Kano, 1992). Female–female sex appears to enhance female–female relationships in several ways (de Waal, 1987; reviewed in Hohmann and Fruth, 2000). First, it is used to reduce tension in the context of feeding, so that females are able to feed close together and even share monopolizable resources, such as meat (Hohmann and Fruth, 1993). Secondly, when conflicts do occur among females, they often reconcile afterwards via sexual interactions. Thirdly, females appear to use sex to express status differences: lower-ranking females typically solicit sex from higher-ranking females, and higher-ranking females usually adopt the top position. Such willingness on the part of subordinates actively to acknowledge lower rank can facilitate more friendly relationships between bonobos of different ranks (de Waal, 1986).

Natural selection apparently also likely favoured genetic and behavioural changes that influenced how females responded to each other emotionally. When a young chimpanzee female joins a new community, she is very shy of well-established adult females, who are often aggressive toward her (Pusey, 1980; Nishida, 1989). By contrast, when an adolescent bonobo enters a new group she develops a 'crush' on a particular adult female, whom she assiduously courts. As their erotic friendship develops, the older female functions as a 'sponsor', easing the youngster's integration into the group (Idani, 1991).

It is likely that these initial changes were amplified over time through positive feedback loops (a major feature of Deacon's emergence theory (Ch. 5)): enhanced female–female bonds led to enhanced female–female cooperation against males, which increased the value of female–female relationships, which favoured enhanced female–female sexuality as a means of facilitating greater social tolerance among females, which in turn enhanced females' tendencies to spend time together, which then increased their ability to ally against males, which tended to promote greater female bonding and thus enhanced female–female sexuality, and so on. The reproductive benefits to individual females of these changes in social relationships would likely have influenced subsequent selection on bonobos in at least two ways: (1) as noted above, these changes would favour genetic mutations that further strengthened female–female alliances, and (2) changes in female relationships altered the way sexual selection operated on males (see below).

Obviously, stronger female alliances and female–female sexual interactions did not seriously disrupt male–female sexuality, which would have been disadvantageous for both females and males. Instead, stronger relationships among females appear to have altered how bonobos competed for mates and how they chose their mates (the two components of sexual selection). Chimpanzee males exhibit the very common male strategy of aggressive competition for high dominance rank, which translates into increased access to mates (Morin et al., 1994). In addition, because males dominate females, they can use aggression to coerce females into mating with them (Goodall, 1986; Smuts and Smuts, 1993). But among bonobos, female–female alliances prevent sexual coercion and allow females freely to determine whom they will mate with (Smuts and Smuts, 1993; Wrangham, 1993; Parish, 1993; 1996; Hohmann and Fruth, 2003). Furthermore, whereas male chimpanzees can apparently perceive the size of the female sexual swelling to identify the timing of female ovulation with a fair degree of accuracy (Deschner et al., 2004), hormonal changes among bonobos (see below) have resulted in concealed ovulation (via a de-coupling between the appearance of the sexual swelling and the timing of ovulation) (Turke, 1984; Wrangham, 1993, Reichert et al., 2002).

Enhanced female mate choice, decreased (or absent) male sexual coercion, and concealed ovulation mean that success in male–male competition is much less important to reproductive success among male bonobos compared with male chimpanzees (Wrangham, 1993; de Waal, 1997).[5] Chimpanzee male status-striving involves strong alliances with other males, and they are less interested in developing close bonds with females. Among bonobos, the reverse is true: male–male competition is less intense, male–male bonds are relatively weak, and they do not form alliances with one another (Kano, 1982; Furuichi, 1989; Vervaecke and van Elsacker, 2000). Males do, however, form strong social bonds with females (Hohmann and Fruth, 2003). In fact, a bonobo male's most important ally is his mother, because she and her female friends will often come to his aid during competition with another male. This translates into a strong maternal effect on male dominance rank (Furuichi, 1989; Ihobe, 1990; Idani, 1991; Gerloff et al., 1999). The significance of maternal power must have further reinforced the power of females in general, another factor contributing to the positive feedback loop mentioned above.[6]

Finally, in another example of emergent social effects, the attraction female bonobos have for other females and the reduction in male–male competition have apparently altered relationships between communities. Chimpanzee males patrol the boundaries of their home ranges, invade neighbouring territories, seek vulnerable individuals, and attack or even kill them (reviewed in Watts and Mitani, 2001; Wrangham, 2003; Wilson et al., 2004). In contrast, the home ranges of neighbouring bonobo communities show extensive overlap, and observers have not witnessed serious aggression between bonobo communities (Idani, 1990; Kano, 1998). When parties from different communities do meet up, males maintain their distance. Females, however, often mingle and engage in sexual encounters with both males and females from the other community (ibid.). As several primatologists have noted, where chimps make war, bonobos make love, demonstrating just how much they have changed in the 2.5 million years since they split from a common ancestor.

---

[5] Humans also evolved a kind of concealed ovulation, but its form and evolutionary context are different. Among humans, ovulation is concealed in part by the *absence* of sexual swelling, whereas among bonobos ovulation is concealed by very *extended* sexual swellings. The absence of sexual swellings is common to the lesser apes (gibbons) and to three of the great apes (orangutans, gorillas, and humans), which suggests that sexual swellings probably evolved among bonobos and chimpanzees after their ancestors split from the rest of the apes, including humans (Wrangham, 1993).

[6] De Waal (1987) suggested that changes in bonobo society began with the extension of female sexual attractiveness followed later by the evolution of female–female alliances against males. While such a scenario is possible, de Waal does not explain why natural selection would have favoured such an initial change. In fact, it seems likely, based on the chimpanzee evidence, that extended sexual attractiveness would most likely have increased female susceptibility to male aggression until female–female alliances became strong enough to prevent male attempts to control females aggressively (Wrangham, 1993).

3. UNDERSTANDING THE EMERGENCE OF BONOBO SOCIETY

In this section I discuss the importance in bonobo social evolution of: (a) multiple feedback loops (including downward causation), (b) history, (c) the emergence of novelty, and (d) individual intentions and consciousness.

i. Feedback Loops and Downward Causation

To understand bonobo society we need to take into account at least three different levels of analysis: individuals, parties, and communities. Clearly, both top-down and bottom-up causation is involved. For example, when THV increased after gorillas disappeared, party size increased because individuals came together more often and stayed together longer (a bottom-up emergent effect). Once many individual proto-bonobos consistently made such choices, new opportunities arose for female–female alliances within parties, as described above. These alliances, through the reproductive benefits they conferred upon females, in turn selected for genetic changes that further strengthened female tendencies to associate with each other, engage in friendly interactions (including sexual ones), and form alliances against males. The change in the female–male balance of power, a party-level phenomenon, also reduced the evolutionary significance of male–male relationships compared with those among chimpanzees.

In addition to the behavioural changes described above, there is evidence that the enhanced importance of female–female relationships also produced important physiological changes. For example, compared with chimpanzees, bonobo females begin showing oestrous cycles earlier in life, resume oestrous cycles after giving birth much sooner (within one year, as compared with 3–4 years), and spend a much larger proportion of each cycle with a sexual swelling. These changes translate into an enormous difference in the percentage of time that females sport a maximal sexual swelling: 48 per cent for bonobos, versus 4 per cent for chimpanzees (Wrangham, 1993). What do these differences mean? Because female bonobos copulate with males much more frequently than chimpanzee females over much greater periods of time, the chances that any given copulation will result in fertilization are much smaller, which greatly reduces the incentive for males to try to control mating access to particular females. Other physiological differences include larger sexual swellings among bonobos, a more prominent clitoris, and the forward rotation of the genital area, changes that appear to enhance the pleasure obtained during G-G rubbing (Wrangham 1993). Such changes seem to indicate a top-down causal relationship between bonobo social evolution and physiological change.

Research on testosterone (T) also shows differences between bonobos and chimpanzees. First, among chimpanzees, as well as gorillas and orang-utans, higher-ranking males show higher T, but among bonobo males, rank and T are not correlated, which is consistent with the reduced importance of male–male competition compared with these other great apes (Sannen et al., 2003; Muller and Wrangham, 2004). Secondly, whereas in chimpanzees there is no overlap between T levels in males and T levels in females, there is considerable overlap among bonobos, although on average females still have lower T than males. This convergence in T levels between the sexes occurs because male bonobos have lower T levels than male chimpanzees, not because female bonobos have higher levels (Sannen et al., 2004). Again, lower T levels in male bonobos appear to reflect the reduced importance of male–male competition. They may also function to reduce male tendencies to be aggressive toward females, facilitating male–female affiliation (Sannen et al., 2003), which positively influences female mate choice (Hohmann and Fruth, 2003). Since these various hormonal changes would provide no apparent benefits until after bonobo social relationships began to change, they provide a particularly striking example of downward causation.

Linked behavioural and physiological changes at the level of individuals in turn influenced the properties of parties of bonobos (bottom-up influences). Among chimpanzees, for example, avoiding the risks of infanticide likely contributes to female reluctance to join foraging parties (de Waal, 1997). Among proto-bonobos, once female–female alliances and concealed ovulation reduced male–male competition and increased female mate choice (as described above), infanticide by males would also decrease, for similar reasons (de Waal, 1987). This, in turn, would likely increase the willingness of mothers to join parties, further enhancing opportunities for female bonobos (especially those with young infants) to develop stronger female–female bonds.

Another example of bottom-up influences concerns the relations between communities. To explain this, I need first to describe community structure and inter-community dynamics among modern-day chimpanzees in somewhat more detail. As mentioned above, owing to feeding competition, chimpanzees tend to travel in small parties or even alone. This means that a large party of males from one community can invade their neighbour's range with a high probability of encountering very small parties or lone individuals, whom they can attack with little risk of retaliatory injuries.[7] The benefits of

---

[7] Lethal aggression between groups is extremely rare in mammals (Manson and Wrangham, 1991) but does occur in a handful of species. Wrangham (1999) has pointed out that all of these species live in social systems in which individuals travel in parties of varying sizes (including alone), which presents opportunities for large parties to attack small parties, or loners, with relative impunity.

successful inter-community competition, and the extreme costs of losing such competitive encounters, are one more reason for male chimpanzees to stick together.[8]

Among bonobos, by contrast, the consistently larger party sizes and the greatly reduced tendency to travel alone make inter-community aggression much more risky for potential attackers as well as much less likely to succeed. This shift in costs and benefits of inter-community aggression has resulted in more peaceful relations between neighbours. Most likely, these changes in community relationships were secondary, following the intra-community changes in social relationships described above. They thus represent another example of bottom-up influences. Once inter-community aggression declined, it would have further reduced the tendency for males to bond with other males, since such bonds would become less important in terms of both the offensive and defensive aspects of inter-community competition—constituting an excellent example of a positive feedback loop.

Before concluding this section, I want to emphasize that the importance of emergent processes (such as positive feedback loops and downward causation) in bonobo social evolution does not depend on whether the exact sequence of changes hypothesized here is completely correct. However bonobo society came about, it is clear that the ways in which bonobos differ from chimpanzees are (a) functionally interrelated (e.g. decreased testosterone and reduced male–male competition are correlated changes produced by the same selection pressures) and (b) causally related (e.g. differences in some variables, such as female–female alliances, altered selection pressures in ways that led to changes in other variables, such as male–male competition). In other words, given the large number of variables and the way they clearly relate to and influence each other, it can be argued that some sort of complex feedback and interrelationship among them must have occurred over evolutionary time, regardless of the precise sequence in which the changes occurred.

ii. Historical Influences

History is critical to our account of bonobo evolution in at least two ways. The first is the causal force of rare or even singular events. The story begins

[8] The benefits to males of successful attacks on males from other communities include reducing competition from neighbouring males (when those males are killed), which can eventually result in taking over part of the neighbour's home range. By attacking females and killing their infants, males decrease the growth of neighbouring communities and perhaps demonstrate to the females that their own males are unable to protect them adequately. The combination of reduced male protection and reduced home range size can induce females from the neighbouring community to transfer into that of the victors (Watts and Mitani, 2001; Wrangham, 2003; Wilson et al., 2004).

with a rare event, a radical change in climate, itself a product of complex interactions among multiple self-organizing and chaotic systems. The change in climate triggered other, one-of-a-kind events (the disappearance of gorillas south of the river and the subsequent increase in THV), which are thought to have launched the bonobo's ancestors on a new evolutionary trajectory.

History is also important in the evolution of bonobos because of how each prior state of the system simultaneously imposed constraints and opened possibilities for future states. On the one hand, once bonobo females began to form alliances that prevented male dominance, success in aggressive competition with other males no longer guaranteed a male access to fertile females and the tendency towards aggression lost much of its value, resulting in reduced male–male competition, weaker male–male bonds, and lower testosterone. On the other hand, an increase in the ability of females to choose their mates favoured those males who courted females by providing favours, such as grooming and food-sharing (Wrangham, 1993). This sort of historical contingency, or path dependence, characterizes all biological evolution because, at any point in time, newly emerging features can only arise out of what already exists—natural selection, unlike the human engineer, can't redesign a system from scratch.

Gould (1989) argued persuasively that the importance in biological evolution of both kinds of historical contingencies implies that, if we could rewind the tape of evolution and then let time move forward again, things would undoubtedly turn out very differently. Bonobo social evolution provides a case in point. Since the climatic changes that led to the disappearance of gorillas were themselves products of chaotic processes, the cold, dry spell that eliminated gorillas might well not occur in the same way or on the same scale, and hence gorillas might not disappear. Or, even if a cold spell did occur, its effects might be quite different if it happened at a different point in time, say two million years earlier or a million years later, when the plant and/or animal composition of the forests might have been quite different from how it was roughly 2.5 million years ago. Finally, even if the climatic changes and the disappearance of gorillas happened all over again, were the plant composition or fruiting pattern of the forest to be even slightly different (e.g. if fruit were scarcer or occurred in smaller patches), the increase in THV might not have made that much difference to party size. Or, even if party size increased, under slightly different conditions it might have led to stronger male–male bonds, rather than stronger female–female bonds, sending these chimpanzee-like animals on a wholly different evolutionary path. Although historical contingencies of this sort may not always be critical to social evolution, I think that most primatologists would agree that the odds of re-inventing what we know as bonobos, if we started all over again, are very slim.

iii. The Emergence of Novelty and its Role in Natural Selection

Evolutionary biologists generally regard evolution by natural selection as a blind, mechanistic process. This is true in the sense that natural selection does not guide evolution in any particular direction; it has no goal. However, this does not necessarily mean that the goals, motivations, and intentions of individuals play no role in evolution. Can we explain the evolution of bonobo society solely in terms of bottom-up mechanistic processes, such as changes in external environments that create new selection pressures that in turn produce changes in gene frequencies over time? Or do we need to invoke bonobos as active agents, or causes, in their own evolution? If so, then the evolution and functioning of at least some animal societies may involve greater similarities with human societies than is sometimes acknowledged.

In the presentation of how bonobos came to be, I discussed the relevant correlations but did not always specify the precise causal sequences. For example, I did not say whether the tendency for bonobo females to form stronger bonds with one another occurred at first because individuals changed their behaviours, or because natural selection, over long periods of time, created friendlier females. Wrangham has argued that, when the amount of THV increased after gorillas disappeared, proto-bonobos took advantage of this opportunity to form larger parties. It is important to realize, however, that individuals of another species might have responded very differently to increased THV; for example, they might have dispersed into smaller parties or even gone solo. Such dispersion is sometimes seen in species that forage on evenly distributed vegetation like THV, because animals are not forced into proximity by clumped resources. The common ancestor of chimpanzees and bonobos, however, was undoubtedly already a highly gregarious creature;[9] these apes wanted to hang out together. It would not take an evolutionary change, therefore, to alter party size. In support of this claim, chimpanzees within the same community forage in larger parties when food becomes temporarily more abundant (Wrangham et al., 1996).

Once larger parties became common, how did stronger female–female bonds come about? Again, a comparison with modern chimpanzees is informative. When a number of chimpanzee females live together in captivity, they tend to form stronger bonds with each other than they do in the wild, and they sometimes form alliances against aggressive males (de Waal, 1982).

---

[9] Since bonobos, chimpanzees, and humans are all very sociable species, the conservative assumption is that the common ancestor of all three was also sociable.

In one captive group, they even showed genito-genital contact, although it was not as intense as that among bonobos and did not appear to lead to orgasm (Anestis, 2004). These findings indicate that before the divergence of chimpanzees and bonobos, at least some females had a tendency to form stronger bonds with each other and to ally against males when circumstances permitted.[10] Because of existing evidence, we equate larger parties with an opportunity for females to increase their power relative to males. But this opportunity did not exist separate from the nature of the animals. It was the fact that individual proto-bonobos were already predisposed to recognize and act upon this opportunity that allowed a new way of life to emerge.

For Wrangham's story of bonobo evolution to be complete, therefore, we must include bonobo minds as active participants in the evolutionary process. From a traditional (reductionist) evolutionary perspective, the mind is a result of natural selection. But the mind can also be a cause of selection. This is because particular minds with particular capacities respond to circumstances in particular ways. These responses can create new behavioural and social patterns prior to any evolutionary change, and these new behavioural dispositions on the part of individuals and groups can in turn have a downward causal effect on subsequent genetic evolution.

For example, as long as female chimpanzees remain highly limited in their ability to associate with one another, any tendencies they might have to form alliances against males will manifest so rarely that whatever reproductive benefits such alliances might provide will not be exhibited often enough for natural selection to strengthen those tendencies. But once the environment changed in a way that allowed proto-bonobos to reveal their potential for female–female alliances, then any genetically based variation in female tendencies to form alliances that was previously 'hidden' (True et al., 2004) could now be subject to natural selection. This could act further to strengthen such bonds by, for instance, enhancing female–female sexuality. In the process just described, 'selection can act in such a manner as to turn an environmentally stimulated phenotype [increased female–female bonding behaviour in larger, more stable parties] into a fixed response to prevalent environmental conditions [a consistent tendency for all females to form female–female bonds]' (Pigliucci and Murren, 2003, p. 1455). This sort of process was identified long ago by C. H. Waddington (1952), who referred to it by the perhaps unfortunate term 'genetic assimilation', but only recently has it received much

---

[10] Similar tendencies toward female–female bonds are seen in wild chimpanzee communities when the habitat allows larger and more stable parties to occur (Sugiyama and Koman,1979; Boesch and Boesch-Achermann, 2000).

attention from evolutionary biologists (Behera and Nanjundiah, 2003; Pigliucci and Murren, 2003). Lest this theory be misinterpreted as non-Darwinian or Lamarckian, note that the orthodox Darwinian Richard Dawkins provides further examples (Dawkins, 2005, e.g. pp. 167, 227).

The intriguing evolutionary process described above has largely been ignored in accounts of social systems and their evolution. This is puzzling because it seems especially likely to occur during social evolution, and this for two reasons. First, social behaviour tends to be one of the most flexible aspects of the phenotype because, by definition, it involves responding to the behaviours of others, which tend to be less predictable than other aspects of the organism's environment (Humphrey, 1976). Secondly, as we have seen through the bonobo example, because of complex feedback loops within social systems, even relatively small changes in social behaviour can become amplified in ways that continue to produce novel patterns with reproductive consequences, resulting in increased opportunities for selection to occur.

iv. Individual Intentions and Consciousness

I implied above that bonobos consciously recognized new opportunities as first their diet, and then their social system, changed. Of course, minds, which are responsible for an animal's capacity to alter behaviour in changed circumstances, play an important role in social evolution whether or not they are conscious; all that is required for 'genetic assimilation' (as described above) to occur are changes in phenotypic expression (due, for example, to a change in the environment) that expose previously 'hidden' or latent genetic variation to selection.

However, when social behaviour sometimes does involve awareness,[11] as is likely in some animals (Griffin, 2001), including chimpanzees and bonobos (see de Waal, 1997, for a fascinating review), this adds still another kind of causation to an already highly complex system. Because conscious mental activity is both intentional and inventive, it can greatly expand the range of behaviours individuals can exhibit. The more aware a mind is, the more likely it will respond to a new situation with novel behaviours that can change the future of all the systems of which this mind is a part. The role of consciousness in altering human society is especially obvious to us humans, because we witness it all the time and because we keep track of our histories. But I suggest that consciousness may also play an important role in the dynamics of some

---

[11] By 'awareness' I mean the ability consciously to anticipate the consequences of their actions and to choose their actions based on that awareness (mental simulation).

non-human animal societies, on both evolutionary timescales and on shorter timescales.

Many other mammals live in social groups that contain multiple females who, in principle, could form highly effective coalitions to restrict male power. In fact, many other mammals live in social groups containing closely related females, which would seem to predispose them toward such cooperation. However, as far as we know, only bonobo females have cooperated in a way that transformed their society from male-dominated to female-dominated, and from aggressive and hierarchical to more egalitarian and peaceful.[12] Equally significant, these transformations did not depend on female kinship bonds (recall that bonobo females migrate into a group from other groups and are not therefore closely related). Is this mere chance, or might it reflect their especially highly developed cognitive capacities, including consciousness?

4. CONCLUSION

This account of bonobo social evolution highlights several important points. First, historically contingent and often chaotic events, such as climate change, can alter a species' evolutionary trajectory in ways we cannot predict. Given the effects of modern human behaviour on global climate change, we are likely soon to face many unanticipated changes in the biotic environment.

Secondly, relatively small changes, such as an increase in the size and stability of foraging parties, can become amplified through multiple recursive feedback loops (Deacon, Ch. 5) to create highly novel phenomena, such as the shift in the balance of power between female and male proto-bonobos and consequent changes in female sexuality, male reproductive strategies, and intercommunity relations.

Thirdly, both bottom-up and top-down causation are involved in these feedback loops. For example, changes in the behaviour of individual females led to alterations in party size and female–male social dynamics (bottom-up causation), and these changes in the social system in turn altered selection pressures in a way that led to genetically based changes in physiology (downward causation).

---

[12] Spotted hyena females also exhibit female–female coalitions and female dominance over males, but hyena society is highly aggressive and competitive and differs from bonobo society in other important ways (e.g. female–female alliances are based on kinship; Engh et al., 2000). However, an attempt to apply some of the ideas in this chapter to spotted hyena social evolution might prove interesting.

Fourthly, it is not always possible to reduce natural selection to the simple formula: favourable new mutations → selection → evolutionary change. As Waddington, Dawkins, and others have described, when phenotypic variation that was previously hidden reveals itself, and if this phenotypic variation is to some degree heritable, and if some variants have higher reproductive success than others, then selection can alter gene frequencies in a way that shifts the entire population toward those more successful variants. Such processes may be especially important in social evolution, because social behaviour is inherently flexible, manifesting differently in different environments.

Fifthly, minds with a degree of conscious awareness may respond to changes in their environments in different and/or more innovative ways than less conscious minds. If some of these creative responses are adaptive, then, through the process just described, they can become more fixed in the population. Individual creativity could thus influence selection, and selection, in turn, could favour increased capacities for awareness and innovation. This sort of positive feedback loop may have played a critical role in the evolution of large brains among mammals such as great apes, dolphins, elephants, and humans. In short, as consciousness and creativity increase in a species over evolutionary time, the innovative actions of individuals may play an increasingly important role in the future evolution of that species.

5. REFERENCES

Anestis, S. F. (2004), 'Female Genito-Genital Rubbing in a Group of Captive Chimpanzees', *International Journal of Primatology*, 25, 477–88.

Behera, N., and V. Nanjundiah (2004), 'Phenotypic Plasticity can Potentiate Rapid Evolutionary Change', *Journal of Theoretical Biology* 226, 177–84.

Boesch, C., and H. Boesch-Achermann (2000), *The Chimpanzees of the Tai Forest* (Oxford: Oxford University Press).

Deschner T, M. Heistermann, K. Hodges, et al. (2004), 'Female Sexual Swelling Size, Timing of Ovulation, and Male Behavior in Wild West African chimpanzees', *Hormones and Behavior* 46, 204–15.

Engh, A. L., K. Esch, L. Smale, and K. E. Holekamp (2000), 'Mechanisms of Maternal Rank "Inheritance" in the Spotted Hyaena, *Crocuta crocuta*', *Animal Behaviour* 60, 323–32.

Furuichi, T. (1989), 'Social Interactions and the Life History of Female *Pan paniscus* in Wamba, Zaire', *International journal of Primatology* 10, 173–97.

Gagneux, P., C. Wills, U. Gerloff, D. Tautz, P. A. Morin, C. Boesche, B. Fruth, G. Hohmann, O. A. Ryder, and D. S. Woodruff (1999), 'Mitochondrial Sequences Show Diverse Evolutionary Histories of African hominoids', *Proceedings National Academy of Sciences* 96, 5077–82.

Gerloff, U., B. Hartung, B. Fruth, G. Hohmann, and D. Tautz (1999), 'Intracommunity Relationships, Dispersal Pattern and Paternity Success in a Wild Living Community of Bonobos (*Pan paniscus*) Determined from DNA Analysis of Faecal Samples', *Proceedings Royal Society of London*, Series B, 266, 1189–95.

Goodall, J. (1986), *The Chimpanzees of Gombe* (Cambridge, Ma: Belknap Press).

Gould, S. J. (1989), *Wonderful Life: The Burgess Shale and the Nature of History* (New York: W. W. Norton).

Griffin, D. R. (2001), *Animal Minds: Beyond Cognition to Consciousness* (Chicago: University of Chicago Press).

Heistermann, M., U. Mohle, H. Vervaecke, L. van Elsacker, and J. K. Hodges (1996), 'Application of Urinary and Fecal Steroid Measurements for Monitoring Ovarian Function and Pregnancy in the Bonobo (*Pan paniscus*) and Evaluation of Perineal Swelling Patterns in Relation to Endocrine Events', *Biology of Reproduction* 55, 844–53.

Hohmann, G., and B. Fruth (1993), 'Field Observations on Meat Sharing Among Bonobos (*Pan paniscus*)', *Folia Primatologica* 60, 225–9.

—— (2000), 'Use and Function of Genital Contacts Among Female Bonobos', *Animal Behaviour* 60, 107–20.

—— (2003), 'Intra- and Inter-sexual Aggression by Bonobos in the Context of Mating', *Behaviour* 140, 1389–413.

—— U. Gerloff, D. Tautz, and B. Fruth (1999), 'Social Bonds and Genetic Ties: Kinship, Association and Affiliation in a Community of Bonobos (*Pan paniscus*)', *Behaviour* 136, 1219–35.

Humphrey, N. K. (1976), 'The Social Function of Intellect', in P. P. G. Bateson and R. A. Hinde (eds.), *Growing Points in Ethology* (Cambridge: Cambridge University Press).

Idani, G. (1990), 'Relations Between Unit-groups of Bonobos at Wamba: Encounters and Temporary Fusions', *African Study Monographs* 11, 153–86.

—— (1991), 'Social Relationships Between Immigrant and Resident Bonobo (*Pan paniscus*) Females at Wamba', *Folia Primatologica* 57, 83–95.

Jurke, M. H., L. R. Hagey, S. Jurke, and N. M. Czekala (2000), 'Monitoring Hormones in Urine and Feces of Captive Bonobos (*Pan paniscus*)', *Primates* 41, 311–19.

Kano, T. (1992), *The Last Ape: Pygmy Chimpanzee Behavior and Ecology* (Stanford, CA: Stanford University Press).

—— (1998), 'Comment on Stanford, C. B. 1998. "The Social Behavior of Chimpanzees and Bonobos: Empirical Evidence and Shifting Assumptions" ', *Current Anthropology* 39, 410–11.

Kinzey, W. G. (1984), 'The Dentition of the Pygmy Chimpanzee, *Pan paniscus*', in R. L. Susman (ed.), *The Pygmy Chimpanzee: Evolutionary Biology and Behavior* (New York: Plenum).

Kuroda, S. (1980), 'Social Behavior of the Pygmy Chimpanzees', *Primates* 20, 161–83.

Malenky, R. K., and R. W. Wrangham (1994), 'A Quantitative Comparison of Terrestrial Herbaceous Food Consumption by *Pan paniscus* in the Lomako Forest, Zaire, and *Pan troglodytes* in the Kibale Forest, Uganda', *American Journal of Primatology* 32, 1–12.

Manson, J., and R. W. Wrangham (1991), 'Intergroup Aggression in Chimpanzees and Humans', *Current Anthropology* 32, 369–90.

Morin, P. J., J. Wallis, J. Moore, and D. Woodruff (1994), 'Paternity Exclusion in a Community of Chimpanzees Using Hypervariable Simple Sequence Repeats', *Molecular Ecology* 3, 469–78.

Muller, M., and R. W. Wrangham (2001), 'The Reproductive Ecology of Male Hominoids', in P. Ellison (ed.), *Reproductive Ecology* (New York: Aldine).

Nishida, T. (1989), 'Social Interactions Between Resident and Immigrant Female Chimpanzees', in P. G. Heltne and L. A. Marquardt (eds.), *Understanding Chimpanzees* (Cambridge, Ma: Harvard University Press).

Parish. A. R. (1993), 'Sex and Food Control in the "Uncommon Chimpanzee": How Bonobo Females Overcome a Phylogenetic Legacy of Male Dominance', *Ethology and Sociobiology* 15, 157–79.

—— (1996), 'Female Relationships in Bonobos (*Pan paniscus*): Evidence for Bonding, Cooperation, and Female Dominance in a Male Philopatric Species', *Human Nature* 7, 61–96.

—— and F. B. M. de Waal (2000), 'How Bonobos (*Pan paniscus*) Challenge Traditional Assumptions About Females, Dominance Intra- and Intersexual Interactions, and Hominid Evolution', *Annals New York Academy of Sciences* 907, 97–113.

Pigliucci, M., and C. J. Murren (2003), 'Perspective: Genetic Assimilation and a Possible Evolutionary Paradox: Can Macroevolution Sometimes be so Fast as to Pass us by?', *Evolution* 57, 1455–64.

Pusey, A. E. (1980), 'Inbreeding Avoidance in Chimpanzees', *Animal Behaviour* 28, 543–52.

Reichert, K. E., M. Heistermann, J. K. Hodges, C. Boesch, and G. Hohmann (2002), 'What Females Tell Males About Their Reproductive Status: Are Morphological and Behavioural Cues Reliable Signals of Ovulation in Bonobos (*Pan paniscus*)?', *Ethology* 108, 583–600.

Sannen, A., L. van Elsacker, M. Heistermann, and M. Eens (2004), 'Urinary Testosterone-Metabolite Levels and Dominance Rank in Male and Female Bonobos (*Pan paniscus*)', *Primates* 45, 89–96.

—— M. Heistermann, L. van Elsacker, U. Mohle, and M. Eens (2003), 'Urinary Testosterone-Metabolite Levels in Bonobos: a Comparison with Chimpanzees in Relation to Social System', *Behaviour* 140, 683–96.

Smuts, B. B., and R. W. Smuts 2003, 'Male Aggression and Sexual Coercion of Females in Nonhuman Primates and Other Mammals: Evidence and Theoretical Implications', in P. B. Slater, J. Rosenblatt, M. Milinski, and C. Snowdon (eds.), *Advances in the Study of Behavior* 2 (New York: Academic Press).

Stanyon, R., B. Chiarelli, K. Gottlieb, and W. H. Patton (1986), 'The Phylogenetic and Taxonomic Status of *Pan paniscus*: A Chromosomal Perspective', *American Journal of Physical Anthropology* 69, 489–98.

Sugiyama, Y., and J. Koman (1979), 'Social Structure and Dynamics of Wild Chimpanzees at Bossou, Guinea,' *Primates* 20, 323–39.

True, H. L., I. Berlin, and S. L. Lindquist (2004), 'Epigenetic Regulation of Translation Reveals Hidden Genetic Variation to Produce Complex Traits', *Nature* 431, 184–7.

Turke, P. W. (1994), 'Effects of Ovulatory Concealment and Synchrony on Protohominid Mating Systems and Parental Roles', *Ethology and Sociobiology* 5, 33–44.

Vervaecke H. (2000a), 'Dominance and its Behavioral Measures in a Captive Group of Bonobos (*Pan paniscus*)', *International Journal of Primatology* 21, 47–68.

—— (2000b), 'Function and Distribution of Coalitions in Captive Bonobos (*Pan paniscus*)', *Primates* 41, 249–65.

—— and L. van Elsacker (2000), 'Sexual Competition in a Group of Captive Bonobos (*Pan paniscus*)', *Primates* 41, 109–15.

—— H. De Vries, and L. van Elsacker (1999), 'An Experimental Evaluation of the Consistency of Competitive Ability and Agonistic Dominance in Different Social Contexts in Captive Bonobos', *Behaviour* 136, 423–42.

Vrba, E. S. (1988) 'Late Pliocene Climatic Events and Hominid Evolution', in F. E. Grine (ed.), *Evolutionary History of the Robust Australopithecines* (New York: Aldine).

de Waal, F. B. M. (1982), *Chimpanzee Politics: Power and Sex among the Apes* (New York: Harper and Row).

—— (1986), 'Integration of dominance and social bonding in primates', *Quarterly Review of Biology* 61, 459–79.

—— (1987), 'Tension regulation and nonreproductive functions of sex among captive bonobos (*Pan paniscus*)', *National Geographic Research* 3, 318–35.

—— (1997), *Bonobo, the Forgotten Ape* (Berkeley: University of California Press).

Waddington, C. H. (1952), 'Selection of the Genetic Basis for an Acquired Character', *Nature* 169, 278.

Watts, D. P., and J. Mitani (2001), 'Boundary Patrols and Intergroup Encounters Among Wild Chimpanzees', *Behaviour* 138, 299–327.

White, F. J., and R. W. Wrangham (1988), 'Feeding Competition and Patch Size in the Chimpanzee Species *Pan paniscus and Pan troglodytes*,' *Behaviour* 105, 148–64.

Wildman, D. E., M. Uddin, G. Liu, L. I. Grossman, and M. Goodman (2003), 'Implications of Natural Selection in shaping 99.4% Nonsynonymous DNA Identity Between Humans and Chimpanzees: Enlarging genus *Homo*', *Proceedings National Academy of Sciences* 100, 7181–8.

Wilson, M. L., W. R. Wallauer, and A. E. Pusey (2004), 'New Cases of Intergroup Violence Among Chimpanzees in Gombe National Park, Tanzania', *International Journal of Primatology* 25, 523–49.

Wrangham, R. W. (1993), 'The Evolution of Sexuality in Chimpanzees and Bonobos', *Human Nature* 4, 47–79.

—— (1999), 'The Evolution of Coalitionary Killing,' *Yearbook of Physical Anthropology* 42, 1–30.

—— C. A. Chapman, A. P. Clark and G. Isabirye-Basuta (1996), 'Social Ecology of Kanyawara Chimpanzees: Implications for Understanding the Costs of Great Ape Groups', in W. C. McGrew, L. F. Marchant and T. Nishida (eds.), *Great Ape Societies* (Cambridge: Cambridge University Press).

—— and D. Peterson (1996), *Demonic Males: Apes and the Origins of Human Violence* (Boston: Houghton Mifflin).

—— and B. B. Smuts (1980), 'Sex Differences in the Behavioural Ecology of Chimpanzees in Gombe National Park, Tanzania', *Journal of Reproduction and Fertility*, Supplement 28, 13–31.

—— and R. W. Wrangham (2003), 'Intergroup Relations in Chimpanzees', *Annual Review of Anthropology* 32, 363–92.

Part III

Consciousness and Emergence

8

Being Realistic about Emergence

Jaegwon Kim

1. INTRODUCTION

The idea of emergence, if not the term, goes back to the Greeks; the distinction between emergent properties of a composite thing and those that are merely 'resultant' (to use later terminology), which is the heart of any concept of emergence, was clearly present in Galen (129–c. 199), as seen in the following passage from *On the Elements According to Hippocrates* (Caston, 1997, Appendix):

Consider the first elements. Even though these substrata are unable to perceive, a body capable of perceiving can at some point come into being, because they are able to act on each other and be affected in various ways in many successive alterations.

For anything constituted out of many things will be the same sort of things the constituents happen to be, should they continue to be such throughout; it will not acquire any novel characteristic from outside, one that did not also belong to the constituents. But if the constituents were altered, transformed, and changed in the manifold ways, something of a different type could belong to the composite that did not belong to its first elements.

Galen is saying that a composite object made up of simpler constituents, when these constituents enter into special complex relationships ('act on each other and be affected in various ways'), can come to exhibit a novel property ('something of a different type') not possessed by its constituents. That of course is the central insight that gave rise to the doctrine of emergent properties and has sustained it over the years.

The concept of emergence as we now know it, and the terms 'emergent' and 'emergence' in something like their present meanings, come from the mid- to late nineteenth century, in works of thinkers like John Stuart Mill and

Henry Lewes.[1] But it was during the first half of the twentieth century that the idea received more intensive attention and elaboration, and 'emergentism' as a set of doctrines concerning the existence and characteristics of emergent properties was formulated. The best-known emergentists were British—Samuel Alexander, C. Lloyd Morgan, and C. D. Broad—but there was also a substantial American presence in the emergentist debates during this period, involving philosophers like Roy Wood Sellars, A. O. Lovejoy, and Stephen C. Pepper. During the mid-twentieth century, when philosophy in the English-language world was dominated by anti-metaphysical movements like logical positivism and various schools of linguistic analysis, emergentism was often trivialized if not ridiculed, and was largely ignored in mainstream philosophy.

Ignored but not forgotten. It seems that there is something inherently natural and appealing in the concept of emergence which has kept it alive through the long period of neglect and disdain, and since the early 1990s there have been strong and visible signs of a revival. Symposia and conferences have been held on emergence and emergentism, and books, anthologies, and special issues of journals on the topic have been published. Especially noteworthy is the fact that the emergence concept has had a special appeal to many practicing scientists. Morgan, an early leader of emergentism, was a comparative zoologist, and Roger W. Sperry, the noted neurophysiologist and Nobel laureate in medicine (1981), was a passionate and prolific advocate of the emergence concept from the 1960s to the end of his life (1994). This trend has continued to this day.[2] Apparently, the hope of these scientists—this clearly was the case with Sperry—is that the concept of emergence will be a productive scientific tool for formulating significant theoretical claims and doctrines about certain scientific domains. For them, the assertion that a given phenomenon, say consciousness, is an emergent phenomenon, or that consciousness emerges from neural processes, is to say something significant and illuminating about consciousness and its relation to neurobiological processes. That is, the claim that phenomenon X is emergent from phenomenon Y is to say something explanatory about the status of X and the relation between X and Y.

But can this hope be realized? Can the concept of emergence, more or less in the form in which it is now understood, be harnessed into useful service, philosophical or scientific? What are the prospects that the concept can be refined, enriched, or reconstructed in a way that would enable it to fulfil the promise some see in it? In this chapter I want to explore these questions in a

[1] John Stuart Mill (1843); George Henry Lewes (1875). It was Lewes who introduced the term 'emergent' to designate those properties of a whole that cannot be deduced from the properties of its parts.

[2] See, for example, Harold J. Morowitz (2002).

preliminary way. I should say up front that what I am going to say will by and large be deflationary if not negative, and I have more questions than I have answers. Lately the emergence concept has, it seems, created a kind of bandwagon effect, engendering high enthusiasms and expectations. What is needed at this point, I believe, is a healthy dose of realism; I think it is important to be realistic about the prospects of the emergence concept. What are the chances that it will turn out to be the kind of magical philosophical or scientific tool that some of its more ardent friends expect it to be, something that will, for example, help us solve the 'mystery' of consciousness? Will emergence enable us to formulate an answer to the question T. H. Huxley raised in 1890, namely how it is that 'anything so remarkable as a state of consciousness comes about as a result of irritating nervous tissue'? Perhaps. I believe, though, that a sober and realistic attitude is what is needed at this point if we are to make meaningful progress in this area.

2. EMERGENCE AND SUPERVENIENCE

Before we can decide whether there really are emergent properties or phenomena, or whether any specific phenomenon, such as consciousness or life, is an instance of emergence, we need a serviceably clear concept of emergence. In spite of the burgeoning literature on emergence (or perhaps because of it), there is little consensus on the exact content of the emergence concept, and it is impossible to escape the impression that the only thing that the proliferating uses of the term 'emergence' have in common may well be the word itself, with its ordinary dictionary meaning—something that isn't fit to bear the theoretical burdens placed on it. This isn't to say that emergence has to be a univocal concept, or that to be useful a concept must be made absolutely precise. It is to ask for a concept that is clear enough and robust enough for the purposes on hand. To make some headway in this direction, it will be useful to begin with a helpful recent survey and analysis by Robert Van Gulick (2001). He distinguishes among three grades of emergence: (1) 'specific value emergence'; (2) 'modest kind emergence'; and (3) 'radical kind emergence'. The first, specific value emergence, is a pretty tame affair exemplified in a situation like this: a whole, say a lump of bronze, has a mass of 1 kilogram whereas none of its parts has this mass. So this is an example in which a whole has a property that none of its parts have. To use philosophical jargon, both the whole and its parts have the same *determinable* property (i.e. mass, or having a mass) but the whole has a *determinate* property under that determinable—that is, a 'specific value' of mass—that none of its constituent parts has. This clearly is not a case of emergent property in which anyone would, or should, be interested.

The second, modest kind emergence, is more promising: 'The whole has features that are different in kind from those of its parts...For example, a piece of cloth might be purple in hue even though none of the molecules that make up its surface could be said to be purple. Or a mouse might be alive even if none of its parts (or at least none of its subcellular parts) were alive' (Van Gulick, 2001, p. 17). The examples offered are of the sort that have traditionally been claimed as emergent properties. What Van Gulick doesn't say here is just in what sense the purple colour of a cloth 'emerges' from the properties of the molecules that constitute the cloth. As characterized, too many properties would count as emergent: this object on my desk has the property of being a ballpoint pen, although none of its parts are ballpoint pens; the brick I am holding is hefty although none of its molecular parts are hefty, and so on. But before going further with this issue, let us look at what Van Gulick says about the third and strongest kind of emergence.

This is 'radical kind emergence' defined as follows: '1. [the emergent property in this sense is] different in kind from those had by its parts, and 2. [it is] of a kind whose nature and existence is not necessitated by the features of its parts, their mode of combination and the law-like regularities governing the features of its parts' (Van Gulick, 2001, p. 17). The second condition, which is what distinguishes it from its weaker sibling, modest kind emergence, amounts to the requirement that an emergent property of a whole not be determined by the properties and relations characterizing its parts; that is, an emergent property of this third kind does not 'supervene' on the microstructure of an object. This has the following consequence: two wholes that have identical lower-level properties and structure (say, they are composed of identical basic physical constituents configured in identical structural relationships) may yet differ in respect of the higher, emergent property. For example, two molecule-for-molecule identical systems may be such that one of them is a live mouse and the other is not, if being a live mouse is emergent in the sense of 'radical kind' emergence. Van Gulick is uncertain whether there are actual cases of radical kind emergence, saying that accepting it would violate 'atomistic physicalism'. However, the real problem with this form of emergence is not atomism or the issue whether any actual cases of emergence fall under it. Rather, the difficulty is whether it is a form of emergence at all. For one thing, classic emergentists accepted microphysical supervenience of emergent properties. C. D. Broad, who held that many properties of chemical compounds are emergent (relative to molecular properties and structure), wrote (Broad, 1925, p. 64): 'No doubt the properties of silver chloride are completely determined by those of silver and of chlorine; in the sense that whenever you have a whole composed of these two elements in certain proportions and relations you have something with the characteristic properties of silver chloride.' Suppose that on a given occasion a mental phenomenon, say pain, emerges from a certain configuration of neural conditions. I doubt that there are serious emergentists who would deny that if the very same configuration of physiological conditions were to recur, the same mental phenomenon would emerge again. If the connection between pain and a neural condition is irregular, haphazard, or coincidental, and not to be relied upon, what reason could there be for saying that pain 'emerges' from that neural condition rather than another? If pain is observed not to occur when the same neural condition is present, emergentists would, I believe, conclude that the real 'basal' condition of pain has not yet been found. If so, what could be the meaning of 'emergence' in Van Gulick's 'radical kind emergence'?

It is clear then that we must consider supervenience as a component of emergence:

[Condition of supervenience] If property M emerges from properties $N_1, \ldots, N_n$, then M supervenes on $N_1, \ldots, N_n$.

Let me give a brief definition of supervenience: to say that M supervenes on $N_1, \ldots, N_n$ is to say that any system that has the base properties $N_1, \ldots, N_n$ will necessarily have the supervenient property M; or, as Van Gulick says, the Ns necessitate M. It is important to see that this is only a claim of determination or necessitation of one property by a set of properties, and that it says nothing about how M can be *derived* or *deduced* from the Ns, or about how the fact that something has M can be *explained* on the basis of the fact that it has the Ns. The relation of determination does not in itself give us a relation of derivability or explainability; for all we know, the determinative relation is a 'brute' fact that cannot be further explained. (This is exactly what the classic emergentists claimed about emergent properties in relation to their basal conditions—Samuel Alexander urged us to accept emergence relationships with 'natural piety'.)

Supervenience, though necessary, is not sufficient for emergence. The surface area of a sphere supervenes on its volume, but it does not emerge from it; the mass of a physical object supervenes on the masses of its parts but does not emerge from them, except in the trivial sense of 'specific value' emergence. In contrast, at least according to most advocates of emergence, mentality both supervenes on and emerges from physical/biological conditions; likewise for biological properties in relation to physicochemical properties. What then must be added to supervenience to yield emergence?

3. MODELS OF REDUCTION

The standard approach, from the very inception of the emergence concept in the modern period, is to invoke concepts like reduction, explanation, prediction, and derivation. The basic idea is that if M emerges from $N_1, \ldots, N_2$, then although M supervenes on the Ns, M is not *reducible* to, *explainable* in terms of, *predictable* on the basis of, or *derivable from*, the Ns. That is, all of the following relationships fail between M and the Ns when emergence holds: reducibility, explainability, predictability, and derivability. I have elsewhere given a detailed unified account of these ideas in terms of a model of reduction that is known as 'functional reduction'.[3] Here I will present a brief summary.

The classic model of reduction that has long served as the backdrop of the debates in this area was developed by Ernest Nagel in the 1950s.[4] According to this model, the essential enablers of reduction are the so-called 'bridge laws', connecting higher-level phenomena to be reduced with phenomena at the reduction base. If our object is a reduction of a theory about conscious sensory experiences to neurophysiology, we shall need bridge laws connecting the various kinds of sensory experiences with their underlying neural substrates, such as:

> pain occurs to an organism at t if and only if neural state N_1 occurs to it at t;
> visual experience of yellow occurs to an organism at t if and only if neural state N_2 occurs to it at t;

and so on. On Nagel's model, a reduction of the theory of sensory experiences would be accomplished if the laws about these phenomena were logically derived from the laws of physiology taken together with these psychoneural bridge laws as auxiliary premises. Well-known traditional antireductionist arguments, notably the so-called multiple realization argument, are based on the claim that the required bridge laws are not available. However, bridge laws are not the problem; even if bridge laws as standardly conceived were available, that would not give us the reduction we want. The trouble is that these bridge laws are contingent empirical laws connecting the properties at the two levels, and it is easy to see that such empirical correlations do not suffice to generate reductive linkages. Here is the reason: when we want to reduce, say, pain to N_1, visual experience of yellow to N_2, and so on, we want to know what it is about N_1 that is responsible for giving rise to pain, what it is about

---

[3] See, e.g. Kim (1998).
[4] The most comprehensive statement is found in Nagel (1961).

N_2 that explains why a visual experience of yellow emerges from it, and so on. Why doesn't a sensation of itch arise from N_1? Why doesn't a visual experience of purple accompany N_2? Why does any conscious experience arise when states like N_1 and N_2 occur? That is to say, what we need is an explanation of the bridge laws themselves. In a serious reduction, therefore, the bridge laws ought to be the explananda. This shows that what is really wrong with Nagelian reduction is that it makes use of bridge laws as premises of reductive derivations, whereas they ought to be the conclusions of such derivations.

Functional reduction does not require Nagelian bridge laws; instead, it relies on the 'functionalization' of the properties to be reduced in terms of properties at the reduction base. Suppose pain can be given a 'functional definition' in terms of physical/physiological input and behavioural output, perhaps thus:

> To be in pain $=_{def.}$ to be in a state that is typically caused by tissue damage and trauma and that typically causes aversive behaviour.

This definition connects pain semantically/conceptually with physical/ behavioural properties. Reduction of pain is accomplished when we are able to identify a 'realizer' of pain so conceived, namely a physical state that fits the functional definition. So suppose neurophysiological research has identified N_1 (say, the activation of a group of neurons in certain cortical areas) as the state that is typically caused by tissue damage and which in turn triggers aversive behaviour. When we have such a neural state for the population of interest to us, say humans or mammals, we have a neural reduction of pain for this population.

One fact to notice is this: a neural reduction of pain does not require a logical derivability of pain from a neural state, or any logical or conceptual connection between pain and its neural reduction base N_1. Looking for such connections between mental phenomena and brain processes would be futile. What we should keep in mind is the fact that in the mind–body problem three players are on the scene, not two; they are pain (and other mental states), the brain, and behaviour. Reduction requires conceptual connections, but these connections connect pain with behaviour, not with the brain. Brain phenomena enter the picture as the realizers of the functionally conceived mental phenomena. It is important to notice that the fact that N_1 is a realizer of pain (for a given group of organisms), or that the brain is the realizer of mentality, is an empirical and contingent fact. What is not contingent is the relation between pain and pain behaviour. I am of course not saying that pain can be reduced this way; what I am saying is that if pain is to be reduced to a brain process, this is what must happen: pain must first be given a functional definition or interpretation and then we must identify its neural realizers.

The first step involves conceptual work: Is the concept of pain functionally definable or interpretable and, if so, how should a functional definition of pain be formulated? The second step, that of discovering the realizers of pain, involves empirical scientific research. It is in effect the research project of finding the neural correlates of conscious experiences. From a philosophical point of view, the crucial question, therefore, is whether pain can be given a functional characterization, in terms of physical input and behavioural output; the rest is up to science. Philosophical functionalism, still the orthodoxy on the mind–body problem, holds that pain, along with other mental phenomena, can be functionalized; if philosophical functionalism is correct, all mental phenomena would be functionally reducible.

I am with those who do not believe pain and other sensory states can be given functional characterizations (Chalmers, 1996). However, this does not change the fact that functionalizability is crucial to reduction and reducibility, and hence to understanding emergence (as we shall shortly see). Conscious experience, or anything else for that matter, is reducible if and only if it is functionally reducible, and it is functionally reducible if and only if it is functionally definable or interpretable.

We can quickly see that functional reduction as defined here is the appropriate concept of reduction for the purposes of defining and clarifying emergence. If pain, say, has been functionally reduced with neural state N_1 identified as its realizer for a given population, this guarantees the following:

(1) Occurrences of pain can be predicted on the basis of knowledge concerning neural and behavioural processes alone (including laws concerning these processes). That is, if M is functionally reduced, the occurrence of M can be predicted exclusively on the basis of information concerning events and processes at the lower reduction base.
(2) Similarly, why an organism has pain at a time can be explained on the basis of information concerning neural and behavioural phenomena. In general, if M is functionally reduced, we can explain why M is instantiated on a given occasion on the basis of knowledge concerning the phenomena at the base level alone.

How might such predictions and explanations be formulated? Consider the following derivation:

System s is in neural state N_1 at t.

N_1 is a neural state such that tissue damage in s and systems like s causes them to go into N_1, and N_1 causes these systems to emit aversive behaviour.

By definition, a system is in pain iff it is in some state P such that P is caused by tissue damage and P in turn causes aversive behaviour.

Therefore, s is in pain at t.

The derivation clearly is valid, and we may take it as a reductive explanation of why *s* is in pain at *t* in terms of *s*'s being in neural state N_1 at *t*. Moreover, this shows that the statement that *s* is in pain can be derived from statements about *s*'s neural-physical states—statements that do not refer to *s*'s pain or other mental states. Note that the third statement in the derivation, though the term 'pain' occurs in it, is a definition, and definitions are free in derivations; they do not count as premisses. If this definition is about anything, it is about the concept of pain, or the meaning of 'pain'; for this reason its use is consistent with the condition that no factual information about pains be used in deriving the conclusion. Thus, the derivation shows that if pain is functionally reducible, with its neural realizer identified for a population of systems of interest to us, we can predict the occurrence of pain solely on the basis of neural and behavioural information about these systems (*plus* facts about the meanings of terms like 'pain'). More generally, the emergentist's question, 'Would complete knowledge of the neurophysiology of an organism suffice for deriving knowledge about the organism's consciousness?' could be answered affirmatively if mentality has been functionally reduced.

This shows that functional reduction gives a unified account of the emergentist idea that an emergent property is irreducible to the basal phenomena and neither explainable nor predictable in terms of them. Moreover, a functional reduction of pain has the following causal and ontological implications:

(3) Each occurrence of pain has the causal powers of its neural realizer; thus if pain occurs by being realized by N_1, this occurrence of pain has the causal powers of N_1. In fact, the pain can be identified with this instance of N_1. In general, if M occurs by being realized by N, the M-instance has the causal powers of the N-instance. Further, the M-instance can be identified with the N-instance.

At this point then our characterization of 'emergent' property looks like this:

[Emergence] Property M is emergent from properties $N_1, \ldots, N_n$ *only if* (1) M supervenes on $N_1, \ldots, N_n$, and (2) M is not functionally reducible with $N_1, \ldots, N_n$ as its realizers.

Thus, supervenience and irreducibility in the sense explained are two necessary conditions of emergence. Are they together sufficient for it? That is, can the connective 'only if' in [Emergence] be upgraded to 'if and only if', thereby making it a complete definition? I believe that the two clauses of [Emergence] capture the concept as it was introduced and intended by the classical emergentists like Samuel Alexander, Lloyd Morgan, and C. D. Broad. When we consider recent proposals concerning emergent properties in complex systems, in terms of such ideas as chaos, nonlinear dynamics, the necessity of simulation (rather than computation), and so forth, we should examine them to see whether they fit the classic conception of emergence encapsulated in [Emergence]. Of course, to judge that one or another of these new proposals does not fit the classic conception does not in itself show that it is not an interesting and potentially fruitful concept. But [Emergence] can serve as a useful benchmark; any deviation from it is a deviation from the classic conception, and new proposals can be analysed and compared with one another in terms of how far, and in what ways, they deviate from [Emergence] as a reference point.

4. DIFFICULTIES WITH THE EMERGENCE CONCEPT

Let me now turn to a couple of problematic aspects of the classic conception of emergence. The first concerns the so-called downward causation—the idea that emergent properties can exert their causal influence 'downward' to affect the processes at the lower basal level. Mental causation—in particular, mind-to-body causation—is a special case of downward causation. Moreover, there is a more general question concerning the causal efficacy of higher-level properties conceived as emergent. Secondly, I want to raise some reasons for thinking that emergence as characterized fails to give us a sufficiently rich and robust concept.

There is no question that emergentists should want downward causation. Emergent properties must do some serious causal work, and this includes their capacity for projecting causal influence downward, affecting the course of events at a purely physicochemical level. Causally impotent properties are explanatorily useless, and there would be little point in positing them or acknowledging their existence in scientific theory. British emergentists like Samuel Alexander and C. Lloyd Morgan thought of emergent properties as active causal agents in the process of cosmic evolution, in producing increasingly richer and more variegated phenomena—from molecules and atoms to life, from life to mind, and so on. Equally clearly, many contemporary advocates of emergence, for example, Roger Sperry, want emergent properties to play a significant explanatory role in scientific theory. Causally inert, epiphenomenal properties obviously are not able to fulfil such roles.

The problem of mental causation has been much discussed in the philosophy of mind during the past three decades. Straightforward reductionism, which identifies mental events with physical events, can give a simple explanation of mental causation. On reductionism, mental events are just a subclass of physical events, and there is no special problem about their causal efficacy. And the clause (3) above states that this indeed is the case under functional reduction. However, physical reducibility in this sense—or in any serious sense—is exactly what emergent properties by definition lack. In combining irreducibility with supervenience, emergent properties are very much like the way mental properties are conceived by advocates of non-reductive physicalism. The difficulties that non-reductive physicalists face with mental causation are well known; in fact, much of the debate over mental causation has been on the question whether there is a way the non-reductivists could overcome these difficulties and vindicate the reality of mental causation.

This is not the place to go into the details of the issues and arguments that have received intense attention in the discussions of mental causation;[5] however, I would like to give an idea of the difficulties that confront anyone who wants causal efficacy for emergent properties. Suppose a claim is made to the effect that an emergent property, M, is a cause of another emergent property, M* (this is short for saying that *an instance* of M causes *an instance of* M*). As an emergent property, M* is instantiated on this occasion because, and only because, its basal condition, call it P*, is present on this occasion. It is clear that if M is to cause M*, then it must cause P*. The only way to cause an emergent property is to bring about an appropriate basal condition; there is no other way. So the M—M* causation implies a downward causal relation, M to P*. But M itself is an emergent property and its presence on this occasion is due to the presence of its basal condition, call it P. When one considers this picture, one sees that P has an excellent claim to be a cause of P*, displacing M as a cause of P*. The deep problem for emergent causal powers arises from the closed character of the physical domain, which can be stated as follows:

> [Causal/Explanatory Closure of the Physical Domain] If a physical event has a cause, it has a physical cause. And if a physical event has an explanation, it has a physical explanation.

Arguably, this principle is presupposed by most working scientists, including of course physicists: if they encounter a physical event for which they are not able to identify a physical cause or explanation, it is highly unlikely that they will consider positing a non-physical causal agent to explain it. Such a move will not only be extremely unusual but it is unlikely to be helpful in framing a testable explanatory and predictive theory. To deny this principle would in effect

---

[5] For details see Kim (1998); Walter and Heckman (2003).

amount to denying the in-principle completability of theoretical physics; that is, it would be equivalent to the assertion that an ideally complete physical theory will not be able to give an account of all physical phenomena (let alone all phenomena), and that to explain some physical phenomena, physical theory must resort to non-physical causal agents.[6] If you are an emergentist, you must make your position clear on this issue of physical causal/explanatory closure; that is, you must either provide sufficient and compelling reasons for rejecting the closure principle or else show that downward causal efficacy of irreducible emergent properties is consistent with physical causal closure.

The second problem I have in mind concerns the question whether emergence as understood in [Emergence] is a genuine relation with explanatory force and metaphysical significance. I have elsewhere argued that supervenience, as it is standardly understood (as it is here), does not represent a unitary relation of metaphysical or explanatory interest and significance. Supervenience can obtain for all sorts of reasons. Consider normative supervenience, that is, the supervenience of normative/evaluative properties on factual/descriptive properties. Why does normative supervenience obtain? Different ethical theorists will give different explanations: (1) normative properties are definable in terms of descriptive properties; (2) there are directly intuitable necessary connections between the two; (3) certain constraints of consistency and rationality regulating normative judgements generate supervenience; and so on. A similarly divergent range of explanations has been offered for mind–body supervenience: (1) mental phenomena are caused by physical phenomena; (2) mental properties are definable in terms of behavioural/physical properties; (3) mind and body are simply two aspects of some deeper reality that is neither mental nor physical in itself; and, of course, (4) the mental emerges from the physical. Since supervenience is consistent with all of these relations, it cannot in itself be a single homogeneous relation. Supervenience simply states an interesting pattern of co-variation between two sets of properties, the normative and the non-normative, the mental and the physical, and so on.

Now consider [Emergence] again. What is added to supervenience to get emergence is irreducibility—the *absence* of a reductive relation. Supervenience, for the reason just stated, cannot make emergence a real, unitary relation. What does irreducibility add that could help? I believe the answer is not much. Reducibility between two domains of properties may well be a real relation; if we know that a domain is reducible to another, we know something interesting and significant about the relationship between them.

---

[6] Moreover, the closure principle is arguably entailed by certain conservation laws of physics, e.g. the law of conservation of energy. See Papineau (2001).

But this does not mean that the negation, or denial, of reducibility is also a unitary and homogeneous relation. Consider properties: being red is a property, and things that are red have something interesting in common. But we cannot say the same of the property of being non-red (if indeed there is such a property). Some non-red things are green, others yellow, still others have no colour; further, numbers, molecules, and black holes are all non-red. Non-red objects do not form a *kind* in the way red objects do. Normally, when K is a kind, or a homogeneous property, non-K is not a kind. I believe relations show a similar characteristic (though perhaps not to the same extent): R may be a significant, homogenous relation but not-R may not be. Being a brother-of is a real and significant relation, but not being a brother-of clearly is not (I am not a brother of George Bush; my computer is not a brother of my car; etc.). Consider irreducibility: shapes are not reducible to colours, and colours are not reducible to shapes. Facts about a country's economy are not reducible to the country's geological facts, nor vice versa. Facts about a person's intelligence are not reducible to facts about his/her kidneys, nor vice versa. Suppose mental facts are not reducible to physical facts, as the emergentist says. Do all these and other possible instances of irreducibility have anything significant in common? Is there a common explanation of the irreducibility for all these cases?

The problem is that the irreducibility component of [Emergence] only gives a *negative* characterization of emergence. It tells us what emergence is not, but it is silent on what it is. What we need is a *positive* characterization in terms of some robust and unitary relation R such that (1) R holds for property families F_1 and F_2 just in case F_1 is emergent, in our pre-analytic sense, from F_2, and (2) the fact that R holds for F_1 and F_2 entails that F_1 is irreducible to F_2. If such an R also entails supervenience of F_1 on F_2, so much the better; but supervenience can always be added as a separate condition. I believe this issue should be the first item on the emergentist agenda.

To conclude, then, there are two challenges for the friends of emergence. The first is to show that emergent properties do not succumb to the threat of epiphenomenalism, and that emergent phenomena can have causal powers vis-à-vis physical phenomena. This must be done without violating the causal/explanatory closure of the physical domain—or, if the physical causal closure is to be given up, a credible explanation and rationale must be offered. The second challenge is to give a positive characterization of emergence that goes beyond [Emergence]—that is, beyond supervenience and irreducibility. Unless this is done, the thesis that minds emerge from bodies remains uninteresting and without much content; we need a positive account of how minds are related to bodies. Saying that they are not reducible to bodies says little about their relationship.

5. REFERENCES

Broad, C. D. (1925), *The Mind and Its Place in Nature* (London: Routledge and Kegan Paul).

Caston, Victor (1997), 'Epiphenomenalisms, Ancient and Modern', *Philosophical Review* 106: 309–63.

Chalmers, David (1996), *The Conscious Mind* (Oxford: Oxford University Press).

Kim, Jaegwon (1998), *Mind in a Physical World* (Cambridge, MA.: MIT Press).

Lewes, George Henry (1875), *Problems of Life and Mind*, vol. 2 (London: Kegan Paul, Trench, Turbner and Co.).

Mill, John Stuart (1943), *A System of Logic*, 8th edn. (London: Longmans, Green, Reader, and Dyer).

Morowitz, Harold J. (2002), *The Emergence of Everything* (New York: Oxford University Press).

Nagel, Ernest (1961), *The Structure of Science* (New York: Harcourt, Brace, and World).

Papineau, David (2001), 'The Rise of Physicalism', in Carl Gillett and Barry Loewer (eds.), *Physicalism and Its Discontents* (Cambridge: Cambridge University Press).

Van Gulick, Robert (2001), 'Reduction, Emergence and Other Recent Options on the Mind–Body Problem: A Philosophic Overview', *Journal of Consciousness Studies* 8, No. 9–10: 1–34.

Walter, Sven, and Heinz-Dieter Heckman (eds.) (2003), *Physicalism and Mental Causation* (Thoverton, UK: Imprint Academic, 2003).

9

In Defence of Ontological Emergence and Mental Causation

Michael Silberstein

> For the contemporary physicalist, I believe there are two problems that truly make the mind–body problem a weltknoten, an intractable and perhaps ultimately insoluble puzzle. These problems concern mental causation and consciousness. The problem of mental causation is to answer this question: How can the mind exert its causal powers in a world that is fundamentally material? The second problem, that of consciousness, is to answer the following question: How can there be such a thing as mind, or consciousness, in a material world? The two problems are interconnected—the two knots are intertwined, and this makes it all the more difficult to unsnarl either of them. (Kim, 2001, p. 271)

Section 1 of this chapter will characterize the kind of emergence I wish to defend and situate it largely in the enactive paradigm of consciousness and cognition. In Section 2 I begin to cast doubt on physicalism and related doctrines in philosophy of mind that would tell against ontological emergence. In the process it will become clear that ontological emergence cum enactivism is philosophically sound and potentially scientifically explanatory.

1. ONTOLOGICAL EMERGENCE CHARACTERIZED

Mental properties, systems, and so on, are ontologically emergent in the following respects:

Mental properties (both phenomenological and intentional) confer causal capacities on the systems that possess them which they would not otherwise have. That is, zombie-me (i.e. a version of me that lacks intentional states)—even if such a being is possible under one or another construal of possibility—does not possess all my causal capacities. The causal capacities of mental properties are not reducible to either the intrinsic or relational physical properties underlying them. Mental properties are therefore irreducibly relational or, if you like, irreducibly dispositional.

Mental properties *qua* mental are causally efficacious with respect to physical or neurochemical properties; such causation is not 'downward' causation, however, but what I call *systemic causation*. It is not downward causation because ontological emergence rejects the layered model of reality as divided into a discrete hierarchy of levels. The universe is not ordered as a hierarchy of closed autonomous levels such as atoms, molecules, cells, and the like. Rather, the universe is intrinsically nested and entangled. The so-called physical, chemical, biological, mental, and social domains of existence are in fact mutually embedded and inextricably interconnected. That is, mental properties are not on a higher level than neurochemical properties, the former are not on a higher level than chemical properties, and so on. It is best to view the world as divided into systems and subsystems, not levels—and even then, such divisions are often not 'carved at the joints' but are nominal and relative to various formalisms and explanatory schemas (see Kitcher, 2002, pp. 459 ff. for more details). As is well known in biology, for example, even in simple cases any attempt to characterize genetic, molecular, immune, neurochemical, or psychological systems will cut across many entangled 'levels' (as they are generally conceived) and will also involve inherently diachronic and environment-wide processes (see Silberstein, 2002). Ontological emergence *does* violate causal closure of the physical (the principle that physics studies a closed causal system), but, as we shall see, that is no reason for concern.

Mental properties, like other properties, can be both diachronic and synchronic in nature, depending on the various details of mental phenomena, including the pragmatic explanatory context. For example, the determining capacities of mental properties need not be exclusively causal, if there are in fact non-causal determination relations in which mental properties could be involved. Note also that there might be non-causal determination relations that are *diachronic* and not synchronic like realization. Such determination might be best described as a kind of systemic holism or self-organization. For example, explanations and characterizations of mental capacities in dynamical systems accounts are inherently diachronic but they are not inherently causally mechanical; or, more specifically, such accounts are not necessarily causal in the sense of efficient causation, but, as discussed below, employ other concepts such as causation-as-constraint.

Mental properties are not intrinsic or categorical properties of brain states. Mental properties are not fully determined (in any sense of determination) by the neurochemical properties of 'underlying' brain states. Mental properties are not identical with, realized by, or constituted by brain states. Mental properties are not even fully nomologically determined by fundamental physical properties and laws. Rather, mental properties are 'wide' and 'external'; they are possessed by systems that are distributed over space-time. Such systems include interactions and inextricable interconnections between mind–brain, the body, and both the physical and social environment. Brain states are physically necessary but not sufficient conditions for the existence of the various mental states that they causally and non-causally support. The full analysis of mental systems requires reference to their evolutionary and historical context as well, indicating the historical dimension of mental properties. Thus ontological emergence rejects both ontological and methodological individualism.

It does not follow from any of this that mental properties are not, in some common-sense way, spatially or physically located 'in the head'. *The question of determination and the question of spatial location are logically distinct.* Nevertheless, as we shall see, mental properties are *not* in the head in the highly specific and technical way intended by the computational theory of mind (CTM) and the representational theory of mind (RTM).

Note as well that this is all consistent with global supervenience, the principle that two worlds that are microphysically identical will be or must be identical in all other macroscopic respects. The reason for the compatibility is that global supervenience can be made true (if it is true) by a number of different metaphysical doctrines, including not just physicalism but also parallelism and various forms of British emergentism, such as that espoused by C. D. Broad. However, given ontological emergence, *if* global supervenience obtains, it is not explained by the determination of everything by fundamental local and intrinsic physical properties, their relations, and the laws that govern them but by some wide, relational, systemic, and diachronic brand of supervenience. The point is that even radical holism is consistent with global supervenience.

Mental properties emerge because one of the capacities of emergent systems is to help generate new emergent systems. That is, systemic causation involves the creation of stable diachronic patterns (systems distributed over space and time) in which the stability and integrity of such patterns is maintained across constant changes in the micro-base of such systems and often even across changes in the macro-environment in which the system is embedded. Explaining such larger-scale systemic causation requires going beyond efficient causation to more self-organization-based notions of causation in terms of order parameters, global or non-local systemic constraints, causal topologies, entrainment, collective effects, configurational degrees of freedom, and even teleological causation more akin to Aristotle's formal and final causes (Silberstein, 1999; Bishop, forthcoming). In this way, emergent chemical and molecular systems beget emergent biological systems, which in turn allows for emergent mental systems. Again, the chemical, biological, and mental are not autonomous levels of reality but inextricably entangled webs with many scales and complex feedback and feed-forward mechanisms involved that are 'guided' by formal and final causes. As we go to larger and larger scales of reality we find more and more robust kinds of teleological (goal-directed) and systemic causation at work (Deacon, 1997; Deacon 2003; Weber, 2003; Bishop, forthcoming).

Mental properties are fundamental properties in the sense that they have irreducible causal capacities and therefore cannot be identified with underlying physical properties, but they are not fundamental in the sense that (if you will) God needed them as fundamental ingredients to bring about a world with mental phenomena. God no more needed phenomenological-intentional properties as basic ingredients to evolve phenomenological-intentional systems than he needed the properties of life as basic ingredients to evolve living systems, for biological systems are ontologically emergent as well. Phenomenal-intentional states are not 'ingredients' within the world. Rather, ontological emergence is a brand of monism which holds that mental properties are grounded in and *emerge from* underlying physical and environmental processes that achieve a certain type or degree of complexity. By 'complexity' I mean biological, functional, teleological, and computational complexity. Quantifying and characterizing complexity, mapping its effects, and so on, is an important step in the future of both developmental biology and cognitive science.

Again, ontological emergence holds that it is not only mental systems, properties, and processes that are ontologically emergent but also some physical, chemical, and biological ones as well. Ontological emergence is therefore not a kind of dualism but a monism that rejects naive essentialism: mental properties or processes are biological, physical, functional, phenomenological, *and* intentional in nature. In the context of ontological emergence we see that metaphysical monism and ontological pluralism are truly compatible. Ontological emergence seeks to eliminate the a priori and merely philosophical question, *what is the mental?*, and replace it with the question, *how do phenomenological-intentional systems arise and what are their causal capacities?* As we shall see, an answer to the former question is often a dodge to answering the latter one.

Mental properties, while not identifiable with non-mental properties, are not in principle brute and inexplicable facts (contra Broad, Chalmers, and others). It is just that the explanation for mental systems cannot be one of identity or of synchronic determination, as in theories of realization or philosophical accounts of intertheoretic reduction. Obviously, ontological emergence also rejects the neural correlates of consciousness (NCC) approach, which explains consciousness as neural correlates (whether viewed diachron-ically or synchronically), which are regarded as a minimally sufficient condition for the conscious state that they underlie. On my view neural correlates are at best necessary but not sufficient conditions for the ment-al states they support. Obviously underlying brain states are an essential element in explaining mental processes, ontological emergence rejects any kind of 'no-brainer' mentality. Ontological emergence embraces explanatory pluralism; various non-reductive causal, nomological, dynamical, or even unifying explanations of mental processes are hoped for and expected.

I see no a priori reason to assign a higher authority to one form of explan-ation over another as this is a matter to be resolved empirically. When it comes to scientific explanation, ontological emergence embraces pragmatic explanatory pluralism and thus rejects exclusivist approaches to explanation. This is pretty much a logical consequence of giving up ontological and methodological individualism. Given that the arrow of determination in ontological emergence is 'side-to-side' (diachronic, entangled, and wide) and not 'bottom-up', so too is the arrow of explanation. The way we divide the world into systems and subsystems is often a matter of pragmatic and perspectival considerations. This is not to invoke a limitless or willy-nilly ontological or explanatory holism; rather, all things being equal, there is a good reason, when it comes to manipulating or intervening in an individual's mental states, for us to start with the brain and not, say, the pancreas. There is no reason why there cannot be more than one type of scientific explanation for the mental or any other phenomena. And there is no a priori reason why one type of explanation must be more fundamental than all the others. Recall that various phenomenological and intentional properties are held to emerge under various kinds and degrees of complexity (for lack of a better word). It is the job of the sciences (both natural and social) to discover exactly what the conditions are (e.g. causal, nomological, dynamical, etc.) from which various mental phenomena emerge. My bet is that explaining many mental capacities will in principle require multiple scientific disciplines ranging from develop-mental biology and neuroscience on one end to cognitive psychology and sociology on the other.

If all of this 'ontological emergence talk' strikes you as just a devilishly evasive way to talk about brute facts parading as explanation, then chances are that you—like most physicalists, dualists, and emergentists—are presuppos-ing exactly what ontological emergence is denying, namely, that all facts in this world are either axioms or theorems, no exceptions. Most people find the very idea of features of the world that are neither fundamental nor follow logically or nomologically from those that are fundamental to be an incoherent proposition. Hence most people are dubious of emergence: the idea that there is real middle ground between identity theories and dualism. If these people are correct, then any non-reductive explanations in science can be nothing more than function of ignorance type explanations, such as the use of classical probability theory to predict the outcomes of dice rolls.

However ontological emergence holds that many complex systems such as cognitive processes are not brute facts, nor do they follow logically or nomologically from fundamental physical facts. According to ontological emergence the arrows of determination and explanation are in principle not strictly bottom-up or even top-down, but rather, in addition, they are (if you will) side-to-side. That is, ontological emergence advocates for an irreducibly contextual and relational ontology and explanatory framework as opposed to the idea that the universe is structured as an axiomatic system with laws of a 'necessitarian' type at bottom 'governing' everything. Making this idea of contextual emergence do scientific work is the goal here. As will be shown in greater detail in the next section, *non-reductive* and inherently contextual explanations of mind are also possible.[1]

The Enactive (Embodied plus Embedded) Paradigm of Consciousness and Cognition

The philosophical view of the mental that I have been characterizing, ontological emergence, can best be placed within the scientific paradigm of consciousness and cognition known as the enactive approach (for more details see Thompson, 2007; Silberstein, 2001; Thompson and Varela, 2001; Varela et. al., 1991; and Hurley, 1998). What follows is my synthesis of the main claims of this tradition as filtered by ontological emergence.

Consciousness and cognition are emerging processes arising from self-organizing networks that tightly interconnect brain, body, and environment at multiple scales. The enactive approach, then, is best situated within the dynamical systems school of cognition and mentality, according to which mental properties emerge as the result of interacting, self-organizing, dynamical systems. Such self-organizing networks are however not merely 'in the head'; numerous mutual interactions between brain and body exist at biochemical scales, for instance in the molecular components of the endocrine,

---

[1] For a more global argument that philosophy of mind is often naive about scientific explanation generally and that mind is not alone as an ontologically and explanatorily emergent phenomena see Silberstein (2001 and 2002). When it comes to theories of scientific explanation, philosophy of mind is often still operating with antiquated accounts, such as the D-N model of explanation (and its variants), which the philosophy of science has long since abandoned.

immune, and nervous systems. The integrity of the entire organism depends on such regulatory cycles involving brain and body at multiple levels. Mental processes are 'constituted' not simply by neural processes in the head, but by the way these processes are integrated into the whole organism's cycles of operation, including physical and social features of the environment as well as its own evolutionary and developmental history. Mental processes (affective, phenomenal, cognitive, etc.), both conscious and unconscious, loop through the physical, social, and cultural environments in which the body is embedded. Cognitive and mental processes are not disembodied mental representations in the head but emerge from the dynamic sensorimotor processes of the entire organism as it is embedded in its physical, evolutionary, and social environment. Cognitive capacities in symbol-using beings such as ourselves are not primarily internal; they are enactive bodily capacities that involve our relations with the world. Cognition and mental states are inherently dynamical, as they involve constant and continuous feedback between perception and action.

Thus it makes no sense to think of brain, body, and environment as internally or externally located with respect to one another. Instead, they are mutually embedding and embedded systems, tightly interconnected on multiple levels. The enactive approach then rejects the picture of mind and cognition shared by RTM, CTM, and connectionism, according to which:

(a) the *external* world provides the input.
(b) the mind–brain engages in *intrinsic, internal,* and *representation*-based cognitive (information) processing either via rules that govern representations, as in RTM, or via neural network patterns of activation that encode various representations, as in connectionism. It is probably best to view connectionism as a halfway house between RTM and the enactive approach.
(c) the output is the behaviour produced as the result of such internal cognitive processing.

In the RTM model that I am rejecting, the relationship between the mind and world is one in which the former abstractly represents the latter via symbols of some sort. In contrast, the enactive approach holds that consciousness and cognition inherently involve embodied action in the world and encompass the complex of mind–brain, body, and environment. These three are connected by means of 'structural couplings' and various other mutual and direct interdependencies.

The external world and the agent's action in that world are an integral part of any scientific explanation of memory, perception, and other cognitive processes. This is a dynamic sensorimotor view of mind which maintains that perception and action *constitute* one another rather than the former being the means to the end of the latter. Consciousness is not an 'interior state' of the brain/body which is caused by events in the outside world and in turn causes behaviour. It is probably best to view mental states as *modes* of these wider processes.

In psychology mental properties, functions, modules, models, and so on, are and must be relationally individuated and cannot be fully explicated in terms of the neural-mechanisms underlying them. Again, the enactive approach rejects both ontological and methodological individualism. This is to say that the enactive approach rejects the following:

(a) the idea that mental states should be taxonomized in the effort to show that they supervene on the properties of states of individuals that are intrinsic to them;
(b) the idea that only such intrinsic properties or states can be causally efficacious;
(c) the idea that the external world or environment is merely secondary to mind and cognition while the internal cognitive processes are where the real action takes place.

The enactive account of mind is a species of 'externalism', though with significant amendments. Externalism has come to mean so many things in the philosophy of mind that multiple qualifications are in order. Content externalism does not necessarily deny that mental states are (in some sense) in the head—just as content internalism does not really deny that what is outside the head plays a major causal role in what goes on inside the head. Both agree that the environment has a substantial causal influence on the content or semantics of mental states. Content externalism goes further, however, and claims that two individuals x and y who share exactly duplicate intrinsic brain states but very different environments—such as me and a 'me' who is actually just a brain in a vat being fed neurological inputs by a supercomputer ('vat-me' for short)—would nonetheless have different mental contents, even though x and y are in exactly the same phenomenological state. Both content internalism and content externalism agree that intrinsic neurochemical properties determine phenomenal experience; thus, if x and y are in exactly the same brain state, then x and y will be having exactly the same experiences.

What content internalism and externalism disagree about is what ultimately *metaphysically* determines the semantic content of intentional psychological states. The latter claims that it is the external environment, while the former holds it is the intrinsic properties of the individual. Notice that both sides essentially agree on the RTM/CTM picture of cognition. They both agree that there is no problem carving off the external environment from the internal and intrinsic states in the head, and they both agree that neurochemical properties are intrinsic features of individuals that determine phenomenal experience. Content externalism only rejects individualism about mental *content*, nothing else.

Now we can fully appreciate the radical kind of externalism that the enactive approach embodies. The latter rejects individualism outright and all the other individualistic suppositions of RTM/CTM. Thus, for the purposes of cognition and consciousness, any distinction between what is in the head (the individual) and the environment is arbitrary at worst and pragmatic at best. The enactive paradigm holds that individuals and their social and physical environment constitute a single complex cognitive system. Nor will the enactive approach grant a hard and fast distinction between mental content or intentionality on the one hand and phenomenological experience on the other. Intentionality and phenomenology are by necessity much more unified in this picture of the mental. From the enactive perspective, the debate about what *metaphysically* fixes the content of propositional attitudes is simply deflated because the individualism of CTM and RTM are wholly rejected.

According to enactivists, the problem with thought experiments involving devices such as 'vat-me' is that they presuppose a falsity, namely, that there are such things as intrinsic mental properties or brain states. The enactive paradigm simply denies that vat-me would be having any coherent experiences at all, because brain states *in the actual world* are only necessary conditions of such experiences and not sufficient. Experience and cognition are inherently embodied and embedded, and vat-me is neither. Thinking and experience require embodied action in the world according to the enactive model. In the actual world the mind–brain–body–nervous-system acquires the states it has as a result of its evolutionary and social history, embodiedness, environmental context, and so on.

Defenders of RTM and CTM, of both the content externalism and internalism varieties, think it absurd to say that vat-me would not be having coherent experiences because these two theories of mind, with their reductive individualism and *internal* abstract representations mediating experiences of the external world, suggest that in many ways we are all brains-in-a-vat! That is exactly what ontological individualism implies. The vat-me thought experiment presupposes that *in principle* a supercomputer manipulating my vat-brain neurons could be causally and functionally equivalent to the environmental, evolutionary, historical, and social forces that actually shape my mental and neurophysical states. This claim is either a non sequitur or simply false from the enactive perspective.

If you find the enactive hypothesis about vat-me absurd as well, then chances are that you are tacitly operating with a representational or computational picture of the mind (RTM or CTM). However, this picture of the mind, which implies that we are all brains-in-a-vat of a sort, bears a rather weighty and weird ontological burden regarding the nature of mental states and their relationship to brain states. According to RTM and CTM, for every possible human experience there exists one (or more) brain state(s) that is sufficient to produce that experience. The ultimate goal of neuroscience then is to generate a huge database of mental state–brain state mappings for the human brain. The enactive approach finds such an idea absurd because it presupposes that the brain is like a 'NATO-standardized' universal Turing machine rather than the contingent, extremely plastic, embedded and embodied dynamical process we know it to be. Brain states and their functional capacities are not best seen as possible universal configurations of (static) neural activation patterns; rather, there are many other features of the brain—such as those which are contextual, dynamical, geometrical, topological, and so on—that play a key role as well.

The enactive approach agrees with ontological individualism that there can be no difference in a person's mental state without some physical difference; yet the enactive approach includes the environmental and historical context, and not just brain states, in the set of the 'physical' states of affairs that can change—that is, the enactive view gives the 'individualist principle' a 'wide' environmental interpretation. The enactive approach agrees with functionalism that the relationship between brain states and mental states is many–one (so-called multiple realizability), but the enactive approach also holds that, conversely, the relationship between mental states and brain states is many–one. The very same brain state narrowly defined can be correlated with different mental states given different contexts.

The emergence of mental processes through collective self-organization is characterized by reciprocal (or two-way) large-scale to small-scale determination, which includes scales involving the environmental context as well as the various scales involved in mind–brain dynamics. Novel systems, mechanisms, and processes emerge as the result of all of these scales. To use my previous language, the enactive approach implies systemic causation, multiple directions for the arrows of determination in general, and thus multiple directions for the arrows of explanations. Thus the enactive paradigm embraces explanatory pluralism. For example, unlike many accounts of cognition such as RTM, connectionism, and the like, the enactive approach often touts the fact that much of human cognition is inherently social as well as biological. This is a fact that cognitive science is just now beginning fully to appreciate via approaches such as ecological theory and social cognition. The social embeddedness of human cognition means that social features of an individual's life will help determine some of his or her psychological and neurochemical properties, not just the other way around. The enactive approach, especially the social version of it described above, is a form of externalism to be sure, but it is not an extreme form of externalism such as behaviourism, eliminativism, or radical anti-nativism. Both the extremes of 'black-boxing' what is in the head, as behaviourists do, and black-boxing what is in the environment, as ontological individualists do, should be avoided when it comes to cognition and the mind.

Ironically, the enactive paradigm has given rise to two very different conceptions of the mental. On the deflationary end there are those who seem to think that the enactive approach supports a kind of eliminativism about self, phenomenal states, and perhaps other mental phenomena that are traditionally conceived as being 'in the head'. The reasoning is, loosely, that just as self-organization and other mechanisms of evolution have done away with any need for a designer to explain biological diversity, so also have they done away with the need for any such 'in the head' in order to explain human behaviour or experience. The argument goes roughly as follows:

(a) There is no central module in the brain that brings everything together prior to action; no Cartesian Theatre where all the sensory information is gathered, processed, and brought to bear on behaviour; no choreographer; or the like. Hence there is nothing that corresponds to a self or executive decision-maker inside the head. When we examine the brain, what we find are multiple processing streams and special-purpose, action-oriented 'representations'—just lots of subsystems doing their own thing without any centralized supervision. As Dennett puts it:

> On my first trip to London many years ago I found myself looking for the nearest Underground station. I noticed a stairway in the sidewalk labeled 'Subway', which in my version of English meant subway train, so I confidently descended the stairs and marched forth looking for the trains. After wandering around in various corridors ... [i]t finally dawned on me that a subway in London is just a way of crossing the street underground. Searching for the self can be somewhat like that. You enter the brain through the eye, march up the optic nerve, round and round in the cortex, looking behind every neuron, and then, before you know it, you emerge into daylight on the spike of a motor nerve impulse, scratching your head and wondering where the self is. (1989, p. 1)

Therefore,

(b) the best interpretation of the enactive approach is an extreme kind of externalism that black-boxes the mental *qua* mental. Dennett holds that the study of self-organizing systems in biology, neuroscience, and artificial intelligence tells us that complex systems can in fact function in what seems to be a thoroughly 'purpose-ful and integrated' way simply by having lots of subsystems doing their own thing without any central supervision. Indeed most systems on earth that appear to have central controllers (and are usefully described as having them) do not. The behaviour of a termite colony provides a wonderful example of it. The colony as a whole builds elaborate mounds, gets to know its territory, organises foraging expeditions, sends out raiding parties against other colonies, and so on. . . . Yet, in fact, all this group wisdom results from nothing other than myriads of individual termites, specialised as different castes, going about their individual business—influenced by each other, but quite uninfluenced by any master-plan (1989, p. 1)

The KISMET project (successor to COG) at MIT and the rhetoric often surrounding it best exemplifies the deflationary interpretation of the enactive approach: given enough modules, and given enough time to interact with the environment, through various self-organizing processes cognitively complex creatures such as humans will emerge. Thus there is no need to posit a robust self, centralized processing, generalized intelligence, phenomenal states, or representations inside the head, because there are only multiple subsystems and their interactions.

The move here is simply to abandon any hope of directly solving the various binding problems (such as pertain to perception, decision, action, etc.). The most extreme expressions of this view sound very much like behaviourism or full-blown eliminativism because we are invited to conclude that, on the enactive view, cognition and mind are all dynamical relations and no relata. The key word for the deflationary interpretation is 'illusion' (see Blackmore, 2004). The self and the phenomenal are illusions as far as this approach is concerned. On the other end of the enactive spectrum are theorists such as myself (2001) who are inclined to think of 'construction' or 'emergence' instead of illusion. For example, instead of claiming that self is an illusion, why not say that cognitive beings are autonomous agents whose selfhood or identity emerges from (or is constructed from) self-organizing patterns of inter-dependent interactions with the (physical and cultural) environment in which they are embedded. It is one thing to say that mental states and dynamics are inherently *relational* and quite another to say that they are wholly *illusory* or empty. The one does not obviously follow from the other. For those of us on the constructive end of the spectrum the enactive paradigm is a theory of emergence and not deflation. I hasten to point out that the difference between these two interpretations of the enactive approach is not merely semantic.

The constructivist interpretation holds that new processes, properties, and systems such as those we designate 'self', 'phenomenal experiences', and so on, really do come into being and are best characterized in terms of ontolog-ical emergence. To say that the self, phenomenological environments, and so on are neither 'in the head' nor located in the 'external world' noumenally designated is not to deny the reality or causal role of such things. Conversely, the deflationist interpretation sees the enactive approach as a way of maintaining that nothing really new emerges; there are just a number of subsystems 'doing their own thing', creating the illusion of something new. Of course, if the deflationists merely want to eliminate highly technical philosophical entities and bugaboos such as Cartesian qualia, the Cartesian ego-self, Cartesian representations, and 'concepts' in the sense of RTM, then the deflationists and constructivists are in agreement. However, the constructivists go on to emphasize that there are other more 'commonsense' notions of self, phenomenal experience, representations and the like best seen in terms of ontological emergence and that the enactive approach is best viewed as a paradigm of such *contextual* emergence.

Take the various binding problems, for example. If one takes phenomenal-intentional processes seriously as ontologically emergent phenomena, then there need not be a central processor in the brain to explain self-governing behaviour; to think otherwise is to commit the 'fallacy of misplaced concreteness' (*à la* Whitehead). Barring some argument to the contrary, the same fallacy is committed when we assume that there must be some obvious isomorphism between neuroanatomy or brain structures on the one hand and mental content or functions on the other (see Noë and Thompson, 2004). Taken seriously, ontologically emergent phenomenal-intentional consciousness might be part of the solution to the binding problem(s) and not just the problem itself; and given ontological emergence this is possible even if there is no central processing module in the brain.

However, if it is the concrete you crave, then cognitive neuroscience now strongly suggests that specific cognitive acts (for instance, the visual recognition of a face) require the transient integration of numerous, widely distributed, constantly interacting, functional brain areas. While more evidence is certainly needed, there is good reason to believe that there are large-scale dynamical patterns of activity at work in the brain. Many neuroscientists and psychologists now believe that conscious mental processes result from a cooperative process in a highly distributed network, rather than from any single brain structure or process. Hence any hypothesis about the neural basis of cognitive acts, including especially conscious cognitive acts, must account for the integrated, coherent operation of large-scale brain activity. We are talking here about long-range phase-locking neural synchrony between widely separated regions of the brain that would allow for such cognitive integration. This conception of consciousness and cognition is generally cashed out in terms of two hypotheses about the brain basis of cognitive acts and conscious mental states: the neural assembly hypothesis and the phase synchrony hypothesis (see Silberstein, 2001; Thompson and Varela, 2001).

As we have seen, one can find such subtler explanations within the dynamical systems approach. The dynamical systems approach rejects the classic view that the firing neuron is the basic brain unit. What motivates this approach? Allow me to quote at length:

The impetus for adopting a dynamical systems perspective in the brain sciences comes from several quarters. First, it is clear that information in the brain is transmitted by far more than action potentials and neurotransmitters. Hormones and neuropeptides impart data through the extracellular fluid more or less continuously in a process known as 'volume transmission.' What is important is that these additional ways of communicating among cells in the central nervous system mean that simple (or even complicated) linear or feedforward models are likely to be inaccurate. The model of the brain as a serial processing computer ignores much important computation and communication in the head. Discovering the importance of global communication in the brain has led some to conclude that it is better to see our brain as a system that works together as a complex interactive whole for which any sort of reduction to lower levels of description means a loss of telling data. Moreover, neurons respond differently when signals arrive simultaneously than when they arrive merely close together. This electrical oscillation affects how the neuron can respond to other inputs. And small changes in the frequency of oscillation (caused by changing the input signals ever so slightly) can produce large changes in a neuron's output pattern. (Hardcastle, 1999, pp. 78–82)

Again, many researchers these days agree that coherent neural activity (in some form or another) is the mechanism by which, in part, the brain supports consciousness (Revonsuo, 2001). In general, such a mechanism will involve synchronous neural activity at high frequencies. Some researchers emphasize complex electrophysiological activity in thalamocortical loops and subcortical circuits, realized by synchronous neural firing 'scanning' the cortex with high frequencies; or synchronous oscillatory activity in the cortex (ibid., p. 6). Others emphasize large-scale, complex electrophysiological or bioelectrical activity patterns involving millions of neurons and billions of synapses. Such large-scale patterns or neural networks would be spatially distributed in the brain. Such patterns (e.g. synchronous oscillations or some other mechanism) would be coherent or unified but would nonetheless change constantly and very rapidly (ibid., p. 7).

The general point is that there may be more subtle dynamical and less mechanistic 'causal mechanisms' in the brain, such as large-scale neural synchrony, that are responsible for binding. Giving an enactive explanation in terms of self-organization certainly implies the absence of a designer, homunculus, or vital force, but it need not preclude ontologically emergent large-scale brain dynamics, or even a phenomenal self that is ontologically emergent and systemically and teleologically causal. Indeed, many of us have argued that ontological emergence is sometimes the best way to view self-organizing phenomena (see Silberstein, 1999; Bishop, forthcoming). Such patterns can be highly distributed, diachronic, irreducibly relational and as causally significant as anything else in the world. Given the enactive view it is also possible that the solution to the various binding problems involves the environment as well as the brain.

2. IN DEFENCE OF ONTOLOGICAL EMERGENCE AGAINST ARMCHAIR PHYSICALISM

If physicalism (PHY), the completeness of physics (CoP), and the causal inheritance principle (CIP) are true then ontological emergence is false. While there is not space to address these claims in great detail, this section will begin to cast doubt on the empirical support for such claims as well as their explanatory value. Let us begin with some standard definitions:

(CoP) All physical events are determined, in so far as they are determined, by prior physical events and the physical laws that govern them. For any physical event e, if e has a cause at time t, then e has a wholly physical sufficient cause at t.

(PHY) All individuals are constituted by, or identical to, microphysical individuals, and all properties are realized by, or identical to, microphysical properties.

(CIP): If mental property M is instantiated on a given occasion by being realized by a basal property P, then the causal powers of this instance M are identical with, or determined by, the causal powers of P.

Kim has been reminding us for years that to give up CoP is to abandon physicalism and/or naturalism as standardly conceived (e.g. Kim, 1998). He has also rightly pointed out that, for those of us defending the causal efficacy of the mental *qua* mental, abandoning physicalism so characterized is a perfectly happy consequence of rejecting CoP. The following passage suggests that physicalists have become a little more sophisticated in their thinking about CoP:

I assumed that the completeness premise was quite uncontentious. Surely, I thought, everybody agrees that the movements of matter, such as the movements of molecules in your arm, can in principle always be fully accounted for in terms of prior physical causes, such as physical activity in your nerves, which in turn is due to physical activity in your brain ... and so on. To my surprise, I discovered that some people didn't agree ... My first response, when presented with this thought, was to attribute it to an insufficient education in the physical sciences. ... However, when they then asked me, not unreasonably, to show them where the completeness of physics is written down in the physics textbooks, I found myself somewhat embarrassed.... I realized that the completeness of physics is by no means self-evident. Indeed further reading has led me to realize, far from being self-evident, it is an issue on which post-Galilean scientific tradition has changed its mind several times. (Papineau, 2001, pp. 13–14)

Ontological emergence and systemic causation are an outright rejection of CoP, PHY and CIP because:

(1) The causal capacities of mental properties are not reducible to either the intrinsic or relational physical properties that 'underlie' them, contra CIP.
(2) Mental properties are not synchronically realized by, composed of, determined by, etc. narrow or intrinsic physical realizer properties; therefore they are irreducibly relational or dispositional in nature, contra CoP.
(3) Mental properties are inherently diachronic and dynamical in that they result from both causal and non-causal (holistic) diachronic processes, and their determining influence is diachronic; for example, they form links in topologically complex causal chains.
(4) Systemic causation means admitting types of causation that go beyond efficient causation to include causation as global constraints, teleological causation akin to Aristotle's final and formal causes, and the like.

The realization relation that figures in PHY is a non-causal *synchronic* determination relation that is supposed to be a superior cousin to the supervenience relation for a variety of reasons. Presumably, unlike the supervenience relation, which is a purely a priori metaphysical invention, the realization relation is scientifically or empirically respectable. Kim and others have noted that global supervenience, strong supervenience, and so on are metaphysically underdetermined relations, such that their truth is compatible with a number of ontological doctrines that are at odds with physicalism, including British emergence, parallelism, and pre-established harmony (Kim, 1993). While there is much less metaphysical underdetermination involved with the realization relation, it is still present; see Melnyk (2003), Gillett (2003), and Shoemaker (2001) for three metaphysically somewhat distinct accounts of the relation. To put the point more strongly, the realization relation is a hodge podge also. The realization relation is supposed to provide an answer to the question, why does strong or global supervenience hold? At the very least, any account of the realization relation had better rule out answers to that question that include or allow for British emergence (i.e. fundamental psycho-physical bridge-laws), dualism, parallelism, and so on. However, nothing stops us from asking: *in virtue of what* does the realization relation hold? Part of the point here is that PHY does not provide a homogeneous determination relation or a single type of scientific explanation, and thus we must look at claims for PHY and CIP in science on a case by case basis.

One problem we immediately encounter is that, outside computer science or Artificial Intelligence (AI), *scientists* do not talk about explanation as realization. The realization relation, like supervenience before it, is a normative a priori philosophical gloss over actual scientific practice. As the following passage conveys, this is equally true even of psychology and cognitive neuroscience, where the concept is supposed to be most at home:

Psychologists and cognitive neuroscientists do not, for the most part, talk of realization, but of the *neural correlates*, or of the *neural mechanisms* for psychological functions and capacities. Cognitive capacities are located in states of the brain. It is part of philosophical lore that such talk is loose-speak for the more metaphysically loaded discussions within the philosophy of mind cast in terms of supervenience and realization. This lore is what justifies the sense that philosophical discussions of the metaphysics of mind are continuous with and contribute to the cognitive sciences, even though one does not hear 'realization' in the mouths of cognitive scientists themselves. It is part of the self-image of naturalistic philosophy of mind. (Wilson, 2004, p. 100)

I think it really only makes sense to talk about PHY and CIP in reference to functional or second-order properties; hence it is unsurprising that no one in science outside philosophy of mind, computer science, and AI talks this way.

Thus the burden is on defenders of PHY to show that it captures actual scientific talk of neural correlates or neural mechanisms. But, with respect to the neural correlates of conscious states, it is not clear that this is a strictly synchronic relation or that it implies CIP. It is just a category mistake to say that neural correlates are identical with, realize, constitute, or otherwise compose phenomenal conscious states. All of these concerns apply even more strongly to neural mechanisms, which are multi-levelled, causal, diachronic, and so on. If realization talk only applies to cooked-up second-order properties and intrinsically functional objects such as mouse traps, Turing machines, and so forth, then we ought to be deeply suspicious of such so-called explanations. As Kim himself admits, functional properties, construed as second-order properties, are not new features of the world: 'by forming second-order expressions we do not bring into existence new properties; we only introduce new ways of talking about properties already in hand' (2002, p. 643). Kim wants to replace second-order 'properties' talk with talk about functional or second-order 'predicates, concepts or designators' (2002). So we are back at square one: how can the mental *qua* mental be nothing but second-order properties, which are in turn nothing but particular first-order realizers, without eliminating the mental? We cannot square reductive functionalism's conception of mental properties as second-order relational properties whose essence involves meeting a causal/relational requirement with the conception of mental properties as phenomenal and intentional. Talk of realization and second-order properties does not answer either of Kim's questions about mental phenomena, it is rather a purely philosophical dodge of no empirical use.

Nor does the identity theory fare any better with respect to empirical justification. According to the identity theory, if every conscious *state* is identifiable with its particular physical realizing *state* (such as a particular brain state), then the problem of mental causation has been solved. But even granting the identity of any given conscious *state* with a particular brain *state*, given CoP, PHY, and the like, conscious states *by virtue of being conscious* will be epiphenomenal because, by hypothesis, only the fundamental physical realizers are truly efficacious: 'There is no way around it. If materialism is true, then all causal efficacy is constituted ultimately by the basic physical properties... [T]hen of course it will turn out that mental properties, along with all other non-basic physical properties, are not efficacious' (Levine, 2001, p. 28). Monism is a necessary but not sufficient condition for accounting for mental causation. Reductive physicalism claims that mental events (or states) are physical events (or states). Let us assume that events are nothing but instantiations of property instances and let us assume the Causal Theory of Properties. Now we can ask reductive physicalism this question: given any action in which properties of a person's brain state (which is identical to a mental state) are efficacious in bringing about his or her action, which properties of that brain state are the efficacious ones? The point is that, given the metaphysical commitments of physicalism, it must answer that the neurophysical properties are the efficacious ones and not the phenomenal-intentional properties *qua* phenomenal-intentional. Reductive physicalism, then, given its identification of mental events with physical events, escapes mental event/state epiphenomenalism but not mental-*qua*-mental property epiphenomenalism.

Why not just go ahead and identify *mental property* instances such as feeling pain with *physical property* instances such as C-fibres firing? The answer is because it is logically impossible to identify the subjective (e.g. feeling pain) with the objective (e.g. C-fibres firing). If it were possible to identify the subjective with the objective, then there would be absolutely no difference between me and zombie-me; yet by hypothesis there is a phenomenal world of subjective experiences that differentiates between me and zombie-me. The bottom line is that, even in the case of reductive physicalism (the identity theory), mental-*qua*-mental properties are causally screened off by the neural properties that are part of the same event.

Reductive physicalism holds that, because what is involved is an identity (between mental states and brain states), there is no explanatory gap to bridge. There are not two things whose linkage needs to be explained; there is just one thing, and it, like everything else, is necessarily identical with itself and not with anything else. If Brian's pain *just is* a certain pattern of brain activity in the *identity* sense of 'is', then there is no gap to be closed any more than there is in any other case of identity. But the case of mind–brain identity does not seem to be like other cases of identity: 'With the standard cases [of identity], once all the relevant empirical information is supplied, any request for explanation of the identities is quite unintelligible, not in this [mind–body] case!' (Levine, 2001, p. 92). For example, if someone asks how H_2O could possibly possess the properties deemed essential to water (such as its liquidity) we can answer their question with an explanation from quantum chemistry. But we cannot answer the analogous question about consciousness and the brain. Accepting the identity theory as a *philosophical* solution to the mind–body problem does not obviate the need for a *scientific explanation* of *how* brain states can have consciousness as one of their properties, just as in the case of water and liquidity.

In fact, in the long run one should only find the identity theory plausible if such a scientific explanation is forthcoming from neuroscience. As Levine puts it, 'if materialism is true, there ought to be an explanation of how the mental arises from the physical: a realization theory... [S]uch a theory should in principle be accessible' (2001, p. 69). Chalmers makes exactly the same point: 'in postulating an explanatory "identity", one is trying to get something for nothing: all of the explanatory work of a fundamental law, at none of the ontological cost' (1997, p. 12). Furthermore, while the identity theory seems plausible when we talk about identifying conscious *states* with brain *states*, we have learned it is not plausible when we consider that each brain state has conscious or subjective *aspects*, such as feeling pain, and non-conscious or objective *aspects*, such as C-fibre activation. These features can only be identified on pain of eliminating the mental, which is prima facie absurd. Reductive physicalism does not yet answer either of Kim's questions regarding the efficacy and existence of conscious states.

In summary, the mind–brain identity theory is as yet *not explanatory* the way other identity theories in science are, because it does not tell us *how* mental states can be nothing but brain states. This explanatory gap seems to be insurmountable in principle, because one cannot identify phenomenal-intentional *properties* with objective physical *properties* without falling into eliminativism. Given that the most one can get is the identification of mental *events* with physical *events*, then, given CoP, the distinct neurophysiological *properties* of conscious brain states causally screen off the phenomenal-intentional features of such states and that removes the very motivation for the identity theory.

Part of the point I want to make here is that a wise defender of physicalism will leave the metaphysical armchair and attend to what the actual mind sciences allege the determination relations are. According to ontological emergence cum enactivism, neural correlates and mechanisms are only necessary conditions for the mental states they support and such mechanisms are not at a 'lower-level' than those mental processes. Rather, 'parts' and 'wholes' throughout the systemic causal environment must be thought of as dynamically co-emerging, in that they mutually specify each other with respect to a certain context that is also part of the wider system (see Bishop, forthcoming). To the extent that emergent wholes have contemporaneous parts, neither the former nor the latter can be characterized independently of each other functionally, causally, or spatio-temporally. Such reflexive global-to-local (and local-to-global) structuring influences by means of self-regulating global patterns or constraints are common in even merely chemical or biological collective self-organizing systems (Wilson, 2004).

Is there talk of synchronic, non-causal determination relations anywhere in science outside computer science and AI? None that I am aware of. For example, it is not even clear that PHY applies to the case of atoms and molecules if PHY is meant to imply some kind of atomism, composition rule, or corpuscularism. It is well known, given the quantum mechanics of bonding relations, that molecules are not nothing but collections or mereological sums of atoms. This is due to the complete spatial overlap of the quantum mechanical wave functions of the electrons involved in bonding. The electrons are indistinguishable in such a case in that one cannot associate a particular electron with a particular atom; there is only a joint probability distribution. Many of us have pointed out repeatedly that atomism generally fails in quantum mechanics and chemistry because of the importance of phenomena such as quantum entanglement (Silberstein, 2002).

One defender of both PHY and reductive functionalism explicitly acknowledges the failure of atomism in physics and goes further still in what he thinks such a view can entertain (Melnyk, 2003, pp. 16–32). Melnyk thinks that PHY and reductive functionalism are compatible with the following *within all (or any branch) of physics*:

(1) The failure of atomism or mereological supervenience, such as found in chemical bonding;

(2) The failure of CIP: causal capacities of wholes are not reducible to the causal capacities of the intrinsic or relational properties of their more basic parts, as in quantum entanglement;

(3) British emergence or 'strong emergence', meaning a truly disunified or 'patchwork' physics, such that physical laws pertaining to some relatively macroscopic scale (such as classical mechanics) might be underivable in principle from some more relatively fundamental physical theory (such as quantum mechanics), which would imply that there are irreducible micro–macro bridge-laws within physics;

(4) The failure of the 'hierarchy of levels' picture, such that the realization relation does not track the micro–macro relation.

Melnyk does think that physical realizer properties must have some 'proper parts', which is to say that they cannot be 'metaphysical simples'. This is consistent, though, with individuals not having atoms and the like as current spatiotemporal parts, but they must still have some kind of physical 'ingredients' or proper parts. Here Melnyk draws an analogy with eggs in a baked cake: the former are ingredients in the cake, yet you cannot retrieve whole individual eggs from a cake just as you cannot retrieve discrete particles from quantum entangled states while so entangled.

Melnyk then does not deny that PHY, CIP, the micro–macro analogue of CoP, and so on, are very possibly violated *within physics itself*. In short, Melnyk is willing to allow for all sorts of emergence and in-principle disunity within physics, so long as these are screened off at some appropriate macroscopic scale such that PHY, CIP, and CoP hold for first-order physical realizers and for the second-order functional properties that they realize. Everything that is not in some sense properly physical will stand in the realization relation to that which is.

Of course, the question that one wants to ask Melnyk is why, if physicalism fails within physics, he is so sure that it holds beyond it? If physics is rife with emergence and disunity, as some of us have suggested might be the case (Silberstein, 2002), then by enumerative induction is it not reasonable to expect that emergence and disunity will also exist beyond physics? On the basis of what we know about complex biological and psychological systems so far, does not ontological emergence, systemic causation, and the failure of physicalism seem even more probable and expected in those domains? Melnyk's primary answer is that the argument from physiology trumps such an enumerative induction for universal ontological emergence—an argument we will consider at a future time.

3. CONCLUSION

In the words of Kim:

What is new and surprising about the current problem of mental causation is the fact that it has arisen out of the very heart of our materialist commitments. This means that giving up Cartesian substantival minds and embracing a materialist ontology does not make the problem go away. On the contrary, our basic physicalist commitments ... can be seen as the source of our current difficulties. (Kim, 2001, p. 272)

At the very least, ontological emergence provides us with a framework for answering Kim's questions: how can the mind exert its causal powers in a world that is fundamentally material, and how can there be such a thing as consciousness in a material world? Kim is right that giving up substance dualism in favour of physicalism does not help with the mind–body problem. However embracing ontological emergence cum enactivism with its rejection of both substance dualism and physicalism does help with the scientific and philosophical aspects of the mind–body problem.

4. REFERENCES

Bishop, R. (2006), 'Downward Causation in Fluid Convection', *Synthese*.

Blackmore, S. (2004), *Consciousness: An Introduction* (Oxford: Oxford University Press).

Chalmers, D. (1996), *The Conscious Mind* (Oxford: Oxford University Press).

Churchland, P. M. (1981), 'Eliminative Materialism and the Propositional Attitudes', *Journal of Philosophy*, 78: 67–90.

Clark, A. (2003), *Natural-Born Cyborgs and the Future of Human Intelligence* (Oxford: Oxford University Press).

Deacon, T. (1997), *The Symbolic Species: the Co-evolution of Language and the Brain* (New York: W. W. Norton and Co).

—— (2003a), 'Multilevel Selection in a Complex Adaptive System: the Problem of Language Origins', in B. Weber and D. Depew (eds.), *Evolution and Learning: the Baldwin Effect Reconsidered* (Cambridge, MA: MIT Press).

—— (2003b) 'The Hierarchic Logic of Emergence: Untangling the Interdependence of Evolution and Self-Organization' in B. Weber and D. Depew (eds.), *Evolution and Learning: the Baldwin Effect Reconsidered* (Cambridge, MA: MIT Press).

Dennett, D. (1989), 'The Origins of Cells', *Cogito*, 3: 163–73.

—— (1991), *Consciousness Explained* (Boston: Little Brown and Co).

Gillett, C. (2003), 'Non-reductive Physicalism, Non-reductive Realization, and Non-reductive Identity: What Physicalism does not Entail', in S. Walter and H-D Heckmann (eds.), *Physicalism and Mental Causation: The Metaphysics of Mind and Action* (Exeter: Imprint Academic).

Hardcastle, V. (1999), *The Myth of Pain* (Cambridge, MA: MIT Press).

Hurley, S. (1998), *Consciousness in Action* (Cambridge, MA: Harvard University Press).

Kim, J. (1993), *Supervenience and Mind* (Cambridge: Cambridge University Press).

—— (1998), *Mind in a Physical World: An Essay on the Mind–Body Problem and Mental Causation* (Cambridge, MA: MIT Press).

—— (2001), 'Mental Causation and Consciousness: the Two Mind-Body Problems for the Physicalist', in C. Gillett and B. Loewer (eds.), *Physicalism and its Discontents* (Cambridge: Cambridge University Press).

—— (2002), 'Precis of *Mind in a Physical World*', *Philosophy and Phenomenological Research*, LXV (3): 640–80.

Kitcher, P. (2002), 'The Third Way: Reflections on Helen Longino's *The Fate of Knowledge*', *Philosophy of Science*, 69(4): 549–59.

Levine, J. (2001), *Purple Haze: The Puzzle of Consciousness* (Oxford: Oxford University Press).

Melnyk, A. (2003a), 'Some Evidence for Physicalism', in S. Walter and H-D Heckmann (eds.), *Physicalism and Mental Causation: The Metaphysics of Mind and Action* (Exeter: Imprint Academic).

Melnyk, A. (2003b), *A Physicalist Manifesto: Thoroughly Modern Materialism* (Cambridge: Cambridge University Press).

Noë, A., and E. Thompson (2004), 'Are There Neural Correlates of Consciousness?', *Journal of Consciousness Studies*, 11(1): 3–28.

Papineau, D. (2001), 'The Rise of Physicalism' in C. Gillett and B. Loewer (eds.), *Physicalism and its Discontents* (Cambridge: Cambridge University Press).

Revonsuo, A. (2001), 'Can Functional Brain Imaging Discover Consciousness in the Brain?', *Journal of Consciousness Studies*, 8(3): 3–23.

Shoemaker, S. (2001), 'Realization and Mental Causation' in C. Gillett and B. Loewer (eds.), *Physicalism and its Discontents* (Cambridge: Cambridge University Press).

Silberstein, M. (2001), 'Converging on Emergence: Consciousness, Causation and Explanation', *Journal of Consciousness Studies*, 8(9–10): 61–98.

—— (2002), 'Reduction, Emergence, and Explanation', in Machamer and Silberstein (eds.), *The Blackwell Guide to the Philosophy of Science* (London: Blackwell Publishers).

—— and J. McGeever (1999), 'The Search for Ontological Emergence', *The Philosophical Quarterly*, 49: 182–200.

Thompson, E. (2007), *Mind in Life: Biology, Phenomenology, and the Sciences of Mind* (Cambridge, MA: Harvard University Press).

—— and F. Varela (2001), 'Radical Embodiment: Neural Dynamics and Consciousness', *Trends in Cognitive Sciences*, 5(10): 418–25.

Varela, F., E. Thompson, and E. Rosch (1991), *The Embodied Mind: Cognitive Science and Human Experience* (Cambridge, MA: MIT Press).

Weber, B. (2003), 'Emergence of Mind and the Baldwin Effect', in B. Weber and D. Depew (eds.), *Evolution and Learning: the Baldwin Effect Reconsidered* (Cambridge, MA: MIT Press).

Wilson, R. (2004), *Boundaries of the Mind: the Individual in the Fragile Sciences* (Cambridge: Cambridge University Press).

10

Emergence and Mental Causation

Nancey Murphy

1. INTRODUCTION

In this chapter my interest is in the question how emergent mental events or properties can have 'downward' causal efficacy without violating the causal closure of the physical world. This is an immensely complex issue, and I cannot hope to address it adequately in this short essay, but I believe I can lay out some resources that will point the discussion in a more fruitful direction than heretofore. I claim that 'emergence' needs to be defined in terms of the *denial* of causal reductionism. Causal antireductionism amounts to *the affirmation of top-down or downward causation*. I define 'downward causation' in terms of the *selection* among lower-level causal processes on the basis of their higher-level (*supervenient*) properties. The mental properties of events have an irreducible role to play in causal processes, then, in that it is only in virtue of the supervenient mental properties that neural processes become subject to the selective pressures of the environment. I shall spell out each of these theses in what follows.

2. EMERGENCE: AN INITIAL APPROACH

Emergence seems to be a concept needed in order to describe how the complex entities we find today, such as living organisms, have come to exist in a universe that used to consist, for instance, only of gases. Attempts to define 'emergence' tend to fall into two categories, epistemic and ontological (Van Gulick, 2001). I believe that epistemic definitions in terms of the unpredictability or non-deducibility of the putatively emergent entity or property are unhelpful: there are many things that cannot be predicted that we do not want to count as emergent, for example, the outcome of certain quantum processes and states of chaotic systems. If we attempt to evade this problem (in the case of chaotic systems) by invoking an omniscient predictor we are unable to *apply* the definition because we have no way to settle disputes about what the omniscient one would or would not know.

An ontological or metaphysical definition, then, is desirable. Robert Van Gulick notes that metaphysical accounts pertain to either (1) properties or (2) causal powers or forces (2001, p. 17). I focus here on causal *powers,* first, because the postulation of new causal *forces* would seem to conflict with our sense of the causal closure of physics, and, secondly, because having causal powers seems to be the best criterion for the existence of a distinct *property.*

If emergence theses, in general, are equivalent to (or at least closely related to) antireductionist theses, then the sort of reductionism on which to focus is causal reductionism. I shall take causal reductionism to be the thesis that in the hierarchy of complex systems all causation is bottom-up. That is, the behaviour of the whole is entirely determined by the behaviour of its parts (or at least by lower-level entities, processes, and laws). The antireductionist thesis asserts that, in addition, there is downward or top-down causation. After a detour to consider downward causation and its role in mental causation I shall return to the topic of emergence.

3. DEFINING DOWNWARD CAUSATION

In one sense the prevalence of downward causation is obvious. It is clearly the case that many systems are influenced by their environments. The system S interacting with its environment is a higher-order system, S'. If S is affected by its environment, then this is downward causation from S' to S.

I believe that causal reductionism nonetheless retains its hold on our imaginations because the claim for downward causation is not clearly distinguished from the *denial* of the causal closure of the lower levels. So the question is, how can downward causation take place without causal over-determination of the lower levels or without the lower level constituents being 'bewitched by larger patterns of action',[1] and without the properties of the higher-level entity or system 'overpowering' the causal forces of the component entities (cf. Sperry, 1983, p. 117)?

---

[1] This is Austin Farrer's description from his 1957 Gifford Lectures. Farrer uses it approvingly but I believe it is the sort of language that makes downward causation appear spooky and unscientific. See Farrer (1958, p. 57).

Here are the ingredients that need to go into an entirely *non-mysterious* account of downward causation in its *complementarity* with bottom-up causation: (1) the distinction between lower-level laws and the initial and boundary conditions within which they operate; (2) the distinction between what Fred Dretske calls 'structuring' and 'triggering' causes (1988); and (3) a definition of downward causation in terms of *selection* among lower-level conditions, structures, or causal processes. To account for this selection process in the realm of biology we need, in addition, to consider the roles of (4) function, (5) information, and (6) feedback. To account for the downward efficacy of the mental we need, in addition, the concepts of (7) nonlinearity, (8) representation, and (9) semiosis.

Space does not allow for consideration of all of these factors. I shall mention briefly the role of initial conditions and structures in my account of downward causation. Robert Van Gulick's is the most helpful account of top-down causation (1995). Van Gulick makes his points about top-down causation in the context of an argument for the non-reducibility of higher-level sciences. The causal reductionist, he says, will claim that the causal roles associated with special-science classifications are entirely derivative from the causal roles of the underlying physical constituents of the objects or events picked out by the special sciences. Van Gulick replies that although the events and objects picked out by the special sciences are indeed composites of physical constituents, the causal powers of such an object are not determined solely by the physical properties of its constituents and the laws of physics, but also by the *organization* of those constituents within the composite. And it is just such patterns of organization that are picked out by the predicates of the special sciences. This fits exactly with Dretske's distinction between triggering and structuring causes. Another way to make the same point is to say that physical outcomes are determined by the laws of physics together with initial and boundary conditions. Thus, Van Gulick concludes, 'we can say that the causal powers of a composite object or event are determined in part by its higher-order (special science) properties and not solely by the physical properties of its constituents and the laws of physics' (1995, p. 251).

The patterns of boundary conditions picked out by the special sciences have downward causal efficacy in that they can affect which causal powers of their constituents are activated or likely to be activated. 'A given physical constituent may have many causal powers, but only some subsets of them will be active in a given situation. The larger context (i.e. the pattern) of which it is a part may affect which of its causal powers get activated. . . . Thus the whole is not any simple function of its parts, since the whole at least partially determines what contributions are made by its parts' (ibid.).

Such patterns or entities, he says, are stable features of the world, often despite variations or exchanges in their underlying physical constituents; the pattern is conserved even though its constituents are not (e.g. in a hurricane or a blade of grass). Many such patterns are self-sustaining or self-reproducing in the face of perturbing physical forces that might degrade or destroy them (e.g. DNA patterns). Finally, the selective activation of the causal powers of such a pattern's parts may in many cases contribute to the maintenance and preservation of the pattern itself. Taken together, these points illustrate that

...higher-order patterns can have a degree of independence from their underlying physical realizations and can exert what might be called downward causal influences without requiring *any objectionable form* of emergentism by which higher-order properties would alter the underlying laws of physics. Higher-order properties act by the *selective activation* of physical powers and not by their *alteration*. (ibid., p. 252, emphasis added)

Donald Campbell's famous example of the production of the termite's jaw structure fits Van Gulick's account of downward causation and also illustrates the roles of function, information, and feedback in selective processes in the biological realm. It is, of course, *feedback* from the environment via differential rates of reproduction that does the selecting of the optimal jaw structure. The selection of one genome over another can only take place because the genes embody *information* about how to form the jaw and because those jaws are either good or bad at fulfilling their *function* in the termite's world.

In the following section I shall try to show that in the mental realm environmental selection of neural structures and processes is made possible because of the supervening *representational* and *semiotic* properties of the neural structures and processes. (In Section 5 I briefly note the role of *non-linear processes*—nerve impulses—in brain function.)

4. MENTAL CAUSATION

i. Stating the Problem

A common move in current philosophy of mind is to say that mental properties or events *supervene* on physical properties or events. I define 'supervenience' as follows:

Property S supervenes on (base) property B if and only if entity *e* possesses S in virtue of *e's* possessing B under circumstances *c*.

Alternatively:

Property S supervenes on property B if and only if *e's* having B constitutes *e's* having S under circumstance *c.*

Thus, I take it that a supervenient property is dependent upon some base property (or set of properties) along with some additional condition(s). For example, the property of being a U.S. penny supervenes on its being a copper disk with Lincoln's head stamped on one side, and so forth, only under the circumstances of its having been made at a U.S. mint, and under a vast number of other, more complex circumstances having to do with the federal government's powers and economic practices. The property of being a sunburn supervenes on a micro-condition of the skin cells under the circumstance of its having been brought about by overexposure to the sun. Fitness supervenes on a particular configuration of biological characteristics only within certain environmental circumstances.

This understanding of supervenience is not the most common, but its value will appear in due course.[2] My definition makes it possible to say that mental properties supervene on brain properties and at the same time one can recognize that (some) mental properties are co-determined by the way the world is.

The typical statement of the problem of mental causation is as follows: if mental states supervene on brain states, and we assume that each brain state has a sufficient cause at the physical level, what causal work is there for the mental to do? The problem can be expressed symbolically as shown in Fig. 10.1. Let the dotted line represent the supervenience relation and the complete arrow the assumed causal relation between brain states.

If B_1 is an adequate cause of B_2, what role does M_1 play? We seem to have a picture of the epiphenomenal character of the mental.

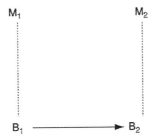

Fig. 10.1

---

[2] For the standard account see Jaegwon Kim's essay in Ch. 8. Others who take my approach include Thomas R. Grimes (1995); Berent Enç (1995); and Paul Teller (1995).

ii. A Simpler Model

The problem with approaching the puzzle of mental causation head-on is that we have so sketchy a grasp on the nature of mental events; the claim that mental events or properties supervene on brain events is really more of a hypothesis than an established conclusion. If Terrence Deacon is correct, mental events are third-order emergent states from brain events,[3] and so their relationship to the physical cannot be captured in a simple diagram such as Fig. 10.1. I shall therefore begin with a simpler example, and will suggest that we can extrapolate from it to provide better directions for solving the problem of mental causation.

Consider a case of classical conditioning. The sound of a bell and a puff of meat powder are paired until a dog is conditioned to salivate on hearing the bell alone. We assume that the dog's hearing the bell (B) is realized by a series of brain events, including neurons firing in its auditory cortex (b), and the taste of meat (M) by another set of neuron firings (m). The simultaneous firing of the two nets or cells of neurons b and m results in neural connections either developing or being strengthened between the two cells so that stimulation of one cell automatically spreads to the other. This explains how the sound of the bell alone becomes a cause of salivation. We can picture the causal relationships at the beginning of the conditioning process as shown in Fig. 10.2.

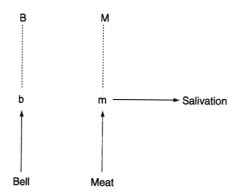

Fig. 10.2

---

[3] See Deacon's essay in Ch. 5; see also Deacon (2003). I shall address his three levels of emergence below.

After conditioning, the causal relations take the form shown in Fig. 10.3.

Now, we are assuming that the dog's awareness of the bell (B) supervenes on the neural processes (*b*) and M on *m*, but these are not the relations with which I shall be concerned here. My interest is in the new (or newly strengthened) *connection* between *b* and *m*. For simplicity's sake we may assume that there is a single neuron connecting cell assemblies *b* and *m*. This neuron has the base property C of being that connection. Once the connection is in place, however, it is *a bearer of information* about the dog's (past) environment—the information that bell-ringing and meat powder occur together. *Thus, I claim that the dog's brain has acquired a new supervenient property, R, the property of being a representation of the relationship between bells and meat.* R supervenes on C, the property of being the connection between *b* and *m*. In Fig. 10.4 the line between *b* and *m* represents our new neuron, *n*, with C and R representing its properties.

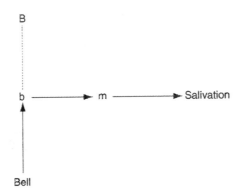

Fig. 10.3

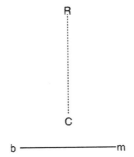

Fig. 10.4

The value of my definition of supervenience may now be clear. If the existence of the neural connection is considered apart from its role in a broader causal system (the dog's history with bells and meat powder), it is just another neuron—its information-bearing character disappears. The information is dependent on the existence of C but also on the *circumstances* under which it was formed.

My ultimate goal is to shed some light on the role of supervenient mental properties. Can we get any guidance from looking at the causal role of this supervenient *representational* property? There are two issues to consider: What is the role of downward causation in this example? And is there a causal role for R?

Clearly it is an instance of downward causation that accounts for the existence of C. The auditory assembly *b* would have been multiply connected to regions throughout the brain. The simultaneous pairing of *b* with *m* resulted in the *selection* of this particular connection for reinforcement. There was no interference with or overriding of the laws of neurobiology, merely the selection of the sites at which the standard process of tuning synaptic weights would take place. From that point on, the brain is restructured so that the ringing of the bell triggers a new effect, salivation.

Does R play any causal role or, once formed, is it epiphenomenal? If we look only at a single instance of the bell being rung and the dog salivating, we can see no causal relevance of R. It does appear to be epiphenomenal, as expressed in Fig. 10.5, rather than as expressed in Fig. 10.6. In epistemological terms, R is relevant for explaining why the connection C is there, but not for explaining how *b* causes salivation now that it is in place.

If we consider the future, however, there is still a (minimal) causal role for R. For example, if the experimenters want to extinguish the dog's response, they can only tamper with the neuron by means of its representational relationship to the environment. It is because of R that the repeated sounding of a bell (rather than any other stimulus), without associated meat powder, will weaken or eliminate the connection.

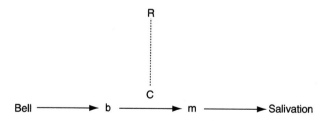

Fig. 10.5

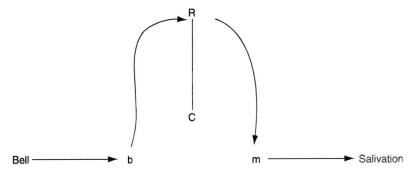

Fig. 10.6

So the supervenient representational property is the 'handle' that allows the environment to have a selective causal impact on a particular neuronal connection. We can see this more clearly in a slightly more complex example. In the example so far, the causal relevance of R is minimal because there is nothing for the dog *to do with* R. So suppose that our dog is now in a cage with meat outside. The latch to the cage door is controlled electronically. The dog discovers that while a bell is sounding the cage door is unlocked. Now we have a (probably more complex) neural connection, n, which has the base property of being the connection C between the neural realization of hearing the bell (b) and the motor instructions for pushing the cage door (m). R is the supervenient property of C's representing a fact about bells and doors in the dog's environment.

Notice that R supervenes on C only under the condition c_1 that the door is unlatched while the bell sounds. It is co-determined by C and c_1. The experimenter can change the situation to c_2 such that the door no longer opens when the bell sounds, and in this case n no longer posses the property R, even though (or because of the fact that) C has *not* changed. In this case, R clearly makes a difference not to the dog's immediate behaviour (it will still for a time push the door when the bell sounds) but to the longer causal chain resulting in its getting or not getting the meat.

So R has no downward efficacy on n (and it is not even clear what this might mean). But R is not eliminable from the causal account. R is a functional property, not a neural property, and it comes and goes depending on the experimenter's changing the circumstances.[4] Behaviour caused by C

---

[4] Note that recognizing the functional character of this supervenient property does not suggest a functionalist account of the mental. Functional roles need to be taken into account but are not sufficient to *define* mental properties.

will succeed in some cases and fail in others. C is necessary and sufficient for some of n's causal roles, but not sufficient for all of them.

I suggest the following as morals of these little stories:

(1) The representational property is a *contextualized* brain state.
(2) We can call R a higher-level property because it involves the brain state in relation to a broader, more complex system: the brain in the body within its environment and with a history.
(3) R is supervenient on the neural state in my sense of 'supervenience' but not in terms of the standard account because it can vary without a change in the base property (that is, due to changed circumstances).[5]
(4) The causal relevance of R is a function of the way it serves to relate the neural property to a broader causal system. It is in virtue of R (its informational, representational content) that C is able to play the causal role that it does. (In the example, it is in virtue of being an accurate representation of the relation between bells and cage doors that the connection C can serve the dog's purpose of getting to the meat.)
(5) It is in virtue of R that agents in the environment have access to C.

iii. Toward an Account of the Downward Efficacy of the Mental

Extrapolating from my conclusions regarding the causal role of supervenient representational properties, I make the following suggestions:

(1) Mental properties are *contextualized* brain states or events.
(2) Mental properties are higher-level properties because they involve the brain state in relation to a broader, more complex system: the brain in the body in its environment, usually with a longer causal history.
(3) Mental properties are supervenient in my sense of 'supervenience' but not in terms of the standard account because they can vary without a change in the base property (that is, due to changed circumstances). For example, a true belief may become a false belief if the world changes.[6]
(4) The causal relevance of supervenient mental properties is a function of the way they serve to relate the neural base property to a broader causal system. It is in virtue of their informational, representational, and semantic content that the base properties are able to play a causal role in the world.
(5) It is in virtue of their mental properties that agents in the environment *and subjects themselves* have access to their own neural causal processes.

---

[5] At this point a discussion of broadening the supervenience base and of global supervenience would be relevant, but space does not permit.

[6] Thus, I agree with the externalist thesis regarding the mental.

These claims need some spelling out. In particular, I want to address the role of consciousness as the means by which subjects have access to the causal processes in their own brains. In so doing, I hope to shed some light on why the problem of mental causation cannot be solved when formulated in the usual manner.

Recall that the problem is usually represented as shown in Fig. 10.1. The question, then, is what causal work does M_1 do?

I claim that this figure is misleading because it represents too little of the causal history. In place of the dog in my simpler examples, consider the case of John Canine, who happens to be in prison. Canine has learnt that when a bell sounds the cell doors unlock to allow the men out for meals. Under condition c_1, when the bell rings Canine hears it, pushes his cell door open, and gets his lunch. Let M_1 represent his hearing of the bell, M_2 represent his belief that the door opens when the bell sounds, M_3 his conscious decision to push the door, and M_4 his enjoyment of lunch; also, let b represent the neural correlate of his hearing the bell, where c is the cell assembly that is the neural realization of Canine's believing that the door will open when the bell rings, m the set of events in the motor cortex that initiate the door-pushing, and l his eating lunch. So the causal picture looks like Fig. 10.7 under condition c_1, when the bell and the locking mechanism are synchronized.

If c_1 changes to c_2 such that the bell and the lock are not synchronized, then the causal picture is as pictured in Fig. 10.8. Notice that M_2 is not necessary to cause m. There need not be a causal arrow downward from M_1 or M_2 in order for m to take place: b and c are jointly sufficient. However, the *relation between* M_2 and c_1 is crucial for the final outcome of getting or not getting lunch. In circumstance c_2, M_2 is qualitatively the same, but its relation to the world has changed *and it no longer has the representational character it had before*. In short, what used to be a true belief has become a false belief, and as such *its neural realization c has a different effect in the world than before*.

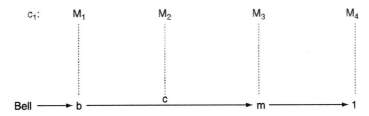

Fig. 10.7

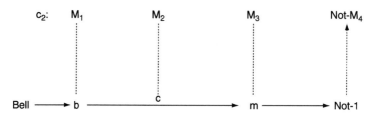

Fig. 10.8

Notice also that if we eliminate M_1 and M_2, b and c together will still have the same *immediate* causal effect. Suppose Canine is hypnotized to make him unable (consciously) to hear the bell and to make him forget his belief about the connection of the bell with the opening of the cell door.[7] We can imagine now that at various times of the day he finds himself pushing on his cell door, *but he has no idea why.*

The presence or absence of M_1 and M_2 does not matter when we look only at a single episode. But notice that it will make a great deal of difference to Canine's ability to change his behaviour appropriately. Without hypnosis he can quickly learn, under condition c_2, that his belief is false—he is able to evaluate M_2, *and thereby evaluate his neural connection c.*[8] With hypnosis, he has no access to the neural processes that shape his behaviour. Thus, the conscious accompaniments are the 'handles' that make our neural states subject to evaluation and change. Whereas in my example of classical conditioning, the representative property of a neural connection was causally relevant for the experimenter wanting to change it, here the conscious mental property is causally relevant to the subject himself when there is need for a change.

In short, what I hope to have shown here is that the downward efficacy of supervenient mental properties or events can only be seen when we understand supervenience in terms of the relation of the base properties to a broader causal system—the supervenient property *is* the base property's relation to a broader system, which entails its enmeshment in a more complex set of causal processes. If downward causation is, in general, a matter of

---

[7] There is controversy about what hypnosis actually accomplishes; suppose for present purposes that such a thing is possible.

[8] Much more needs to be said about *levels* of mental processing and the role of downward causation from higher-level evaluation in shaping lower-level processes.

selection among lower-level causal processes, then the supervenient mental property is what constitutes the criterion for that selective process.[9]

5. BUT IS THIS EMERGENCE?

If all of the foregoing is correct, then I could simply end this essay with the claim to have shown that mental properties and events are emergent. I want to proceed, however, to relate my work here to some of the recent literature on emergence. If I am able to do so I shall have strengthened my case for the relation between the concepts of emergence and downward causation.

Terrence Deacon's work on emergence is, in my view, the most interesting. In several essays, including the one in this volume, he describes three levels of emergence. First-order emergence occurs when 'properties emerge as a consequence of shape interactions'. An example is the generation of the surface tension of water from the interaction of water molecules. Second-order emergence occurs 'as a consequence of shape interactions played out over time, where what happens next is highly influenced by what has happened before' (Deacon, Ch. 5), as in the formation of a snowflake, 'where initial and boundary conditions become amplified in effect over time'. Third-order emergence occurs 'as a consequence of shape, time, and "remembering how to do it"'. An example is in biology,

where genetic and epigenetic instructions generate materials for and place constraints upon first- and second-order systems and thereby specify emergent outcomes called biological *traits*. These traits then become substrates for natural selection by virtue of the fact that (1) their instructions are mutable and replicable, and (2) they endow organisms with adaptive properties. (Goodenough and Deacon, 2003, p. 1)

In his essay in this volume Deacon describes the differences among the three levels of emergence in terms of the topology of causality; 'nature tangles its causal chains into complex knots' (Deacon, Ch. 5, p. 124). Here he also emphasizes the role of amplification processes in pattern formation. These processes account for how 'certain minor or even incidental aspects of a

---

[9] Questions about mental causation can be approached in either of two ways: by asking what difference the qualia make or by asking about the informational content. I hope that the relevance of qualia could be incorporated into my account in so far as qualia add to (are essential for) the informational content. For example, if I am colour blind I am lacking the information that will prepare me for having other people look with amusement at my socks.

componential process can come to be the source of [their] dominant features' (Deacon, Ch. 5, p. 125).

We can better appreciate the way in which third-order emergence of mental properties incorporates and builds on first- and second-order emergence if we draw examples of first- and second-order emergence from the realm of neurobiology.

If we abstract a neuron from its evolutionary origins and consider only its structure, it is an extremely complex example of first-order emergence. The structure of its parts gives it causal powers that none of its parts alone possesses. For example, the peculiar structure of its membrane gives it the capacity selectively to admit a variety of ions.

Deacon speaks of first-order emergence as 'flame-like', that is, the dynamic nature of a flame is not reducible to its parts (cf. Deacon, 2003). Alwyn Scott compares a nerve impulse to a flame travelling along a wick or fuse. The neuron in the process of transmitting an impulse is a second-order emergent system. It exemplifies symmetry breaking and downward causation. A neuron in its resting state contains potassium ions in relatively high concentrations. As the potassium ions diffuse outward through the cell membrane there is a balanced tendency to pull potassium ions in. Thus, the net flow of potassium is zero (Scott, 1995, p. 46)—there is symmetry. At the same time the sodium ion concentration outside the cell is high and is kept that way because the membrane is not permeable to sodium ions in its resting state (ibid., p. 47).

A nerve impulse is a pulse of electrical charge. Once it begins, a charge travels along the length of the cell by the coordinated alternating intake and discharge of charged sodium and potassium ions. Just as the burning of one section of a wick or fuse heats the next section and causes it to burn, the change in ion concentrations at one active node in the neuron changes the permeability at the next node, and so the process of ion exchange travels along the length of the axon (ibid., p. 49).

This system nicely illustrates most of the features I listed in Section 3 as ingredients that explain the insufficiency of bottom-up accounts of causation. There is the *structure* of the neuron with its *initial* (rest) *condition*. The nerve impulse is *triggered* by a chemical signal from another neuron, and the impulse itself is a *nonlinear* process—what happens next depends on what happened before. The Hodgkin–Huxley equations that describe the velocity of nerve impulses are nonlinear diffusion equations (ibid., p. 53). Finally, the impulse has a *downward causal impact* on the states of the ion channels. In Deacon's terms, 'micro-configurational states can be amplified to determine macro-configurational regularities, . . . where these in turn further constrain and/or amplify subsequent micro-configurational regularities' (Deacon, Ch. 5, p. 136).

The very simple example I presented above of learning by classical conditioning exemplifies several layers of third-order emergence in the sense of incorporating information and memory. The neural substrate (*b*) involved in recognizing the sound of the bell would involve the formation of a cell assembly, which is a network of neurons trained by means of a repeated stimulus to act briefly as a closed system (Scott, 1995, p. 81). This is an instance of memory. Cell assemblies deliver facilitation to other such systems, and the conditioning alters neural structure (probably synaptic weights of neurons already in place) so that stimulation of assembly *b* results in stimulation of the neural instructions to salivate. As I suggested above, this connection embodies information regarding the (past) association of the bell with meat powder.

Regarding third-order emergence Deacon says: 'The result is that specific historical moments—either of higher-order regularity or of unique micro-causal configurations—can additionally exert a cumulative influence over the entire causal future of the system' (Ch. 5, p. 137). Here the higher-order system is the dog's whole brain and nervous system in its body and in this particular environment. The higher-order regularity is the pairing of the bell with meat. This causes a repeated micro-causal configuration—the simultaneous firing of the bell and meat-taste assemblies, *b* and *m*. The cumulative effect is to make a long-term change at the micro-level such that the causal future of the system is different—namely, the bell has taken on the causal power of causing the dog to salivate.

Regarding third-order emergence Deacon says, in addition, that it occurs when there is both 'amplification of the global influences' and 'a redundant "sampling" of these influences which reintroduces them into different realizations of the system' (Ch. 5, p. 137), but I do not see how to apply this to my example. Perhaps selection is an adequate key to understanding emergence, and amplification and reintroductions of the selected features is a special case of selection.

Finally, Deacon says that third-order emergent processes require semiotic analysis for adequate description. To have full-fledged symbolic meaning we need to consider much more complex learning, involving the communal development of a linguistic system.[10] Nonetheless, the dog's conditioning involves what Deacon (following C. S. Peirce) calls iconic and indexical signs. The development of cell assemblies allowing for *recognition* of a stimulus enables iconic signification. The associative relationship between the bell and the meat power is indexical—the bell comes to signify meat for the dog (Deacon, 1997, ch. 3).

[10] An account that runs to 500 pages in Deacon's *Symbolic Species* (1997).

6. CONCLUSION

Recall that my approach to the issue of emergence (in Section 2) was as follows: the claim that there is emergence is equivalent to the claim that there are causal powers or processes that are not solely the result of the laws governing the lower-level entities composing them. This would be the case if there is indeed downward causation as well as bottom-up causation. I explained (in Section 3) how downward causation could take place without violating the causal closure of the lower level: it is by means of *selection* among lower-level boundary conditions, structures, or causal processes. I then tried to show (in Section 4) that representational properties and, by analogy, mental properties and events, which supervene on neural properties, provide the criteria by which the neural structures and processes are selected for causal roles in the interaction of an organism with its environment. Thus, mental properties and events have causal roles that are not reducible to their neural base properties.

In section 5 I hope to have shown the parallels between an account of downward causation in general and Deacon's account of emergence, and in particular to have shown the parallels between my account of the downward efficacy of the mental and Deacon's account of third-order emergence.

7. REFERENCES

Deacon, Terrence W. (1997), *The Symbolic Species: The Co-evolution of Language and the Brain* (New York and London: W. W. Norton and Co.).
—— (2003), 'The Hierarchic Logic of Emergence: Untangling the Interdependence of Evolution and Self-Organization', in Bruce Weber and David Depew (eds.), *Evolution and Learning: The Baldwin Effect Reconsidered* (Cambridge, MA: MIT Press).
Dretske, Fred (1988), *Explaining Behavior: Reasons in a World of Causes* (Cambridge, MA: MIT Press).
Enç, Berent (1995), 'Nonreducible Supervenient Causation', in Elias Savellos and Ümit D. Yalçin (eds.), *Supervenience: New Essays* (Cambridge: Cambridge University Press), 169–80.
Farrer, Austin (1958), *The Freedom of the Will* (New York: Charles Scribner's Sons).
Goodenough, Ursula, and Terrence W. Deacon (2003), 'From Biology to Consciousness to Morality', unpublished paper, adapted from an article published in *Zygon* 38: 801–19.
Grimes, Thomas (1995), 'The Tweedledum and Tweedledee of Supervenience', in Elias Savellos and Ümit D. Yalçin (eds.), *Supervenience: New Essays* (Cambridge: Cambridge University Press), 110–23.
Heil, John, and Alfred Mele (eds.) (1995), *Mental Causation* (Oxford: Clarendon).
Savellos, Elias E., and Ümit D. Yalçin (eds.) (1995), *Supervenience: New Essays* (Cambridge: Cambridge University Press).
Scott, Alwyn (1995), *Stairway to the Mind: The Controversial New Science of Consciousness* (New York: Springer-Verlag).
Sperry, Roger (1983), *Science and Moral Priority: Merging Mind, Brain, and Human Values* (New York: Columbia University Press).
Teller, Paul (1995), 'Reduction', in Robert Audi (ed.), *The Cambridge Dictionary of Philosophy* (Cambridge: Cambridge University Press), 679–80.
Van Gulick, Robert (1995), 'Who's in Charge Here? And Who's Doing All the Work?', in John Heil and Alfred Mele (eds.), *Mental Causation* (Oxford: Clarendon Press), 233–56.
—— (2001), 'Reduction, Emergence and Other Recent Options on the Mind/Body Problem: A Philosophic Overview', *Journal of Consciousness Studies* 8, 9–10: 1–34.

11

Strong and Weak Emergence

David J. Chalmers[1]

1. TWO CONCEPTS OF EMERGENCE

The term 'emergence' often causes confusion in science and philosophy, as it is used to express at least two quite different concepts. We can label these concepts *strong emergence* and *weak emergence*. Both of these concepts are important, but it is vital to keep them separate.

We can say that a high-level phenomenon is *strongly emergent* with respect to a low-level domain when the high-level phenomenon arises (in some sense) from the low-level domain, but truths concerning that phenomenon are not *deducible* even in principle from truths in the low-level domain.[2] Strong emergence is the notion of emergence that is most common in philosophical discussions of emergence, and is the notion invoked by the British emergentists of the 1920s.

We can say that a high-level phenomenon is *weakly* emergent with respect to a low-level domain when the high-level phenomenon arises from the low-level domain, but truths concerning that phenomenon are *unexpected* given the principles governing the low-level domain. Weak emergence is the notion

[1] Most of this chapter was written for discussion at the Granada workshop on emergence. One section (the last) is modified from a posting to the Usenet newsgroup comp.ai.philosophy, written in February 1990. I thank the editors and the participants in the Granada workshop on emergence for their feedback.
[2] In philosophers' terms, we can say that strong emergence requires that high-level truths are not conceptually or metaphysically necessitated by low-level truths. Other notions in the main text can also be formulated in these modal terms, but I will mainly talk of deducibility to avoid technicality. The distinction between conceptual and metaphysical necessity will not be central here, but in principle one could formulate finer-grained notions of strong emergence that take this distinction into account.

of emergence that is most common in recent scientific discussions of emergence, and is the notion that is typically invoked by proponents of emergence in complex systems theory. (See Bedau 1997, for a nice discussion of the notion of weak emergence and its relation to strong emergence.)

These definitions of strong and weak emergence are first approximations which might later be refined. But they are enough to exhibit the key differences between the two notions. As just defined, cases of strong emergence will likely also be cases of weak emergence (although this depends on just how 'unexpected' is understood). But cases of weak emergence need not be cases of strong emergence. It often happens that a high-level phenomenon is unexpected given principles of a low-level domain, but is nevertheless deducible in principle from truths concerning that domain.

The emergence of high-level patterns in cellular automata—a paradigm of emergence in recent complex systems theory—provides a clear example. If one is given only the basic rules governing a cellular automaton, then the formation of complex high-level patterns (such as gliders) may well be unexpected, so these patterns are weakly emergent. But the formation of these patterns is straightforwardly deducible from the rules (and initial conditions), so these patterns are not strongly emergent. Of course, to deduce the facts about the patterns in this case may require a fair amount of calculation, which is why their formation was not obvious to start with. Nevertheless, upon examination these high-level facts are a straightforward consequence of low-level facts. So this is a clear case of weak emergence without strong emergence.

Strong emergence has much more radical consequences than weak emergence. If there are phenomena that are strongly emergent with respect to the domain of physics, then our conception of nature needs to be expanded to accommodate them. That is, if there are phenomena whose existence is not deducible from the facts about the exact distribution of particles and fields throughout space and time (along with the laws of physics), then this suggests that new fundamental laws of nature are needed to explain these phenomena.

The existence of phenomena that are merely weakly emergent with respect to the domain of physics does not have such radical consequences. The existence of unexpected phenomena in complex biological systems, for example, does not on its own threaten the completeness of the catalogue of fundamental laws found in physics. As long as the existence of these phenomena is deducible in principle from a physical specification of the world (as in the case of the cellular automaton), then no new fundamental laws or properties are needed: everything will still be a consequence of physics. So if we want to use emergence to draw conclusions about the structure of nature at the most fundamental level, it is not weak emergence but strong emergence that is relevant.

Of course, weak emergence may still have important consequences for our understanding of nature. Even if weakly emergent phenomena do not require the introduction of new fundamental laws, they may still require in many cases the introduction of further levels of explanation above the physical level in order to make these phenomena maximally comprehensible to us. Further, by showing how a simple starting point can have unexpected consequences, the existence of weakly emergent phenomena can be seen as showing that an ultimately physicalist picture of the world need not be overly reductionist, but rather can accommodate all sorts of unexpected richness at higher levels, as long as explanations are given at the appropriate level.

In a way, the philosophical morals of strong emergence and weak emergence are diametrically opposed. Strong emergence, if it exists, can be used to reject the physicalist picture of the world as fundamentally incomplete. By contrast, weak emergence can be used to support the physicalist picture of the world, by showing how all sorts of phenomena that might seem novel and irreducible at first sight can nevertheless be grounded in underlying simple laws.

In what follows, I will say a little more about both strong and weak emergence.

2. STRONG EMERGENCE

We have seen that strong emergence, if it exists, has radical consequences. The question that immediately arises, then, is: are there strongly emergent phenomena?

My own view is that the answer to this question is yes. I think there is exactly one clear case of a strongly emergent phenomenon, and that is the phenomenon of consciousness. We can say that a system is conscious when there is something it is like *to be* that system; that is, when there is something it feels like from the system's own perspective. It is a key fact about nature that it contains conscious systems; I am one such. And there is reason to believe that the facts about consciousness are not deducible from any number of physical facts.

I have argued this position at length elsewhere (Chalmers, 1996; 2002) and will not repeat the case here. But I will mention two well-known avenues of support. First, it seems that a colourblind scientist given complete physical knowledge about brains could nevertheless not deduce what it is like to have a conscious experience of red. Secondly, it seems logically coherent in principle that there could be a world physically identical to this one, but lacking consciousness entirely, or containing conscious experiences different from our own. If these claims are correct, it appears to follow that facts about consciousness are not deducible from physical facts alone.

If this is so, then what follows? I think that even if consciousness is not deducible from physical facts, states of consciousness are still systematically *correlated* with physical states. In particular, it remains plausible that in the actual world, the state of a person's brain determines his or her state of consciousness, in the sense that duplicating the brain state will cause the conscious state to be duplicated too. That is, consciousness still *supervenes* on the physical domain. But importantly, this supervenience holds only with the strength of laws of nature (in the philosophical jargon, it is natural or nomological supervenience). In our world, it seems to be a matter of law that duplicating physical states will duplicate consciousness; but in other worlds with different laws, a system physically identical to me might have no consciousness at all. This suggests that the lawful connection between physical processes and consciousness is not itself derivable from the laws of physics but is instead a further basic law or laws of its own. The laws that express the connection between physical processes and consciousness are what we might call fundamental psychophysical laws.

I think this account provides a good general model for strong emergence. We can think of strongly emergent phenomena as being systematically determined by low-level facts without being deducible from those facts. In philosophical language, they are naturally but not logically supervenient on low-level facts. In any case like this, fundamental physical laws need to be supplemented with further fundamental laws to ground the connection between low-level properties and high-level properties. Something like this seems to be what the British emergentist C. D. Broad had in mind, when he invoked the need for 'trans-ordinal laws' connecting different levels of nature.

Are there other cases of strong emergence, besides consciousness? I think that there are no other clear cases, and that there are fairly good reasons to think that there are no other cases. Elsewhere (Chalmers, 1996; Chalmers and Jackson, 2001) I have argued that given a complete catalogue of physical facts about the world, supplemented by a complete catalogue of facts about consciousness, a Laplacean super-being could, in principle, deduce all the high-level facts about the world, including the high-level facts about chemistry, biology, economics, and so on. If this is right, then phenomena in these domains may be weakly emergent from the physical, but they are not strongly emergent (or if they are strongly emergent, this strong emergence will derive wholly from a dependence on the strongly emergent phenomena of consciousness). In short, with the exception of consciousness, it appears that all other phenomena are weakly emergent or are derived from the strongly emergent phenomenon of consciousness.

One might wonder about cases in which high-level *laws*, say in chemistry, are not obviously derivable from the low-level laws of physics. How can I know now that this is not the case? Here, one can reply by saying that even if the high-level laws are not deducible from the low-level laws, it remains plausible that they are deducible (or nearly so) from the low-level *facts*. For example, if one knows the complete distribution of atoms in space and time, it is plausible that one can deduce from there the complete distribution of chemical molecules, whether or not the laws governing molecules are immediately deducible from the laws governing atoms. So any emergence here is weaker than the sort of emergence that I maintain is present in the case of consciousness.

Still, this suggests the possibility of an intermediate but still radical sort of emergence, in which high-level facts and laws are not deducible from low-level *laws* (combined with initial conditions). If this intermediate sort of emergence exists, then if our Laplacean super-being is armed only with low-level laws and initial conditions (as opposed to all the low-level facts throughout space and time), it will be unable to deduce the facts about some high-level phenomena. This will presumably go along with a failure to be able to deduce even all the low-level facts from low-level laws plus initial conditions (since if the low-level facts were derivable, the demon could deduce the high-level facts from there). So this sort of emergence entails a sort of incompleteness of physical laws even in characterizing the systematic evolution of low-level processes.

The best way of thinking of this sort of possibility is as involving a sort of *downward causation*. Downward causation means that higher-level phenomena are not only irreducible but also exert a causal efficacy of some sort. Such causation requires the formulation of basic principles which state that when certain high-level configurations occur, certain consequences will follow. (These are what McLaughlin (1993) calls configurational laws.) These consequences will themselves either be cast in low-level terms, or will be cast in high-level terms that put strong constraints on low-level facts. Either way, it follows that low-level laws will be incomplete as a guide to both the low-level and the high-level evolution of processes in the world.[3]

---

[3] In such a case, one might respond by trying to introduce new, highly complex, low-level laws to govern evolution in these special configurations, in the effort to make low-level laws complete once again. But the point of this intermediate sort of emergence will still remain. It will just have to be rephrased, perhaps as the claim that non-configurational low-level laws are an incomplete guide to the evolution of processes. See Meehl and Sellars (1956) for related ideas here.

To be clear, one should distinguish *strong* downward causation from *weak* downward causation. With strong downward causation, the causal impact of a high-level phenomenon on low-level processes is not deducible even in principle from initial conditions and low-level laws. With weak downward causation, the causal impact of the high-level phenomenon is deducible in principle, but is nevertheless unexpected. As with strong and weak emergence, both strong and weak downward causation are interesting in their own right. But strong downward causation would have more radical consequences for our understanding of nature, so I will focus on it here.

I do not think there is anything incoherent about the idea of strong downward causation. I do not know whether there are any examples of it in the actual world, however. While it is certainly true that we can't *currently* deduce all high-level facts and laws from low-level laws plus initial conditions, I do not know of any compelling evidence for high-level facts and laws (outside the case of consciousness) that are not deducible in principle. But I think it is possible that we will encounter some. (See Kim (1992; 1999) for some doubts.)

Perhaps the most interesting potential case of downward causation is in the domain of quantum physics, at least on certain collapse interpretations of quantum mechanics. On these interpretations, there are two principles governing the evolution of the quantum wave function: the linear Schrödinger equation, which governs the standard case, and a nonlinear measurement postulate, which governs special cases of 'measurement'. In cases of measurement, the wave function is held to undergo a sort of 'quantum jump' quite unlike the usual case. A key issue is that no one knows just what is the criterion for a measurement taking place. Yet it is clear that for the 'collapse' interpretation to work, measurements must involve certain highly specific causal events, most likely at a high-level. If so, then we can see the measurement postulate as itself a sort of configurational law, involving downward causation.

Both consciousness and the quantum measurement case can be seen as strong varieties of emergence in that they involve in-principle non-deducibility and novel fundamental laws. But they are quite different in character. If I am right about consciousness, then it is a case of a strongly emergent quality, while if the relevant interpretations of quantum mechanics are correct, then it is more like a case of strong downward causation.

In principle, one can have one sort of radical emergence without the other. If one has strongly emergent qualities without strong downward causation, one has an epiphenomenalist picture on which there is a new fundamental quality that plays no causal role with respect to the lower level. If one has strong downward causation without strongly emergent qualities, one has a picture of the world on which the only fundamental properties are physical, but on which their evolution is governed in part by high-level configurational laws.

One might also in principle have both strongly emergent qualities and strong downward causation together. If so, one has a situation in which a new fundamental quality is involved in new fundamental causal laws. This last option can be illustrated by combining the cases of consciousness and quantum mechanics discussed above. In the familiar interpretations of quantum mechanics according to which it is consciousness itself that is responsible for wave-function collapse, the emergent quality of consciousness is not epiphenomenal but plays a crucial causal role.

My own view is that, relative to the physical domain, there is just one sort of strongly emergent quality, namely, consciousness. I do not know whether there is any strong downward causation, but it seems to me that if there *is* any strong downward causation, quantum mechanics is the most likely locus for it. If both strongly emergent qualities and strong downward causation exist, it is natural to look at the possibility of a close connection between them, perhaps along the lines mentioned in the last paragraph. The question remains wide open, however, as to whether or not strong downward causation exists.

3. WEAK EMERGENCE

Weak emergence does not yield the same sort of radical metaphysical expansion in our conception of the world as strong emergence, but it is no less interesting. I think that understanding weak emergence is vital for understanding all sorts of phenomena in nature, and in particular for understanding biological, cognitive, and social phenomena, as is demonstrated in many of the other chapters in this volume.

I gave a quick definition of weak emergence earlier. But it is more satisfactory to understand the notion by example, and then attempt to analyse it. The concept of emergence is often tacitly invoked by theorists in cognitive science and in the theory of complex systems, in such a way that it is clear that a notion of other than the notion of strong emergence is intended. We can take it that something like weak emergence is at play here, and we can then use the examples to make sense of just what weak emergence comes to.

It will help to focus on a few core examples of weak emergence:

(A) The game of Life: high-level patterns and structure emerge from simple low-level rules.
(B) Connectionist networks: high-level 'cognitive' behaviour emerges from simple interactions between simple threshold logic units.

(C) The operating system (Hofstadter 1977): the fact that overloading occurs just around when there are thirty-five users on the system seems to be an emergent property of the system.

(D) Evolution: intelligence and many other interesting properties emerge over the course of evolution by genetic recombination, mutation, and natural selection.

Note that in all these cases, the 'emergent' properties are in fact deducible (perhaps with great difficulty) from the low-level properties, perhaps in conjunction with knowledge of initial conditions, so strong emergence is not at play here.

One sometimes hears it suggested that emergence is the existence of properties of a system that are not possessed by any of its parts. However, this phenomenon is too ubiquitous for our purposes. Under this definition, filing cabinets and packs of cards, and even XOR gates, have many 'emergent' properties. So this is surely not what theorists generally mean by 'emergence'.

One might suggest that weak emergence involves 'deducibility without reducibility'. Of course the notion of reducibility is itself controversial and somewhat unclear. Biological and psychological laws and properties are frequently said not to be reducible to physical laws and properties, simply on the grounds that they might be found associated with all kinds of different physical laws and properties as substrates. However, some standard examples of weak emergence, such as the emergence of thermodynamics from statistical mechanics, involve phenomena that are 'reducible' in this sense. And other phenomena that are not 'reducible' in this sense, such as the functioning of a telephone, are not obviously emergent. So reducibility in this sense does not seem to be the key to weak emergence.

We might instead understand weak emergence in terms of the *ease of understanding* one level in terms of another. Emergent properties are usually properties that are more easily understood in their own right than in terms of properties at a lower level. This suggests an important observation: *weak emergence appears to be an observer-relative property*. Properties are classed as 'emergent' based at least in part on (1) how interesting the high-level property at hand is to a given observer, and (2) how difficult it is for an observer to deduce the high-level property from low-level properties. The properties of an XOR gate are an obvious consequence of the properties of its parts; emergent properties aren't. To capture this, we might suggest that weakly emergent properties are *interesting, non-obvious consequences* of low-level properties.

This still cannot be the full story, though. Every high-level physical property is a consequence of low-level properties, usually in a non-obvious fashion. It feels unsatisfactory, for instance, to say that computations performed by a COBOL program are an emergent property relative to the low-level circuit operations—at least this example feels much less naturally classed as 'emergent' than a connectionist network. So something is missing. The trouble seems to lie with the complex, jury-rigged *organization* of the COBOL system. The low-level processes may be simple enough, but all the complexity of the high-level behaviour is due to the complex *structure* that is given to the low-level mechanisms (by programming). By contrast, in the case of connectionism or the game of Life there is simplicity both in low-level mechanisms and in their organization. Consequently, in those cases the high-level processes have more of the character of 'something for nothing'.

To capture this, one might suggest that weak emergence is the phenomenon wherein complex, interesting high-level function is produced as a result of combining simple low-level mechanisms in simple ways. I think this is much closer to a good definition of emergence. Note that COBOL programs, and many biological systems, are excluded by the requirement that not only the mechanisms but also their principles of combination be simple. (Of course simplicity, complexity, and interestingness are observer-relative concepts, at least for now, although some have tried to explicate them in terms of Chaitin–Kolmogorov–Solomonoff complexity.) Note also that most phenomena that satisfy this definition should also satisfy the previous definition, as complex and interesting consequences of simple processes will typically be non-obvious.

This conclusion captures the feeling that weak emergence is a 'something for nothing' phenomenon. And most of our examples fit. The game of Life and connectionist networks are clear cases: interesting high-level behaviour emerges as a consequence of simple dynamic rules for low-level cell dynamics. In evolution, the genetic mechanisms are very simple, but the results are very complex. (Note that there is a small difference, in that in the latter case the emergence is diachronic, i.e. over time, whereas in the first two cases the emergence is synchronic, i.e. not over time but over levels present at a given time.)

A residual problem is that it is not clear how (C), the operating system example, fits this paradigm of a way of understanding emergence. But an appeal to principles of design should get us the rest of the way. We *design* the game of Life according to certain simple principles, but complex, interesting properties leap out and *surprise* us. Similarly for the connectionist network—we only design it at a low level, and we hope that complex high-level properties will emerge. For more traditional computer programs, by contrast, what one gets out is much closer to what one puts in. The operating system example also fits in well. The design principles of the system in this case are quite complex—unlike the other cases that fit our definition above—but still the figure 'thirty-five' is not a part of that design at all.

So we might suggest an alternative: A weakly emergent property of a system is an interesting property that is unexpected, given the underlying principles governing the system. Here the notion of 'underlying principles' is deliberately vague, so that it can be understood in multiple ways. One way to understand it is in terms of the principles according to which a principle is designed. Doing so will help capture cases discussed above. But we can also apply the definition to cases where the underlying principles are not, strictly speaking, designed at all. Corresponding to different ways of specifying the underlying principles of a system, we will have different sets of emergent properties.

In the case of evolution, for example, we might see the underlying principles as operating at the level of the gene. In this case the complex, interesting, high-level properties, such as intelligence, are unexpected relative to the underlying principles, and hence qualify as emergent. Alternatively, we might see the underlying principles as operating at the level of the organism. On this construal, the most salient adaptive phenomena like intelligence are no longer unexpected in the same way, so they are less clearly emergent. However, there will then be other kinds of emergent phenomena, such as unexpected by-products of the evolutionary process (e.g. Gould and Lewontin's 'spandrels'). This construal also allows a potential account of one sense in which consciousness seems emergent. Raw consciousness may not have been selected for, but it somehow emerges as an unexpected by-product of selection for adaptive processes such as intelligence.

Overall, our initial understanding of weak emergence, in terms of phenomena that arise from a low-level domain but that are unexpected given the principles of that domain, seems to fit the cases quite well. But of course there is little point in deciding just which of these notions is the definitive analysis of 'weak emergence' as the notion is used in the sciences, just as there is little point in deciding just which of the notions in this chapter is the definitive analysis of 'emergence' itself. Typical uses of the term 'emergence' may well express cluster concepts with many different elements.

Still, we can reasonably hope that most or all of the notions discussed in this chapter may play some role in understanding the many uses of the term 'emergence' in the sciences and in philosophy. More importantly, we can hope that they can play some role in understanding the phenomena to which the term has been applied.

4. REFERENCES

Bedau, M. (1997), 'Weak Emergence', *Philosophical Perspectives*, 11: 375–99.

Broad, C. D. (1925), *The Mind and its Place in Nature* (New York: Routledge).

Chalmers, D. J. (1996), *The Conscious Mind: In Search of a Fundamental Theory* (Oxford: Oxford University Press).

—— (2002), 'Consciousness and its Place in Nature', <http://consc.net/papers/nature.html>.

—— and F. Jackson (2001), 'Conceptual Analysis and Reductive Explanation', *Philosophical Review* 110:315–61.

Hofstadter, D. R. (1977), *Gödel, Escher, Bach: An Eternal Golden Braid* (New York: Basic Books).

Kim, J. (1992), 'The Nonreductivist's Trouble With Mental Causation', in J. Heil and A. Mele (eds.), *Mental Causation* (Oxford: Oxford University Press).

—— (1999), 'Making Sense of Emergence', *Philosophical Studies* 95: 3–36.

McLaughlin, B. P. (1992), 'The Rise and Fall of British Emergentism', in A. Beckermann, H. Flohr, and J. Kim (eds.), *Emergence or Reduction?: Prospects for Nonreductive Physicalism* (Berlin: De Gruyter).

Part IV

Religion and Emergence

12

Emergence, Mind, and Divine Action: The Hierarchy of the Sciences in Relation to the Human Mind–Brain–Body

Arthur Peacocke

1. HIERARCHIES OF COMPLEXITY: 'EMERGENTIST MONISM'

i. 'Levels' in a Philosophical Perspective

The natural and human sciences increasingly give us a picture of the world as consisting of a complex hierarchy—or more accurately, hierarchies—a series of levels of organization and matter in which each successive member of the series is a whole constituted of parts preceding it in the series.[1] The wholes are organized systems of parts that are dynamically and spatially interrelated—a feature sometimes called a 'mereological' relation. Furthermore, all properties also result, directly in isolation, or indirectly in larger patterns, from the properties and relations inherent within the complexity of microphysical entities. This feature of the world is now widely recognized to be of significance in relating our knowledge of the various levels of complexity—

---

[1] Conventionally said to run from the 'lower', less complex to the 'higher', more complex systems—from parts to wholes—so that these wholes themselves constitute parts of more complex entities, rather like a series of Russian dolls. In the complex systems I have in mind here, the parts retain their identity and properties as isolated individual entities. So the systems referred to are those which, loosely speaking, were the concern of the first phase of general systems theory. In those systems the parts (or 'elements') of the complex wholes are physical entities (e.g. atoms, molecules, cells) which are either individually stable or which undergo processes of change (as e.g. in chemical reactions) themselves analysable as being the interchange of stable parts (atoms in that case). The *internal* relations of such elements are not regarded as affected by their incorporation into the system.

that is, the sciences which correspond to these levels.[2] It also corresponds not only to the world in its present condition but also to the way complex systems have evolved in time out of earlier simpler ones.

I shall presume at least this with the 'physicalists': all concrete particulars in the world (including human beings)—with all of their properties—are constituted only of fundamental physical entities of matter/energy at the lowest level and manifested in many layers of complexity—a 'layered' physicalism. I share this view in so far as it is a *monistic* one (a constitutively ontologically reductionist one), namely, that everything can be broken down into whatever physicists deem to constitute matter/energy, and that no extra *entities* are deemed to be operating at higher levels of complexity in order to account for their properties. However, what is even more significant about natural processes and about the relation of complex systems to their constituents is that the concepts needed to describe and understand them—as indeed also the methods needed to investigate each level in the hierarchy of complexity—are specific to and distinctive of those various levels. It is very often the case (but not always) that the properties, concepts, and explanations used to describe the higher-level wholes are not logically reducible to those used to describe their constituent parts, themselves often also constituted of yet smaller entities. This is an epistemological assertion of a non-reductionist kind, and its precise implications have been much discussed. With reference to a *particular* system, whose constitutive parts (or 'elements') are stable, it is possible to affirm that there can indeed be 'theory' autonomy in the sense already indicated above (that is, the logical and conceptual non-reducibility of predicates, concepts, laws, etc. of the theories applied to the higher level) without there being 'process-autonomy' (defined to mean that the processes occurring at the higher level are *more than* an interlocking, in new relations, of the processes in which the constituent parts participate) (Peacocke, 1986, 1994, chs. 1, 2).[3]

When the epistemological non-reducibility of properties, concepts, and explanations applicable to higher levels of complexity is well-established, their employment in scientific discourse can often, *but not in all cases*, lead to a putative and then to an increasingly confident attribution of reality to that to which the higher-level terms refer. Because of widely influential reductionist presuppositions, there has been a tendency to regard the level of quarks (or whatever physicists currently regard as the basic building blocks

---

[2] See, e.g. Arthur Peacocke (1993), 36–43, 214–18, and Fig. 12.1 (based on a scheme of W. Bechtel and A. Abrahamson's (1991), fig. 8.1).
[3] Whether or not this statement about theory- and process-autonomy applies to the relations *between* distinctive systems is another matter.

of the natural world) as alone being 'real'. However, there have long been good grounds for not granting any special priority to this level of description.

In this regard W. C. Wimsatt[4] has argued effectively for the need for a variety of independent derivation, identification, or measurement procedures, which he calls 'multiple determination'. When one is looking for what is invariant (or identical) in any phenomenon, object, or result, one must employ the whole variety of these procedures in order to ascertain the existence and character of the phenomena. What is invariant, at whatever level the procedures are directed, Wimsatt calls 'robust', which implies that what is yielded by the procedures appropriate to each level can be said to be real. *In other words, 'reality' is what the various levels of description and examination (e.g. of living systems) actually refer to.* These levels, so ascertained, are often regarded as having determinative ('causal') efficacy, a proposal discussed further below.

'Reality' is thus not confined to the physico-chemical alone. One must accept a certain 'robustness' of the entities postulated (or, rather, discovered) at different levels, resisting any attempts to regard them as less real in comparison with some favoured lower level of 'reality'. Each level has to be regarded as a 'cut' through the totality of reality, if you like, in the sense that we have to take account of nature's mode of operation at that level. From this perspective, there is no sense in which, for example, subatomic particles—with their properties—are to be regarded as 'more real' than, say, a bacterial cell, a living organism, or a human person. New and distinctive kinds of realities at the higher levels of complexity may properly be said to have *emerged*. This can occur with respect either to moving synchronically up the ladder of complexity or diachronically through cosmic and biological evolutionary history.

ii. 'Levels' in a Research Perspective

Although I have given it only in outline, the foregoing argument for the putative reality—and hence for the 'emergence'—of that to which higher-level terms refer, has been used frequently in the contemporary philosophical debate about reductionism in science. Philosophers have concentrated on the relations between already established theories on different 'levels' in order to determine whether new ontological commitments are warranted with respect

---

[4] W. C. Wimsatt (1981) has elaborated these criteria of 'robustness' for such attributions of reality to emergent properties at higher levels.

to the higher levels or whether statements in higher-level theories can in fact be reduced to those of lower-level theories (perhaps via 'bridge laws').

However, this way of examining the question of reductionism is less appropriate in the context of the biological and social sciences, since in these fields knowledge hardly ever resides in theories with distinctive 'laws'. In these sciences, what is sought is usually a *model* of a complex system which explicates how its components interact to produce the properties and behaviour of the whole system: organelle, cell, multi-cellular organism, ecosystem, and so on. These models are not presented as sentences using terms that must be translated into lower-level terms if reduction is to be successful. Rather, models in the biological and social sciences generally function as visual systems, structures, or maps; they represent multiple interactions, multiple connecting pathways of causes and determinative influences, between entities and processes. In these sciences investigators are generally attempting to explain the properties and interactions of a particular system by asking how the parts of the system give it those properties and interactions at that level. They often find that they have to use new terms, sometimes brought in from other scientific disciplines, in the process of seeking an explanation. When the systems are not simply aggregates of similar units, then it can turn out that the behaviour of the system is due principally, and sometimes entirely, to the distinctive way its parts are put together—which is what models attempt to make clear. Being incorporated into a system constrains the behaviour of the parts and can lead to behaviours at the level of the system as a whole which is often unexpected and unpredicted.

As W. Bechtel and R. C. Richardson have expressed it, '[The behaviours] are *emergent* in that we did not anticipate the properties exhibited by the whole system given what we knew of the parts' (Bechtel and Richardson, 1992, p. 266, emphasis added). They illustrate this from an historical examination of the controversies over fermentation and oxidative phosphorylation, showing how the understanding of a system,

in which the contributions of the parts are recognised, but the organization is understood to generate unanticipated behaviours in the whole system, usually develops later, after those pursuing the more reductionistic path discover that the parts are insufficient to explain the behaviour of the system and turn more to examining how the organization of the system might affect the activities of the parts. (p.267)

What is crucial here is not so much the unpredictability of the results, but rather the inadequacy of explanations when only the parts are focused upon, rather than the whole system.

For example, the yeast fermentation of glucose to produce energy involved a 'highly orchestrated, interlocking *system* of reactions.... This functional organization creates a fermentation system at a level of organization which resides above that at which chemical reactions... occur. Fermentation is thus a distinctive *activity* of a system at a higher level' (pp. 273, 274, emphasis added).

An even more striking example is afforded by the case of research into oxidative phosphorylation. Here again, unpredictability pointed the way, though it is not in itself a unique criterion. Oxidative phosphorylation could not be understood until a model was developed that involved *both* a chemical structure of a special kind (a membrane), without which the process could not occur, *and* a structural organization (the mitochondrion), which turned out to be critical for the cyclic system of reactions to be organized in a particular way:

One had to develop new sorts of models, foreign to the lower level. In these models, the processes associated with the lower level were no longer construed to operate as they would in isolation, but were altered by being constrained to operate in a highly structured system. The complexity made possible sorts of phenomena which could not be generated by the components alone or when put together in a simple manner. Moreover, the effects of such structures could not be anticipated simply by knowing the components. This constitutes a sense in which the phenomena in question are *emergent*: they are different in kind from the phenomena that can be generated without the structured system and can only be understood once we understand the structured systems... (p. 278)

With emergent phenomena, it is the interactive organization, rather than the component behaviour, that is the critical explanatory feature. (p. 285, emphasis added)

There are, therefore, good grounds for re-introducing the concept of 'emergence' into our interpretation of naturally occurring, hierarchical, complex systems constituted of parts which themselves are, at the lowest level, made up of the basic units of the physical world. I shall denote this position as that of *emergentist monism*.[5]

2. WHOLE–PART INFLUENCE (OR 'TOP-DOWN CAUSATION')

If we do make such an ontological commitment about the reality of the 'emergent' whole of a given total system, the question then arises how one

[5] As does Philip Clayton. Note that the term 'monism' is emphatically *not* intended (as is apparent from the non-reductive approach adopted here) in the sense in which it is taken to mean that physics will eventually explain everything (which is what 'physicalism' is usually taken to mean).

is to explicate the relation between the state of the whole and the behaviour of parts of that system at the micro-level. It transpires that extending and enriching the notion of causality now becomes necessary because of new insights into the way complex systems in general, and biological ones in particular, behave.

A more substantial ground for attributing reality to higher-level properties and the entities associated with them is given when the complex wholes possess a distinctive determinative efficacy. This has the effect of making the separated, constituent parts behave in ways they would not do if they were not part of that particular complex system (that is, in the absence of the inter-actions that constitute that system). For *to be real is to have causal power.*[6] New determinative ('causal') powers and properties can then properly be said to have *emerged* when these conditions obtain.

A deeper understanding of how higher levels influence the lower levels of the natural world has allowed application in this context of the notion of a determining ('causal') relation from whole to part (or: from system to con-stituent). Accounts of this whole–part influence must of course never ignore the 'bottom-up' effects of parts on the wholes, for they depend on the distinctive properties of the parts being what they are—albeit now in the new, complex, interacting configuration of the whole. In recent years a number of related concepts have been developed to describe these part–whole relations in both synchronic and diachronic systems—that is, both those in some kind of steady state with stable characteristic emergent features of the whole, and those that display an emergence of new features over the course of time.

The terms *'downward causation'* and *'top-down causation'* were employed by Donald Campbell (1974, pp. 179–86) to denote the way in which an organism's behaviour patterns and the network of its relationships to its environment together determine, over the course of time, the actual DNA sequences at the molecular level present in the evolved organism—even though, from a 'bottom-up' viewpoint of that organism, a molecular biologist would tend to describe its form and behaviour as a consequence of those same DNA sequences. Campbell cites the instance of the evolutionary development of efficacious jaws made of suitable proteins in a worker termite. Because of a certain imprecision and a lack of generalizability in Campbell's example, I prefer to use actual complex systems to clarify this suggestion (see Peacocke, 1983). Consider, for example, the Bénard phenomenon. At a critical point, a fluid heated uniformly from below in a containing vessel ceases to manifest the entirely random 'Brownian' motion of its molecules and begins to display

---

[6] A dictum attributed to S. Alexander by J. Kim (1993), 204, and separately in (1992),134–5.

up-and-down convective currents of literally millions of molecules in columns of hexagonal cross-section—while the individual molecules themselves continue to obey the normal laws covering their motion and interaction. Additionally, certain auto-catalytic reaction systems (e.g. the famous Zhabotinsky reaction and glycolysis in yeast extracts), often after a time interval from the point when first mixed, spontaneously display rhythmic temporal and spatial patterns the forms of which can even depend on the size of the containing vessel. Indeed Harold Morowitz has identified some twenty-eight different emergent levels in the natural world (Morowitz, 2002).

Moreover, many examples of dissipative systems are now known (Peacocke, 1983) which, because they are open, a long way from equilibrium, and non-linear in certain essential relationships between fluxes and forces, can display large-scale patterns in spite of the random motions of the units—'order out of chaos', as Prigogine and Stengers (1984) dubbed it.

In these examples, the ordinary physico-chemical descriptions of the interactions at the micro-level simply cannot account for the observed phenomena. It is clear that what the parts (molecules and ions, in the Bénard and Zhabotinsky cases) are doing and why the patterns they form are what they are *because* of their incorporation into the system-as-a-whole—in fact these are patterns *within* the systems in question. This fact is even clearer in the much more complex (and only partly understood) systems of genes switching on-and-off. The genes' interplay with cell metabolism and with specific protein production is crucial in the processes by which biological forms develop. The parts would not be behaving as observed if they were not parts of that particular system (the 'whole'). The state of the system-as-a-whole is influencing (i.e. acting like a 'cause' on) what the parts, the constituents, actually do. Examples of this kind arise not only in self-organizing and dissipative systems but also, for example, in the literature on economic and social systems.

Terrence Deacon (2001) has usefully categorized emergent phenomena into three levels or 'orders';[7] I draw on his descriptions in what follows:

(1) *First order.*[8] Distribution relationships among micro-elements determine statistical dynamics, which produce the higher-order collective properties. An example is the statistical properties of large aggregates of water molecules. These emergent phenomena are typically synchronic.

---

[7] See Deacon's essay in Ch. 5. A similar proposal is made by Deacon (2003). See also B. Weber and T. Deacon (2000).

[8] Somewhat ambiguously—in view of the intense philosophical discussion concerning the meaning of the term—Deacon calls this 'supervenience', because there is a strict correspondence relation between the higher-level and lower-level properties.

(2) *Second order.* Spatially distributed re-entrant (i.e. feedback) causality allows microstate variation to amplify and influence macrostate development, leading to progressive amplification of microstate influences, increasing divergence, and decreasing predictability—macro-relationships undermine, constrain, and bias micro-relationships. Examples include snow crystal growth, chemical networks (the Zhabotinsky reaction), biochemical cycles (glycolysis), and chaotic and self-organizing (autopoietic) systems (Gregersen, 1998). These emergent phenomena are typically diachronic, developing in time, with symmetry-breaking.

(3) *Third order.* Causality is distributed across time as well as space via memory (i.e. re-presentation of ensemble properties in properties of ensemble elements). The result is a progressive amplification of adaptation and increasing divergence, complexity, and self-organization—a 'self-referential self-organization'. Specific historical moments can exert a cumulative influence over the entire causal future of the system. Third-order emergence inevitably exhibits a developmental and/or evolutionary character; it involves an amplification of global influences on the parts, but also a redundant 'sampling' (= 'natural selection') of these influences. Whereas second-order emergent phenomena exhibit locally and temporally restricted whole-to-part influences, third-order evolutionary emergent phenomena can exhibit amplification of these effects as well. The key example is the evolution of living organisms.

These three subcategories of emergent phenomena can be arranged into a hierarchy of increasing complexity because higher-order forms are composed of lower-order ones. In so far as higher-order emergent phenomena are dependent on lower-order ones, their probability of formation is substantially lower, so that there are vastly more examples of (1) than of (2) than of (3).

For such systems we do not have available any account of events in terms of temporal, linear chains of causality as previously conceived ($A \rightarrow B \rightarrow C \dots$), for the term 'causation' has tended to denote simply a regular chain of events in time (sometimes, too, simply in terms of a Humean conjunction). A wider use of 'causality' and 'causation' is now needed, one that includes the kind of whole–part, higher-to-lower-level relationships that the sciences have themselves recently been discovering in complex systems, especially the biological and neurological ones. One should perhaps better speak of '*determinative influences*' rather than of 'causation', which can have misleading connotations. Where such determinative influence of the whole of a system on its parts occurs, one is justified in attributing reality to those emergent properties and features of the whole system which produce the consequences. This understanding accords with the pragmatic attribution, both in ordinary life and in scientific investigation, of the term 'reality' to that which we cannot avoid taking into account in our diagnosis of the course of events in experience or experiments. Real entities have influence and play irreducible roles in adequate explanations of the world.

Hence the term *whole–part influence* will be used to represent the net effect of all those ways in which a system-as-a-whole, operating from its 'higher' level, is a determining factor in what happens to its constituent parts, the 'lower' level. With arrows representing such influences, the determining relations between the higher (H) and lower (L) levels in such systems and their succession of states (1, 2, 3 ...) may be represented as shown in Fig. 12.1. The vertical lines in the figure represent the mereological relation between the state of the whole system H and the entities of which it is constituted at the lower level L at particular times (1, 2, 3 ...). The diagonal arrow implies that the holistic state H_2 (which is composed of constituents L_2) is determined by ('caused by'), and is a consequence of, the holistic state H_1 *jointly with* L_1 Perhaps it would be better, then, since we are trying to represent holistic states together with their constituents (L), to depict the succession as in Fig. 12.2. This figure attempts to emphasize that there can be a *joint* effect of states H ... with the L ... on successor states at any one time. It is important to stress what these representations still fail to show adequately, namely, that the 'higher levels' (H ...) just are the systems-as-a-whole exerting a determinative influence on the behaviour of their own constituents (the 'lower levels', L ....). Fig. 12.3 is also an attempt to depict this.

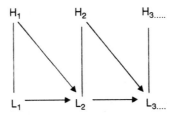

Fig. 12.1

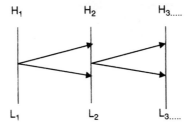

Fig. 12.2

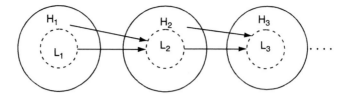

Fig. 12.3

3. THE MIND–BRAIN–BODY RELATION

Much of the discussion of the relation of higher- to lower-levels in hierarchically stratified systems has centred on the mind–brain–body relation, on how mental events are related to neurophysiological events in the human-brain-in-the-human-body—in effect, on the whole question of human agency and what we mean by it. In this context a hierarchy of levels[9] can also be delineated, each of which is the focus of a corresponding scientific study, from neuroanatomy and neurophysiology to psychology. Those involved in studying 'how the brain works' have come to recognize that

[p]roperties not found in components of a lower level can emerge from the organization and interaction of these components at a higher level. For example, rhythmic pattern generation in some neural circuits is a property of the circuit, not of isolated pacemaker neurons. Higher brain functions (e.g., perception, attention) may depend on temporally coherent functional units distributed through different maps and nuclei. (Sejnowski et al., 1988, p. 1300)

Even a traditional physicalist such as Patricia Churchland can express (with T. J. Sejnowski) the aim of research in cognitive neuroscience thus:

The ultimate goal of a unified account does not require that it be a single model that spans all the levels of organisation. Instead the integration will probably consist of a chain of models linking adjacent levels. When one level is explained in terms of a lower level this does not mean that the higher level theory is useless or that the high-level phenomena no longer exists. On the contrary, explanations will co-exist at all levels, as they do in chemistry and physics, genetics and embryology. (Churchland and Sejnowski, 1988, p. 744)

---

[9] The physical scales of these levels are, according to P. S. Churchland and T. J. Sejnowski (1988), 741–5, as follows: molecules, 10^{-10}m.; synapses, 10^{-6}m.; neurones, 10^{-4}m.; networks, 10^{-3}m.; maps, 10^{-2}m.; systems, 10^{-1}m.; central nervous system (CNS), 1m., in human beings.

The still intense philosophical discussion of the mind–brain–body relation has been broadly concerned with attempting to elucidate the relation between the 'top' level of human mental experience and the lowest, bodily physical levels. The question of what kind of 'causation', if any, may be said to be operating from a 'top-down' direction, in addition to the obvious and generally accepted 'bottom-up' direction, is still much debated in this context.

I suggest a clue to this problem is available from the foregoing discussion concerning the general relation of wholes to constituent parts in a hierarchically stratified complex system of stable parts. I have in the past used the term 'whole–part influence'[10] and maintained that a non-reductionist view of the predicates, concepts, laws, and so on applicable to the higher level could be coherent. Reality could putatively be attributed to these non-reducible, higher-level predicates, concepts, laws, and the like, which, together with their distinctive properties, could properly be called 'emergent' and be said to influence the behaviour of their constituent parts. When this emergentist monist approach is applied to the mental activity of the human-brain-in-the-human-body, then, in order to elucidate its nature, 'we must look to vernacular ["folk"] psychology and its characteristic intentional idioms of belief, desire, and the rest, and their intentional analogues in systematic psychology' (Kim, 1993, p. 193). Mental properties are now widely, and in my view rightly, regarded by many philosophers as epistemologically irreducible to physical (that is, neurological) ones.

In the mind–brain–body case the idea that mental properties can be 'physically realized' has also been much deployed in association with the 'non-reductive physicalist' view of the mind–brain issue.[11] This latter view has been summarized by J. Kim (1993, p. 198) in the form of four theses:

---

[10] It must be stressed that the 'whole–part' relation is *not* regarded here necessarily, or frequently, as a spatial one. 'Whole–part' is synonymous with 'system–constituent'.

[11] The idea of mental states being 'physically realized' in neurones was expanded as follows by John Searle (1984), 26 (emphasis added): 'Consciousness ... is a real property of the brain that can cause things to happen. My conscious attempt to perform an action such as raising my arm causes the movement of the arm. At the higher level of description, the intention to raise my arm causes the movement of the arm. At the lower level of description, a series of neuron firings starts a chain of events that results in the contraction of the muscles ... the same sequence of events has two levels of description. *Both of them are causally real,* and the higher level-causal features are both caused by and realised in the structure of the lower level elements.' What follows in the main text here shows that I am not satisfied with Searle's parallelism between the causality of the mental and physical; it is not enough–and I argue later on for a notion of *joint,* rather than parallel causality as being more useful in this context.

(i)   *Physical Monism*: all concrete particulars are physical;
(ii) *Anti-Reductionism*: mental properties are not reducible to physical prop-
      erties;
(iii) *The Physical Realization Thesis*: all mental properties are physically
      realized; that is, whenever an organism, or system, instantiates a mental
      property *M*, it has some physical property *P* such that *P* realizes *M* in
      organisms of its kind;
(iv) *Mental Realism*: mental properties are real properties of objects and
      events; they are not merely useful.

This view is usually represented in a diagram of the form shown in Fig. 12.4.

Kim has argued (1993, pp. 202–5) that this concept (which is complexly
related to the concept of 'supervenience' in many treatments) is paradoxical.
It is usually taken to mean that a microstructure physically realizes a mental
property by being a *sufficient* cause for that property. According to the
physicalist perspective there is complete causal closure at the physical level
alone, which means that mental properties cannot, in fact, have real causal
powers irreducible to physical ones. However, if for mental properties to be
real is for them to have new, irreducible causal powers, as I have argued, then
the *non-reductive* physicalist is committed to downward causation from the
mental to the physical levels. Hence, Kim argues, there is a conflict between
the postulate of downward causation (derived from the non-reducibility,
and the need for causal efficacy, of the mental) and the physicalist's assumption that a complete physical theory can in principle account for all phenomena (causal closure). S. D. Crain has succinctly summarized Kim's conclusion:
'the *non-reductive* physicalist cannot live without downward causation, and
the non-reductive *physicalist* cannot live with it' (Crain, 2004).

What light can be thrown on this particular impasse for non-reductive
physicalism by the above treatment of relations between higher- and lower-
level states in many natural complex systems? I suggest that what Kim is
illicitly assuming is that, when a physical microstructure 'physically realizes' a

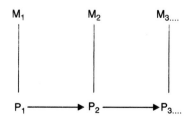

Fig. 12.4

higher-level property (in this case, putatively, a mental one), then a *sufficient* account of the determinative relations can be given in terms of microphysical events at the realizing level, an account entirely (if only eventually) explicated by the laws and theories of physics. However, I have argued that, in the wider range of physical, biological, and other systems previously discussed, the determining effects of the higher levels on the lower ones are real but different in kind from the effects the parts have on each other operating separately at the lower level. The patterns and structures of the higher levels make a real difference in the way the constituents behave. Hence what happens in these systems at the lower level is the result of the *joint* operation of both higher- and lower-level influences. The higher and lower levels could be said to be *jointly* sufficient determinants of the lower-level events, a proposition which has also been developed philosophically in terms of higher- and lower-level properties by Carl Gillett.[12] Recognizing the existence of *jointly* sufficient determinants of lower-level events by including *both* higher- and lower-level influences can illuminate the paradox in non-reductive physicalism as normally propounded, which Kim has accurately identified with respect to the mind–brain issue.

How can we apply this recognition to the relationship between the levels that operate in the mind–brain–body complex? Three graded possibilities suggest themselves, working 'upwards', as it were, from the purely physical.

(1) *Levels H are states of the brain; levels L are individual neuronal events.* Here by a 'state of the brain' is meant the 'temporarily coherent functional

---

[12] See, among other papers, Carl Gillett (2003). After rejecting the hypothesis of the completeness of physics (in the sense that all microphysical events are determined by prior such events and the laws of physics), he explores the possibility that microphysical properties could be *heterogeneous* in their contribution of certain powers and could do so only under conditions when they realize certain properties.

Given that the ontologically fundamental microphysical properties/relations, 'P1', 'P2', 'P3',... 'Pn', instantiated in microphysical individuals 'a1', 'a2', 'a3', etc. realize an instance of a property 'H' in 's', where *s* is constituted by a1, a2, a3, etc. he considers the situation in which P1, a micro-physical realizer of H, contributes one of its causal powers, C^*, causing microphysical effect 'Pz', to individuals only conditionally upon realizing an instance of H. In that case, 'the property H partially determines the contribution of causal power to an individual, since P1 only contributes C^* to individuals when realizing H... The crucial point is that in the particular circumstances, H is a necessary member of the properties which are only jointly sufficient for determining the contribution of C^* to a1. There is thus a prima facie reason to believe, in this situation, first, that the realised property H is a causally efficacious property, since it partially determines the contribution of a power to an individual, and, second, that HCE [Higher Causal Efficacy—that there are causally efficacious realised properties] is consequently also true' (p.96). Gillett concludes that 'it very well may be the case that PHY [Physicalism—all individuals are constituted by, or identical to, physical individuals, and all properties are realized by, or identical to, physical properties] and HCE can both be true when we purge ourselves of CoP [the completeness of physics]' (p.98).

units distributed through different maps and nuclei' (Churchland and Sejnowski, 1988)—that is, it refers to the spatial and temporal *patterns* of activity at the brain level, as can be observed externally by empirical techniques. When the higher–lower level relation under consideration is the one that pertains to brain activity and its constituent neurones, the same considerations should apply as in those other natural complex systems already discussed—so that the relation of these particular higher to lower levels may be represented as in Figs. 12.1–12.3.[13] That is, L_1, L_2 ... in those diagrams would represent micro-component (individual neuronal) states, and H_1, H_2 ... would represent the succession of brain states constituted by the micro-components *together with* their complex activity and distributed patterns of interaction.

What is significant about this proposal is the presence in Fig. 12.1 of those diagonal arrows (from H_1 to L_2, H_2 to L_3 ...), which now can be taken to represent the influence of holistic brain states (H) on individual neuronal micro-states (L), the succession of which is therefore caused *jointly* by the preceding states of both H and L. As with those other complex systems, this diagonal arrow implies that the holistic brain state H_2 is what it is because of the determinative influence of the holistic brain state H_1, jointly with L_1. Thus in this instance the interrelations could also be depicted as in Figs. 12.2 and 12.3.

(2) *Levels H are mental-with-brain states; levels L are individual neuronal events.* In (1) the 'higher' states H being referred to were holistic brain states, patterns of neurophysiological activity—and so basically *physical* states. However, the increasingly empirically confirmed tight link between, on the one hand, patterns of brain activity and, on the other, particular *mental* activities means that the succession of brain states is *at least* covariant with a particular succession of mental events, even though there is an irreducible relation between the language of mental events and those of neural events.[14] We shall now call them 'mental-with-brain states' because of this tight empirical association of epistemologically irreducible mental events with brain states. I suggest that it is reasonable to apply to this relation—the relation of mental-with-brain states to neural events—the same interpretation that I have applied to the complex systems already considered. That is, the patterns of higher-level holistic states (the H_1 ... of Figs. 12.1–12.3) can be *jointly* determinative influences, together with the lower-level constituents (the

---

[13] Niels H. Gregersen (2000) has usefully extended depictions of this kind by adding 'above' the higher level the effect of the realm of cultural contents on mental events; and 'below' the 'lower' level the global physical situation as a factor influencing that level (see his Fig.2).

[14] It is, of course, this enigma that the languages of the 'physical realization' and the 'supervenience' of mental events have attempted to explicate.

$L_1 \ldots$ of Figs. 12.1–12.3), on the succession of states of the whole complex—what may be depicted as $(H_1 - L_1)$, $(H_2 - L_2)$, and so on.[15] This is to postulate that the higher-level, now mental-with-brain states (the $M_1 \ldots$ of Fig. 12.4) have a determinative influence, *jointly* with the lower-level neural states (the $P_1 \ldots$ of Fig. 12.4), on the succession of mental-with-brain states, $(M_1 - P_1)$, $(M_2 - P_2)$, and so on. The sequence of mental-with-brain states is itself then a determinative influence on the succession of *its own* neuronal constituents, as already elaborated, so that on this proposal diagonal arrows should be added to Fig. 12.4, as in Fig. 12.1 (and other versions corresponding to Figs. 12.2 and 12.3).

Note that, in this perspective, mental events have a determinative influence on events at the neuronal 'micro'-level—the level that the non-reductive physicalist has hitherto been taking as alone doing the causal work, that is, as determining the succession not only of their own states but those of the mental-with-brain states too. Hence the physicalist's assumption that all causation is mediated through physical entities[16] (which includes the brain) does not, even in this perspective, preclude an influence of the patterns of mental events. Mental events, which are tightly linked with brain states and their associated patterns, can also exert determinative whole–part influences on their micro-neuronal constituents.

(3) *Levels H are mental states; levels L are brain states.* Since mental activity, the content of consciousness, appears in the hierarchy of complexity of natural systems only at the level of the human-brain- in-the-human-body, it has a strong claim to be regarded as a genuine *emergent* in the strong sense already discussed—especially because of the irreducibility of mental to physical language. Our experience of willed action supports the postulate that in some way mental events are indeed causally effective; and this, together with the irreducibility of mental language just mentioned, is a strong pointer to attributing a new level of reality to the mental. In this perspective, mental activity—the content of our consciousness describable in first-person language—is a real emergent *from* brain activity. As such, it could be causally effective on successive brain states, as in other H–L systems. In the other cases, however, the higher-level states are all capable of physical descriptions, even if complex ones. Since a succession of mental states—unlike the succession of states, say, in oxidative phosphorylation—is not so describable, one has to recognize that

---

[15] Dashes replacing the vertical lines in the figures.

[16] But, as is apparent elsewhere in this chapter, I do *not* take this to mean that 'all micro-physical events are determined, insofar as they are determined, by prior microphysical events and the laws of physics', as C. Gillett (2003) defines the 'Completeness of Physics'.

this proposal extrapolates from a known kind of relationship in the hierarchy of physical and biological complexity to a new level of relation (mind-to-brain).

However, extrapolating from the known to the unknown or, rather, from the understood to the not-understood, has frequently been a successful ploy in investigating the natural world. Doing so under Postulate (3) would then entail the same kind of 'diagonal' *joint* efficacy of the higher level (mental states) and of the lower level (brain states) on the simultaneous and covariant succession of mental and brain states, as in the physical systems already described and understood. Note that this is still a *monist*, not a dualist, proposal, for, according to it, mental states are emergent only upon brain states.[17] Nonetheless, it does imply that this mental emergence is a distinctive reality which has its own determinative efficacy.

Most non-reductive physicalists hold a much less realistic view of these higher-level mental properties than I wish to affirm here in this emergentist monist perspective.[18] The difference is particularly evident in their talk of the 'physical realization' of the mental in the physical when such talk is not supplemented by any further discussion of whole–part influences. Non-reductive physicalists also generally do not attribute determinative (causal) powers to that to which higher level concepts refer. Just as the complex brain states can be said to emerge from the states of the individual neurones, so similarly mental states can coherently be regarded as emergent from brain states, as having determinative efficacy, and therefore as also being real. The content of 'consciousness' then putatively becomes how we describe to ourselves the holistic higher-level state of the component neurones, synapses, etc. of our brains.

The foregoing cannot pretend to explicate fully the relation between the content of mental events and holistic brain states, but at least it rests on empirical observations of the intimacy and tightness of that relation. Perhaps the capacity of mentalistic language to refer to its own activity in the experience of consciousness may one day be understood. In the meantime it is legitimate to postulate, with respect to human persons, a whole–part determinative influence (top-down causation) of holistic mental states via lower brain states on the 'micro-physical' neuronal level, and so on the body.

---

[17] Themselves emergent only from micro, neuronal events.

[18] This emergentist monist perspective emphasizes that the higher level in this context is real and has determinative ('causal') efficacy in a way that, in general, the purely epistemological assertion of 'dual-aspect monism' (affirming that mind–brain events may be *viewed* from two different perspectives) does not. Talk of two 'aspects' does not imply any *determinative ('causal')* relation between the aspects—any more than between the similarly postulated wave and particle 'aspects' of the electron.

In this instance, mental events, such as intentions—whatever they are onto-logically—have determinative ('causal') efficacy in the physical world, a view that can scarcely be doubted in view of the ability of human agents to act in the world (e.g. intending, then effecting, the picking up of an object). *How* this might be so, consistent with well-understood relations in complex systems, is the issue to which the preceding discussion is addressed.

4. PERSONS

Up to this point, I have been taking the term 'mental' to refer to that activity which is an emergent reality especially distinctive of human beings. But in many wider contexts, not least that of philosophical theology, a higher and more inclusive term for this emergent reality would be 'person', and its cognate 'personal'. These terms represent the total psychosomatic, holistic experience of the human being in all its modalities: conscious and unconscious, rational and emotional, active and passive, individual and social, and so on. The concept of personhood recognizes that, as Philip Clayton puts it,

We have thoughts, wishes and desires that together constitute our character. We express these mental states through our bodies, which are simultaneously our organs of perception and our means of affecting other things and persons in the world... [The massive literature on theories of personhood] clearly points to the indispensability of embodiedness as the precondition for perception and action, moral agency, community and freedom—all aspects that philosophers take as indispensable to human personhood and that theologians have viewed as part of the *imago dei*. (Clayton, 1998, p. 205)[19]

There is a strong case for designating the highest level, the whole, in that unique system which is the human-brain-in-the-human-body-in-social-relations by means of the term 'person'. The reality of the person then stands at the apex of the complex systems of the world. For to speak only of mental states as having downward determinative ('causal') efficacy on lower-level brain and neuronal events does not do justice to the rich complexity of the actual higher level of the *person*, namely, of the human-brain-in-the-human-body-in-social-relations. Persons as such experience themselves as *inter alia* determinative agents with respect to their own bodies and the surrounding world (including other persons), so that the exercise of personal *agency* by individuals transpires to be a paradigm case and supreme exemplar of

---

[19] See also, Clayton (1997), ch.4.

whole–part influence. Persons can, moreover, report with varying degrees of accuracy to themselves (and by language also to others) on aspects of their internal mental states, and so implicitly on their brain states concomitant with their actions. In other words, 'folk psychology' is unavoidable and the real reference of the language of 'personhood' is justified. Be it noted, too, that at the personal level, human beings experience those 'signals of transcendence' which are the universal spiritual possession of humanity and the impetus of the religious quest.

5. 'WHOLE–PART INFLUENCE' AS A MODEL FOR GOD'S INTERACTION WITH THE WORLD

In a world that is a closed causal nexus, increasingly explicated by the sciences, how might God be conceived of as influencing particular events, or patterns of events, in the world without interrupting the regularities observed at the various levels studied by the sciences? Initially, let us prescind from any analogy with the mind–brain–body relation or with personal agency.

A model I have proposed is based on the recognition that the omniscient God uniquely knows, over all frameworks of reference of time and space, everything that it is possible to know about the state(s) of all-that-is, including the interconnectedness and interdependence of the world's entities, structures, and processes. This is a pan*en*theistic[20] perspective, for it conceives of the world as, in some sense, being 'in' God, who is also 'more' than the world. It also follows that the world would be subject to any divine determinative influences that do not involve matter or energy (or forces). Thus, mediated by such whole–part influences on the world-as-a-whole (as a *System*-of-systems) and thereby on its constituents, God could bring about the occurrence of particular events and patterns of events—those which express God's intentions. These would then be the result of 'special, divine action', as distinct from the divine holding in existence of all-that-is, and so would not otherwise have happened had God not so intended. By analogy with the exercise of whole–part influence in the natural systems already discussed, such a unitive, holistic effect of God on the world could occur without abrogating[21] any of

---

[20] For a contemporary discussion of panentheism see Philip Clayton and Arthur Peacocke (2004).
[21] N.B., the same may be said of *human* agency in the world. Note also that this proposal recognizes more explicitly than is usually expressed that the 'laws' and regularities which constitute the sciences usually apply only to certain perceived, if ill-defined, levels within the complex hierarchies of nature.

the laws (regularities) which apply to the levels of the world's constituents. This influence would be distinguished from God's universal creative action in that particular intentions of God for particular patterns of events to occur are thereby effected; *inter alia*, patterns could be intended by God in response to human actions or prayers.

The ontological 'interface' at which God must be deemed to be influencing the world is, on this model, that which occurs between God and the totality of the world (= all-that-is), and this may be conceived of panentheistically as within God's own self. What passes across this 'interface', I have also suggested,[22] may perhaps be conceived of as something like a flow of information—a pattern-forming influence. Of course, one has to admit that, because of the 'ontological gap(s)' between God and the world which must always exist in any theistic model, this is only an attempt at making intelligible that which we can postulate as being the initial effect of God experienced from, as it were, our side of the ontological boundary.[23] Whether or not this use of the notion of information flow proves helpful in this context, we do need some way of indicating that the effect of God at this level, and hence at all levels, is that of pattern-shaping in its most general sense. I am encouraged in this kind of exploration by the recognition that the Johannine concept of the *Logos*, the Word of God, may be taken to emphasize God's creative patterning of the world and also God's self-expression *in* the world.

On this model, the question arises at what level or levels in the world such divine influences might be coherently conceived as acting. By analogy with the operation of whole–part influence in natural systems, I have in the past suggested that, because the 'ontological gap(s)' between the world and God is/ are located simply *everywhere* in space and time, God could affect holistically the state of the world (the whole in this context) at all levels. Understood in this way, the proposal implies that patterns of events at the physical, biological, human, and even social levels could be influenced by divine intention without abrogating natural regularities at any of these levels. In this form it poses in a particularly acute form the challenge of 'special divine action' to current scientific understandings of the world as a closed nexus of webs of causes and whole–part influences. The sharpness of this challenge is arguably less if the top-down influence of God is conceived as operating mainly, or even exclusively, at the level of the human person, the emergent reality of which we have already located as at the apex of the systems-based

[22] *TSA*, pp.161, 164. John Polkinghorne (1996, pp. 36–7) has made a similar proposal in terms of the divine input of 'active information'.
[23] I would not wish to tie the proposed model too tightly to a 'flow of information' interpretation of the mind–brain–body problem.

complexities of the world. God would then be thought of as acting in the world in a top-down manner by shaping human personal experience which thereby effects events at the physical, biological, and social levels.

These two limiting forms of the proposal of special divine action by top-down divine influence are not mutually exclusive. However, divine action in a form that is confined to the personal level is less challenged by (has more 'traction' with) the general scientific account of the world than when such divine action is proposed to be at *all* levels. At this stage in formulating my response, I am inclined to postulate divine top-down influences at all levels, but with an increasing intensity and precision of location in time from the lowest physical levels up to the personal level, where they could be at their most intense and most focused. More general theological considerations need to be brought to bear on how to formulate this model of special divine action. One relevant consideration might be developed as follows.

I hope the model as described so far has a degree of plausibility in that it depends only on an analogy with complex natural systems in general and on the way whole–part influence operates in them. It is, however, clearly too impersonal to do justice to the *personal* character of many (but not all) of the profoundest human experiences of God. So there is little doubt that it needs to be rendered more cogent by recognizing, as I have argued above, that among natural systems the instance *par excellence* of whole–part influence in a complex system is that of personal agency. Indeed I could not avoid speaking above of God's 'intentions' and implying that, like human persons, God had purposes to be implemented in the world. For if God is going to affect events and patterns of events in the world, we cannot avoid attributing personal predicates such as intentions and purposes to God—inadequate and easily misunderstood as they are. So we have to say that, though God is ineffable and ultimately unknowable in essence, yet God 'is at least personal', and personal language attributed to God is less misleading than saying nothing! That being so, we can now legitimately turn to the exemplification of whole–part influence in the mind–brain–body relation as a resource for modelling God's interaction with the world. When we do so, the cogency of the 'personal' as a category for explicating the wholeness of human agency reasserts itself and the traditional, indeed biblical, model of God as in some sense a 'personal' agent in the world, acting especially on persons, is rehabilitated—but now in a quite different metaphysical, non-dualist framework, and coherent with the worldview which the sciences engender.[24]

---

[24] See *TSA*, pp.160–6, for an elaboration of this move. For the history and development of this proposal see Peacocke (1995), *note* 1, p.263; see also *note* 1, p.215, in Peacocke (1999).

6. REFERENCES

Bechtel, William and A. Abrahamson (1991), *Connectionism and the Mind* (Oxford and Cambridge, Mass: Blackwell).

—— and Robert C. Richardson (1992), 'Emergent Phenomena and Complex Systems', in A. Beckermann, H. Flohr, and J. Kim (eds.), *Emergence or Reductionism?* (Berlin and New York: Walter de Gruyter).

Campbell, D. T. (1974), ' "Downward causation" in Hierarchically Organised Systems', in F. J. Ayala and T. Dobhzhansky (eds.), *Studies in the Philosophy of Biology: Reduction and Related Problems* (London: Macmillan).

Churchland, P. S., and T. J. Sejnowski (1988), 'Perspectives in Cognitive Neuroscience', *Science* 242, 741–5.

Clayton, Philip (1997), *God and Contemporary Science* (Edinburgh: Edinburgh University Press).

—— (1998), 'The Case for Christian Panentheism', *Dialog* 37/3 (Summer 1998), 201–8.

—— and Arthur Peacocke (eds.) (2004), *In Whom We Live and Move and Have Our Being: Panentheistic Reflections on God's Presence in a Scientific World* (Grand Rapids, MI: Eerdmans).

Crain, Steven D. (2004), Unpublished Paper.

Deacon, Terence (2001), 'Three Levels of Emergent Phenomena', Paper Presented to the *Science and Spiritual Quest Boston Conference,* 21–3 October 2001.

—— (2003), 'The Hierarchic Logic of Emergence: Untangling the Interdependence of Evolution and Self-Organization', in B. Weber and D. Depew (eds.), *Evolution and Learning: The Baldwin Effect Reconsidered* (Cambridge, MA: MIT Press).

Gillett, Carl (2003), 'Strong Emergence as a Defense of Non-Reductive Physicalism: A Physicalist Metaphysics for "Downward Causation" ', *Principia,* 6: 83–114.

Gregersen, N. H. (1998), 'The Idea of Creation and the Theory of Autopoietic Processes', *Zygon* 33: 333–67.

—— (2000), 'God's Public Traffic: Holistic Versus Physicalist Supervenience', in N. H. Gregersen, W. B. Drees, and U. Görman (eds.), *Human Person in Science and Theology* (Edinburgh: T. & T. Clark), 153–88.

Kim, J. (1992), ' "Downward Causation" in Emergentism and Nonreductive Physicalism', in A. Beckermann, H. Flohr, and J. Kim (eds.), *Emergence or Reduction? Essays on the Prospects of Nonreductive Physicalism* (New York: Walter de Gruyter).

—— (1993), 'Non-Reductivism and Mental Causation', in J. Heil and A. Mele (eds.), *Mental Causation* (Oxford: Clarendon Press).

Morowitz, Harold (2002), *Emergence* (New York: Oxford University Press).

Peacocke, Arthur (1983, 1989), *The Physical Chemistry of Biological Organization* (Oxford: Clarendon Press).

—— (1993), *Theology for a Scientific Age: Being and Becoming - Natural, Divine and Human* (Minneapolis: Fortress and SCM Press)—'TSA'.

Peacocke, Arthur (1994), *God and the New Biology* (London: Dent, 1986, repr. Peter Smith, Gloucester, MA).

—— (1995), 'God's Interaction with the World: The Implications of Deterministic "Chaos" and of Interconnected and Interdependent Complexity', in R. J. Russell, N. Murphy, and A. R. Peacocke (eds.), *Chaos and Complexity: Scientific Perspectives on Divine Action* (Notre Dame, IN: University of Notre Dame Press), 263–87.

—— (1999), 'The Sound of Sheer Silence: How Does God Communicate With Humanity?', in R. J. Russell, N. Murphy, T. C. Meyering and M. A. Arbib (eds.), *Neuroscience and the Person: Scientific Perspectives on Divine Action* (Notre Dame, IN: University of Notre Dame Press), 215–47.

Polkinghorne, John (1996), *Scientists as Theologians*, (London: SPCK).

Prigogine, I., and I. Stengers (1984), *Order Out of Chaos* (London: Heinemann).

Searle, John (1984), *Minds, Brain and Science* (Cambridge, MA: Harvard University Press).

Sejnowski, T. J., C. Koch, and P. Churchland (1988), 'Perspectives in Cognitive Neuroscience', *Science* 241, 1300.

Weber, Bruce, and Terence Deacon (2000), *Cybernetics & Human Knowing* 7: 21–43.

Wimsatt, W. C. (1981), 'Robustness, Reliability and Multiple-determination in Science', in M. Brewer and B. Collins (eds.), *Knowing and Validating in the Social Sciences: A tribute to Donald T. Campbell*, (San Francisco: Jossey-Bass).

13

Emergence: What is at Stake for Religious Reflection?

Niels Henrik Gregersen

1. INTRODUCTION

The world of nature exhibits many examples of emergence: the crystalline structure of water under low temperature, which we call ice; the reaction chains of fire and gunpowder that result in explosions; the formation of flocks when there are enough birds; the awakening of awareness in embryos; and the incessant creation of new words and meaning in human languages. Nature is a continuous source of surprise.

So far everyone agrees. The natural leaps of evolutionary novelty are to be accepted as empirical facts with an attitude of 'natural piety', to use Samuel Alexander's famous phrase.[1] What is up for debate, however, is the onto-logical status of emergent phenomena. Are emergent properties merely the epiphenomenal outcomes of fundamental microphysical processes? Or do higher-order systems acquire new forms of causal influence which affect the lower-level entities by which they are constituted? There are emergentists who make weak epistemological claims and emergentists who make strong ontological claims.

In both cases, however, the concept of emergence generally remains within the confines of natural explanations. Referring to natural piety, therefore, does not mean invoking supernatural explanations.[2] On the contrary, the idea

---

[1] See Alexander's expression in *Space, Time and Deity* (1927, vol. II, pp. 46–7): 'The existence of emergent qualities thus described is something to be noted, as some would say, under the compulsion of brute empirical fact, or, as I should prefer to say in less harsh terms, to be accepted with the "natural piety" of the investigator. It admits no explanation.'

[2] C. Lloyd Morgan, who saw God as the ultimate cause of evolution, likewise emphasized the naturalistic thrust of the idea of emergence in *Emergent Evolution*, p. 2: 'In other words the position is that, in a philosophy based on the procedure sanctioned by progress in scientific research and thought, the advent of novelty of any kind is loyally to be accepted wherever it is

of emergence arose within the climate of established evolutionary thinking. Scientists as well as philosophers and theologians are today prepared to accept that more can come out of less. Novelty is produced through new material constellations, which are able to do things that the individual parts cannot perform on their own. Thus, the change from potential to actual states does not depend on the prior existence of a fully actualized being (like God), as had been claimed in Aristotelian and medieval metaphysics. The Thomistic principle, itself derived from Aristotle, stated that 'the perfections of effects pre-exist in their causes'; for example, fire, which is actually hot, causes wood, which is only potentially hot, to inflame (Aquinas, *Summa Theologiae*, Ia, q. 4 a. 2). The early twentieth-century emergentists superseded this principle by recognizing that 'the effects' do in fact include distinctively new properties that did not exist prior to their evolutionary appearance—neither in God nor as pre-existing seminal forces in matter. As pointed out by Alexander, '[t]o call it [i.e. a physico-chemical structure] organism is but to mark the fact that its behaviour, its response to stimulation, is, *owing to the constellation*, of a character different from those which physics and chemistry are ordinarily concerned with, and in this sense something new with an appropriate quality, that of life' (Alexander, 1927, p. 62, italics added). It's not always matter that matters, but frequently also the arrangements or patterns of material entities. Alongside mass and energy, information and informational structures are quintessential to the understanding of nature (see Gregersen, 2004).

This naturalistic thrust, however, does not preclude a religious interpretation of the emerging world. From the outset, the idea of emergence was embraced by religious thinkers of various kinds. Samuel Alexander developed a position which lingered between a Spinozistic pantheism and an evolutionary theism; Lloyd Morgan combined his naturalistic view of emergence with a classical theism, claiming that all-that-is ultimately depends on God as an 'immaterial source of all' (Morgan, 1923, p. 298); other emergentists, such as Roy Wood Sellars (1922), carefully wanted to avoid any religious interpretation of nature.

As the history of emergentism since the 1920s has shown, the discussion of emergent phenomena can take place at three distinct, yet nonetheless correlated, levels: scientific, philosophical, and theological. The scientific question is *how* emergent properties come about under specific *causal* conditions. It seems obvious that even though the same term 'emergence' is

---

found, without invoking any extra-natural Power (Force, Entelechy, Élan, or God) through the efficient Activity of which the observed facts may be explained.'

used for describing a vast variety of processes, this scientific question can best be dealt with on a case-to-case basis. It's not very likely that the emergence of language (which evolves through an intricate interplay between the central nervous system and historically evolved social institutions) can be scientifically explained by employing the same model that is used in explaining ice crystals, which supervene on a clearly defined subvenient base of chemical bonds.[3] Secondly, we have the philosophical issue of clarifying the diverse meanings of emergence as we go from one domain to another. This task involves sorting out the distinctive claims of emergence, weaker or stronger. But thirdly and finally, we have the task of formulating a metaphysical and/or theological synthesis, one that aims to explain in a coherent manner what the phenomena of emergence may tell us about the world that we inhabit, when interpreted in light of other features of experience and other well-tested scientific theories.

In what follows I will briefly present some of the major philosophical positions at the second level, the level of philosophical analysis. But my main effort will be devoted to the third task. Five distinct models for appropriating the idea of emergence from a religious perspective will be presented. These I shall dub as (1) Flat Religious Naturalism, (2) Evolving Theistic Naturalism, (3) Atemporal Theism, (4) Temporal Theism, and (5) Eschatological Theism. My aim is to present a typology that can serve as an overview of the current situation and at the same time offer a pathway for further explorations. The order of models to be presented will follow the range of theological claims at stake, so that I begin by presenting positions with minimal religious claims and end up referring to positions with stronger religious claims. As will become evident, emergent properties and processes are central to some theological views, whereas emergence plays a more subordinate role in other theological positions. It will also become clear that some theological positions will require a strong view of emergence, whereas others can rest content with weak emergence. I therefore begin with a brief analysis of strong and weak claims of emergence.

---

[3] In his book, *The Emergence of Everything: How the World became Complex*, Harold Morowitz (2002) uses the term 'emergence' in a manner very similar to John Maynard Smith's and Eörs Szatmáry's concept of 'evolutionary transitions'; see their *The Origins of Life: From the Birth of Life to the Origins of Language*. While I fully acknowledge the attraction of choosing emergence as a covering term for these processes, it remains pertinent to clarify the different meanings of emergence and the variety of causal claims involved in the notion of emergence.

2. WEAK AND STRONG: EPISTEMOLOGICAL VERSUS
ONTOLOGICAL VERSIONS OF EMERGENCE

How can one define the difference between 'emergents' and mere 'resultants', to use the distinction first introduced by G. H. Lewes in his *Problem of Life and Mind* (Lewes, 1877, p. 412)? Think of a musical chord in a Beethoven symphony: the symphony certainly consists of distinct sounds from the many instruments, but the 'chordiness' of the performance is more than the sum of individual sounds. Reflecting on the phenomenon of chordiness, C. Lloyd Morgan argued that there may often be uncorrelated resultants without emergence, but there exist no emergents without resultants, since the latter provide the continuity that underlies any new steps in emergence (Morgan, 1923, p. 5). It is not quite clear, however, what this example may tell us about the ontological status of emergent phenomena in general. That an organized whole is more than the sum of the parts is an insight that already Plato formulated when he pointed out that the meaning of a word is more than the sum of the letters, each taken individually (*Theaetetus* 203 E; cf. *Laws* 903 B–C). Both Plato's and Morgan's examples, however, draw on qualia, the felt qualities of experience, and on the apprehension of meaning among human beings. While human experience certainly makes up one of the strongest candidates for emergence, consciousness may be too specific a case to support a fully comprehensive theory of emergence.

Let me instead focus on the case of bird flocking. The movements of the individual birds seem to depend on the concerted formation of bird flocks, and on an evolved system for signalling and responding, which only comes into being at the level of entire bird populations. Groups of geese are able to move in the spring from Denmark over Svalbard to the east coast of Greenland, a remarkably long route of around 10,000 kilometres. It seems reasonable to suggest that such transport of organisms, limbs, tissues, cells, molecules and atoms, and so on, could never be explained from the micro-physical level of physical or biochemical laws alone. A scientific explanation of bird migration obviously requires the inclusion of evolutionary explanations of historically evolved macro-patterns, which, according to the general consensus within theoretical biology, are not reducible to physical or chemical explanations (see Mayr, 1982). It is also likely that, in addition to long-term selection pressures under specific environmental conditions, a fuller explanation of migration patterns will eventually demand the inclusion of learning processes as well (see Weber and Depew, 2003).

The question is, then, how this scientific state of the art is to be understood philosophically. Let me here confine myself to two major philosophical options.[4] The first position holds that the emergence of holistic patterns in fact *could* be fully explained by the constituent parts of the configuration, so that emergent phenomena, in reality, are nothing but the supervenient properties arising out of the subvenient physical parts; it's the latter that are responsible for all the causal work. On this view, higher-order emergent properties may not be *expressible* in terms of lower-level properties, but the higher-order emergent properties are nonetheless, at least in principle, *causally reducible* to lower-level microphysical causation. That is, if we imagined a mathematical archangel, or a Laplacean calculator with infinite computational capacities, she would be able to explain the movements of higher-order systems (at each given level B, C, D, ...) from her full knowledge of the entities at the constituent level (level A).

Interestingly, we find this notion of emergence expressed in a seminal paper from 1948 by Carl Hempel and Paul Oppenheimer, in which they present their famous Covering Law Model of scientific explanation. They argue that 'emergence of a characteristic is not an ontological trait inherent in some phenomena: rather it is indicative of the scope of our knowledge at a given time. Thus it has no absolute, but a relative character; and what is emergent with respect to the theories today may lose its emergent status tomorrow' (Hempel and Oppenheimer, reprinted in Pitt, 1988, p. 21). A closer analysis reveals that Hempel and Oppenheimer make four moves to circumvent an ontological interpretation of emergence. They first make the proper observation that the characterization of something as emergent is indeed relative in character, that is, relative to a presupposed explanatory theory; they secondly make the 'in principle'—or 'not yet'—argument that future research may be able to reduce what cannot be reduced in the light of today's science; they thirdly argue that the emergent character of biological and psychological phenomena is 'trivial' (Pitt, 1988, p. 22), since emergence is only about the failure of deductive inference from physics to biology at the level of intra-scientific explanations; and fourthly, they conclude that emergence is predicated only about 'characteristics' or properties of an object, but not about real-world objects or systems, since all-that-exists is comprised by micro-physical entities. Accordingly they propose the following definition of emergence: 'The occurrence of a characteristic W in an object w is emergent relative to a theory T, a part relation Pt, and a class G of attributes if that occurrence cannot be deduced by means of T from a characterization of the Pt-parts of w with respect to all the

---

[4] A very helpful analysis of the philosophical discussion is Timothy O'Connor and Hong Yu-Wong (2002). See also various other chapters in this volume, where these issues are discussed in great detail, esp. in Philip Clayton's introductory chapter.

attributes in *G'* (Pitt, 1988, p. 21). What Hempel and Oppenheimer do not acknowledge, however, is that it will hardly ever—in fact, never—be possible for any future science (which has to work within the *finite* computational resources available in our universe) to escape the fact of the intra-scientific non-reducibility of explanations from evolutionary biology to physics.[5] Neither do they discuss the possibility that new causal capacities (e.g. selection principles) come to work at the level of higher-order systems (such as organisms, populations, and macro-evolutionary developments), which in fact do have positive and negative feedback effects on the constituent level of those systems. The simple example of migration of groups of geese, considered above, may count as one such example.

On the epistemological view of emergence, proposed by Hempel and Oppenheimer, talk of emergence is only a useful shorthand for referring to delicate complex structures; even though proponents of this view always admit that we do not actually have in hand bridging laws that connect lower-level types to higher-level, they simply assume a token–token causation from microphysics to macrophysics.[6] Accordingly, emergence is perceived as a rather trivial affair that does not have any special implications for expanding our current scientific world view. In short, emergent phenomena are not based on new real-world systems; they are merely properties with the following two characteristics:

(1) *the feature of epistemic novelty:* something distinctively new appears (relative to our present-day theories);
(2) *the feature of conceptual non-reducibility:* higher-order emergent levels are not (yet) expressible or explainable in terms of the explanatory models at hand concerning the micro-physical elements.

This view is what henceforth will be termed 'weak emergentism'. The other option, explored by a number of authors in this volume, is that higher-order emergent properties and processes are also ontologically real in terms of being causally efficient. This stronger view of emergence bases itself on the additional requirement of a causal influence of the higher-order structures upon their constituent level:

---

[5] Based on computational arguments, the molecular biologist and director of the Max-Planck Institute in Tübingen, Alfred Gierer, argued for a 'finitistic epistemology' (1988). On the basis of the physical nature of our present universe, Paul Davies has recently made a similar argument in his unpublished paper, 'Emergent Biological Principles and the Computational Properties of the Universe' (2004).

[6] Or at least a fully determinable functional explanation is assumed, as in Jaegwon Kim's position in Ch. 8.

(3) *the feature of top-down causality:* higher or more comprehensive levels of organization do exercise a dynamic influence on their constituent levels, for example, by positive feedback, negative feedback, or selective emphasis.

This view would also imply that higher-order systems are ontologically 'real' by virtue of their causal efficacy. It is important to note, however, that this stronger view of ontological emergence also presupposes an antecedent bottom-up influence from the constituent physico-chemical level which has led to the emergence of the biological, psychological, or social levels of organization. There exist no emergents that are not *also* resultants; strong emergentists will therefore embrace reductionist analysis, though they will argue that in some cases a causal reduction to the constituent parts will not offer a sufficient explanation.

Also, in order for the causal efficacy of higher-order systems to work, it is not necessary to postulate new physical or energetic forces at the constituent level. As Terrence Deacon argues, the top-down causal constraints and influences depend on the particular topologies or patterns that make up the context in which emergent processes take place:

What needs to be explained, then, is not a new form of causality, but how some systems come to be dominated by their higher-order topical properties so that these appear to 'drag along' component constituent dynamics, even though, at the same time, these higher-order regularities are also constituted by lower-order interactions.... I believe that we can understand emergent phenomena as all being variant forms of what might be called *topological reinforcement or amplification in pattern formation.* (Deacon, 2003, p. 283)

On this basis, Deacon suggests a typology of three forms of emergence. First we have the often trivial cases of *first-order emergence* through supervenience relations, in which the properties of the higher-order systems depend on the subvenient level, such as the 'aquosity' of water, which depends on the chemical bonding between hydrogen and oxygen, the presence of many H_2Os, and the appropriate thermal conditions. A *second-order* variant of emergence takes place through chaos and self-organization, where the environmental conditions play a formative role in combination with the history of the system. An example is the formation of snow crystals, which are caused not only by the first-order physical properties of ice (which yield a preference for hexagonal structures), but also by the radial symmetry of heat dissipation and the unique history of temperature and humidity of each snow crystal. At this level the diachronic parameter of time begins to be important. But only at the level of *third-order emergence* do we observe an evolution in the strict sense, in so far as systems 'remember' their history by including their own prehistory in their own organizational program. One example is the nucleic acids in genomes; but of course many other sorts of evolutionary learning can be mentioned, from the intra-organismic coordination of parts in an organism to the emergence of inter-organismic communication at the group level. At that point evolutionary systems begin to be self-referential, in the sense that they maintain and develop themselves according to internal programs. In short, they develop themselves by *autopoiesis*, or self-productivity (Deacon, 2003, pp. 288–301).[7]

In Deacon's account all three variants of emergence are understood within a naturalistic framework, in which *top-down causality operates not in contrast to, but on the basis of, bottom-up causality.* What is emerging biologically is propagated out of the physical capacities of matter. But once the emergent systems have become established, they are able to exercise additional causal influences by constraining and channelling ('from above') what is dynamically possible ('from below').

As we are now going to see, some theological appropriations of emergence demand this stronger view of emergence, whereas other religious interpretations need only a weak version of emergence in order to support their religious vision.

3. RELIGIOUS REFLECTIONS ON EMERGENCE

Let us now explore how the idea of emergence has already been accommodated within religious reflection. By the term 'religious reflection' I mean two distinct, yet correlated tasks of theology: one offers an *internal* presentation of a given religious point of view, while the other provides, from an *external* perspective, more general conceptual schemes that allow for a controlled comparison between different religious and non-religious points of view. I take both these tasks of religious reflection to be public in nature, that is, both are open to a process of mutual understanding that crosses the boundaries between distinct communities of religious and non-religious groups. Whether we understand ourselves as religious naturalists, as theists of various shades, or as critics of religion, religious positions (in so far as they are clearly expressed) can be made intelligible also to those who do not want to take a specific, or even any, religious stance. One doesn't need to *share* a religious view in order to understand its formal structure and semantic content.

[7] On the concept of autopoiesis as involving more than just self-organization, see Niels Henrik Gregersen, 'The Idea of Creation and the Theory of Autopoietic Processes' (Gregersen, 1998).

The following five views are ordered according to the strength of their religious commitments.[8] They are chosen on the belief that they are live options in current religious life. They are also chosen not only because they make reference to the phenomena of emergence, but also because they cover substantial parts of the theological discussions that have taken place since the early twentieth-century British Emergentists.

The first model, *Religious Naturalism*, differs from the others by being unconcerned about the specific theoretical claims of either weak or strong emergentism; religious naturalism celebrates the manifold products of evolution, which are seen as nothing but the results of a prosaic physico-chemical history, which is 'all that is'.[9] The other end of the spectrum, *Eschatological Theism*, differs from the others by not sharing the broad naturalist assumption found in standard versions of emergence. In order for eschatological theism to be coherent, it must be assumed that higher-order emergent phenomena cannot be fully explained by the causal factors that precede them, since the advent of God into the world is here taken to be the immediate cause of evolutionary novelty.

Thus only models (2)–(4) fall into the broad category that may be termed 'Theistic Naturalism'. The second model, *Evolving Theistic Naturalism*, is distinctive in so far as it conceives God as the emergent result of natural processes; as such, it has a certain affinity to pantheism. By contrast, models (3) and (4), *Atemporal* and *Temporal Theism*, follow the lead of the great monotheistic religions: Judaism, Christianity, Islam, and some of the Hindu traditions. God is here understood as the creative principle, which retains a causal priority in relation to the world of nature. The difference between Atemporal and Temporal Theism lies in whether or not the emerging world has a feedback influence on the divine nature. According to Atemporal Theism, God remains self-identical in all respects as the unchanging creative principle; according to Temporal Theism, God not only gives to but also receives from the world, so that there are two poles in the ellipse of divine being: God's essential nature and God's changing nature in relation to the world of creation.

---

[8] See a parallel typology developed by Philip Clayton, who proposes a typology according to the strength of emergentist commitments; see 'Towards a Constructive Christian Theology of Emergence' (Clayton, forthcoming)

[9] Religious Naturalism, thus defined, should therefore be distinguished from the position of Theistic Naturalism, in which God the creator is seen as united with the world of creation, while also being 'more than the world'; see, e.g. David Ray Griffin (2004), p. 2.

Model 1: Flat Religious Naturalism

By 'Flat Religious Naturalism' I refer to the ontological position that 'nature is all that is', thus excluding God from the inventory of reality. Religious naturalism, however, may well be religiously deep in the sense of expressing the inner value of natural events and celebrating their manifestations. In the American religious tradition, we find this view among the nineteenth-century transcendentalists such as Ralph Waldo Emerson, Henry David Thoreau, and Walt Whitman. More recently we find this view nicely presented by Ursula Goodenough in her book, *The Sacred Depths of Nature*. Referring to emergence, she seems fully satisfied with weak emergence: 'Emergence. Something more from nothing but. Life from nonlife. Like wine from water, it has long been considered a miracle wrought by gods or God. Now it is seen to be the near-inevitable consequence of our thermal and chemical circumstances' (Goodenough, 1998, pp. 28–9).

Goodenough explicitly dissociates herself from any attempt to explain the cases of emergence from a notion of divine purpose, or as a result of divine coordination of the basic laws of physics with the intent of producing the world as we know it. No miracles come from outside into the world, but the world of nature itself abounds in miracles. According to Goodenough, no covenant should be made with a transcendent God; instead, a covenant of silence should be made with the Mystery of life which invites to a sacred celebration. As put in poetic prose: 'The religious naturalist is provisioned with tales of natural emergence that are, to my mind, far more magical than traditional miracles. Emergence is inherent in everything that is alive, allowing our yearning for supernatural miracles to be subsumed by our joy in the countless miracles that surround us' (Goodenough, 1998, p. 30). What happens here is that the divine becomes the predicate of Nature, and not the creative author of the world of emergence. Creativity resides in Nature, whereby Nature is transformed into 'the divine'.

Model 2: Evolving Theistic Naturalism

Evolving Theistic Naturalism shares with Flat Religious Naturalism the view that nature is prior to God and that the divine is a quality of nature, not its source. In Samuel Alexander's *Space, Time, and Deity* we find the first sketch of a theology that uses emergence as the central concept for an evolving theistic naturalism. The ladder of emergence, according to Alexander, has its roots in the striving of Space-Time (or evolution) towards ever more complex modes of realization. Proceeding analogically from the bottom towards the top, Alexander posits the quality of deity as a further step in this process of evolution:

For we become familiar with levels of different quality, and we may by analogy conceive a higher type unfolded by the onward pressure of Time. There is no intervention here, but only extension of a series whose principle is known, to use another term. Even without the religious emotion, we could on purely speculative evidence postulate deity, on the ground of the general plan on which Space-Time works vol. II (Alexander, 1927,. p. 381)

This is a very clear expression of a fully naturalized view of providence. Here purpose is rooted in the Space-Time that structures nature, whereas deity is the quality that results from the upward strife and movement of nature's capacity of evolution. Accordingly, the concept of emergence is used as a global concept that applies without restriction to God as well as to life and consciousness. The world of nature is 'tending to deity'. The world is God's body: it is in the process of producing the quality of deity, of which God is said to be the 'possessor'. Accordingly, God's deity is lodged only in a portion of the big universe, since the divine qualities, on Alexander's view, supervene on the emergent qualities of life and mind: 'God includes the whole universe, but his deity, though infinite, belongs to, or is lodged in, only a portion of the universe' (ibid, p. 357). In this sense, deity is subject to the same laws that apply elsewhere in the emergent universe, for deity is 'an empirical quality like mind or life'. Accordingly, God (being the possessor of deity) is itself an emerging reality like everything else in the universe. Only the basic Space-Time continuum—with its internal tendency or 'nisus' towards deity—forms the ultimate creative ground of being. Space-Time is prior to the actuality of God, for 'God as an actual existent is always becoming deity but never attains it. He is the ideal God in embryo' (ibid., p. 365).

Samuel Alexander's philosophical theology may be difficult to interpret in detail, but Alexander nonetheless presents a particularly interesting case. He is prepared to apply the idea of emergence without qualifications to God's nature. The actuality of God (and with it the qualities of deity) is emerging along with, and as a result of, the upward drive of evolutionary history. To this extent Alexander's position may be termed a historicized pantheism. But in so far as the universe is also understood as the body of God, God is also co-extensive with the universe, and may even be termed creative: 'as being the whole universe God is creative, but his distinctive character of deity is not creative but created' (ibid., p. 397).[10]

---

[10] The similarities to Alfred North Whitehead's dipolar concept of God are striking here, but cannot be dealt with at this juncture.

While the specifics of Samuel Alexander's theology have not found many followers, the general form of his theological logic nonetheless reappears again and again in new forms. In a recent article, 'Emergence of Transcendence', the biophysicist Harold Morowitz suggests that the idea of emergence may in fact be used to map theological conceptions. For Morowitz the laws of nature, though ultimately shrouded in mystery, are statements of the operations of the immanent God: 'The transition from mystery to complexity would be, in theological terms, the divine spirit.' Thus, the transcendence of God is not the external source of the world, but is itself a *result* of nature's evolution and unfolding, which with human beings has now reached a new level: 'The emergence of the societal mind resonates with the theologians' concept of "the Son" or "being made in God's image". This argues that the human mind is God's transcendence, and miracles are what humans can do to overcome "the selfish gene" and other such ideas in favour of moral imperatives' (Morowitz, 2003, p. 185). This theology is sketched in broad strokes, as Morowitz himself admits, yet the idea of an emergent deity is no doubt appealing to religiously inclined scientists. Morowitz's theology, like Alexander's, can be criticized for applying the idea of emergence too directly to God, thereby employing an analogical method that derives ontological statements too directly from analogies. Morowitz may also be charged for thinking too anthropomorphically about the transcendence of God. But the general outcome is inevitable if emergentist thinking is written large, metaphysically speaking. On this view, nature works bottom-up; but somewhere along the ladder of complexity, new features evolve which are then able to influence the course of evolution in a top-down manner. Thus, the construal of God as an emergent deity is inherently linked to the stronger version of emergence. It cannot be satisfied by weak emergence alone, as in the case of Flat Religious Naturalism.

Model 3: Atemporal Theism

While the first two models are distinctively modern approaches to speaking about the divine as an emerging reality, Atemporal Theism can be said to be a classic position in philosophical theology. That God cannot change is an axiom inherited from ancient Greek philosophy, and in the Middle Ages it was the shared position among Jewish, Christian, and Muslim philosophical theologians such as Moses Maimonides, Thomas Aquinas, and Avicenna.[11]

---

[11] See, e.g. David B. Burrell (1993).

Although God is the creator of a temporal world, God is unimaginatively beyond time and change.

In early modernity this idea of a timeless God found a new shape in the wake of the scientific idea of the physical closure of nature. Whereas the timelessness of God was earlier professed to safeguard the otherness of God, the idea now became that God could not interfere with the world subsequent to its creation. The world was now conceived as a mechanistic world-system, obeying the deterministic laws of physics. In its extreme form, atemporal theism grew into a deism which construed God only as the great initiator of the clockwork universe. More typically, God was seen as not only creating the universe, but also sustaining the existence and order of the universe at every moment, including the laws of nature. This idea is usually referred to as uniformitarianism.

Whereas traditional theism asserted God's sovereignty over the course of nature, also in terms of being able to act above the confines of the laws of nature, naturalized versions of atemporal theism argue that God either cannot (or does not) act in ways that are additional to, or that abridge, God's role in upholding the system of nature as a whole.[12] In early nineteenth-century theology we find this uniformitarian position encapsulated and expanded in the work of the founder of modern theology, Friedrich Schleiermacher, who stated without equivocation that our 'absolute dependence on God coincides entirely with the view that all...things are conditioned and determined by the interdependence of Nature' (Schleiermacher, 1989, p. 170). Being preserved by God and being part of the causal nexus of nature is one and the same thing.

A contemporary proponent of this view is the Dutch physicist-theologian Willem B. Drees. Accepting the principle of the causal closure of physical reality (and assuming the completeness of a naturalist account), Drees does not see any room for a divine interaction with a developing world (Drees, 1996, p. 104). Rather, God is so unique and different from the world of creation that no temporal, personal, or causal characteristics can be attributed to God. Drees therefore prefers

to think of God as the sustaining Ground of Being who is also at the ground of the natural order and its integrity. To use an image from the novelist John Fowles, one might perhaps say that like the silence that contains a sonata and the white paper that contains a drawing, God sustains our existence. God would be considered as a sense of potentiality, of non-existence, a 'dimension in and by which all other dimensions exist'. (Drees, 2002)

---

[12] A fine analysis of 18th-century positions can be found in John Hedley Brooke (1991), 152–91.

Being a committed naturalist, Drees may appear to be a proponent of a Flat
Religious Naturalism as defined above (model 1). Both Drees and Goodenough combine a belief in the completeness of bottom-up scientific explanations with a sense of mystery. But although Drees's reference to God as non-
existing may appear to be atheistic, he only distances himself from the
presentation of God as one existing entity among others and as describable
in terms borrowed from the created world. What makes Drees a theist (in the
more general sense of the term) is his view that God—as the sea of possibilities—is prior to the world of nature and is its creative 'Ground of Being'. God
is affirmed as metaphysically ultimate, even in relation to the space-time
continuum that makes up the world of creation. Owing to the uniformitarian
view of the God–world relation, however, Drees takes no particular interest in
emergent phenomena, since the latter will be no more revelatory of God than
more ordinary phenomena. Although he does not deal with the varieties of
weak and strong emergence in particular, he would be inclined to allow for
weak emergence only.

A more complex version of Atemporal Theism has recently been proposed
by the physicist Paul Davies. Davies also takes his point of departure from the
uniformitarian view of the God–world relation, but he is far more interested
in the new causal capacities of emergent phenomena. By focusing on the way
in which the basic laws of physics, in combination with ever-changing
environments, seem to be fine-tuned for the emergence of organized complexity, Davies offers what he calls a 'modified uniformitarianism'. No divine
supervision of the details of evolution is needed; yet, says Davies,

I am proposing that God 'initially' selects the laws, which then take care of the
universe, both its coming-into-being at the big bang and its subsequent creative
evolution. Without the need for direct supernatural intervention. By selecting judi-
ciously, God is able to bestow a rich creativity on the cosmos, because the actual laws
of the universe are able to bestow a remarkable capacity to canalise, encourage, and
facilitate the evolution of matter and energy along pathways leading to greater
organizational complexity. (Davies, 1998, p. 158)[13]

Central to this view is a theistic interpretation of the so-called cosmic fine-
tuning of laws and initial conditions for the production of a world consisting
of life and consciousness. What are important on Davies's view are not only
the laws of nature, but also the balanced proportion of order and chance that
gives to creation its inherently emergent features. Emergent phenomena are
not just pale manifestations of deterministic laws, for not only are some
laws of nature probabilistic, but their outcomes often depend on fragile

---

[13] Also to be found in Philip Clayton and Arthur Peacocke (2004), 104.

environmental conditions. It is thus the felicitous interplay between necessity and chance that 'leads to the emergence of *a different sort of order*—the order of complexity—at the macro-, holistic level' (Davies, 1998, p. 159).

Davies's position urges him to be genuinely interested in emergent phenomena—not only in Terrence Deacon's 'first-order' sense of supervenient emergence, but also in Deacon's category of second-order emergence (which includes the phenomena of chaos and self-organization), where novelties depend on the interplay between rule-governed systems and their ever-changing environments. God, on this view, would be the creative mind who is both selecting the laws and giving room for the appropriate portions of chance—for the purpose of emergent complexity. Davies thus proposes a sort of teleology in nature, yet one without a divine teleology 'tinkering' with the detailed processes. Rather, God is like the inventor of a game such as chess: God sets up the rules while leaving open the space for the self-development of the game of creation.

On Davies's model there is no explicit feedback from the world to God, however. One could nevertheless argue that his model would imply at least a certain successiveness in the divine mind, as a result of God's coming-to-know what is coming-to-be in the world of creation. Furthermore, Davies is open to the additional possibility of God acting together with the natural capacities of the world—provided that one could develop a consistent theory for how God could do so without violating the laws and statistical distributions of nature. However, only Temporal Theism, to which we now turn, requires the development of a theory of divine interaction in conjunction with a developing world.

Model 4: Temporal Theism

As we saw above, the idea of temporal change in God was unheard of in antiquity and in the Middle Ages. During the twentieth century, however, various versions of temporal theism have been developed within philosophical theology, and today temporal theism is probably the majority position in philosophical theology as well as in systematic theology. Process theology, drawn on the canvas of the philosophical theology proposed by the mathematician Alfred North Whitehead, was among the first to argue for a dipolar concept of God. According to process theology, God not only possesses a 'primordial nature' which is essentially unchanging, but also a 'consequent nature', which appears as a result of the ongoing divine absorption of temporal developments into the mind of God (Whitehead, 1978, pp. 342–52).[14]

[14] See also the classic exposition in John B. Cobb, Jr. and David Ray Griffin (1977), 41–62.

Other versions of the same idea have reappeared in many forms in more recent theology (both philosophical and doctrinal); in the field of science-and-religion, temporal theism is shared by many authors.[15]

Temporal theism has a particular affinity to strong emergence. Although some form of temporal theism—understood as a passive divine responsive-ness—is indeed possible on the premise of an exclusively weak emergentism, the view that God interacts with a developing world is particularly congenial to the notion of a God whose experience grows along with the emergent realities in relation to which (or whom) God is seen to be actively involved.

In the work of the biochemist Arthur Peacocke we find a particularly clear way of combining temporal theism and strong emergence. For God to be omniscient, God must know all that is logically possible. But in so far as the future is not yet determinable, and (owing to strong emergence) not deter-mined prior to the actual selection of emergent properties, God cannot know all future actualities. God can know the phase space of future possibilities, but not the exact route of emergent evolution. This limitation on divine know-ledge may be seen by critics as an external limitation on God. But if God creates the world by setting nature free for a process of fertile self-exploration, this limitation is not external to God; it is ultimately rooted in the generosity of divine love. God's self-limitation, or *kenosis*, is motivated by the goal of the self-realization of divine love.

Peacocke combines this 'letting-go' view of the divine creativity that under-lies all things with a strong affirmation of a God who accompanies and actively responds to the world in a manner analogous to whole–part causation. The world of nature, as perceived by science, consists of myriads of individual systems, some hierarchically stratified (such as organisms and groups), others only loosely connected in coupled networks (such as ecosystems). As different as the individual systems are, Peacocke claims that nature remains an inter-connected and interdependent 'System-of-systems', in which nature-as-a-whole exercises an influence on the individual systems. Against this backdrop, Peacocke suggests that we can view God as the 'Circumambient Reality' of the universe. God, however, is not to be perceived as a far-away external environ-ment to the universe, for, being immanent in the world, God is ubiquitously present and incessantly active as God works out the divine intentions 'in, with, and under' the nexus of nature as a whole. It is in this context that Peacocke appeals to top-down (or 'whole–part') causality as an analogy for the manner in which God influences the process of emergent evolution:

---

[15] Without necessarily following Whitehead's cosmology, temporal theists include, for example, Ian Barbour, Arthur Peacocke, John Polkinghorne, Keith Ward, Robert John Russell, and many others.

By analogy with the operation of whole-part influence in real systems, the suggestion is that, because the ontological gap between the world and God is located simply everywhere in space and time, *God could affect holistically the state of the world-system.* Hence, *mediated by the whole-part influences of the world-system on its constituents, God could cause particular patterns of events to occur which would express God's intentions.* These latter would not otherwise have happened had God not so specifically intended. (Peacocke, 2001, p. 110)[16]

As is evident from this quotation, Peacocke is not only seeing whole–part causation as an epistemological analogy for divine action, but is suggesting that God actually works in and through a world of emergent processes. These processes, which he views as a potential means for divine action, appear to be inherently flexible, such that they are open for God to exert a continuous influence on the course of evolution.

Note, though, that Peacocke is not arguing that there are in-principle gaps in scientific explanation. He locates only two sources of ontological indeterminacy in the world of nature: quantum indeterminacy and consciousness, and neither of them is on his view sufficient for a theology of a transformative divine presence in nature. It is rather *nature as whole* that exhibits cases of emergence and that moves in the direction of ever greater complexity. Consequently, Peacocke's theological explanation is primarily related to the world as a whole. He thus hypothesizes that, analogous to the way in which higher-level systems (e.g. a flock of migrating birds) exercise an informational influence on lower-level systems (the individual birds), God may likewise exert a persistent flow of information on the world-as-a whole. Since no information flows without some exchange of matter-and-energy, it is important for Peacocke to acknowledge that God's influence is not seen as an additional supernatural causality, but rather as a causality always couched in, and hidden by, natural processes.

The immanence of the transcendent God is thus quintessential to Peacocke's position. One would never be able to extract 'a divine factor' from the natural flow of information, for it is exactly in nature's operations themselves that God is active. Hence the rational character of his theistic understanding of reality does not depend on gaps in scientific explanations; instead, it appears as a meta-reflection on the trajectory of evolution as a whole. The epistemic support for Peacocke's religious interpretation, in other words, is cumulative and refers mainly to the outcomes rather than to specific causal loopholes in nature.

---

[16] Also see Peacocke (2001), 43–8 (on God and time) and 51–9 (on whole–part causation). A more technical and comparative account is also given in Peacocke (1999).

Peacocke has been criticized for hypostasizing 'the world-as-a whole', but he insists that the world does in fact constitute such an emergent System-of-systems. He admits, though, that the causal work is often done in the interplay between distinctive, type-different systems (such as systems of sound and meaning). He is therefore prepared to argue that, *ex hypothesi*, relatively autonomous processes are launched over the course of history which acquire new modes of causality (especially what Aristotle would have called formative causality) (Peacocke, 1999, pp. 227–8). In so far as this occurs, not only will scientific theories evidence a certain degree of autonomy relative to one another, but real-world emergent processes will also exert their own special forms of causality (e.g. negative and positive feedback, constraining and propagating specific patterns). Peacocke would here accept a strong version of emergence, including not only the first-order and second-order varieties of *supervenience* and *self-organization*, but also Terrence Deacon's third-order variety of *autopoiesis*, or 'top-down' evolved self-productivity. The development of genetic pools, immune systems, brains, signal systems, and language may serve as examples. As I have argued earlier,

By its acceptance of a constitutive materialism, autopoietic theory denies an autonomy of existence of higher level systems; these always depend ontologically on lower level systems. Autopoietic theory, however, does claim a process autonomy since type-different systems operate on the basis of their internal codes. Thus, the fact that type-different systems cannot be written together in a uniform causal scheme has an ontological basis in pluriform evolution itself. (Gregersen, 1998, p. 363)

For example, immune systems select antibodies to be cloned; birds and mammals produce species-specific warning signals; bird flocks produce population-specific cycles of migration; and the production of meaning in human language selects sounds to be uttered.

As pointed out by the philosophical theologian Philip Clayton, a strong version of emergence will thus require a correspondingly weaker notion of supervenience, since the claim is that the latter cannot grasp the whole causal story enacted in the evolutionary processes. Supervenience may well explain the genesis of higher-level systems (for example, the emergence of life or of central neural systems); yet once these systems have appeared through evolution, they take on an autonomous causative role in co-determining the use of the available energy budget. Such a formative role of higher-order systems is exhibited both in the world of biology and in human experience. As aptly formulated by Clayton, the same thought pattern may apply also to God's influencing the world:

Information biology provides us with a way of conceiving the introduction of information into the environment, and such information could guide the development of life-forms in a sort of proto-purpose fashion (think of Kant's 'purposiveness without purpose'). Given the analogy, God could guide the process of emergence by introducing new information (formal causality) and by holding out an ideal or image that could influence development without altering the mechanical mechanisms of evolution or adding energy from the outside (final causality). (Clayton, 2002, p. 273)

What we see here is that emergentist concepts can be used to model an understanding of divine causality. The critic may then ask, *How* exactly is all this possible? Neither Peacocke's more holistic account, nor Clayton's or my own more pluralistic account, will be able to answer this question directly. For the question denies precisely what is presupposed by these theological proposals, namely, that God and nature are so intimately intertwined that the presence of the living God cannot be subtracted from the world of nature and still leave the world as it is. Nature equals God-and-nature. For the same reason, the arguments that have been put forward are not part of a natural theology that attempts to argue for the 'existence of God' against the background of emergence. Rather, what we have here are examples of a theology of nature that engages in a type of hypothetical reasoning: *if* nature includes cases of strong emergence, and *if* God is the creator at work in, with, and under creation, then there is a natural fit—a strong case of coherence—between the emergentist view of nature and the tradition of temporal theism.

Of course, it remains possible to affirm strong emergence without affirming a religious explanation. At the level of ultimate explanations, however, both the theist and the non-theist will be asked how they are able to account for the fact that the laws of nature are as fertile as they are, and why evolution exhibits the 'upward' drive that we observe. No metaphysics can escape the need to explain these facts.[17]

Model 5: Eschatological Theism

So far we have explored several examples of how the defenders of certain live options in religion have appropriated more recent scientific and philosophical discussions of weak and strong emergence. It has sometimes been forgotten, however, that some religions have already developed a high sensitivity to novelties as pointers to the presence of the living God. Not the least of these is in Jewish religion, in which new and unforeseen events—in nature as well as in history—have been experienced as the work of the almighty God. This reflects a situation in which the orderliness of nature and the regularities in

[17] See further Niels Henrik Gregersen, 'From Anthropic Design to Self-Organized Complexity', in Gregersen (2003).

human experience were seen as dependent on the divine will from moment to moment. On this view, the laws of nature are not viewed as prescriptive for how natural events *must* turn out; they are rather interpreted as generalized descriptions of how things *usually* work themselves out under divine providence. 'Laws of nature' are conceived by analogy to positive legislation in human societies. It follows that laws of nature permit of exceptions and may be changed over time.

The German theologian Wolfhart Pannenberg has reminded us of this historical background for present-day discussions of the pervasive features of emergence in natural history. In a seminal article, 'Contingency and Natural Law', he addresses the issue of how we today should perceive the laws of nature. Are laws of nature to be treated as Platonic forms, which have their existence prior to the occurrences that are regulated by them? Or should the laws of nature instead be conceived as abstractions in relation to the much more subtle occurrences of contingency? Pannenberg is in favour of the latter view. For example, we observe first-case instantiations of new laws, such as the Mendelian laws of inheritance, which did not exist prior to the emergence of DNA–RNA networks. Thus, having argued that occurrences are prior to regularities, Pannenberg proposes to reverse the order between emergents and resultants. Persisting patterns often arise *as the result of* contingent occurrences; the patterns could well have been otherwise but, as a matter of fact, they have turned out to be this particular way. And once the patterns have established themselves, they initiate new habits of nature. This theologically motivated position shows strong parallels to the philosophy of nature advanced by Charles Sanders Peirce and, more recently, in the work of the philosopher of science Nancy Cartwright (Cartwright, 1999). In all three cases, the concrete instantiations of emergence and the formation of novel structures take precedence over the subsequent formulation of laws of nature.

As a result, the typically naturalistic orientation of emergentism appears in a new light. On the basis of this argument, Pannenberg suggests an eschatological ontology, according to which it is the coming-into-being of novel possibilities that determines what the constituent things in reality are. Only in the light of *future* constellations are we able to discover the full gamut of potentialities possessed by constituents in the past:

Every event throws new light on earlier occurrences; this now appears in new connections. This fact seems to have possessed considerable weight for the thinking of the Israelites. Their thinking implied, one might say, an eschatological ontology: if only the future will teach us what is the significance of an event, then the 'essence' of an event or occurrence is never completely finished in the present. Only after the larger connection of occurrences to which an event belongs has been completed can the true essence of the individual event be recognized. In the last analysis, only the ultimate future will decide about its peculiarity.(Pannenberg, 1993, p. 83)

Not only epistemology is at stake here. Pannenberg's position does not turn merely on the claim that we cannot discover who we are and what we can accomplish without proceeding through our contingent life-histories. This conception is also about ontology: without experiencing our particular life-histories, we would not be who we are. Moreover, this observation does not only pertain to personal and social histories; it also applies to natural entities and processes. For instance, without being part of the circuits of a brain, the capacities of the individual neurons would not at all come into effect. What fundamentally 'is', and what the various entities can 'do', depends on the networks of which they are part. Therefore only the future—or the concrete instantiations in the future—will reveal (and realize) what the networks and their particular functions are going to be.

I have chosen Pannenberg as a particularly explicit proponent of what I have called Eschatological Theism. The point here is that potentialities do not simply reside in the past configurations of matter; they result from an interplay between creaturely potencies and the coming into being of the divine possibilities offered to the world. Accordingly, the past and the present must be seen in light of the future, rather than the future being explained out of the past or the present.

Pannenberg is famous for his insistence on an eschatological ontology. But he is by no means alone in this regard. The tendency to understand God more as the attractive force of the future than as the pulling power of the past can also be found among philosophers such as Alfred North Whitehead and Teilhard de Chardin. The insistence that the future cannot be sufficiently explained by the past likewise finds ample expression in modern Continental theology. Similarly, Pannenberg's German colleague Jürgen Moltmann has argued extensively that the future cannot be exclusively predicted by means of prolongations of the past and the present into the future; emergent novelties are instead to be seen as advents of the future flowing into the present from the realm of possibilities (Moltmann, 1985).[18]

On views such as these, weak emergence is not enough. Something new, with new causal capacities, emerges during evolutionary history. We can now see more clearly the difference between models (4) and (5): the latter claims that one will never be able to offer a sufficient explanation of emergence only by referring to the causal powers of nature, as in model 4. The transformative

---

[18] Similarly, Moltmann's colleague Eberhard Jüngel asserts, 'What in a strict theological sense deserves to be called *new* is at any case a predicate of a divine act'; see E. Jüngel, 'Das Entstehen vom Neuem' ['The Emergence of Novelty'], in Jüngel (1990), 142.

presence of God must be part of any ultimate explanation of why, finally, the course of evolution is moving upwards in the direction of increased complexity.

4. CONCLUSION

So many and variegated are the religious appropriations of the idea of emergence. There are, of course, more possibilities to be explored than those that fall within the five-fold typology that I have presented here. Still, these five approaches do represent some important voices within current religious self-reflection that may at least count as live options in current theology. How they will fare in the long run depends not only on their ability to establish their relations to future scientific theories concerning emergent phenomena; it will also depend on the extent to which they are able to compete with one another as metaphysical alternatives. Perhaps knock-down arguments do not exist in the fields of metaphysics and theology. But there certainly do exist rational criteria of comprehensiveness, coherence, and experiential adequacy that will be employed in future discussions of the religious and anti-religious interpretations of emergent processes.

5. REFERENCES

Alexander, Samuel (1927), *Space, Time, and Deity,* vols I–II. (New York: The Humanities Press).

Aquinas, Thomas (1962), *Summa Theologiae* (Roma: Alba Paulinae Editiones).

Brooke, John Hedley (1991), *Science and Religion: Some Historical Perspectives* (Cambridge: Cambridge University Press).

Burrell, David B. (1993), *Freedom and Creation in Three Traditions* (Notre Dame: University of Notre Dame Press).

Cartwright, Nancy (1999), *The Dappled World: Study of the Boundaries of Science* (Cambridge: Cambridge University Press).

Clayton, Philip (2002), 'Divine Causes in the World of Nature', in Ted Peters, Muzzafar Iqbal, and Syed Nomanul Haq (eds.), *God, Life, and the Cosmos: Christian and Islamic Perspectives* (Aldershot: Ashgate).

—— (forthcoming), 'Towards a Constructive Christian Theology of Emergence' in Nancey Murphy and William Stoeger (eds.) (forthcoming), *Emergence: From Physics to Theology* (Oxford: Oxford University Press).

—— and Arthur Peacocke (eds.) (2004), *In Whom We Live and Move and Have Our Being: Panentheistic Reflections on God's Presence in a Scientific World* (Grand Rapids: Eerdmans).

Cobb, Jr., John B., and David Ray Griffin (1977), *Process Theology: An Introductory Exposition* (Belfast: Christian Journals Limited).

Davies, Paul (1998), 'Teleology Without Teleology', in Robert John Russell, William R. Stoeger, and Fransisco J. Ayala (eds.), *Evolutionary and Molecular Biology: Scientific Perspectives on Divine Action* (Vatican City/Berkeley: Vatican Observatory Publications and Center for Theology and the Natural Sciences).

—— (2004), 'Emergent Biological Principles and the Computational Properties of the Universe', unpublished paper.

Deacon, Terence (2003), 'The Hierarchic Logic of Emergence: Untangling the Interdependence of Evolution and Self-Organization', in Bruce H. Weber and David J. Depew (eds.), *Evolution and Learning* (Cambridge, Mass.: MIT Press).

Drees, Willem B. (1996), *Religion, Science, and Naturalism* (Cambridge: Cambridge University Press).

—— (2002) *Creation: From Nothing until Now* (London: Routledge).

Gierer, Alfred (1988), *Die Physik, das Leben, und die Seele: Anspruch und Grenzen der Naturwissenschaft* (München: Piper), 37–64.

Goodenough, Ursula (1998), *The Sacred Depths of Nature* (New York: Oxford University Press).

Gregersen, Niels Henrik (1998), 'The Idea of Creation and the Theory of Autopoietic Processes', *Zygon* 33:1, 333–68.

—— (2003), 'From Anthropic Design to Self-Organized Complexity', in Niels Henrik Gregersen (ed.), *From Complexity to Life: On the Emergence of Life and Meaning* (New York: Oxford University Press), 206–34.

Gregersen, Niels Henrik (2004), 'Complexity: What is at Stake for Religious Reflection?', in Kees van Kooten Niekerk (ed.), *The Significance of Complexity: Approaching a Complex World through Science, Theology, and the Humanities*, (Aldershot: Ashgate).

Griffin, David Ray (2004), *Two Great Truths: A New Synthesis of Scientific Naturalism and Christian Faith* (Louisville: Westminster/John Knox Press).

Hempel, C. G., and P. Oppenheimer (1948), 'Studies in the Logic of Explanation', *Philosophy of Science* 15, 567–79, in Joseph C. Pitt (ed.) (1988), *Theories of Explanation* (New York: Oxford University Press), 9–50.

Jüngel, E. (1990), 'Das Entstehen vom Neuem', in *Wertlose Wahrheit: Zur Identität und Relevanz des Christlichen Glaubens* (München: Chr. Kaiser Verlag).

Lewes, G. H. (1877), *Problems of Life and Mind*, vol II. (London: Kegan Paul).

Mayr, Ernst (1982), *The Growth of Biological Thought: Diversity, Evolution, and Inheritance* (Cambridge, MA.: Harvard University Press).

Moltmann, Jürgen (1985), *God in Creation: An Ecological Doctrine of Creation* (Minneapolis: Fortress Press).

Morgan, C. Lloyd (1923), *Emergent Evolution* (London: Williams and Norgate).

Morowitz, Harold (2002), *The Emergence of Everything: How the World became Complex* (New York: Oxford University Press).

—— (2003), 'Emergence of Transcendence', in Niels Henrik Gregersen (ed.), *From Complexity to Life: On the Emergence of Life and Meaning* (New York: Oxford University Press).

O'Connor, Timothy, and Hong Yu-Wong (2002), 'Emergent Properties', in Edward N. Zalta (ed.), *Stanford Encyclopedia of Philosophy* (Winter 2002 Edition), <http://plato.stanford.edu/entries/properties-emergent/>.

Pannenberg, Wolfhart (1993), *Toward a Theology of Nature: Essays on Science and Faith*, Ted Peters (ed.) (Louisville: John Knox Press).

Peacocke, Arthur (1999), 'The Sound of Sheer Silence', in Robert John Russell, Nancey Murphy, Theo C. Meyering, and Michael A. Arbib (eds.), *Neuroscience and the Person: Scientific Perspectives on Divine Action* (Vatican City/Berkeley: Vatican Observatory Publications/Center for Theology and the Natural Sciences), 215–48.

—— (2001), *Paths from Science Towards God: The End of all our Exploring* (Oxford: One World).

Schleiermacher, Friedrich (1989), *The Christian Faith*, trans. H. R. Mackintosh and J. S. Stewart (Edinburgh: T & T Clark).

Sellars, Roy Wood (1992), *Evolutionary Naturalism* (Chicago: Open Court).

Smith, John Maynard, and Eörs Szatmáry (2000), *The Origins of Life: From the Birth of Life to the Origins of Language* (Oxford: Oxford University Press).

Weber, Bruce H., and David J. Depew (eds.) (2003), *Evolution and Learning: The Baldwin Effect Reconsidered* (Cambridge, MA.: MIT Press).

Whitehead, Alfred North (1978), *Process and Reality: An Essay in Cosmology*, Corrected edition by David Ray Griffin and Donald W. Sherburne (New York: The Free Press).

14

Emergence from Quantum Physics to Religion: A Critical Appraisal

Philip Clayton

I am of the opinion that all the finer speculations in the realm of science spring from a deep religious feeling, and that without such feeling they would not be fruitful. I also believe that this kind of religiousness, which makes itself felt today in scientific investigations, is the only creative religious activity of our time. (Albert Einstein, 1930)[1]

I am a deeply religious nonbeliever.... This is a somewhat new kind of religion. (Einstein, 1954)[2]

It's been an interesting, and possibly unique, collection: a series of essays spanning the entire range from quantum physics to the question of God. The interest of the concept of emergence lies in part in the number of fields in which it is currently being applied. Even in the hands of more cautious authors, emergence continues to represent a 'bold hypothesis'. And yet it could hardly be said that the chapters in this book represent uncritical enthusiasm; indeed, most of the authors would not call themselves 'emergence theorists' at all. Instead, the authors have taken a concept that is in many cases not part of the standard vocabulary in their home disciplines, and they have tested the concept against core data and theories in their various fields.

Several tasks thus fall to this final summary chapter. First, we should attempt to draw into sharper focus what are the diverging ways in which the term 'emergence' has been used in these chapters. Openly acknowledging the differences, and knowing in advance that one will at best discover a series of family resemblances, we must nonetheless work to discover any common-alities that run across the vast array of scientific disciplines here summarized. Secondly, I put on the philosopher's hat and attempt the task of constructing a

---

[1] Albert Einstein (1930), quoted from Max Jammer (1999), p. 32.
[2] See Einstein (1954), quoted in Calaprice (1996).

philosophy of emergence, using the data that results from the first, compara-tive section as a constraint. As is inevitable in philosophy, a constructive theory of emergence will go beyond what any of the sciences individually can provide. But since the present volume so clearly raises the question whether there *is* any unified theory of emergence, the volume would remain incomplete if it did not offer at least the sketch of a hypothetical answer to the question. Philosophy being by nature a comparative discipline, the only way to test a claim is to consider a number of the competing options and to ask which one does the best job of explaining the entire domain that one is considering.

Finally, we must consider the implications of emergence theories for the understanding of religion in an age of science. It could be that the data on emergence leave religion untouched. It could be that they deeply undercut the sorts of claims to knowledge traditionally made by at least some systems of religious belief, such as classical theism. Or it could be that emergence theory suggests a way to transform religious truth claims in order to bring them more into line with the view of reality being offered by the sciences today. The effort to connect emergence and religion will at any rate occupy us in the closing pages of this closing chapter.

1. PIECES OF THE PUZZLE

For many, the most valuable contribution of emergence, and for some its only real function, lies in its ability to express analogies between patterns of development studied in various particular sciences. Many of the preceding chapters offer careful examinations of emerging patterns and structures within the specific sciences and at the boundaries between them. A brief comparative analysis of the results is crucial if we are to look for broader similarities.

Erich Joos charts the emergence of the classical world from the quantum world. Here 'emergence' does not represent the application of a concept from any other field; in Joos's work it is a technical term that describes the highly specific connections that link quantum phenomena to the macro-physical world. Paul Davies also begins by treating a technical theme in physics, 'the physics of downward causation'. Actually, however, his argument is of much broader significance. For if the world in fact manifests the sorts of downward causal relationships that he discusses, the idea of a 'theory of everything'—one that attempts to build upwards from fundamental physics to explain every-thing in the universe—would turn out to be deeply problematic. As Davies shows, the implications will be different depending on whether one construes the physics of downward causation in terms of whole–part causation or of level entanglement. We return to these implications below.

The three chapters in the biology section at first appear highly diverse; taken together, however, they provide a fascinating picture of the range of thinking about emergence across the biological sciences. Terry Deacon's article draws the closest connections with physics. One sees in his well-known 'three orders of emergence' a careful and sophisticated attempt to describe the precise manner in which the phenomena of evolving organisms emerge naturally as a result of the orders of increasing complexity in the physical world (thermodynamics and 'morphodynamics'). Deacon uses the concept of the 'hole at the centre of the hub' as a way of insisting that the origin and subsequent evolution of life not be understood as 'magical' or as involving any leap out of or beyond physical explanation. At the same time, Deacon's precise post factum reconstruction of the orders of emergence in the natural world is clearly opposed to any reductive account of the physics–life relationship. In one sense, evolving life forms are 'nothing but' a complex topological relationship of the same matter and energy that physics studies; in another sense, however, life clearly offers a 'something more'—a set of structures, causes, 'topologies', and phenomena that require different types of explanations from those that preceded them. To what extent this process of development should be interpreted as ontological novelty is a complicated question to which we will return.

Lynn Rothschild and Barbara Smuts clearly stand closer to one another methodologically, even though they specialize in opposite ends of the evolutionary spectrum. Both authors study a scale of increasing complexity—of structures, functions, and behaviours—that begins below their particular area of study, extends through it, and includes behaviours at yet higher levels as well. In both cases they chronicle a complex set of interactions between organisms and their environments, such that the explanatory story can only be told by means of the dynamic of parts and whole. And both defend a model of study that one recognizes as distinctively *bio*logical rather than physical or chemical. Still, both are in their different ways concerned with disciplinary transitions: Rothschild with the transition from biochemistry to a distinctively biological study of unicellular organisms, and Smuts with the transition from the highly complex, morally significant social interactions between bonobos, on the one hand, to similar studies of social interactions in *homo sapiens* on the other. Clearly there are both similarities and differences between these two sets of transitions.

A philosopher must be extremely cautious in commenting on the intense debates that take place among the four philosophers who have written on the emergence of mind; clearly any evaluative comments that might be made here are a *part* of the ongoing discussion rather than standing outside or above it. Teasing out a few of the underlying questions and naming a few of the disputes might nonetheless be helpful. One of the most contentious questions in this section is whether 'mind' should be explained as an emergent phenomenon arising out of brain states and, if so, what precisely it means to call mental phenomena 'emergent'. Jaegwon Kim is clearly the most sceptical of the four authors with regard to such claims: either emergentist explanations of mind break with the causal closure of the physical world and are thus at least crypto-dualist, or they accept that all causes are ultimately physical causes, in which case they provide a redundant explanation of mental phenomena. Kim argues that the case for emergence as a *tertium quid* has not yet been made success-fully. David Chalmers and Nancey Murphy are clearly more sympathetic to emergentist explanations, though they do not make the strong ontological claims that Silberstein and Ellis have made. Where Chalmers accepts emergen-tist (non-reductive) explanations as one attractive option among the compet-ing models of mind, Murphy argues strongly that our explanations of mental and social phenomena must be non-reductive, even though, in a broad sense, they remain physical explanations. Michael Silberstein, by contrast, locates and defends an emergence-based theory of mind as a distinct competitor over against physicalist and dualist explanations. His 'enactive (embodied plus embedded) paradigm of consciousness and cognition' accepts a clear ontology of emergence; he brings a variety of arguments against the viability of physicalist explanations and for a distinctively emergence-based theory of mental causation.

I deferred the treatment of George Ellis's chapter to this point because it pairs most naturally and closely with the contribution of Michael Silberstein. In fact, Ellis has contributed one of the most boldly synthetic essays in this volume. He considers detailed examples drawn from specific emergence relationships across the natural sciences, interpreting these cases not as *contrasting* instances to mental causation but as offering supporting evidence for it. As an astrophysicist, Ellis stands closest to Joos in his professional work. Yet his chapter locates the broad range of emergent phenomena discussed by the other authors along an extremely broad spectrum running from quantum physics through macrophysics, chemistry, biochemistry and molecular biol-ogy, zoology, environmental science, and the neurosciences. All of these cases taken together, Ellis argues, constitute a single, comprehensive case for an ontology of emergence.

Arthur Peacocke and Niels Gregersen, like George Ellis, believe that the phenomenon of emergence is relevant to our understanding of religious phen-omena and that it can be theologically productive. Gregersen's essay shows that emergence can be interpreted in such a way that it is consistent with more traditional views of the divine in the various monotheistic traditions (Judaism, Christianity, Islam, and some forms of Hindu thought)—even though other lines of emergence-based reflection have given rise to very different models of God, as well as to various naturalistic metaphysics that eschew the concept of God altogether. Among the five models Gregersen discusses (Flat Religious Naturalism, Evolving Religious Naturalism, Atemporal Theism, Temporal Theism, and Eschatological Theism), he himself seems to advocate a version of temporal theism with at least some eschatological elements.

Ellis and Peacocke (in this and other works) have reconceived the nature of deity from the standpoint of the sciences of emergence. Ellis's notion of God (see Murphy and Ellis, 1996) is linked with what he calls 'the moral nature of the universe' and, presumably, with a continuing divine lure that pulls all things toward the actualization of their intrinsically moral nature, in a manner consistent with the traditional Quaker understanding of 'the light within'. Peacocke likewise revises traditional theology in an emergentist direction. God is 'co-creator' with finite agents, luring them without coercion and without pre-determining the outcome. Having established the parameters for the emerging universe that our sciences are now discovering, God allows the open-ended process of evolution to construct more and more complex organisms and interacting systems, leading to (but not necessarily culminating with) rational, moral, aesthetic beings such as ourselves. Presumably a God of this type would not be timeless or utterly distinct from the world but temporal in its very nature. Such a God is involved in an immanent fashion 'in, with, and under' all things. We return to the religious significance of emergence in the final section of this chapter.

2. TOWARD A CONSTRUCTIVE THEORY OF EMERGENCE

The differences between the authors are great enough that one cannot claim that all, or even most, would endorse a single unified theory of emergence—not even a purely naturalistic one, and far less one that makes robust religious claims. This book should therefore be read not as a systematic apologetic for a single theory of emergence, but rather as a sourcebook: it contains the data and theoretical resources necessary for evaluating whether a unified theory of emergence is possible, without actually providing such a theory.

Still, one can't help but wonder whether the scientific developments presented here are of broader philosophical significance. Taken together, do they constitute a sort of cumulative case for an emergence-based understanding of the natural world? More precisely, do insights from recent science and philosophy support a view of natural evolution as producing new levels of reality over time: new types of objects with new forms of causal powers, which therefore require types of explanation unique to each level? If the evidence does support a distinctively emergentist view of the world, what might such a view look like? In what follows I offer a sketch of such a theory—not with the claim that it is the only such theory available, or that all (or even most) of the authors in this volume would endorse it, but as a plausible inference to draw from the data and arguments presented in these pages. *Not* to raise the question of a general theory of emergence at the end of this collection would be to draw back from an obvious possibility when one ought rather to formulate and explore it in a critical and constructive manner.

Unitary theories of emergence come in various types, ranging from those that are emphatically naturalist to those that include a significant role for some transcendent dimension. In emergence theories, however, the relationship between the two ends of the spectrum is not fully symmetrical: one can endorse levels of emergence up to a certain point without being required to accept higher and more speculative levels of emergence, yet those who endorse the 'higher' levels must acknowledge that these levels remain dependent on the levels that precede them. Thus, although I follow the lines all the way to the religious questions, readers are free to exit the cumulative argument at any point at which they can show that it is more rational to stop than to proceed.

i. Emergence in the Natural World

We begin, then, with a fully naturalistic emergence theory of the relationships between the sciences and the reality that they reveal to us. Perhaps the best way to start is to say what, according to most of the authors in this volume, this natural reality seems *not* to be. The world has not turned out to be explainable solely in terms of the matter and energy relations of physics as we know it. One can postulate that the universe as a whole is a closed system, but most of the smaller systems that we are interested in explaining are thermodynamically open systems. Many of these systems may therefore not finally be deterministic, and this for one of several reasons. A system would be indeterminate for 'bottom-up' reasons if the indeterminacy that we know to hold at the quantum level is still manifested in macrophysical systems (and it has been experimentally shown that at least some macrophysical systems evidence quantum indeterminacy effects). Conversely, a system would be indeterminate for 'top-down' reasons if it receives inputs of energy or information from outside the system that cannot be expressed in terms of the laws of that system.

Only a fully determinate system would be fully knowable (predictable) in scientific terms. And yet indeterminacy does not represent the only limitation on knowledge; so-called chaotic systems, for example, are determinate systems for which it is impossible to predict the future evolution of the system. In these particular systems, knowing the system's future states requires knowing the values of initial conditions to a level of precision far beyond anything that we could ever measure empirically. Hence in such cases the future remains unknowable to us, even though the processes in question are fully law-like.

One could list other examples of intrinsic limits on the scientific knowledge that we can have of the world. Nevertheless, to paraphrase Mark Twain, reports of the demise of the scientific project are premature. As it turns out, none of the known limits has taken a form that would undercut the results we do have or the prospects for massive increases in what we can still learn by scientific methods. The limits imposed by chaotic dynamics, quantum uncertainty, and thermodynamically open systems in biology are compatible with a continually expanding knowledge of the physical structures and causal mechanisms that underlie phenomena in the world. It's just that they put an end to hopes that we will someday possess an exhaustive ('bottom-up') knowledge of natural systems.

The theory of emergence argues that this 'yes, but...' expresses a broad pattern in nature, which is discernable in the relations between a large number of sciences. Put differently, emergence represents a hypothesis about our knowledge of the world which takes the form of a two-fold prediction. On the one hand, the door for increasing scientific knowledge remains open. To take three examples: it has not proven impossible to explain the origin of life from non-life; organs and organisms do not present us with an 'irreducible complexity' that eludes biological explanation and that only a God could have produced; and we have not discovered that thought or mind is a separate substance altogether, functioning independently of brain structures and processes. In all these cases, claims of the demise of the natural causal explanatory project and for the necessity of depending on supernatural explanations *within the domain covered by the sciences* are premature: emergentists predict that scientists will continue to make progress toward a fuller understanding in all three cases.

On the other hand, there is evidence that a certain dream called 'the unity of science'—the hoped-for reduction of all things and explanations to fundamental physics—was misguided. It *could* have been the case that more complex systems turned out merely to be extensions of the physics of the underlying systems, so that by adding the right additional variables, constants, and subordinate laws to the existing lower-order laws and equations one could compute the dynamics of higher-order systems. But the evidence currently suggests that the world does not work that way, and the constructive theory of emergence (as I construe it) predicts that further scientific advances will not overturn this result.

ii. Types of Non-reducibility, and a Wager

As this volume shows, theories of emergence can be and have been developed with high levels of detail and philosophical sophistication. Here there is space to highlight only three key claims made by many of the prominent emergence theorists concerning the relationships between the scientific disciplines. First, the evolution of more and more complex systems in the natural world turned out not to be continuous but to involve the periodic appearance of new systems with qualitatively different structures, evidencing ever more intricate forms of interaction with their environments. Secondly, although emergent systems, organisms, and properties are not reducible—the dynamics of self-reproducing cells cannot be explained in terms of the sorts of dynamics that physics studies—emergent entities don't contradict the physics on which they continue to depend. *Every* natural system is constrained by the constants, laws, and regularities that specify what is physically possible. A biological or psychological system can no more overcome these constraints than the software on your computer can achieve results that are inconsistent with the fundamental physical limitations of your computer's circuitry and motherboard.

Thirdly, to say that a given system is emergent is to say that *it is explanatorily, causally, and hence ontologically irreducible to the systems out of which it has evolved.*[3] That nature forms more complex systems, and that we are right to use labels such as 'cell' or 'kidney' or 'monkey' to designate these systems, is beyond dispute. Systems that evidence some but not all of these forms of irreducibility are generally called 'weakly' emergent. Since the claims represented by the three italicized adverbs become increasingly contentious, a word on each individually is in order.

Explanatory irreducibility is the easiest to establish. Not only has there been a complete failure to achieve the sort of downward reduction once triumphantly proclaimed by the unity of science movement, but we also now have good empirical reasons to think that such reduction is not even possible in

---

[3] All authors in this book endorse explanatory irreducibility. Causal irreducibility is the more controversial claim. I take it that if a system is explanatory and causally irreducible, it is also ontologically irreducible.

principle.[4] Newtonian physics was 'reduced' to relativistic physics when it was mathematically demonstrated that the former was a special case of the latter for velocities $<< c$.[5] But our best evidence today suggests that explanatory reductions of this sort are not possible in most cases of the evolution of new complex systems.

The debate concerning *causal* irreducibility is represented in the papers by Jaegwon Kim and Michael Silberstein above. Without seeking to reiterate that debate here, I note merely that theories of 'strong emergence' presuppose, with Silberstein, that causal interactions between organisms complex enough to evidence mental properties are not reducible to (complex forms of) micro-physical causality. It's crucial for emergence theories that causal irreducibility not hold only at the level of mental properties. Thus George Ellis, in a recent presentation to the Royal Society, argued that three features allow for the emergence of biological complexity out of the underlying physical substra-tum: 'top-down action in the hierarchy of complexity, the causal efficacy of biological information, and the origin of that information through evolu-tionary adaptation of the first two' (Ellis, 2004).

The third type, *ontological* irreducibility, might seem to be a natural consequence of the first two, but some authors in this text find it the most contentious of the three. If new structures emerge that have new phenomenal properties, if these structures require explanations given in terms of that particular level of emergence and not reducible to explanations at a lower level, and if the resulting structures or organisms exercise causal powers that are likewise irreducible, why would one *not* want to speak of them as emer-gent objects? I cannot think of any more sophisticated and science-oriented set of criteria for determining the parameters of one's ontology than this. Of course, one could claim that she has no idea what the word 'ontology' means and is not comfortable with using it; yet this hardly represents a serious philosophical critique of an emergentist ontology, since it's a rejection of ontological reflection *tout court*. More typically, resistance to ontological emergence takes the form of asserting that ultimate ontological priority must be given to fundamental physics. But, I would respond, the *appropriate* ontological priority is already granted to physics by the asymmetry presup-posed in each of the emergentist accounts: all more complex systems remain dependent upon the fundamental constraints of physics, whereas physics is not itself dependent on the laws and regularities of, say, biology or psychology.

---

[4] See Brown and Smith (2003); Rothman (2002); Looijen (2000). For an argument that self-reproducing cells cannot be explained at any level lower than the Darwinian–biological, see Kauffman and Clayton (2006).

[5] And now, philosophers of science such as Don Hardy at Notre Dame University are arguing, even that claimed reduction is contentious.

With these constraints in place, why would one need to claim in addition that only micro-physical causes exist and hence that all existing objects are 'really' micro-physical objects or events?

Perhaps there is a sort of wager being made here, with the two parties betting on opposite sides. (I used this framework in the debate with Michael Arbib on the nature of mind and mental causation that lay behind our diverging articles in Russell, Arbib et al., 1999.) Take the debate about mind. Both sides agree that we cannot at present explain all the phenomenal properties of thought in terms of neurophysiological causes. Arbib and others believe that the more plausible bet is that in the long run we will be able to do so. But I claim that the more rational course of action, given all that we now know, is to wager on the other side. I wager that no level of explanation short of irreducibly mental explanations will finally do an adequate job of accounting for the human person. This means wagering on the causal efficacy of the conscious or mental dimension of human personhood. And of course, if it's causally efficacious, it must exist.

What's true of that wager, I suggest, is also true of the entire debate concerning emergence. Reductionists, and even weak emergentists, argue that the best bet is that *apparently* qualitative differences in evolutionary history are in principle explainable in terms of lower-level causes and structures. Strong emergentists argue by contrast that, as much as science will gain a vastly greater understanding of the correlations between 'lower' and 'higher' levels, nevertheless the causes and explanations of higher-order events, even in the long run, will have to be given in terms intrinsic to each particular level of natural reality. If the advance of science continues to support this wager, is that not sufficient justification for speaking of the new levels, objects, and causes as ontologically emergent?

iii. Emergence in Science

Two types of work follow from this realization, one scientific and one philosophical. I presuppose that the lion's share of the work belongs to the first category. For any given system or organism on the emergence ladder of natural history, it's the competition among scientific theories that must establish the best theoretical framework for explaining the data. Generally it is science that brings new phenomena and new types of organization to public attention, and it remains the goal of scientific research to establish the closest possible correlations with phenomena at lower levels of organization. Sometimes this research leads to the recognition of new types of causal interactions which require their own forms of explanation.

Of course, one could argue that physics is undercut by irreducibly biological phenomena, that neo-Darwinian biology is undercut by the dynamics of the evolution of culture, or that neurophysiology is undercut by our necessary reliance on first-person reports. But why would one not instead view these three examples as signs that empirical or scientific inquiry into the natural world has continued to advance by producing new, distinct, yet interrelated fields of inquiry? The physical sciences have spawned the biological sciences as their offspring; they in turn have produced the human and social sciences, resulting in a much more variegated account of the natural world than any single science alone could provide. The social sciences rely crucially on natural scientific data (e.g. cognitive neuroscience, evolutionary psychology) without themselves *becoming* natural sciences. Why would one view this rich and complex network of interlocking explanations as anything other than good news for human inquiry? An emergentist framework for science is therefore not a retreat into irrationality, but a rich form of 'parallel processing' aimed at producing the most successful possible network of knowledge about the natural world.

What place then remains for philosophical reflection? Certainly the role of the philosopher (or the theologian!) is not to compete with the scientist within the area of her own specialization. But understanding the interrelationships between the sciences, and their broader implications, inevitably includes a philosophical component. After all, the relationship between any two disciplines A and B cannot be comprehended from the standpoint of A or B alone—unless B is subsumed under A (in which case it becomes a part of the domain of A), or A and B are both subsumed under a separate scientific discipline C (with similar results). In the absence of such results, scientists and philosophers must work together, as they have done in this text, to specify the relationships between the disciplines in the most conceptually rigorous fashion possible. Some of the resulting proposals may later be strengthened by concrete empirical results; others will be overturned; and some may long remain matters for philosophical speculation.

iv. The Philosophy of Emergence

What then of the more philosophical dimensions of emergence theory? Viewed as a claim about the nature of reality, emergentism represents a species of monism; call it *emergentist monism*. Monism rejects multiple kinds of substance, as in Descartes' theory of 'thinking stuff' and 'extended stuff' (*res cogitans* and *res extensa*), arguing instead that all objects and phenomena in the universe arise out of one basic matter-energy 'stuff'. Yet a physics-based monism cannot be the last word, since it's equally obvious that the universe produces more and more complex levels of organization. *Emergentist* monism emphasizes continuity through process, the fundamental ontological affinity between all existing things.

Attempting to do justice to the radically new structures and phenomena that arise in universal history, one might however be just as inclined to use the term *emergentist pluralism,* which expresses an ontology of continual becoming. To espouse pluralism is to reject any privileged level of analysis. Combine this emphasis with the previous paragraph, and one obtains the most balanced, and I believe the most justified, view: the universe evidences *both* a downward dependence on the constraints of the lower or earlier levels, *and* an upward dependence of parts on the wholes in relation to which they exist. Hence one should be just as sceptical of the claim, 'Well, in the end it's all about physics', as one is of the claim, 'The universe exists ultimately in order to produce human consciousness.' The emergence of human thought, self-reflection, and consciousness was a surprising and novel occurrence in the history of the universe, but there is no reason to conclude that this level of emergence is ontologically any more fundamental than the emergence of self-reproducing life forms on which the dynamics of natural selection could act. A chauvinism of the highest known level is no less pernicious than a chauvinism of the lowest level currently known to us.

Philosophy becomes increasingly necessary as one turns one's attention toward the upper end of the ladder of emergence, where our ability to express laws and mathematical relationships is now—and presumably will always be—more limited. Given that our knowledge of the genetic structure of the cell is only fifty years old, and theories of gene interactions and gene expression are younger still, it's not surprising that we have but a limited grasp of the phenomena associated with the human brain, with its billions of nerve cells and roughly 10^{14} neural connections. This vast complexity has tempted theorists to respond in two diametrically opposed directions. Both responses are based on the assumption that the brain could never give rise to the properties associated with thought, mentality, consciousness, and subjective sensations (*qualia*), properties that are phenomenologically quite different from the electrochemical properties of individual neurons. But from this assumption—which emergentists reject—two opposite conclusions have been drawn. The one group maintains that, since the brain could not possibly produce the world of mentality by itself, mental phenomena must be grounded in another world altogether: the world of mental substances, spirits, or souls. The other group, arguing from the same assumption, holds that the appearance of mentality must therefore be an illusion. Mental properties cannot play a role in the correct causal account of human thought and should thus be eliminated from truly scientific accounts of the world (see Patricia Churchland (1996; 2002); Churchland and Sejnowski (1992); Paul Churchland (1988; 1989); cf. McCauley (1996)). Yet one finds surprising properties all the way up the scale of increasing complexity; should one be surprised to find yet more novel emergent properties associated with the brain, the most complex natural system yet discovered in the universe? We may not fully understand the emergent relationship, in part because it involves the co-evolution of neural structures, language, and culture (Durham (1991); Deacon (1997)). But that a relationship is difficult to understand does not prove that it doesn't exist.

When one looks over the massive literature of the last few decades in the philosophy of mind, one can't help but walk away with the impression that we are really quite uncertain about what to say regarding human consciousness. Some use the strength of the correlations between brain states and first-person experiences as grounds for concluding an identity relationship between them; some use the felt difference of subjective properties to argue for dualist connections; and some use the disanalogies between mental properties and other properties in the natural world as grounds for urging that 'folk psychology' be eliminated from our final account of human persons. Distinct from each of the other responses, the emergence programme amounts to the wager that mental phenomena can be understood—without being explained away (Dennett, 1991)—by analogy to other emergent relationships in the world. Such an analogy preserves the *differences* between mind and lower-level phenomena while removing the sense that mind is 'spooky' or ontologically unique in the history of evolution. Instead, emergentists argue, the question of mind can best be addressed by looking for the ways in which mental phenomena emerge from neurological structures and processes, and by studying how these phenomena in turn begin to play a role within broader wholes or contexts (language, culture, social structures and institutions, value judgements, the construction of self-identity), in terms of which alone they can be understood. Think, for example, of Nancey Murphy's emphasis (in Chapter 10) on the broader social and cultural contexts within which concepts are located and explained.[6]

Some will complain that the emergence approach makes mental phenomena *too much* like other natural phenomena, and others will complain that it allows them to be *too different.* Some will complain that the emergentist approach does not demand a method of study that is distinct enough from

---

[6] See also Murphy and Brown (forthcoming). I have also emphasized the study of the human person in the context of the social or human sciences in Clayton (2004), chapters 4–5, and in my contribution to Russell, Arbib et al., (1999).

physics and biology, and others will protest because the approach endorses the use of distinctively social scientific and phenomenological methods of inquiry, which diverge too greatly from the natural sciences. But I take the fact that the emergence position can be (and often is) criticized from both sides as sign that it just may have found the right balance between the extremes that tend to dominate the discussion.

Finally, a few words are necessary for those who are made uneasy by the fact that the philosophy of emergence appears metaphysical—those who worry that the empirical grounds for positions of this type are necessarily so minimal as to render them suspect. First, readers are welcome to construe all the unifying language in this proposal in a 'regulative' fashion. According to Kant, some usages of language express the drive toward unified under-standing that is intrinsic in the human quest to comprehend the world, even while they go beyond the kind of knowledge we have in the ordinary theoretical ('constitutive') use of language.[7] Of course, if you go on to claim to *know* that emergence theories are always only regulative, and hence that one could *never* have any reason to believe they are true, I would be sceptical. Nevertheless, for present purposes it's sufficient if one acknowledges that the human quest to understand and to unify leads us inevitably to appeal to the narrative of emergence across natural history.

Similarly, it's sufficient if the reader acknowledges that *some impetus* toward broader theories of emergence is provided by results within a wide variety of the natural sciences, as well as data from cognitive psychology, the social sciences, and the philosophy of mind. It may be that the data are suggestive but not conclusive; it may be that at some point the lines emerging from the various sciences get lost in the swirling clouds of metaphysical reflection and disappear from sight, as it were, so that one can't quite claim to have estab-lished a comprehensive emergence theory of reality. (Yet how will one know exactly where that point of disappearance is unless one attempts to follow the lines as far as one possibly can?) Nonetheless, it will have been enough if we can establish *the pattern of emergence* that runs (like a second-order derivative) through the domains that are open to sight. More metaphysically minded thinkers will seek to express the pattern as a theory of reality. For the meta-physically more cautious, however, it may suffice to recognize, in light of the contributions to this volume, that considering the connections between the various sciences suggests a pattern of emergence that the individual sciences

---

[7] I have explored the relationship between regulative and 'constitutive' knowledge in chapter 1 of (2000) and Kant's application of regulative theories to the question of knowledge of God in chapter 5 of the same work. On regulative language and transcendental arguments see Bieri et al. (1979) and Stern (1999).

alone cannot establish—a pattern that sets the mind on a journey of reflection and speculation that cannot be avoided by traditional appeals to empirical criteria or to some supposedly clear 'line of demarcation' between science and metaphysics. If the questions raised by the essays in this volume are not an invitation to do philosophy, I don't know what is.

3. RELIGION AND EMERGENCE

Several chapters explicitly consider the religious implications of emergence, and a number of others do so implicitly. Peacocke considers downward causation, or what he calls 'whole–part influence,' as a model for God's interaction with the world. He understands the divine influence as 'something like a flow of information—a pattern-forming influence' (Ch. 12, p. 275). Gregersen includes a version of Peacocke's model, which he calls 'temporal theism', alongside his four other theological models. The five models taken together, Gregersen suggests, reflect the most significant forms of religious reflection on emergence (Ch. 13, p. 281). Only the middle three, which he groups together under the heading 'theistic naturalism', on his view actually represent distinctively emergentist positions, in so far as the first (religious naturalism) is 'unconcerned about the specific theoretical claims of weak or strong emergentism' (Ch. 13, p. 287), and the last (eschatological theism) does not share 'the broad naturalist assumption found in standard versions of emergence' (ibid.). That leaves only evolving theistic naturalism, atemporal theism, and temporal theism as candidates, which he argues are represented, respectively, by Samuel Alexander (and perhaps Willem Drees and Paul Davies); by the classical theists (Maimonides, Aquinas, and Avicenna); and by Whitehead and the process theologians (and perhaps by Peacocke and Clayton).

In these final paragraphs I should like to step back from the particular names and essays, in order to reflect for a moment on the religious dimension of emergence and on its potential significance for religious thought. As Gregersen's analysis shows—and his analysis is supported by cross-cultural approaches in contemporary religious studies—it would be difficult to find a view of the world (a metaphysic) that *could not* be seen as having religious significance. As Ursula Goodenough graphically puts it, one may feel the same sense of awe and wonder in observing a transduction cascade as she feels in standing before an ancient Aztec ruin by moonlight: 'same rush, same rapture' (Goodenough, 1997, p. 46). Hence any attempt to prove a priori that only certain sorts of views about the world should pass as religious—say, those containing the term 'God' or those that postulate a transcendent dimension of reality—are doomed to failure. A fortiori, emergence cannot be a necessary condition for a religious response to the world; nor can one conclude that, because a viewpoint espouses naturalistic emergence, it *cannot* be religious.

This recognition radically changes the nature of the discussion. As soon as the former worries about necessary and sufficient conditions for religiosity have been dispelled, the central question now becomes: what forms might the human religious response take, given the recognition that we are products of emergent evolution within a world of continual process and development? Three major options suggest themselves, depending on whether the religious response focuses on the natural, the emerging and unknown, or the transcendent. The first type, as Gregersen points out, need not depend specifically on emergence. Religious naturalism or 'ecstatic naturalism' incorporates the classically religious human responses of awe, wonder, amazement, the appreciation of beauty, and the sense of mystery—all in response to the natural world in the form that the sciences reveal it to us. Only an idiosyncratic definition of religion, say, one that links religion exclusively to belief in God or organized religious communities, could exclude such responses from the realm of the religious.

Religious responses of the second type (responses to the new, novel, surprising, or mysterious) are more diverse. At least three subcategories can be identified, and more could be found as well. The religious response may be evoked by the remarkable, almost mysterious manner in which qualitatively new forms arise out of complex interrelationships of parts-in-systems. Thus people express amazement that a set of biochemical interactions could produce self-reproducing cells or more complicated life forms, which become agents in a new sort of system, the biological. A similar response may be engendered by the remarkable fact that the amazingly complex organ we call the brain manifests such diverse properties as cognition, awareness, rational decision-making, and a sense of self. Note that this response can have different foci, depending on whether one emphasizes the qualitatively emergent properties themselves or the complexity, regularity, and law-likeness of the underlying structures and processes that give rise to the novel properties. A third religious response in this category arises out of the recognition that the process of emergence is open-ended, that it leads beyond the known and normal toward emergent levels of reality which may be altogether different from the world that we have known up to this point. A number of religiously oriented texts over the last several decades, and even some new religious movements, depend upon the belief that cultural evolution, and perhaps even cosmic evolution, is producing new and remarkable forms of reality, whether one speaks of the future in terms of the 'Age of Aquarius' or the paranormal powers that Michael Murphy chronicles in *The Future of the Body* (1992). The enduring interest in the work of Samuel Alexander (1920) is surely related to the fact that he postulated the most radical possible form of emergence: the emergence of deity. Alexander was a naturalist who believed that only the natural world exists; and yet he argued that, as the universe evolves, it gradually takes on the properties formerly associated with deity (it 'deises' itself).

The final form of religious response to emergence involves the belief that emergent evolution as we perceive it is linked in some way to a transcendent ground, power, or mind. Those who respond in this way have the sense that the law-like order of nature somehow reflects the 'mind of God' (cf. Davies, 1992). The theistic worldview expressed in all three of the great Abrahamic traditions reflects the conviction that the amazing fecundity of natural evolution in the end expresses the intentional creative structuring of God. This response to the emerging world is strengthened if one also holds that God is also being affected by and responding to each new level of emergent reality, as occurs within the various versions of process and temporal theism (see Chapter 13). On the Whiteheadian view, the 'primordial nature' of God is responsible for providing the range of possibilities for evolution and the creative lure toward ever greater complexity; the 'consequent nature' of God then responds to each occasion of experience, internalizing and valuing all moments of emergent evolution in their distinctness and uniqueness (Griffin, 2001).

The religious response is further intensified for those who hold that the world is somehow located *within the divine*, as is maintained by recent versions of *panentheism* (see Hartshorne, 1948; Griffin, 2001; Clayton and Peacocke, 2004). Panentheists maintain not only that the patterns of emergence are grounded in the divine order and that God continually responds to the evolutionary process, but also that the world is located within the divine being. Standing closer to the classical metaphysical systems of the East, this view questions the notion of God creating a separate world, set over against the divine, although (in contrast to pantheism) it continues to understand God as also more than the world. Panentheists seek to formulate a single ontological vision rather than sharply separating the becoming of the world from the timelessness and aseity of the divine being. As a result, the emergent processes and features of the world become religiously significant in and of themselves, and not only because of their divine origin or telos.

Given the various compatibilities just sketched, it is obvious that emergentist results in the sciences do not need to exclude all forms of theism. (Of course, if one endorses a completely naturalistic emergence theory, one will have to dispense with all non-naturalistic beings and forces, but in that case it's the naturalism that does the excluding, not the emergence theory as such.) The framework of emergence does however undercut some traditional forms of theism. It undercuts purely atemporal understandings of the God–world relationship, in so far as such views tend to underestimate the importance of time, process, and pervasive change within the natural world. It also at least indirectly undercuts static views of the divine nature, for it would be surprising, though not impossible, that a natural reality characterized by ubiquitous process and interconnection would be the result of a creator whose nature is essentially non-relational and non-responsive.

It seems to me, finally, that emergence theory tends to undercut dogmatic knowledge claims about the nature of God. Such claims tend to presuppose that one can have timeless knowledge, a view that implicitly lifts the epistemic agent above and hence out of the flow of history in which she is immersed. If emergence is right, our epistemic situation is constantly changing, in so far as we are products of a pervasive process of biological and cultural evolution. Acknowledging this fact should make one far more suspicious of any knowledge claims that imply, however tacitly, that the knower stands above the march of history and has direct and immediate access to timeless truths.[8]

In this final chapter I have sought to draw together some of the lines of reflection introduced in this volume. The book's essays were not intended to defend a single viewpoint, and the discerning reader will find clear and sometimes deep conceptual differences between them. Nonetheless, in presenting arguments for (and sometimes against) emergence across the scientific fields, the various contributions have raised an intriguing and significant possibility: an emergence-based view of the world that links together a wide variety of specific results and patterns. Moving beyond the particular scientific results is not mandated by science, of course, and nothing propels the bench scientist to engage in philosophical reflection of this sort. Yet the more successful emergence-based explanations become in the various particular sciences, the more one wonders what might be their broader significance. This closing chapter has offered one version of a philosophical theory of emergence, albeit certainly not the only possible version. Perhaps it has helped to establish the point that emergence theories, in whatever specific form they may be advanced, are not only of scientific, but also of philosophical and perhaps even religious, interest.

---

[8] Obviously, there is much more to be said about the relations between emergence theory and theism in general, and Christian theism in particular. For a fuller statement on the former see Clayton (2004), chapter 5; on the latter, see my contribution in Murphy and Stoeger (forthcoming).

4. REFERENCES

Alexander, Samuel (1920), *Space, Time, and Deity,* the Gifford Lectures for 1916–18, 2 vols. (London: Macmillan).

Bieri, Peter, Rolf P. Horstmann, and Lorenz Krüger (eds.) (1979), *Transcendental Arguments and Science: Essays in Epistemology* (Dordrecht, Boston: D. Reidel).

Brown, Terrance, and Leslie Smith (eds.) (2003), *Reductionism and the Development of Knowledge* (Mahwah, N. J.: L. Erlbaum).

Calaprice, Alice (ed.) (1996), *Quotable Einstein* (Princeton: Princeton University Press).

Churchland, Patricia Smith (1996), *Neurophilosophy: Toward a Unified Science of the Mind–Brain* (Cambridge, MA.: MIT Press).

—— (2002), *Brain-Wise: Studies in Neurophilosophy* (Cambridge, MA.: MIT Press).

—— and Terrence J. Sejnowski (1992), *The Computational Brain* (Cambridge, MA.: MIT Press).

Churchland, Paul M. (1988), *Matter and Consciousness: A Contemporary Introduction to the Philosophy of Mind,* rev. edition (Cambridge, MA.: MIT Press).

—— (1989), *A Neurocomputational Perspective: The Nature of Mind and the Structure of Science* (Cambridge, MA: MIT Press).

Clayton, Philip (2000), *The Problem of God in Modern Thought* (Grand Rapids: Eerdmans).

—— (2004), *Mind and Emergence: From Quantum to Chaos* (Oxford: Oxford University Press).

—— and Arthur Peacocke (eds.) (2004), *In Whom We Live and Move and Have Our Being: Scientific Reflections on a Panentheistic World* (Grand Rapids: Eerdmans).

Davies, Paul (1992), *The Mind of God* (New York: Simon & Schuster).

Deacon, Terrence (1997), *The Symbolic Species: The Co-Evolution of Language and the Brain* (New York: W. W. Norton).

Dennett, Daniel C. (1991), *Consciousness Explained* (Boston: Little, Brown and Co.).

Durham, William (1991), *Coevolution: Genes, Culture, and Human Diversity* (Stanford: Stanford University Press).

Einstein, Albert (1930), 'Science and God', *Forum and Century* 83: 373–79.

—— (1954), Letter to Hans Muehsam of March 30, 1954, Einstein Archive 38–434.

Ellis, George (2004), 'On the Causal Incompleteness of Physics', response presented to the Royal Society on December 9, 2004 (expanded version forthcoming in *Physics Today,* 2005).

Goodenough, Ursula (1997), *The Sacred Depths of Nature* (New York: Oxford University Press).

Griffin, David Ray (2001), *Reenchantment Without Supernaturalism: A Process Philosophy of Religion* (Ithaca, N.Y.: Cornell University Press).

Hartshorne, Charles (1948), *The Divine Relativity: A Social Conception of God* (New Haven: Yale University Press).

Jammer, Max (1999), *Einstein and Religion* (Princeton: Princeton University Press).

Kauffman, Stuart, and Philip Clayton (forthcoming), 'On Emergence and Agency', *Biology and Philosophy*.

Looijen, Rick C. (2000), *Holism and Reductionism in Biology and Ecology: The Mutual Dependence of Higher and Lower Level Research Programmes* (Dordrecht and Boston: Kluwer Academic Publishers).

McCauley, Robert N. (1996), *The Churchlands and their Critics* (Cambridge, MA.: Blackwell).

Murphy, Michael (1992), *The Future of the Body: Explorations into the Further Evolution of Human Nature* (Los Angeles: J. P. Tarcher).

Murphy, Nancey, and George F. R. Ellis (1996), *On the Moral Nature of the Universe: Theology, Cosmology, and Ethics* (Minneapolis, MN.: Fortress Press).

—— and Warren S. Brown (forthcoming), *Did My Neurons Make Me Do It? Philosophical and Neurobiological Perspectives on Moral Responsibility and Free Will*.

—— and William R. Stoeger (eds.) (forthcoming), *Emergence: From Physics to Theology* (Oxford: Oxford University Press).

Rothman, Stephen (2002), *Lessons from the Living Cell: The Limits of Reductionism* (New York: McGraw-Hill).

Russell, Robert J., Michael Arbib, et al. (eds.) (1999), *Neuroscience and the Person* (Vatican City State: Vatican Observatory Publications).

Stern, Robert (ed.) (1999), *Transcendental Arguments: Problems and Prospects* (New York: Oxford University Press).

Notes on Contributors

David J. Chalmers is currently Professor of Philosophy and Director of the Centre for Consciousness Studies at the Australian National University. His formulation of the 'hard problem' of consciousness and his own proposals for addressing the problem—in numerous papers and in *The Conscious Mind: In Search of a Fundamental Theory* (1996)—have had a significant impact on the discussion of consciousness within the philosophy of mind over the last decade. Chalmers is one of the founders of the Association for the Scientific Study of Consciousness; he also edits the *Philosophy of Mind Series* at Oxford University Press and is an editor for the *Stanford Encyclopedia of Philosophy*. He has a book forthcoming, *The Character of Consciousness*.

Philip Clayton is Ingraham Professor at the Claremont School of Theology and a professor of philosophy and of religion at the Claremont Graduate University. Out of his twin intellectual foci on the interface between science and religion and the history of modern metaphysics came *The Problem of God in Modern Thought* (2000). He recently co-edited *In Whom We Live and Move and Have Our Being: Panentheistic Reflections on God's Presence in a Scientific World* with Arthur Peacocke. His most recent book is *Mind and Emergence: From Quantum to Consciousness*, published by Oxford University Press in 2004, and he is currently involved in preparing *The Oxford Handbook of Religion and Science*.

Paul C. W. Davies is the Professor of Natural Philosophy in the Australian Centre for Astrobiology at Macquarie University. His research has spanned the fields of cosmology, gravitation, and quantum field theory, with particular emphasis on black holes and the origin of the universe. Dr. Davies is also widely known as an author. He has written more than twenty-five books, both popular and specialist works, including *The Physics of Time Asymmetry*, *Quantum Fields in Curved Space* (co-authored with Nicholas Birrell), *The Mind of God*, *About Time*, *How to Build a Time Machine*, and, most recently, *The Origin of Life*, which was published by Penguin in 2003.

Terrence W. Deacon is Professor of Anthropology at the University of California, Berkeley, with research specializations in biological anthropology and the neurosciences. Professor Deacon's work focuses on the evolution and adaptation of the brain; he is best known for his work on the evolution of language abilities and the human brain. His neurobiological research has also utilized cross-species transplantation of embryonic brain tissue to study the evolution and development of brains. In addition to numerous research papers he has authored *The Symbolic Species* (1997) and is currently finishing a book on evolution and consciousness, *Homunculus*, to be published by W. W. Norton.

George F. R. Ellis has, for the past thirty years, been a professor of applied mathematics at the University of Cape Town while lecturing throughout the world. Dr. Ellis has also served as President of the Royal Society of South Africa and of the International Society of General Relativity and Gravitation. His scientific work has focused on the mathematical foundations of general relativity and cosmology. His latest studies are (with John Wainwright) *The Dynamical Systems Approach to Cosmology* (Cambridge University Press, 1996), (with Nancey Murphy) *On the Moral Nature of the Universe: Theology, Cosmology, and Ethics* (Fortress Press, 1996), and (with Peter Coles) *Is the Universe Open or Closed? The Density of Matter in the Universe* (Cambridge University Press, 1997).

Niels Henrik Gregersen is Professor of Systematic Theology at the University of Copenhagen. His primary fields of research are systematic theology and the intersection of science and religion. Formerly general editor of *Studies in Science and Theology*, he is systematic theology editor of the *Danish Journal of Theology* and associate editor of the *Encyclopedia of Science and Religion*, as well as a member of the editorial advisory boards of *Zygon: Journal of Religion and Science, Theology and Science*, and *Dialog: A Journal of Theology*. Recently he has edited or co-edited books such as *The Human Person in Science and Theology*, (T & T Clark and Eerdmans, 2000), *Design and Disorder* (T & T Clark, 2002), *From Complexity to Life* (Oxford University Press, 2003), and *Gift of Grace: The Future of Lutheran Theology* (Fortress Press, 2005).

Jaegwon Kim is the William Herbert Perry Faunce Professor of Philosophy at Brown University. His research interests have recently focused on philosophy of mind and his groundbreaking work on the notion of supervenience. He currently serves on the editorial boards of *Philosophy and Phenomenological Research*, the Macmillan *Encyclopedia of Philosophy Supplement*, and *Philosophical Issues*, as well as on the board of editorial consultants of *Philosophical Papers and Philosophical Explorations*. Dr. Kim's book *Mind in a Physical World: An Essay on the Mind–Body Problem and Mental Causation* was published in 1998 by MIT Press/Bradford Books, and his most recent monograph, *Physicalism, or Something Near Enough*, was published in 2005 by Princeton University Press.

Nancey Murphy, a philosopher of science and a Christian theologian, teaches at Fuller Theological Seminary where she is Professor of Christian philosophy. Recent publications indude *Anglo-American Postmodernity* (Westview Press, 1977); (with Willam R. Stoeger, ed.) *Emergence—From Physics to Theology* (Oxford University Press, 2007); and (with Warren S. Brown) *Did My Neurons Make Me Do It? Philosophical and Neuroscientific Perspectives on Moral Responsibility and Free Will* (Oxford University Press, forthcoming). Dr. Murphy serves on the editorial advisory boards of *Zygon Theology and Science, Theology Today,* and *Brazas Press: Journal of Religion and Science.* Her most recent studies are *Anglo-American Postmodernity: Philosophical Perspectives on Science, Religion, and Ethics* (Westview Press, 1997) and *Reconciling Theology and Science: A Radical Reformation Perspective* (Pandora Press, 1997). She is currently completing a book with Warren S. Brown on neuroscience and philosophy of mind (expected publication in 2006).

Arthur Peacocke, the 2001 winner of the Templeton Prize for Progress in Religion, devoted the first twenty-five years of his career to teaching and research in the field of physical biochemistry, specializing in biological macromolecules and making significant contributions to our understanding of the structure of DNA. His principal interest during the past twenty-five years has been in exploring the relation of science to theology. From this most recent interest, he has authored ten books exploring the relationship between science and religion. His studies include *Theology for a Scientific Age* (1990 and 1993), winner of a Templeton Foundation Outstanding Book Prize, *From DNA to Dean: Reflections and Explorations of a Priest–Scientist* (1996) and *God and Science: A Quest for Christian Credibility* (1996). His most recent book, *Paths From Science Towards God: The End of All Our Exploring,* was published in 2001 by Oneworld Publications.

Lynn J. Rothschild, a research scientist in earth system science, is Director of the Astrobiology Strategic Analysis and Support Office for NASA, located at the Ames Research Center in Moffett Field, California, does research on the evolution and physiological ecology of unicellular animals and plants. Her work is helping to create a model of Precambrian ecosystems and to predict the impact of carbon dioxide pressure and ultraviolet light on global change over millennia. She has served as co-editor-in-chief of the *International Journal of Astrobiology* and was formerly on the editorial board of *Origins of Life and Evolution in the Biosphere* and on the board of reviewers of the *Journal of Eukaryotic Microbiology.* Dr. Rothschild is co-editor (with A. Lister) of *Evolution on Planet Earth: The Impact of the Physical Environment,* which was published in 2003 by Academic Press.

Erich Joos has conducted research at the Universities of Heidelberg, Texas, and Hamburg, and is currently conducting independent research in Hamburg, Germany. His current research interests have focused on decoherence theory, interpretations and foundations of quantum theory, and the interface between classical mechanics and quantum theory. In 1985, he published the first paper (with H.D. Zeh) quantifying the quantum–classical transition via decoherence. His most recent book is *Decoherence and the Appearance of a Classical World in Quantum Theory*, published by Springer in 2003. More information on Erich, and on decoherence, can be found at <www.decoherence.de>.

Michael Silberstein is Associate Professor of Philosophy at Elizabethtown College and an adjunct at the University of Maryland where he is also a faculty member in the Foundations of Physics Program and a Fellow on the Committee for Philosophy and the Sciences. His primary research interests are philosophy of physics and philosophy of cognitive neuroscience. He is especially interested in how these branches of philosophy bear on more general questions of reduction, emergence, and explanation. His most recent book is *The Blackwell Guide to the Philosophy of Science* (co-edited with Peter Machamer), published in 2002, in which he has a chapter on reduction, emergence, and explanation. He is currently working on a book entitled *Contextual Emergence: On the Relational Nature of Reality.*

Barbara Smuts is a Professor in the Psychology Department, University of Michigan, Ann Arbor. She is a co-editor of *Primate Societies* and author of *Sex and Friendship in Baboons* as well as many journal articles on animal behavior. She has studied social relationships in wild chimpanzees, baboons, and bottlenose dolphins and is currently studying social behaviour among domestic dogs.

Index